Guide to the
Atlanta
Campaign

The U.S. Army War College
Guides to Civil War Battles

Guide to the
Atlanta Campaign

Rocky Face Ridge to
Kennesaw Mountain

Edited by
Jay Luvaas
and Harold W. Nelson

University Press of Kansas

© 2008 by the University Press of Kansas

Published by the University Press of Kansas (Lawrence, Kansas 66045), which was organized by the Kansas Board of Regents and is operated and funded by Emporia State University, Fort Hays State University, Kansas State University, Pittsburg State University, the University of Kansas, and Wichita State University

Library of Congress Cataloging-in-Publication Data

Guide to the Atlanta campaign : Rocky Face Ridge to Kennesaw Mountain / edited by Jay Luvaas and Harold W. Nelson.
    p.   cm.
    Includes bibliographical references.
    ISBN 978-0-7006-1569-8 (cloth : alk. paper) — ISBN 978-0-7006-1570-4 (pbk. : alk. paper)
    1. Atlanta Campaign, 1864. 2. Kennesaw Mountain, Battle of, Ga., 1864. 3. Historic sites—Georgia—Guidebooks. I. Luvaas, Jay. II. Nelson, Harold W.
    E476.7.G85 2008
    973.7′371—dc22   2008003944

British Library Cataloguing-in-Publication Data is available.

Printed in the United States of America

10   9   8   7   6   5   4   3   2   1

The paper used in this publication is recycled and contains 50 percent postconsumer waste. It is acid free and meets the minimum requirements of the American National Standard for Permanence of Paper for Printed Library Materials Z39.48-1992.

CONTENTS

MAPS AND ILLUSTRATIONS ·

Maps

Illustrations

ACKNOWLEDGMENTS

We acknowledge a debt of gratitude to the many people who helped to make this book possible. Maj. Gen. Paul Cerjan, commandant of the U.S. Army War College when we began this project, offered command support that was essential to moving from the simple "battle" topics that had characterized the early War College Guides into the broader "campaign" approach evidenced most clearly in this volume and the Vicksburg Guide that preceded it. Maj. Gen Richard Chilcoat was the commandant who encouraged us to give this project renewed momentum before we retired, and Gen. Gordon Sullivan made it possible for the team to work together one final year before that retirement took place. Without that fortunate combination of high-level support we might not have finished the draft.

Col. Dave Hansen and Dr. Gary Guertner, serving successively as chairmen of the Department of National Security and Strategy, found ways to cover some of our departmental duties so that we could find time for reconnaissance, research, and staff rides of the campaign.

The staff at the U.S. Army Military History Institute was, as always, essential to our work. Dr. Richard Somers and Louise Arnold Friend were expert guides to manuscript and published materials, and Michael J. Winey and Randy W. Hackenberg aided us in selecting photographs and other images to support the text. Unfortunately, much of their early work with the Army War College photo lab in support of this volume was lost when the manuscript languished.

Col. (Ret.) Stephen Riley, executive director of the Army War College Foundation, found funds to produce the maps, and Darin Graugberger of the University of Kansas did outstanding work, taking our rough sketches and transforming them into clear, useful, accurate maps. Some readers will note similarities to maps in Albert Castel's *Decision in the West,* also published by the University Press of Kansas, and we are grateful for the permission to derive aspects of these maps from that source.

Michael Briggs, editor-in-chief at the University Press of Kansas, has been an active collaborator in all efforts to see this project through to completion. He understood the reasons that other volumes needed to take precedence in the War College's Guidebook series, but he never lost sight of the potential of our early manuscript for this book. Without his patient guidance the project would have been abandoned.

A group of special friends who share our love of walking old battlefields to find new insights, the "Army of the Cussewago," walked this ground with us twice—first while Interstate 75 was under construction, and later when we had a workable manuscript. They provided excellent advice and helped us improve the sequence of stops we used to interpret the campaign.

We owe special thanks to Chris Hockensmith, who typed, edited, and proofed our early drafts. She then updated digital files from floppy disks and primitive word-processing programs as the years passed, solving the inevitable reformatting problems that accompany that work.

Finally our wives, Linda and Janet, have been tolerant "Civil War widows" while we worked on this book. When we were sneaking away to Gettysburg for a few hours at a time in the early 1980s, our absences might have been tolerable, but the many week-long trips to Georgia were a burden. We compounded the problem by agreeing to conduct far too many staff rides to other battlefields while still finding hours to polish this manuscript. We thank them for their patience and understanding.

Jay Luvaas

Harold W. Nelson

THE U.S. ARMY WAR COLLEGE GUIDES

The Army War College guidebooks are a by-product of the historical staff-ride program. When we came to Carlisle Barracks in 1982 we began to take students on weekend trips to nearby battlefields, using extracts from the Official Records to reconstruct commanders' decisions and unit actions on the ground. The materials we used at Gettysburg were so popular that we eventually published them as a guidebook in 1986, and several additional volumes followed in quick succession.

While we were putting finishing touches on those books we began work on Sherman's Atlanta campaign. Several factors impeded completion of the project. When we returned to the manuscript after we retired in 1995, we found that we brought new perspective to the work. Both of us had led far more staff rides with senior officers. We had studied generals Ulysses S. Grant and William T. Sherman more carefully, and we were ready to lead readers on a staff ride of General Sherman's mind.

By 1864, the leaders of the Union Army had forged a powerful instrument that resembled earlier armies in many ways while introducing new capabilities that were changing the nature of warfare. As we follow Sherman down the railroad toward Atlanta we are moving with a leader who was inventing military applications for the important industrial developments of his day. He used staff experts equipped with telegraphic communications to prioritize shipments and optimize use of carrying capacity, inventing a primitive "industrialized logistics" that would be filled with lessons for soldiers in the ensuing century. His "pipeline" to the rear was filled with replacements as well as supplies, so that his armies were as strong numerically after Kennesaw Mountain in July as they had been when he embarked on offensive operations in May. Given the attrition accompanying long marches, the privation of living in the field, and the bloody battles fought around Resaca, New Hope Church, and Kennesaw Mountain, this was a remarkable accomplishment in his day, and it would become the standard for armies operating in the next century.

As we went on staff rides with generals who were building an Information Age army, we considered how generals such as Sherman and Grant had shaped the future, coordinating and conducting large, complex operations unlike any that had come before them. The generals who accompanied

us knew that the microchip, precision weapons, and improved communications were pulling them into a new era just as the railroad, the rifle
musket, and the telegraph had pulled Sherman into the Industrial Age,
enabling him to find new solutions to old problems. That insight shaped
our selection of the materials in this guidebook.

HOW TO USE THIS BOOK

A noted English historian declared some ninety years ago that "the skilled game of identifying positions on a battlefield innocent of guides, where one must make out everything for oneself—best of all if no one has ever done it properly before—is almost the greatest of outdoor pleasures."

This guide is designed to help you enjoy this experience with the Atlanta campaign. The stops are arranged to present the most important phases of the campaign as it developed, recognizing that in this particular campaign we cannot take a strictly chronological approach to all events as they unfolded. The selections were chosen to enable you to appreciate what it must have been like for the officers and men in both armies as they fought intense battles across varied terrain.

This is not intended to serve as a *history* of the campaign—for that you should consult more standard works on the Civil War or narrative histories relating to this campaign. Those who visit battlefields with us report that the most productive study begins *after* they have stopped at key points, viewed the terrain, and shared the recollections of participants—the approach you will experience by using this guide.

We have included full names and military ranks at the first mention of major figures in the Atlanta campaign; when the first mention appears within an excerpt, this information is enclosed in brackets. We have omitted the full name and rank for many of the minor figures.

The convention used in this book is that all Confederate names are italicized. Union names are in roman type.

Key to Maps

Military units–size

Federal Forces		Confederate Forces
Infantry		Infantry
MCPHERSON	ARMIES	**JOHNSTON**
DODGE	CORPS	**POLK**
Wood	DIVISIONS	**Cantey**
Kilpatrick	BRIGADES	Vaughn

General military symbols

▬▬▬▬▬	Infantry Lines	▬▬▬▬▬
• • • • •	Cavalry Lines	• • • • •
⊥⊥⊥⊥⊥⊥⊥⊥	Forts/ Trenches	⊥⊥⊥⊥⊥⊥⊥⊥
╫	Artillery	╫

Military movements

➤	Attack	◀
──────▶	March	◀──────
------------▶	Retreat	◀------------

Geographical symbols

────────	Historic Major Roads
════════	Modern Tour Route
────────	Modern Major Roads
────────	Modern Minor Roads
RINGGOLD	Battlesites/ Stops
DALTON	Major Cities
Euharlee	Minor Cities
Dug Gap	Historical Markers / Information
⌣	Bridge
✝	Cemetery
✝	Church
▲	Hill / Mountain
Ⓗ	Historical Marker
1 **8**	Stop Locations

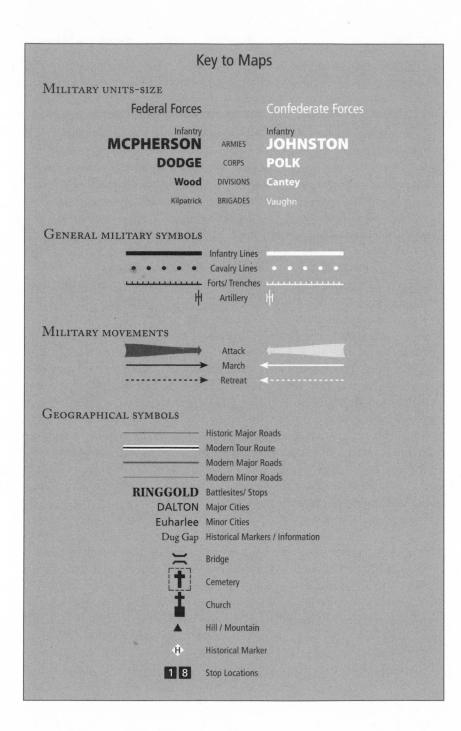

INTRODUCTION

Maj. Gen. William T. Sherman's Atlanta campaign was a vital part of the strategic plan devised by Lt. Gen. Ulysses S. Grant in the spring of 1864. Pressure against the Confederacy would be applied simultaneously in Virginia by the Army of the Potomac and subsidiary offensives in the Shenandoah Valley and against Richmond from the south; two Union columns would penetrate deep into West Virginia while another Union army was to advance from New Orleans against Mobile. Sherman, recently appointed to command the Military Division of Mississippi, was to move against Confederate Gen. *Joseph E. Johnston's* army in north Georgia. His mission: to break up the opposing army "and to get into the interior of the enemy's country as far as you can, inflicting all the damage you can against their War resources."

Sherman functioned as an army group commander in this campaign, for his field force comprised three armies—Maj. Gen. George Thomas's Army of the Cumberland (60,773 effectives), Maj. Gen. James B. McPherson's Army of the Tennessee (24,465 effectives), and Maj. Gen. John M. Schofield's Army of the Ohio (13,559 effectives), in all nearly 100,000 troops and 254 guns. The estimated strength of the Confederate forces under *Johnston* was 64,000, including Lt. Gen. *Leonidas Polk's* corps from the Army of Mississippi, which joined *Johnston's* Army of Tennessee about one week after active operations began.

Both armies spent the winter of 1863–1864 in northern Georgia. *Johnston*, who had been placed in command after the Confederate defeat at Chattanooga the previous November, occupied Rocky Face Mountain west of Dalton, Georgia, and the dominant hills to the north. Because the rigors of the past six months had greatly reduced the condition of the army's horses and his infantry lacked sufficient shoes, blankets, and small arms, *Johnston* spent the winter working to improve the morale and discipline of his troops.

Sherman's overriding concern was logistics: he had sufficient men and equipment, but he had to accumulate vast quantities of food and forage in the storehouses at Chattanooga and make arrangements to bring forward the supplies needed to sustain his armies throughout a long and arduous campaign. On the eve of the campaign, the Army of the Cumberland was

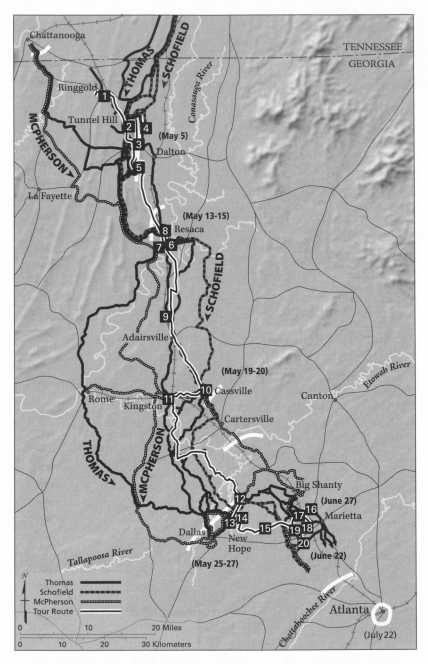

Movement of Sherman's Armies and Guidebook Stops in the Theater of Operations

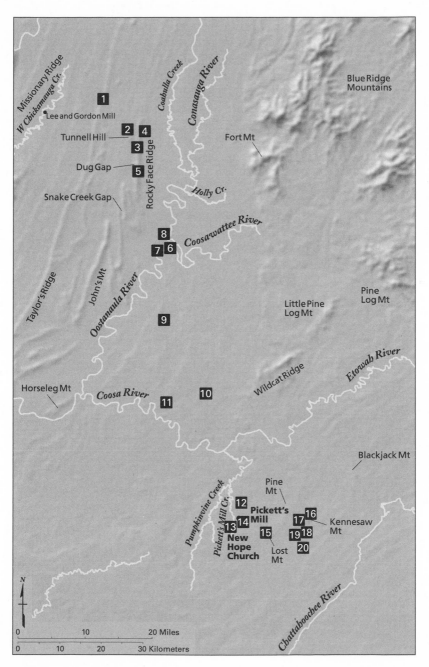

Major Physical Features and Guidebook Stops

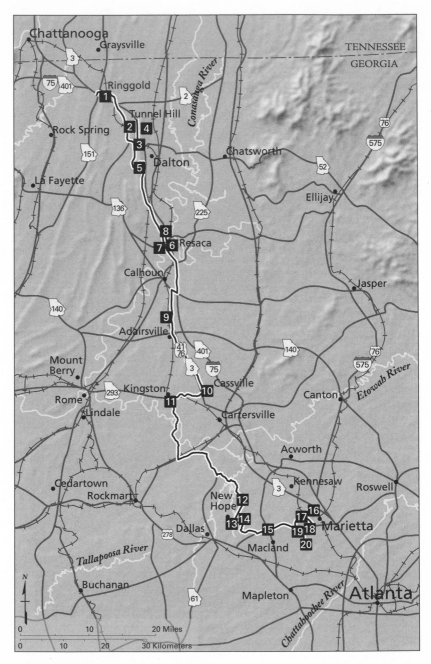

Modern Highways and Guidebook Stops

in position near Ringgold, the Army of the Ohio was poised on the Georgia line north of Dalton, and the Army of the Tennessee was marching from its winter camps in northern Alabama to Chattanooga and Gordon's Mills.

The campaign began on May 7, when Thomas moved forward to occupy Tunnel Hill. From the high hill beyond, Sherman could see the Confederate defenses in Buzzard Roost, as the gorge through the precipitous Rocky Face Mountain was called. Ordering Thomas and Schofield to press strongly at all points, Sherman sent McPherson on a wide turning movement through Snake Creek Gap to attack the railroad near Resaca and then to occupy a strong defensive position from which he could menace *Johnston's* line of communications and "stand ready to fall on the enemy's flank when he retreated." McPherson reached Snake Creek Gap on May 8, and on the ninth Schofield and Thomas pressed hard against the Confederate lines, "pushing it almost to a battle." McPherson failed, however, either to seize Resaca, which was strongly held, or to cut the railroad, and on the thirteenth the Confederates withdrew from Dalton to Resaca. Two of Thomas's corps and Schofield's Army of the Ohio marched through Snake Creek Gap to reinforce McPherson, while Maj. Gen. Oliver O. Howard's Fourth Corps, of the Army of the Cumberland, followed the retreating Confederates through Dalton.

On May 12 McPherson's troops moved forward to occupy a ridge overlooking Camp Creek about two miles west of town, with Thomas and then Schofield prolonging the line to the north, while Howard pressed the rear of units retreating from Dalton. By the fourteenth the Confederates occupied a strong position behind Camp Creek, occupying forts previously constructed and entrenched on some high hills north of town. There was heavy fighting along the entire line. A strong Confederate counterattack against the Union left flank nearly succeeded, but on the Union right Sherman's forces seized Confederate earthworks and lodged themselves on the east side of Camp Creek. On the fifteenth *Johnston* slipped away, his line of communications threatened by artillery occupying high ground within range of the railroad bridge across the Oostenaula River and exposed to a Union division that had crossed the river downstream.

Elements of the two armies met again at Adairsville two days later, where the Confederates delayed but could not check the advance of Sherman's mobile columns. After stubborn skirmishing, the Confederates fell back from one line of breastworks to another, gaining time for the army to retreat to Kingston and then on to Cassville, where *Johnston* occupied "an excellent position" from which he intended to assault Sherman's

General Joseph E. Johnston (Library of Congress).

converging columns on May 19. He called off his attack, however, when misleading reports suggested that Lt. Gen. *John B. Hood's* corps, on the right, would be threatened by an attack against his right flank and rear, and the Confederates withdrew instead to a high hill south and east of the town. Although it was a formidable position, their lines on the right were soon enfiladed by Union artillery posted on higher ground, and *Johnston* once again abandoned his position. On May 20 the Confederates crossed the Etowah River and prepared to defend Allatoona Pass.

Sherman, recalling the topography of the area from the days twenty years earlier when he had been assigned to Marietta, resolved not to force Allatoona Pass, where the Confederates occupied a strong position. He would instead cross the Etowah downstream and converge by separate

General William T. Sherman (Collection of the
Military Order of the Loyal Legion of the United
States, U.S. Army Military History Institute;
hereafter MOLLUS).

columns on Dallas, an important road junction from which he could
threaten Marietta and Atlanta. This move would also force *Johnston* to
abandon Allatoona Pass, thus enabling Sherman to regain use of the railroad, his only line of supply.

On May 23 *Johnston* learned that Sherman had crossed the river, and
that afternoon he ordered Lt. Gen. *William J. Hardee* to move his corps to
the Dallas-Atlanta road via New Hope Church. *Polk's* corps marched by a
route farther to the south, and *Hood's* corps, bringing up the rear, reached

New Hope Church on the 25th. Here the Confederates encountered the leading division of Maj. Gen. Joseph E. Hooker's Twentieth Corps, which had crossed Pumpkin Vine Creek from the west and was fighting its way to the crossroads. Both sides quickly threw up breastworks, and for the next five days there was constant firing and sporadic heavy fighting in the thickly forested hills and ravines from Dallas to New Hope Church, which quickly became known to survivors as the "hell-hole." On both sides the men were almost constantly under fire. Engaged each night in fatigue duty, building breastworks, and digging rifle pits, they had little opportunity for rest and poor facilities for cooking, and were required to be constantly on the alert to resist any attack day or night. "It is useless to look for the flank of the enemy," Sherman concluded, "as he makes temporary breast-works as fast as we travel. We must break his line without scattering our troops too much, and then break through."

This, however, he was unable to do, and on May 27 Sherman moved two divisions behind his lines to the left in an endeavor to get around Johnston's entrenchments. After a difficult flank march "through dense forests and the thickest jungle," Brig. Gen. Thomas J. Wood's division, of Howard's Fourth Army Corps, moved forward in a column of three brigades to attack the Confederate right flank. Struggling through thick undergrowth and rough ravines, this division encountered one brigade behind breastworks and was struck by two other brigades from Maj. Gen. *Patrick R. Cleburne's* division, which had been sent at the last minute to prolong the Confederate line. During the next several hours Wood lost about 1,400 killed, wounded, and missing, producing a dismal scene that reminded one Union general of the carnage of Antietam and Gettysburg. *Cleburne* lost about 450 killed and wounded.

Sherman now decided to shift to the left, capture Allatoona, and re-establish his line of communications on the railroad. As McPherson's Army of the Tennessee prepared to pull away from Dallas, however, it was fiercely attacked by Maj. Gen. *William P. Bate's* Confederate division, and he could not withdraw until June 1. His army again united, Sherman kept edging to his left to gain possession of the roads leading to Allatoona and Ackworth. On June 2 Union cavalry under two generals, Maj. Gen. George Stoneman and Brig. Gen. Kenner Garrard, occupied the Allatoona pass, causing *Johnston* to evacuate his lines at Dallas, New Hope, and Pickett's Mill and fall back to a new position, about ten miles in length, in which "three prominent hills" forming a triangle—Lost Mountain, Pine Mountain, and Kennesaw Mountain—served as impregnable redoubts.

Even such strong points, however, are useless against troops that can maneuver, and on June 10, having shifted McPherson's army to his extreme left, Sherman moved his columns forward—McPherson along the railroad, Thomas toward the right at Pine Mountain, and Schofield to the vicinity of Lost Mountain. The next day the bridge over the Etowah was completed and supplies by railroad began to arrive. Sherman's superior numbers enabled him to keep maneuvering on the flanks, and when Thomas's Army of the Cumberland threatened to break the line between Kennesaw and Pine mountains, *Johnston* was forced to abandon the latter and fall back by stages to a new line in which Kennesaw Mountain served as a salient. Both Confederate flanks were now refused and the entire line was heavily fortified. By this time, to quote Sherman, the whole country was "one vast fort"; he saw Kennesaw as "the key to the whole country" and estimated that *Johnston* had "fifty miles of connected trenches." On June 22 *Hood's* corps made a sudden but unsuccessful attack on one of Hooker's divisions at Kolb's Farm.

Faced with the alternative of continuing his turning movements or assaulting the Confederate earthworks, Sherman now decided on a frontal attack. "An army to be efficient must not settle down to a single mode of offensive," he explained (or perhaps rationalized), and by changing his pattern he hoped to catch the enemy by surprise. Orders specified that "each attacking column will endeavor to break a single point of the enemy's line, make a secure lodgment beyond, and be prepared for following it up toward Marietta and the railroad in case of success." On June 27 two Union columns advanced upon the left center of the Confederate lines; within two hours the assaults failed, with losses three times that of the Confederates.

On the extreme Union right, however, a portion of Schofield's Army of the Ohio crossed the creek protecting the Confederate left and entrenched, which prompted Sherman to move McPherson's entire army from the left to his extreme right. To counter this new threat to his line of retreat, *Johnston* abandoned his lines at Kennesaw on the night of July 2 and fell back to a line at Smyrna Church, blocking the road to Atlanta. Three days later the Confederates withdrew to a previously fortified bridgehead covering the railroad bridge and ferry crossing the Chattahoochie River. From nearby hills Sherman could now see buildings in Atlanta.

This ends the first and the most critical phase of the Atlanta campaign. The Union Army did not enter Atlanta until September 2, but much of the ground over which the armies fought and maneuvered in that phase is now under asphalt and concrete. Moreover, by then the military situation had changed significantly in Sherman's favor. He was out of the mountains, with his army united and his line of communications secure. Despite some 20,000 or more casualties thus far in the campaign, Sherman had nearly 30,000 more troops on hand or within supporting distance at the end of June than were present for duty when active operations commenced, thanks to his system of moving men forward from furloughs and hospitals and bringing fresh divisions to reinforce his armies in the field. *Johnston reported losses of about 10,000.*

The day after Sherman's repulse at Kennesaw, Grant authorized him to make movements "entirely independent of any desire to retain *Johnston's* forces where they are," which changed significantly his original mission to break up the opposing army and to capture and destroy Confederate war resources in Atlanta. He now had greater flexibility than before.

On July 18, however, Sherman learned that *John B. Hood* had replaced *Johnston* as general. Two of Sherman's army commanders had been *Hood's* classmates at West Point and remembered him as "a brave, determined, and rash man," and Sherman assumed that *Johnston* had been relieved because he had been overly cautious. Sherman and his principal subordinates therefore "agreed that we ought to be unusually cautious and prepared at all times for sallies and for hard fighting."

This pretty much describes the nature of the battles fought for Atlanta, in which *Hood* delivered a series of hard blows to Sherman's army as it tightened its grip around the city. Sherman had more troops and better subordinate commanders, and above all, he commanded an army of seasoned veterans. *Hood's* sorties could only postpone—not prevent—the fall of the city.

On September 3 Sherman wired the Washington authorities: "So Atlanta is ours, and fairly won. . . . Since May 5 we have been in one constant battle or skirmish, and need rest."

From Rocky Face to Kennesaw Mountain, the Atlanta campaign was a masterpiece of *both* offensive and defensive maneuver. With greater numbers and mobility, Sherman managed to outflank or threaten the communications of every position occupied by his opponent, while, for his part, *Johnston* succeeded, against formidable odds, in keeping his army intact and always between Sherman and Atlanta. Through constant maneuvering, Sherman forced his opponent from one strong position to another, despite the fact that Sherman's objective was known, his line of advance was dependent upon a single railroad, and he had to negotiate every river and mountain range from Dalton to Kennesaw.

The most significant aspect of the campaign, however, was not the battles or even the maneuvers themselves. Sherman's special genius was in his mastery of logistics—his ability to move reinforcements and supplies forward over such hostile and immense territory in the face of a skilled opponent. If the greater industrial capacity and manpower of the North was the basic reason why the North won the war, it was Sherman's concepts and organization that brought this power together before Atlanta.

1. SHERMAN AND GRANT PREPARE FOR ACTIVE OPERATIONS

Interstate Highway 75 is now the high-speed route through the terrain covered by this campaign. Whether you are approaching this first stop from north or south, exit I-75 at Interchange 348. Follow the signs toward Ringgold, driving about 0.5 mile north to the "T" intersection. Turn right on U.S. 41. Follow this highway through Ringgold. Near the far edge of town the highway passes under the railroad that was the transportation backbone of the campaign. Mark your odometer reading at the railroad underpass. Drive about 0.4 mile farther to a picnic site with historical markers on the right side of the road (Ringgold Gap Historical Site). Park there and walk to the large bronze plaque portraying the movements of the Northern and Southern armies.

STOP 1, RINGGOLD

Report of Maj. Gen. William T. Sherman, USA, Commanding Military Division of the Mississippi

On the 14th day of March, 1864, at Memphis, Tenn., I received notice from General Grant . . . that he had been commissioned Lieutenant-General and Commander in Chief of the Armies of the United States, which would compel him to go East, and that I had been appointed to succeed him as commander of the Division of the Mississippi. He summoned me to Nashville for a conference, and I . . . accompanied him on his journey eastward as far as Cincinnati. We had a full and complete understanding of the policy and plans for the ensuing campaign, covering a vast area of country, my part of which extended from Chattanooga to Vicksburg.

I returned to Nashville, and on the 25th began a tour of inspection, visiting Athens, Decatur, Huntsville and Larkin's Ferry, Ala.; Chattanooga, Loudon, and Knoxville, Tenn. During this visit I had interviews with General McPherson, commanding the Army of the Tennessee, at Huntsville; Major-General Thomas, commanding the Army of the

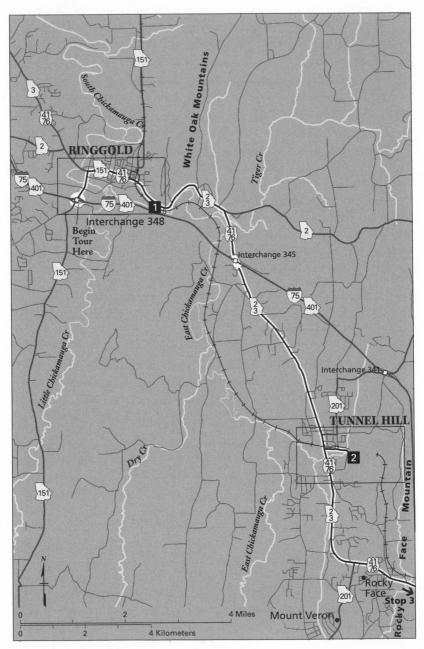

Ringgold to Tunnel Hill

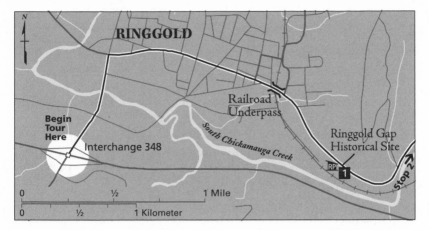

Ringgold Gap Historical Site (Stop 1)

Cumberland, at Chattanooga, and General Schofield, commanding the Army of the Ohio, at Knoxville. We arranged in general terms the lines of communication to be guarded, the strength of the several columns and garrisons, and fixed the 1st day of May as the time when all things should be ready.

Leaving these officers to complete the details of organization and preparation, I returned again to Nashville on the 2d of April and gave my personal attention to the question of supplies. I found the depots at Nashville abundantly supplied, and the railroads in very fair order, and that steps had already been taken to supply cars and locomotives to fill the new and increased demand of the service, but the impoverished condition of the inhabitants of East Tennessee, more especially in the region around Chattanooga, had forced the commanding officers of the posts to issue food to the people. I was compelled to stop this, for a simple calculation showed that a single railroad could not feed the armies and the people too, and of course the army had the preference, but I endeavored to point the people to new channels of supply. [*The War of the Rebellion: A Compilation of the Official Records of the Union and Confederate Armies,* 129 vols. (Washington, D.C.: Government Printing Office, 1891), vol. XXXVIII, pt. 1, pp. 61–62. Hereafter cited as *O.R.*]

General Orders No. 6, Nashville, Tennessee, 6 April 1864

To enable the military roads running from Nashville to supply more fully the armies in the field, the following regulations will hereafter be observed:

I. No citizen, nor any private freight whatever, will be transported by the railroads, save as hereinafter provided.

II. Officers traveling under orders, or on leave of absence, sick or furloughed soldiers departing from or returning to their regiments, and small detachments of troops, will be transported on the orders of post commanders, of Brigadier General Andrew Johnson, Military Governor of Tennessee, or of the commanding officer of either of the Departments of the Ohio, the Cumberland, or the Tennessee, or of the Military Division of the Mississippi. Bodies of troops will not be transported by railroads when it is possible for them to march, except upon the order of the commanding officer of some one of the Military Departments above named. Civil employees of the various Staff Departments will be transported on the order of the senior and supervising Quartermaster, Department of the Cumberland, at Nashville . . . or of the commanding officer of either of the Military Departments above named. Employees of the railroads will be transported on the order of the superintendent or chief engineer of the railroads.

III. No citizens will be allowed to travel on the railroads at all except on the permit of the commanding officer of one of the three Military Departments, or of the Military Division of the Mississippi, and when their transportation will not prevent that of any army supplies, of which the proper officer of the Quartermaster's Department will be the judge.

IV. Express companies will be allowed one car per day each way, on each military road, to carry small parcels for soldiers and officers. One car per day more for sutlers' goods and officers' stores, may be allowed by the senior and supervising Quartermaster at Nashville, at his discretion; these cars to be furnished by the express companies and attached to the passenger trains. When a sufficient surplus of stores has been accumulated at the front the senior and supervising Quartermaster . . . may increase this allowance, but not before.

V. Stores exclusively for officers' messes in very limited quantities, after due inspection by the Inspecting Officer at Nashville . . . of sutlers' goods, and all private stores, shipped to the front, will be passed

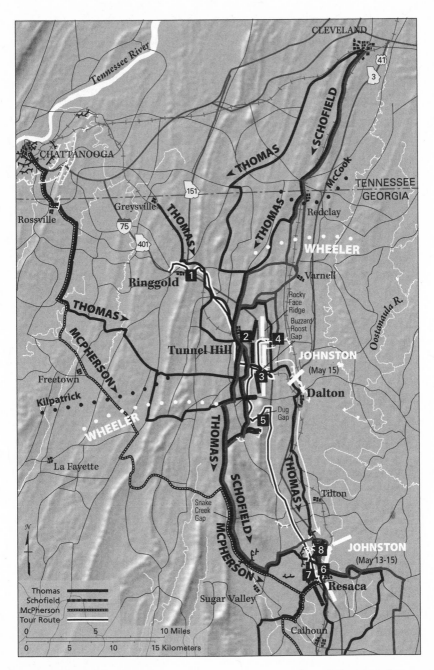

Initial Movements of Union Armies and Disposition of Confederate Defenses

free on the several roads, on the order of the senior and supervising Quartermaster, Department of the Cumberland, at Nashville. . . .

VI. Horses, cattle, or other live stock, will not be transported by railroad, except on the written order of the Commanding General of the Military Division, or of one of the Military Departments.

VII. Trains on their return trips will be allowed to bring up private freight, when the shipment thereof does not interfere with the full working of the roads, of which the senior and supervising Quartermaster at Nashville will be the judge.

VIII. Provost Marshals have nothing to do with transportation by railroads. Their passes merely mean that the bearer can go from one point to another named in their pass, but not necessarily by rail. The railroads are purely for army purposes.

IX. When the rolling stock of the railroads is increased, or when a due accumulation of stores has been made at the front, increased facilities may be extended to passengers and private freight, of which due notice will be given. Until that time citizens and sutlers must use wagons.

X. Until the railroad is relieved all military posts within thirty-five miles of Nashville, and twenty miles of Stevenson, Bridgeport, Chattanooga, Huntsville, and Loudon, must haul their stores by wagons.

XI. The general manager of the railroads, and his duly appointed agents and conductors, will control the trains, and will be authorized to call on every passenger for his orders for transportation by railroad, that they may be returned to the general manager or superintendent. The military guard will enforce good order, and sustain the agents and conductors of the roads in their rightful authority, but will report any mismanagement or neglect of duty, through their officers, to these Headquarters.

XII. Until other arrangements are perfected, commanding officers, on the request of the railroad managers, will furnish details for providing wood or water at such points as may be necessary to supply the trains. [*Military Orders of General William T. Sherman, 1861–65* (Washington, D.C.: 1869), pp. 233–235. Hereafter cited as *Orders.*]

Report of Maj. Gen. William T. Sherman, USA (continued)

At first my orders operated very hard, but the prolific soil soon afforded early vegetables, and ox-wagons hauled meat and bread from

Kentucky, so that no actual suffering resulted, and I trust that those who clamored at the cruelty and hardships of the day have already seen in the results a perfect justification of my course. At once the store-houses at Chattanooga began to fill so that by the 1st of May a very respectable quantity of food and forage had been accumulated there, and from that day to this stores have been brought forward in wonderful abundance, with a surplus that has enabled me to feed the army well during the whole period of time, although the enemy has succeeded more than once in breaking our road for many miles at different points.

During the month of April I received from Lieutenant-General Grant a map, with a letter of instructions. [O.R., XXXVIII, pt. 1, p. 62.]

Lt. Gen. Ulysses S. Grant, USA, Commanding General, U.S. Army, to Maj. Gen. William T. Sherman, 4 April 1864

Private and Confidential

It is my design, if the enemy keep quiet and allow me to take the initiative in the spring campaign, to work all parts of the Army together and somewhat toward a common center. For your information I now write you my programme as at present determined upon. I have sent orders to [Maj. Gen. N. P.] Banks . . . to finish up his present expedition against Shreveport with all dispatch; to turn over the defense of the Red River to General [Frederick] Steele and the navy, and return your troops to you and his own to New Orleans; to abandon all of Texas except the Rio Grande, and to hold that with . . . four thousand men; to reduce the number of troops on the Mississippi to the lowest number necessary to hold it, and to collect from his command not less than 25,000 men. To this I will add 5,000 from Missouri. With this force he is to commence operations against Mobile as soon as he can. It will be impossible for him to commence too early.

[Maj. Gen. Q. A.] Gilmore joins [Maj. Gen. B. F.] Butler with 10,000 men, and the two operate against Richmond from the south side of James River. This will give Butler 35,000 men to operate with. . . . I will stay with the Army of the Potomac, increased by Burnside's Corps of not less than 25,000 effective men, and operate directly against Lee's Army wherever it may be found. [Maj. Gen. Franz] Sigel collects all his available force in two columns . . . to move against the Virginia and Tennessee Railroad. . . .

You I propose to move against *Johnston's* army, to break it up and to get into the interior of the enemy's country as far as you can, inflicting all the damage you can against their War resources.

I do not propose to lay down for you a plan of campaign, but simply to lay down the work it is desirable to have done, and leave you free to execute in your own way. Submit to me, however, as early as you can, your plan of operation. . . . I want to be ready to move by the 25th instant if possible. . . . I know you will have difficulties to encounter getting through the mountains to where supplies are abundant, but I believe you will accomplish it. [O.R., XXXII, pt. 3, pp. 245–246.]

Sherman to Grant, 10 April 1864

Private and Confidential

Your two letters of April 4 . . . afford me infinite satisfaction. That we are now all to act in a common plan, converging on a common center, looks like enlightened war.

Like yourself you take the biggest load, and from me you shall have thorough and hearty cooperation. I will not let side issues draw me off from your main plan in which I am to knock *Joe Johnston*, and do as much damage to the resources of the enemy as possible. . . . I have seen all my army, corps and division Commanders and have signified only to . . . Schofield, Thomas and McPherson our general plans. . . . I am pushing stores to the front with all possible dispatch. . . . Each of the three armies will guard by detachments of its own their rear communications.

At the signal given by you, Schofield will leave a select garrison at Knoxville and Loudon, and with 12,000 men drop down to Hiwassee and march on *Johnston's* right by the old Federal Road. Stoneman, now in Kentucky organizing the cavalry forces of the Army of the Ohio, will operate with Schofield on his left front. . . . Thomas will aim to have 45,000 men of all arms and move straight on *Johnston* wherever he may be, fighting him cautiously, persistently, and to the best of advantage. He will have two divisions of cavalry to take advantage of any offering. McPherson will have . . . full 30,000 of the best men in America. He will cross the Tennessee at Decatur and Whitesburg, march toward Rome, and feel for Thomas.

If *Johnston* fall behind the Coosa, then McPherson will push for Rome, and if *Johnston* then fall behind the Chattahoochee, as I believe he will, then McPherson will cross and join with Thomas. McPherson has no cavalry, but I have taken one of Thomas' divisions, viz., Garrard's, 6,000 strong, which I now have at Columbia, mounting, equipping and preparing. I design this division to operate on McPherson's right rear or front, according as the enemy appears. . . .

Should *Johnston* fall behind the Chattahoochee I would feign to the right, but pass to the left, and act on Atlanta or on its eastern communications, according to developed facts. . . . I would ever bear in mind that *Johnston* is at all times to be kept so busy that he cannot, in any event, send any part of his command against you or Banks. [*O.R.*, XXXII, pt. 3, pp. 312–314.]

Report of Maj. Gen. William T. Sherman, USA (continued)

Subsequently I received from him notice that he would move from his camp about Culpeper, Va., on the 5th of May, and he wanted me to do the same from Chattanooga. My troops were still dispersed, and the cavalry, so necessary to our success, was yet collecting horses at Nicholasville, Ky., and Columbia, Tenn.

On the 27th of April I put all the troops in motion toward Chattanooga, and on the next day went there in person. My aim and purpose was to make the Army of the Cumberland 50,000 men, that of the Tennessee 35,000, and that of the Ohio 15,000. These figures were approximated, but never reached, the Army of the Tennessee failing to receive certain divisions that were still kept on the Mississippi River, resulting from the unfavorable issue of the Red River expedition. But on the 1st of May the effective strength of the several armies for offensive purposes was about as follows:

Army of the Cumberland, Major-General Thomas commanding: Infantry, 54,568; artillery, 2,377; cavalry, 3,828; total, 60,773. Guns, 130.

Army of the Tennessee, Major-General McPherson commanding: Infantry, 22,437; artillery, 1,404; cavalry, 624; total, 24,465. Guns, 96.

Army of the Ohio, Major-General Schofield commanding: Infantry, 11,183; artillery, 679; cavalry, 1,697; total, 13,559. Guns, 28.

Grand aggregate: Troops, 98,797; guns, 254.

About these figures have been maintained during the campaign, the number of men joining from furlough and hospitals about compensating for the loss in battle and from sickness.

These armies were grouped on the morning of May 6 as follows: That of the Cumberland at and near Ringgold; that of the Tennessee at Gordon's Mills, on the Chickamauga; and that of the Ohio near Red Clay, on the Georgia line, north of Dalton.

The enemy lay in and about Dalton, superior to me in cavalry ([Maj. Gen. *Joseph*] *Wheeler's*), and with three corps of infantry and artillery, viz.: *Hardee's, Hood's*, and *Polk's*, the whole commanded by General *Joe Johnston*. . . . I estimated the cavalry under *Wheeler* at about 10,000, and the infantry and artillery about 45,000 to 50,000 men. [*O.R.*, XXXVIII, pt. 1, pp. 61–62.]

General Orders No. 7, 18 April 1864

II. When troops are ordered to march for action . . . all encumbrances must be left in store at the most safe and convenient point. Mounted officers (general, regimental, or Cavalry) will be expected to carry on their own or led horses the necessary bedding and changes of clothing, with forage and provisions for themselves for three days—which must last five days. Infantry officers and soldiers must carry on their persons or led horses . . . the same; to which end will be allowed to each company, when practicable, one led horse or pack mule. Artillery can carry the same on their caissons, so that all troops must be in readiness for motion, without wagons, for a five days' operation.

III. For longer periods of service the Generals . . . will indicate in orders beforehand the number of wagons to each Headquarters and subdivision of command. In no event will tents be carried, or chests, or boxes, or trunks. Wagons must be reserved for ammunition proper, for cooking utensils, for provisions consisting exclusively of bread or flour, salt, sugar, coffee, and bacon or pork—in the proportion of thirty days' sugar and coffee, double of salt, twenty days' of bread or flour, and six of pork or bacon. The meat ration must be gathered in the country or driven on the hoof. Officers must be restricted to the same food as soldiers, and the general knows that our soldiers will submit to any deprivation, provided life and health can be sustained and they are satisfied of the necessity.

IV. One or two ambulances and one wagon should follow each regiment; all other wheeled vehicles should be made up into trains of convenient size, always under command of some Quartermaster, with a proper escort; and minute instructions should be imparted to the officers in charge of trains as to keeping closed up, doubling up on the roads when they are wide enough, or parking in side fields when there is any cause of delay ahead, so that the long periods of standing in a road, which fatigue the troops so much, may be avoided. [*Orders,* pp. 235–236.]

General Orders No. 10, 26 April 1864

I. There will be established, at or near Nashville, one or more Camps of Instruction, in which will be collected all regiments arriving from the rear which are not assigned to any one of the . . . armies in the field, all detachments or individuals who have got astray from their commands, and all convalescents discharged from hospitals. These camps will be under the general supervision of the commanding officer of the District of Nashville, who will assign to each a General Officer, who will . . . organize and equip for service all such regiments and detachments, and subject them to a thorough system of instruction in the drill and guard duties. . . .

III. Soldiers' Homes are merely designed for the accommodation of men in transit; and when delayed from any cause, the men will be sent to the Camp of Instruction. Officers, and men also, in and about Nashville awaiting orders, will be sent to the Camp of Instruction. . . .

V. Patrols will, from time to time, be sent to collect men and officers who are in Nashville without proper authority. All who are not in possession of written orders that warrant their presence in Nashville will be arrested and taken to the Camp of Instruction. [*Orders,* pp. 237–238.]

Sherman to Grant, 24 April 1864

General: I now have, at the hands of Colonel [Cyrus B.] Comstock, of your staff, the letter of April 19, and am as far prepared to assume the offensive as possible: I only ask as much time as you think proper to enable me to get up McPherson's two divisions from Cairo. . . .

McPherson is ordered to assemble the Fifteenth Corps near Larkin's, and to get [Maj. Gen. G. M.] Dodge and [Maj. Gen. Francis P.] Blair [Jr.] at Decatur at the earliest possible moment, and from these two points he will direct his forces on Lebanon, Summerville, and La

Fayette, where he will act against *Johnston* if he accepts battle at Dalton, or move in the direction of Rome if he gives up Dalton and falls behind the Oostenaula or Etowah. I see there is some risk in dividing our forces, but Thomas and Schofield will have forces enough to cover all the valley as far as Dalton, and should *Johnston* turn his whole force against McPherson, the latter will have his bridge at Larkin's and the route to Chattanooga via Will's Valley and the Chattanooga, and if *Johnston* attempts to leave Dalton, Thomas will have force enough to push on through Dalton to Kingston, which would checkmate him.

My own opinion is *Johnston* will be compelled to hang to his railroad, the only possible avenue of supply to his army, estimated from 45,000 to 60,000 men. At La Fayette all our armies will be together, and if *Johnston* stands at Dalton we must attack him in position. Thomas feels certain that he has no material increase of force, and that he has not sent away *Hardee* or any part of his army.

Supplies are the great question. I have materially increased the number of cars daily. When I got here they ran from 65 to 80 per day. Yesterday the report was 193, today 134, and my estimate is 145 per day will give us daily a day's accumulation.

McPherson is ordered to carry in wagons twenty days' supplies and rely on the depot at Ringgold for the renewal of his bread ration. Beeves are now being driven to the front. . . .

Our weakest point will be from the direction of Decatur, and I will be forced to risk something from that quarter, depending on the fact that the enemy has no force available with which to threaten our communications from that direction. Colonel Comstock will explain much that I cannot commit to paper. [*O.R.*, XXXII, pt. 3, pp. 465–466.]

2. GENERAL SHERMAN'S OPENING MOVES

Continue driving in the same direction on U.S. 41. After traveling about 2.75 miles you will cross I-75. Stay on U.S. 41; 3.9 miles beyond the interstate you will approach a railroad overpass. Immediately after passing over the tracks, near the crest of the overpass, turn left on Oak Street. Follow Oak Street as it parallels the railroad for about 0.2 mile and then continue straight on Clisby-Austin Road where Oak Street turns left to cross the tracks. Drive about 0.3 mile on Clisby-Austin Road, crossing Tanyard Creek on a one-way bridge and passing the Austin House, General Sherman's headquarters during this phase of the campaign. Turn left into the crushed rock parking lot and park your vehicle here. Walk toward Tunnel Hill until you can see the old tunnel to the right of the modern tunnel.

STOP 2, TUNNEL HILL

5–7 May 1864

Narrative of Maj. Gen. William T. Sherman, USA, Commanding Military Division of the Mississippi

On the 5th I rode out to Ringgold, and on the very day appointed by General Grant from his headquarters in Virginia the great campaign was begun. . . . My general headquarters and official records remained back at Nashville, and I had near me only my personal staff and inspectors-general, with about half a dozen wagons, and a single company of Ohio sharp-shooters . . . as headquarters or camp guard. I also had a small company of irregular Alabama cavalry . . . used mostly as orderlies and couriers. No wall-tents were allowed, only the flies. Our mess establishment was less in bulk than that of any of the brigade commanders . . . because I wanted to set the example, and gradually to convert all parts of that army into a mobile machine, willing and able to start at a minute's notice, and to subsist on the scantiest food. To reap absolute success might involve the necessity even

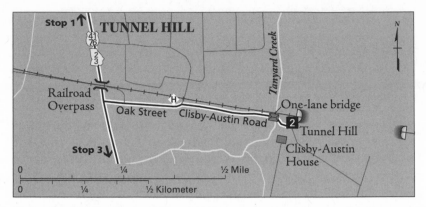

Sherman's Headquarters at Tunnel Hill (Stop 2)

of dropping all wagons, and to subsist on the chance food which the country was known to contain.

I had obtained not only the United States census-tables of 1860, but a compilation made by the Controller of the State of Georgia for the purpose of taxation, containing in considerable detail the "population and statistics" of every county in Georgia. One of my aides (Captain Dayton) acted as assistant adjutant general, with an order-book, letter-book, and writing paper that filled a small chest not much larger than an ordinary candle-box. The only reports and returns called for were the ordinary tri-monthly returns of "effective strength." As these accumulated they were sent back to Nashville, and afterward were embraced in the archives of the Military Division of the Mississippi. [William Tecumseh Sherman, *Memoirs of General W. T. Sherman*, 2 vols. (New York: Library of America, 1990), vol. II, pp. 31–32. Hereafter cited as Sherman, *Memoirs*.]

Report of Maj. Gen. William T. Sherman, USA, Commanding Military Division of the Mississippi

To strike Dalton in front was impracticable, as it was covered by an inaccessible ridge known as the Rocky Face, through which was a pass between Tunnel Hill and Dalton known as the Buzzard Roost, through which lay the railroad and wagon road. It was narrow, well obstructed by abatis, and flooded by water caused by dams across Mill Creek. Batteries also commanded it in its whole length from the spurs on either side, and more especially from a ridge at the farther end like a traverse directly across its debouche. It was, therefore, necessary to turn it. On its north front the enemy had a strong line of works behind Mill Creek, so that my attention was at once directed to the south. In that direction I found Snake Creek Gap, affording me a good practicable way to reach Resaca, a point on the enemy's railroad line of communication, eighteen miles below Dalton. Accordingly I ordered General McPherson to move rapidly from his position at Gordon's Mills. . . . During the movement General Thomas was to make a strong feint of attack in front, while General Schofield pressed down from the north. [O.R., XXXVIII, pt. 1, p. 63.]

Maj. Gen. William T. Sherman to Maj. Gen. James B. McPherson, USA, Commanding Army of the Tennessee, 5 May 1864

Sir: The enemy still lies about Dalton, and from all appearances is on the defensive, guarding approaches mostly from the north and west. He occupies in some force the range of hills known as the Tunnel Hill. By tomorrow night our forces will be about as follows: Schofield at Red Clay; Thomas at Ringgold—his left, Catoosa Springs, center at Ringgold, and right (Hooker) near Wood's Station; and you at Gordon's Mills. If you are all ready I propose on Saturday morning [May 7] to move against the enemy—Thomas directly on Tunnel Hill; Schofield to Varnell's and the gap between it and Catoosa Springs, feeling toward Thomas; Hooker will move through Nickajack Gap on Trickum and threaten the road which runs from Buzzard Roost to Snake [Creek] Gap.

As these are in progress I want you to move, via Rock Spring, Tavern Road, to the head of Middle Chickamauga; then to Villanow; then to Snake [Creek] Gap, secure it and from it make a bold attack on the enemy's flank or his railroad at any point between Tilton and Resaca. I am in hopes that Garrard's cavalry will be at Villanow as soon as you, for, you know, I have sent General Corse to meet him at Shellmound and conduct him across the mountain to La Fayette and to you. But, in any event, his movement will cover your right rear and enable you to leave all encumbrances either at Ship's Gap or Villanow, as you deem best.

I hope the enemy will fight at Dalton, in which case he can have no force there that can interfere with you. But, should his policy be to fall back along his railroad, you will hit him in flank. Do not fail in that event to make the most of the opportunity by the most vigorous attack possible, as it may save us what we have most reason to apprehend—a slow pursuit, in which he gains strength as we lose it. In either event you may be sure the forces north of you will prevent his turning on you alone.

In the event of hearing the sound of heavy battle about Dalton, the greater necessity for your rapid movement on the railroad. It once broken to an extent that would take them days to repair, you can withdraw to Snake [Creek] Gap and come to us or await the development according to your judgment or information you may receive. I want to put this plan in operation, beginning with Saturday morning if possible. The sooner the better for us. [O.R., XXXVIII, pt. 4, pp. 39–40.]

Maj. Gen. William T. Sherman to Maj. Gen. George H. Thomas, USA, Commanding Army of the Cumberland, 5 May 1864

The position of our troops tomorrow night, the 6th instant, will be, Schofield at Red Clay, you at Ringgold, and McPherson at Gordon's Mills. The plan of action will be: You move in force on Tunnel Hill, secure it and threaten Dalton in front, but not to attack its defenses until further orders, unless the enemy assumes the offensive against either of our wings, when all must attack directly in front toward the enemy's main army and not without orders detach to the relief of the threatened wing. . . . I want you, with cavalry or infantry, to fill well up Dogwood Valley, and communicate with McPherson at Villanow. Trains likely to embarrass our movements should not be taken east of Taylor's Ridge, till we have observed the effect of these first movements. [O.R., XXXVIII, pt. 4, p. 35.]

Maj. Gen. William T. Sherman to Maj. Gen. John M. Schofield, USA, Commanding Army of the Ohio, 5 May 1864

I want you to keep up communication with Howard, and as he moves toward Tunnel Hill you move on Varnell's Station, inclining to your right so as to hold the road between Varnell's and Catoosa Springs. If you have reason to apprehend encountering a force superior to your own, you can cross the hills to your right and make for Catoosa. As you perceive I do not propose to attack Dalton from the north, but the west and south, therefore the movement should continue to Varnell's except with almost a certainty of the case I make of a superior force there. . . . As soon as Tunnel Hill is secured to us, I shall pause to give McPherson time for his longer march, but we must occupy the attention of all the enemy lest he turn his whole force on McPherson, which must be prevented. Therefore, on the sound of heavy battle always close up on Howard and act according to circumstances. We will not be able to detach to McPherson's assistance, but can press so closely from this direction that he cannot detach but a part of his command against him. [*O.R.*, XXXVIII, pt. 4, p. 38.]

Report of Maj. Gen. George H. Thomas, USA, Commanding Army of the Cumberland

The army got into position by the first, and stood as . . . directed, communication having been fully established from the right to the left of the whole command. According to instructions . . . the army moved on Tunnel Hill at daylight on the 7th in three columns—[Maj. Gen. John M.] Palmer's corps on the direct road from Ringgold, Howard via Lee's house, and Hooker's via Nickajack Gap and Trickum. The enemy made some show of resistance in Palmer's front, but evacuated Tunnel Hill on the appearance of Howard's column on his flank and fled toward Buzzard Roost, our troops occupying Tunnel Hill Ridge. Palmer's command was then moved forward and took position on Howard's right along the ridge, and both corps remained there for the night. [*O.R.*, XXXVIII, pt. 1, p. 139.]

Report of Brevet Maj. Gen. Jefferson C. Davis, USA, Commanding Second Division, Fourteenth Army Corps, Army of the Cumberland

On the morning of the 5th the division passed through the gap at Ringgold, and went into bivouac near the stone church, at the forks of the Dalton and Cleveland roads. The enemy's pickets were encountered . . . in small force. On the morning of the 7th, the advance of the army was assigned to my division, and at Daylight [Col. Daniel] McCook's brigade, followed by the rest of my command, moved on the direct road to Tunnel Hill. The enemy's cavalry was soon encountered and some sharp skirmishing kept up until the head of the column reached Smith's house, within cannon range of the enemy's position at Tunnel Hill. At this point the enemy opened his artillery, but being familiar with the ground, I soon made disposition of my troops and placed a few guns in position, and ordered them to return the fire, which was promptly executed. In accordance with the general plan for the advance upon that place, Major General Howard's corps moved from Cherokee Springs, from the direction of Cleveland, and formed a junction with my command at this point. General Howard sent a force to operate on the north end of Tunnel Hill, while a strong line of skirmishers from McCook's brigade . . . attacked the enemy's position below the town near where the road leading to Dalton crosses the hill. These movements, assisted by the action of the batteries, caused the enemy to withdraw from his position and retreat toward Buzzard Roost. [*O.R.*, XXXVIII, pt. 1, p. 626.]

Sherman to Schofield, Tunnel Hill, 7 May 1864, 2 p.m.

Thomas took Tunnel Hill with scarcely any opposition. I have been all over it. It is a stony ridge . . . and looks right toward a break of Rocky Face Ridge, through which pass the rail and common roads. In this gorge is the Buzzard Roost, which is the place where *Johnston* expects to fight us. Tonight McPherson will be at Ship's Gap, tomorrow at Villanow and Snake Creek Gap, and the next day should strike or threaten the railroad. Tomorrow I want to occupy all of *Johnston's* attention. Thomas will threaten in front. I want you to hold well the gap toward Varnell's, and to reconnoiter up the point of Rocky Face near Lee's, and get a foothold on the ridge, so as to move on the ridge toward Buzzard Roost. If possible, get some point where you can see Dalton, and I want to guard against the possibility of *Johnston* turning on McPherson. Hooker is about Trickum. Reconnoiter the ridge tonight, and make a lodgment tomorrow morning, but don't be drawn into a battle. [*O.R.*, XXXVIII, pt. 4, p. 65.]

Schofield to Sherman, 7 May 1864, 8:15 p.m.

Lieutenant Twining has returned from reconnaissance of the north point of Rocky Face. The ascent from the north is not very difficult. The summit is now occupied by an infantry picket only. A considerable infantry force is encamped along the valley at the foot of the ridge extending to about two miles and a half from Buzzard Roost. This was estimated from the sound of the drums. The first high point is about three miles from Buzzard Roost. Lieutenant Twining and his guide think Dalton can be plainly seen from that point. I presume the point can be carried without much difficulty, unless it be occupied by the enemy in force tonight. I will be ready to march at daylight, and await your instructions. [*O.R.*, XXXVIII, pt. 4, pp. 65–66.]

8 May 1864

Sherman to Thomas, Tunnel Hill

The reconnaissance today has not drawn a single gun of the enemy, nor has any one seen a gun certain. I sat on the hill three hours and don't think [Maj. Gen. Daniel] Butterfield's skirmishers more than got abreast of the hill used as signal hill, certainly not within 300 yards of the gap. Schofield reports extensive works the other side of the ridge, I suppose in Crow's Valley, but not many men. I fear *Johnston* is annoying us with small detachments, whilst he will be about Resaca in force. Have you any more definite reports than I indicate. Are you prepared to make an attack on the Buzzard Roost, and how? [*O.R.*, XXXVIII, pt. 4, p. 71.]

Sherman to Schofield, 12 Noon, Tunnel Hill

When you get to the summit make a lodgment, and feel along the ridge southward till you can see down into the Buzzard Roost Gap. Being now in communication with Howard's troops you can easily be reinforced. I doubt the strength of the enemy in Dalton, else they would not permit this movement. Develop the truth, for if *Johnston* is moving south we should be on his heels all the time. [*O.R.*, XXXVIII, pt. 4, p. 82.]

When Schofield reached the gap at the northern end of Rocky Face Ridge, he found Brig. Gen. Charles G. Harker's brigade of Brig. Gen. John Newton's division, Fourth Army Corps, already on the ridge ahead of him. Accordingly he deployed two brigades in the gap and brought forward another division to the left and rear, within supporting distance. From this position he could see the Confederate works on the ridge in the rear of Rocky Face, some five or six miles north of Dalton, which he reported as being "strongly occupied" by enemy infantry. While he could see no Confederate infantry in the valley, he reported to Sherman that he lacked sufficient information to "justify" an advance toward Dalton.

Sherman to Schofield, Tunnel Hill

If you are satisfied that the enemy is in Dalton in force you may take up a position as strong as possible, covering the road to Varnell's and Dalton, and connect with Newton. I am surprised the enemy does not use artillery to any of our approaching parties. The absence of artillery surprises me. Are you certain his works are occupied in force? That is the point I want to develop. McPherson was passing Villanow at 2 p.m. today. Use every bit of daylight to study the ground, and report to me with sketch and letter at dark. [*O.R.*, XXXVIII, pt. 4, p. 83.]

Schofield to Sherman, 8:30 p.m.

I have spent most of the day until dark in studying the ground east of Rocky Face, and understand it pretty well. If Newton holds this gap at the end of Rocky Face, where [Brig. Gen. Henry M.] Judah's left brigade now is, I can take a strong position running about east northeast from this point and covering the roads from Lee's and Varnell's to Dalton and connect with Newton. How much my left would be exposed I cannot say, as I have not yet been able to see beyond the range of hills to the east of Varnell's and Dalton road. I think there would be little risked in taking the position, even if it should not be afterward deemed advisable to maintain it or to advance.

I am not able to say whether the enemy is in force at Dalton. The defenses I saw were only those on the north point of the high ridge east of Rocky Face. The general line of defense is not visible from any point I have reached today. One thousand men would be a strong garrison for the works I saw.

I sent General Judah this afternoon with one of his brigades up to General [Charles G.] Harker's position near the rebel signal station, Harker being in front and awaiting orders relative to attacking. Judah did not attack. He thinks he can carry the signal station in the night without very much loss. From the descriptions given me by General Newton and my staff officers, who have been on the ridge, it seems impossible to take that position by daylight. The chances of success at night would be better. After carrying that point it would take a long time to reach the immediate vicinity of Buzzard Roost. If the possession of the signal station is in itself of great importance, it may be worth the risk. . . . If only as means of reaching Buzzard Roost, I judge not. . . .

I send a sketch of the country I have seen today. It is not very accurate because the topographers have not had time to plot their work. The valleys leading north and south are open fields, while the ridges are steep, stony, and wooded. I have indicated . . . my proposed position for tomorrow, also that which I now occupy. [O.R., XXXVIII, pt. 4, p. 83.]

Sherman to Schofield, Midnight, Tunnel Hill

I am just in receipt of your valuable sketch and note. My direction for you to pass along the top of the ridge till you could look into Buzzard Roost was based on the idea that the top, like Lookout [Mountain], was a kind of plateau, but, according to General Harker's report, it must be a perfect couteau, knife edge, a sharp ridge. Tomorrow you keep up communication with that force, tying to it strong, and let your left move up, not too much, but enough for a change, and keep up the idea of advance. Keep skirmishers out, with orders to act with boldness, but not rashness, to feel the enemy's position from your direction. . . . At the earliest possible moment get a look into the enemy's lines and act on the knowledge of the state of facts to your front and rear.

McPherson passed Villanow at 2 p.m. for Snake Creek Gap, which he is ordered to secure good and operate from it on the enemy's line and rear. We must not let *Johnston* amuse us here by a small force whilst he turns on McPherson. Therefore I want the earliest possible information from all points what *Johnston* does when he finds not a mere detachment, but a large, strong army within five miles of Resaca, covered against him by the very mountains he chose to cover himself. Hooker can go to McPherson's rear in about eight miles, his right by two and a half to three below Trickum; therefore keep touched to the right, your lines on strong ground but your vedettes out as boldly as possible for knowledge. All of McCook's cavalry will be on your left, and the effect of Stoneman's coming up will soon be felt. [*O.R.*, XXXVIII, pt. 4, p. 84.]

Brig. Gen. William D. Whipple, USA, Chief of Staff,
Army of the Cumberland, to Maj. Gen. William T. Sherman,
Midnight

General: Inclosed I have the honor to forward . . . [the] statement of a prisoner of war.

I was captured late this evening, about half a mile from Buzzard Roost Gap, near the railroad. I belong to the Thirty-sixth Alabama infantry, [Brig. Gen. *Henry D.*] *Clayton's* brigade, [Maj. Gen. *Alexander P.*] *Stewart's* division [*Hood's* Corps]. There are about 42,000 infantry about Dalton, unless reenforced [*sic*] since last night. Of these there are 11,000 men posted in Buzzard Roost Gap, comprising *Stewart's* and [Maj. Gen. *John C.*] *Breckinridge's* old divisions, commanded, I think, by [Maj. Gen. *William B.*] *Bate.* [Maj. Gen. *Thomas C.*] *Hindman's* and [Maj. Gen. *Carter L.*] *Stevenson's* divisions, numbering about 10,000, are stationed about five miles and a half north of Dalton, lying between the East Tennessee railroad and the mountain. *Cleburn[e]'s* division, about 6,000 strong, is on *Hindman's* right, between him and the railroad. The position of the three latter divisions is strongly entrenched. There is a good deal of artillery, none of it heavier than 10-pounder caliber. The horses are not in good condition, and would not stand a long march. The rebels were working all last night fortifying Buzzard Roost Gap, and have masked batteries at points all along through it. The low ground has been all overflowed by dams, so that you can't travel the road, except close up to the hill. The dams are covered over with brush to conceal them. [Maj. Gen. *Nathan B.*] *Forrest* was reported last night to be within ten hours' ride of Resaca. *Johnston* is reported to have said that he wished the Federals would go to his (rebel) left; that he would rather have them attempt a flank there than on his right. The army is full of confidence in *Johnston* and of whipping the United States forces, and intend to make a desperate struggle. [*O.R.*, XXXVIII, pt. 4, pp. 71–72.]

3. MILL CREEK GAP AND ROCKY FACE

Retrace your route on Oak Street. Note the historical markers on your right at that point. You may wish to stop to read them before returning to U.S. 41. Turn left onto that highway. Drive about 3.6 miles to Mill Creek, move into the right lane, and turn right at about 4.1 miles into the Georgia State Patrol facility. Make your right turn just before the Georgia State Patrol sign. Turn left immediately into the site with historical markers on the hillside below and in front of the Georgia State Patrol building. Park and orient yourself using the historical markers.

EXCURSION

If you are dressed for walking and wish to view remnants of Confederate defensive positions, walk up the hill on the west side of the Georgia State Patrol building. Follow the narrow concrete road marked "Personnel Only" up past the rear of the First Church of the Nazarene and through the parking lot of Tipton's Family Life Center to the guardrail near the southeast corner of the parking area. The George Dewey Memorial Trail parallels the back of the lot, and you can follow white blazes uphill to the right (west). After a few hundred yards the trail bends sharply to the left. Here you can see well-preserved artillery positions, part of the extensive earthworks that were manned by General *Johnston's* soldiers. This should give you a sense of the strength of the positions he commanded at this site.

Retrace the route to your car and orient yourself using the historical markers.

STOP 3, BUZZARD'S ROOST

9–12 May 1864

OPERATIONS

Report of Gen. Joseph E. Johnston, CSA, Commanding Army of Tennessee

I assumed command of the Army of Tennessee at Dalton on the 27th of December. . . . The effective total of the infantry and artillery of the army, including two brigades belonging to the Department of Mississippi, was 36,826. The effective total of the cavalry, including *Roddey's* command at Tuscumbia, was 5,613. The Federal force in our front, exclusive of cavalry, and the Ninth and Twenty-third Corps at Knoxville, was estimated at 80,000. The winter was mainly employed in improving the discipline and equipment of the army and bringing back absentees to the ranks. At the end of April more than 5,000 had rejoined their regiments. [*O.R.*, XXXVIII, pt. 3, p. 612.]

Narrative of Gen. Joseph E. Johnston, CSA, Commanding Army of Tennessee

An active campaign of six months, half of it in the rugged region between Chattanooga and Dalton, had so much reduced the condition of the horses of the cavalry and artillery, as well as of the mules of the wagon-trains, that most of them were unfit for active service. The rest they had been allowed at Dalton had not improved their condition materially; for, from want of good fuel, the railroad-trains had not been able to bring up full supplies of forage. This continued until near the end of January, when the management of the railroad had been greatly improved by the intervention of Governor [*Joseph E.*] Brown [of Georgia], and a better system introduced in the manner of forwarding military supplies.

This scarcity of food made it necessary to send almost half of the artillery-horses and all of the mules not required for camp-service to the valley of the Etowah, where long forage could be found, and the sources of supply of grain were nearer. . . . I find, in a letter to the President dated January 15th, this passage:

> Since my arrival, very little long forage has been received, and nothing like full rations of corn—that weevil-eaten. The officer commanding the artillery of a division that I inspected today reported that his horses had had but thirteen pounds each, of very bad corn, in the last three days.

Normally each horse required daily about fourteen pounds of hay and twelve pounds of grain, while each mule required the same amount of hay and nine pounds of grain.

In the course of the inspection . . . I found the condition of the army much less satisfactory than it had appeared to the

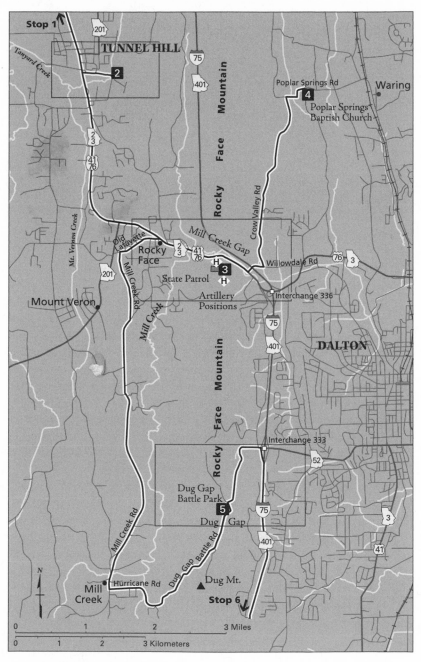

Tunnel Hill to Dug Gap

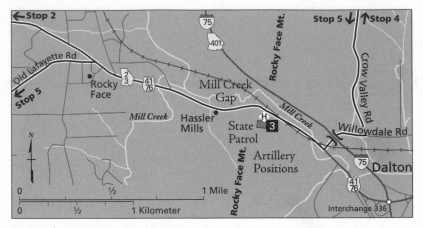

Mill Creek Gap (Stop 3)

President. . . . There was a great deficiency of blankets; and it was painful to see the number of bare feet in every regiment. . . . Two of the four brigades inspected by me that day were not in condition to march, for want of shoes. There was a deficiency, in the infantry, of six thousand small-arms. The artillery-horses were generally still so feeble from long, hard service and scarcity of forage, that it would have been impossible to manoeuvre our batteries in action, or to march with them at any ordinary rate on ordinary roads. It was long before they could draw the guns through fields. Early in February, when the supply of forage had become regular, and the face of the country almost dry, after the review of a corps, the teams of the Napoleon guns were unable to draw them up a trifling hill, over which the road to their stables passed.

On the 15th and 16th, [Brig. Gen. *William A.*] *Quarles's* and [Brig. Gen. *William E.*] *Baldwin's* brigades, "the last two sent from Mississippi," returned to that department in obedience to orders from the Secretary of War. At the same time Governor Brown transferred two regiments of State troops to the army. These were placed as guards for the protection of the railroad-bridges between Dalton and Atlanta. Intrenchments for this object were then in the course of construction, under the direction of the chief-engineer of the army, Brigadier General *Leadbetter*. . . .

The time of winter was employed mainly in improving the discipline and instruction of the troops, and attention to their

"Buzzard's Roost Pass." Union infantry columns advance under friendly artillery fire (*Harper's Pictorial History of the Great Rebellion* [New York: Harper Bros., 1866–1868], 603).

comfort. . . . Military operations were confined generally to skirmishing between little scouting parties of cavalry of our army with
pickets of the other. [Joseph E. Johnston, *Narrative of Military Operations* (New York: D. Appleton, 1874), pp. 279–280. Hereafter cited as
Military Operations.]

Report of Gen. Joseph E. Johnston, CSA (continued)

On February 17 the President ordered me by telegraph to detach
Lieutenant-General *Hardee* with the infantry of his corps, except *Ste-
venson's* division, to aid Lieutenant-General *Polk* against Sherman in
Mississippi. This order was obeyed as promptly as our means of trans-
portation permitted. The force detached was probably exaggerated to
Major-General Thomas, for on the 23d the Federal army advanced to
Ringgold, on the 24th drove in our outposts, and on the 25th skirmished at Mill Creek Gap and in Crow's Valley, east of Rocky Face
Mountain. We were successful at both places. At the latter, *Clayton's*
brigade, after a sharp action of half an hour, defeated double its number. At night it was reported that a U.S. brigade was occupying Dug
Gap, from which it had driven our troops. [Brig. Gen. H. B.] *Granbury's* (Texas) brigade, returning from Mississippi, had just arrived. It
was ordered to march to the foot of the mountain immediately and to
retake the gap at sunrise next morning, which was done. In the night
of the 26th the enemy retired. On February 27 I suggested to the Executive by letter through General [*Braxton*] *Bragg* [general in chief]
that all preparations for a forward movement should be made without
further delay.

In a letter dated 4th of March General *Bragg* desired me "to have
all things ready at the earliest practicable moment for the movement
indicated." . . . On the 18th a letter was received from General *Bragg*
sketching a plan of offensive operations, and numerating the troops to
be used in them under me. . . . I suggested modifications, and urged
that the additional troops named should be sent immediately to enable us, should the enemy advance, to beat him and then move forward; or should he not advance, do so ourselves. General *Bragg* replied
by telegraph on the 21st:

> Your dispatch . . . does not indicate acceptance of plan
> proposed. Troops can only be drawn from other points for

advance. Upon your decision of that point further action must depend.

I replied by telegraph on the 22d:

In my dispatch of 19th I expressly accept taking offensive. Only differ with you as to details. I assume that the enemy will be prepared for advance before we will, and will make it, to our advantage. Therefore I propose, both for offensive and defensive, to assemble our troops here immediately.

This was not noticed. Therefore, on the 25th I again urged the necessity of re-enforcing the *Army of Tennessee*, because the enemy was collecting a larger force than that of the last campaign, while ours was less than it had been then. On the 3rd of April Lieut. Col. *A. H. Cole* arrived at Dalton to direct the procuring of artillery horses and field transportation to enable the army to advance. On the 4th, under Orders [No.] 32, of 1864, I applied to the chief of the conscript service for 1,000 Negro teamsters. None were received.

On the 8th of April Col. *B. S. Ewell*, assistant adjutant-general, was sent to Richmond to represent to the President my wish to take the offensive with proper means, and to learn his views. A few days after Brigadier-General [*William N.*] *Pendleton* arrived from Richmond to explain to me the President's wishes on that subject. I explained to him the modification of the plan communicated by General *Bragg* (which seemed to me essential), which required that the intended re-enforcements should be sent to Dalton. I urged that this should be done without delay, because our present force was not sufficient even for defense, and to enable us to take the offensive if the enemy did not.

On the 1st of May I reported the enemy about to advance. On the 2d Brigadier-General [*Hugh*] *Mercer's* command arrived—about 1,400 effective infantry. On the 4th I expressed myself satisfied that the enemy was about to attack with his united forces, and again urged that a part of Lieutenant-General *Polk's* troops should be put at my disposal. I was informed by General *Bragg* that orders to that effect were given. Major General [*William T.*] *Martin*, whose division of cavalry, coming from East Tennessee, had been halted on the Etowah to recruit its horses, was ordered . . . to observe the Oostenaula from Resaca to Rome; and Brigadier-General [*John H.*] *Kelly* was ordered, with his command, from the neighborhood of Resaca, to report to Major-General *Wheeler*.

The effective artillery and infantry of the *Army of Tennessee* after the arrival of *Mercer's* brigade amounted to 40,900; the effective cavalry to about 4,000. Major-General Sherman's army . . . on the 5th of May was in line between Ringgold and Tunnel Hill, and, after skirmishing on that and the following day, on the 7th pressed back our advanced troops to Mill Creek Gap. [*O.R.*, XXXVIII, pt. 3, pp. 613–615.]

Narrative of Gen. Joseph E. Johnston, CSA (continued)

The position of Dalton had little to recommend it as a defensive one. It had neither intrinsic strength nor strategic advantage. It neither fully covered its own communications nor threatened those of the enemy. The railroad from Atlanta to Chattanooga passes through Rocky Face Ridge by Mill Creek Gap, three miles and a half beyond Dalton, but very obliquely, the course of the road being thirty degrees west of north, and that of the ridge about five degrees east of north.

As it terminates but three miles north of the gap, it offers little obstacle to the advance of a superior force from Ringgold to Dalton. Between Mill Creek and Snake Creek Gaps, this ridge protects the road to Atlanta on the west, but at the same time covers any direct approach from Chattanooga to Resaca or Calhoun—points on the route from Dalton to Atlanta—or flank movement in that direction, by an army in front of Mill Creek Gap. These considerations would have induced me to draw the troops back to the vicinity of Calhoun, to free our left flank from exposure, but for the earnestness with which the President and Secretary of War . . . wrote of early assumption of offensive operations and apprehension of the bad effect of a retrograde movement upon the spirit of the Southern people. [*Military Operations*, pp. 277–278.]

TACTICS

Narrative of Gen. Joseph E. Johnston, CSA (continued)

On the 5th, the Confederate troops were formed to receive the enemy. *Stewart's* and *Bate's* divisions, in Mill Creek Gap, in which they had constructed some slight defensive works—the former on the right of the stream, [Maj. Gen. *Benjamin F.*] *Cheatham's* on *Stewart's* right, occupying about a mile of the crest of the mountain; [Maj. Gen. *William H. T.*] *Walker's* in reserve; *Stevenson's* across Crow Valley, its left joining *Cheatham's* right, on the crest of the mountain; *Hindman's*, on the right of *Stevenson's*; and *Cleburn[e]'s* immediately in front of Dalton, and behind Mill Creek, facing toward Cleveland.

On the same day the Federal army was formed in order of battle, three miles in front of Tunnel Hill, and in that position skirmished with our advanced guard until dark. It was employed all of the next in selecting and occupying a position just beyond the range of the field-pieces of the Confederate advanced-guard, on which it halted for the night.

In the evening, a telegram from Lieutenant-General *Polk* informed me that he had been ordered to join the *Army of Tennessee* with all his infantry. At daybreak on the 7th, the Federal army moved forward, annoyed and delayed in its advance by dismounted Confederate cavalry, firing upon it from the cover of successive lines of very slight entrenchments, prepared the day before. Its progress was so slow that the Confederates were not driven from Tunnel Hill until eleven o'clock A.M., nor to Mill Creek Gap until three P.M. In the afternoon the Federal army placed itself in front of the Confederate line, its right a little south of Mill Creek Gap, and its left near the Cleveland Road.

In the evening, intelligence was received of the arrival of [Brig. Gen. *James*] *Cant[e]y's* brigade at Resaca. It was ordered to halt there, to defend that important position.

On the 8th, the cavalry, which had been driven through Mill Creek Gap the day before, was divided, [Col. *J. Warren*] *Grigsby's* (Kentucky) brigade going to the foot of the mountain, near Dug Gap, and the remainder to the ground then occupied by *Kelly's* troops, in front of our right.

About four o'clock P.M., a division of Hooker's corps . . . assailed our outpost in Dug Gap. . . . A sharp attack was also made upon the angle where the Confederate right and center joined on the crest of the mountain. This point was held by [Brig. Gen. *Edmund W.*] *Pettus's* brigade, by which the assailants, Newton's division of the Fourth Corps, were quickly and handsomely repulsed. [Brig. Gen. *John C.*] *Brown's* brigade was then moved from *Stevenson's* right to the crest of the mountain, joining *Pettus's* left.

On the 9th another assault was made upon the troops at the angle . . . and much more vigorous than that of the day before, by a larger force advancing in column and exhibiting great determination. It was met, however, with the firmness always displayed when *Pettus* or *Brown* commanded, and their troops fought; and the enemy was driven back with a loss proportionate to the determination of their attack.

Similar assaults upon *Stewart* and *Bate* in the gap, made with the same resolution, were in like manner defeated. . . .

The Confederate troops suffered little in these engagements, for they fought under the protection of intrenchments. But we had reason to believe that the enemy, who were completely exposed, often at short range and in close order, sustained heavy losses. . . .

On the same day Major General *Wheeler,* with [Col. *George C.*] *Dibrell's* and [Brig. Gen. *William W.*] *Allen's* brigades, encountered a large body of Federal cavalry near Varnell's Station. Dismounting all of his troops but two regiments, he made a combined attack of infantry and cavalry, by which the enemy was put to flight. . . .

At night Brigadier General *Cant[e]y* reported that he had been engaged at Resaca until dark with troops of the Army of the Tennessee . . . commanded by Major-General McPherson, and had held his ground. As intelligence of the arrival of that army in Snake Creek Gap had been received, Lieutenant-General *Hood* was ordered to move to Resaca immediately with three divisions—those of *Hindman, Cleburne,* and *Walker.* . . .

On the 10th . . . skirmishing . . . near Dalton continued all day, to our advantage—both at the gap and on *Stevenson's* front. Near night an attack, especially spirited, was made upon *Bate's* position, on the hillside facing the gap on the south. It was firmly met . . . and repulsed. At night reports were received from the scouts in observation near the south end of Rocky Face, to the effect that General McPherson's troops were entrenching their position in Snake Creek Gap. [*Military Operations,* pp. 304–308.]

Report of Maj. Gen. Alexander P. Stewart, CSA, Commanding Division, Hood's Corps, Army of Tennessee

On the morning of Saturday, May 7, the enemy being reported advancing from Ringgold on Dalton, my command was placed under arms, and with [Maj. *John W.*] *Eldridge's* battalion of artillery, took position on the ridges in front of Mill Creek Gap and on the right of the railroad, *Bate's* division prolonging the line on the left of the railroad. The cavalry fell back and the enemy appeared on Tunnel Hill Ridge in heavy force. After nightfall, in obedience to orders from Lieutenant

General *Hood*, the division retired to the line we had entrenched on the south or Dalton side of the gap. On Monday, the 9th, the troops were disposed as follows. *Clayton's* brigade on the main mountain (Rocky Face) on the right, [Brig. Gen. *Alpheus*] *Baker's* and [Brig. Gen. *Marcellus A.*] *Stovall's* on the ridge to the right of the creek and railroad, [Brig. Gen. *Randall L.*] *Gibson's* on the advanced ridge on left of the railroad, *Bate's* division on left of *Gibson's*, occupying the main mountain to Trail Gap.

Sunday evening (8th) the enemy's skirmishers occupied the line we abandoned Saturday night—the front line of the gap—and from that time until Thursday night (12th) a constant and heavy skirmishing continued. In fortifying the gap I had caused lines of breast-heights for skirmishers to be constructed in front of the main lines of battle, artillery proof. The enemy repeatedly charged them and were as often repulsed with severe loss. It is believed the skirmishers occupying these advanced works could have held them successfully against any force that could have been brought against them. During these affairs my own loss was but trifling. *Gibson's* line was occasionally enfiladed by the enemy's artillery, from which he suffered, though not heavily.

It is proper here to say that the defenses of the gap were constructed by my division, Lieut. *John W. Glenn* being the engineer officer superintending. I desire to bear testimony to his zeal, skill, and energy. Mill Creek had been dammed at the two railroad bridges by the division pioneer company, aided by the pioneers of *Stevenson's* division. [*O.R.*, XXXVIII, pt. 3, p. 816.]

Report of Maj. Gen. Oliver O. Howard, USA, Commanding Fourth Army Corps, Army of the Cumberland

My part of this movement was to endeavor to put a force on Rocky Face Ridge, and make a demonstration toward Buzzard Roost Gap in conjunction with the Fourteenth Corps. General Newton's division on the morning of the 8th of May moved to the north end of Rocky Face, some two miles above Buzzard Roost Gap, where he pushed up a small force at first, driving the enemy along the crest. He succeeded in taking about one-third of the height from the enemy, and establishing a signal station upon a prominent point. He had attempted to get possession of a rebel station, but owing to the rugged nature of the heights, and the ability of the enemy to defend so narrow a path, he could not reach it.

In the meantime Generals [David S.] Stanley and [Thomas J.] Wood pushed strong skirmish lines, well supported, as far up the western slope as possible.

During the night following, General Newton succeeded in getting two pieces of artillery upon the ridge. The next morning, 9 May, he attempted to make farther progress and succeeded in driving the enemy from 50 to 100 yards. General Stanley during the afternoon . . . made a reconnaissance into the pass of Buzzard Roost, developing a strong musketry and artillery fire. . . . The casualties in my command resulting from these operations were between 200 and 300 killed and wounded.

In accordance with instructions from General Thomas, the Fourth Corps made preparations to remain near Buzzard Roost Gap for the purpose of holding the enemy at Dalton, if possible, while the rest of the army, excepting Stoneman's cavalry, was moving through Snake Creek Gap to turn the enemy's flank.

May 11 the troops of the corps were disposed as follows: General Stanley to hold the gap, General Newton to hold Rocky Face and the roads leading around the north end of it, with General Stoneman's cavalry covering his left flank, and General Wood in reserve on Tunnel Hill. During the evening . . . and on the morning of the 12th the general movement was progressing, and the Fourth Corps found itself alone, confronted by the entire rebel army.

From the signal station on Rocky Face the enemy's movements could be distinctly seen. About 10 a.m. he moved out a strong force as if to turn my left flank and give battle, but after pressing in the skirmishers the column returned within his works. The threat, however, was so strong that General Wood's division was moved to the support of General Newton.

During the night following the enemy evacuated Dalton. [*O.R.*, XXXVIII, pt. 1, p. 189.]

Report of Brevet Maj. Gen. Jefferson C. Davis, USA, Commanding Second Division, Fourteenth Army Corps, Army of the Cumberland

In compliance with orders, I moved my entire division beyond the town and took position on the right of the Dalton road, and sent a regiment from [Brig. Gen. James D.] Morgan's brigade to take possession of a high round hill, immediately in my front, known to us as Signal Hill. This duty was well performed by the Tenth Illinois Regiment. . . . McCook's brigade had the advance during the day, and most of the fighting . . . in driving the enemy's pickets and skirmishers was gallantly performed by his troops. . . . The division remained in this position until the forenoon of the 9th, when an advance into the gap of Buzzard Roost was determined upon. [Col. John G.] Mitchell's brigade was ordered to advance along the left of the road and drive in the enemy's pickets, occupying a little group of round-shaped hills in front of the enemy's works, which obstructed the gap.

During the succeeding three days my troops were kept more or less under fire. The enemy, after persistent and sometimes heavy skirmishing, was driven into his works in the gorge and upon the top of Rocky Face. The operations of these three days were mostly executed and the fighting done by General Morgan's brigade. Much of the fighting consisted in heavy skirmishing, and on several occasions, when attempts were made to feel of the enemy's works, it became almost a general engagement in severity. Captain [Charles M.] Barnett, my chief of artillery, with much difficulty succeeded in getting a part of his artillery in position, and operated very successfully with it against the enemy's batteries and works. The privations and hardships my troops were compelled to undergo during these few days' operations, and their constant exposure to the fire of the enemy's artillery, as well as his skirmish line and sharpshooters, and the consequent heavy loss in killed and wounded, gave the highest proof of their discipline and courage, and the zeal with which they were entering upon the long and arduous campaign before them.

On the 12th my command was relieved from its position in the gap by troops from the Fourth Corps, and, following the other divisions of the corps, marched at sunrise for Snake Gap Creek. . . . [*O.R.*, XXXVIII, pt. 1, pp. 626–627.]

Report of Col. John G. Mitchell, USA, Commanding
Second Brigade, Second Division, Fourteenth Army Corps,
Army of the Cumberland

May 7, marched to Mill Creek Gap (Buzzard Roost) and formed line, connecting on my left with Fourth Army Corps.

May 8, moved my command to the track of Atlantic and Western Railroad, covered the front with double line of skirmishers, under command of Colonel [Henry B.] Banning, the Seventy-eighth Illinois and the One hundred and thirteenth Ohio on the right and left of the front line, the remaining three regiments in rear line. With this disposition attacked and drove the enemy from the summit of the first spur of Rocky Face Ridge, which stood directly in the mouth of Mill Creek Gap. The second spur, immediately in front of the first, was taken in the same manner by a strong skirmish line.

At the same time I deployed two companies, A and F, of the Thirty-fourth Illinois . . . to occupy a hill on the right of the railroad, and to the right rear of the crest first taken. These men, in reaching this hill, were compelled to wade the backwater of Mill Creek, waist deep. They plunged into the water, crossed, and scaling the hill at a point where it was so steep that they were compelled to hold on by the undergrowth, drove a battalion of the enemy from it, and held it until the Ninety-eighth Ohio relieved them.

May 9 to 12: position unchanged; constant skirmishing. [*O.R.*, XXXVIII, pt. 1, pp. 678–679.]

Report of Lt. Col. Oscar Van Tassell, USA, Commanding Thirty-Fourth Illinois Infantry, Second Brigade, Second Division, Fourteenth Army Corps, Army of the Cumberland

On the 8th day of May [we] were ordered to support the skirmish line, whose duty it was to clear the hill in front of Rocky Face Ridge of rebel sharpshooters. Arrived on the top of the hill, I was directed to send a company of skirmishers to clear the knob on the right of the railroad. . . . Company H . . . was deployed and sent forward for this purpose; the men plunging waist deep into a creek, crossed the railroad, and charged up the hill on the double-quick, drove off the rebel sharpshooters, afterward repulsing two lines of skirmishers who advanced to retake the position, and holding their ground until relieved. The enemy having dammed the creek running through this gap, it had overflowed the low ground between the knob and this hill . . . and I was called on by Colonel Mitchell to furnish a party to see whether the dam could be cut. Sergeant Elhannon C. Winters and Privates John Crichton, Henry Coryell, and George Garnick, of Company A, volunteered to perform the work.

Moving cautiously down the railroad to within a few yards of the rebel pickets, Sergeant Winters concealed his men and went forward to see how the land laid. Gaining a position within twenty feet of the rebel sentinel, he discovered a strong picket reserve close to the sentinel, and seeing the impossibility of going farther with the force at his command he cautiously withdrew his men, and went back to report progress, and was excused from further duty at the time.

During the night, however, Colonel Mitchell sent for Sergeant Winters, and giving him another detail of about twenty men, directed him to cut the dam, if possible. On the approach of this party, the rebel sentinel and reserve withdrew, moving up the hill-side and around in rear of the party, evidently with the intention of capturing them; seeing his danger, Sergeant Winters sent a man back to report; Colonel Mitchell then sent a stronger force in charge of a commissioned officer, and the whole number moved forward to perform their task, which the rebels perceiving, they advanced upon the party, firing rapidly. As it had now become so light that every movement was easily seen by the enemy, the officer in charge of the party ordered a retreat. . . . I have been thus particular in giving an account of this adventure, because I wished to do justice to a gallant young noncommissioned officer in one of his numerous deeds of coolness in danger since he has been under my command.

In the afternoon of the next day I received orders to support a skirmish line which was ordered to dislodge the sharpshooters of the enemy from Rocky Face Ridge, but on arriving at the position indicated in the order, I was informed by the officer in charge of the skirmishers that his men were out of ammunition, and unless they were relieved, he would be obliged to abandon the line; accordingly, I sent forward Companies D and I, as skirmishers, who held the line until after dark. . . . [O.R., XXXVIII, pt. 1, pp. 683–684.]

Report of Capt. Charles M. Barnett, USA, Battery I, Second Illinois Light Artillery, Second Division, Fourteenth Army Corps, Army of the Cumberland

On the . . . 9th [of May], this battery worked all night, placing three guns in position on a hill fronting Rocky Face Ridge, and relieved three guns on the left of the railroad with the other three. 10th, fired 196 rounds at the enemy; at night fell back, and took the harness off for the first time in thirty-six hours. 11th, placed three pieces in the gap on the railroad and fired forty rounds. 12th, marched at 6 a.m. for Snake [Creek] Gap. [*O.R.*, XXXVIII, pt. 1, p. 829.]

Report of Brig. Gen. Richard W. Johnson, USA, Commanding First Division, Fourteenth Army Corps, Army of the Cumberland

On the 7th . . . I marched at daylight in rear of General Davis' division . . . By direction of the major-general commanding corps, I filed to the right and formed my division, with two brigades on the line and one in reserve, on the right of General Davis. . . . Later in the day, General Davis having driven the enemy out of Tunnel Hill and within their works at Buzzard Roost Pass, I advanced my line, swinging to the left to conform to the movement of Davis' troops, and again formed line of battle . . . upon his right. . . . The 8th was occupied in maneuvering in front of Buzzard Roost, my final position being with my left resting near the high knob, known to us as Signal Hill, and my line stretching southwardly so as to command and practically close up all roads leading out of Buzzard Roost Gap to the west and southwest. Toward evening I caused a section [2 guns] to be placed in position on the ridge which terminated the open field to the westward of the gap, and opened upon a line of the enemy's works beyond the pass. This, with the advance of part of General Davis' division and part of Wood's brigade, of Butterfield's division, to the ridge beyond the field, developed to batteries of determined strength, one upon the point of Chattoogata Mountain, to our right, the other in the rear of the pass, on our left. . . .

Early on the morning of the 9th I advanced [Brig. Gen. William P.] Carlin's brigade across Mill Creek to relieve some of the regiments of Wood's brigade, which had been thrown in there on the evening previous, and was occupying the ground at the base of Chattoogata Mountain. About 11 a.m. I was . . . at department headquarters, to receive instructions, and heard it reported . . . by an officer of General Wood's staff, that the troops of that command had felt all along Chattoogata; that they found but a small force here, and that . . . it would not be difficult to carry the crest of the mountain by assault. To verify the report . . . I was instructed to advance Carlin's brigade, so as, if possible, to clear the mountain to its top, supporting him with another brigade; this was accordingly done. Carlin, with a strong but well-extended skirmish line, seized the long, isolated ridge, which, lying south of the railroad, almost closed up the westerly mouth of the gap, and swept the mountain of the enemy's skirmishers clear to the foot of the abrupt palisade which crowns the slope. In the hope that some path might be found at which we could force our way, relying confidently on the tried troops of Carlin's brigade, to advance wherever footing could be found, I ordered my reserve brigade . . . across Mill Creek, to within close supporting distance.

A careful reconnaissance by General Carlin all along his line, and to a considerable distance below his right, disclosed no practical footway to the crest of the ridge. An attempt to jump round the nose of the mountain, so as to ascend from the reverse side, which was supposed to be less abrupt, developed a heavy force of infantry and artillery, strongly entrenched, in our front, upon the line by which we must at first advance, and so posted as to enfilade us wherever we should wheel to ascend the mountain. To have assaulted this position would have brought my command within the fire of nearly the whole of the enemy's artillery, and that of perhaps a superior force of infantry, without the possibility of receiving adequate support. To attempt to carry the mountain without first clearing this position would have been hopeless; accordingly, after a stubborn and well-pressed attack, by a strong line of skirmishers . . . had verified my own previous observations and the report of Brigadier General Carlin, I ordered the attempt to be given up. My loss from the enemy's artillery in this affair was unusually heavy, the battery on Chattoogata Mountain and one near their left . . . on the eastern slope of Rocky Face, burst their shell among us with remarkable accuracy. [O.R., XXXVIII, pt. 1, pp. 519–520.]

4. CONFEDERATE DEFENSES EAST OF ROCKY FACE

Use the exit ramp on the east end of the lot to leave the parking area, rejoining U.S. 41 in the same direction you were traveling before stopping. Move into the left lane as soon as traffic permits. Drive a little more than 0.2 mile and turn left onto Willowdale Road. Cross over the railroad tracks and under the interstate, and immediately turn left on Crow Valley Road. Follow Crow Valley Road for approximately 3.3 miles. When you come to a "T" intersection with Poplar Springs Road, turn right. Follow Poplar Springs Road about 0.5 mile to the cemetery of the Poplar Springs Baptist Church, which will be on your right. The parking lot for the cemetery begins in front of the steps. Park, then stand in front of the steps facing Poplar Springs Road, with the cemetery on your left. The right flank of the Confederate lines was on the prominent hill (Potato Hill) about half a mile to your right.

The Confederate works along the northern military crest of Potato Hill are so well preserved that they are visible from this position in the winter months. Guns on the hill dominated the railroad from Red Clay and anchored the right flank of *Stevenson's* line.

STOP 4, STEVENSON'S LINE

9–13 May 1864

Report of Maj. Gen. Carter L. Stevenson, CSA, Commanding Division, Hood's Corps, Army of Tennessee

During the latter part of . . . [April] I received orders to break up my winter camp on the Sugar Valley road and move my division to the position assigned it in front of Dalton. I went into bivouac in Crow's Valley and immediately went to work to complete the defense of the portion of the line allotted me, from the signal station upon Rocky Face Mountain, on my left, to Alt's Creek, on my right. General *Pettus* was placed upon the left, General [*Alexander W.*] *Reynolds* on the left center, General [*Alfred*] *Cumming* on the right center, and General *Brown* on the right. General *Pettus* was ordered to hold the

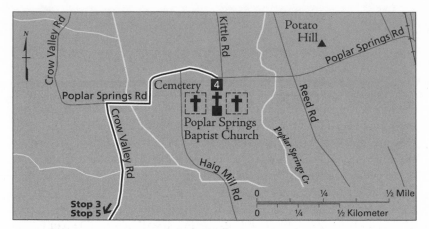

Confederate Defenses East of Rocky Face (Stop 4)

mountain with a regiment of rifles. The movements of the enemy very soon showed that his greatest efforts would be against the mountain, which was, in fact, the key to my position, and accordingly . . . General *Pettus* was ordered to occupy the mountain with his brigade, and the vacancy in the trenches created by his removal filled by extending intervals to the left.

On the 8th . . . the enemy pushed forward his skirmishers vigorously, supported by a line of battle against the angle in *Pettus*' line at the crest of the mountain. This attack was quickly and handsomely repulsed by that portion of his line which occupied the angle. In compliance with instructions from the lieutenant-general, *Brown's* brigade was then moved from its position on my right to the left of *Pettus*, on the crest of the mountain, who was thus enabled to contract his lines and strengthen his weak point—the angle. . . . *Brown's* place in the works was first supplied by *Mercer's*, then by [Brig. Gen. *Edward C.*] *Walthall's*, and then by [Brig. Gen. *Daniel C.*] *Govan's* brigade. General *Brown*, as senior officer, was directed to take charge of the defense of that portion of the mountain occupied by my troops.

On the 9th . . . the enemy, formed in column of divisions, made a heavy assault upon the angle in *Pettus*' line. The fight was obstinate and bloody, but resulted in a complete success to us. . . . In the meantime the enemy had advanced his sharpshooters close upon the line of *Brown's* brigade on the mountain, and *Reynolds* and *Cumming's* in the valley.

Soon after the assault upon *Pettus* the enemy maneuvered considerably in the valley, and seemed at one time disposed to assault the position of Generals *Cumming* and *Reynolds*. In front of General *Cumming* he appeared several times in line of battle, but was checked by the fire of skirmishers and of those guns of Maj. J. W. *Johnson's* battalion of artillery that could be brought to bear upon him. From this time until we retired from the position there was constant skirmishing, first along my whole line, and later mainly in front of *Brown's* and *Pettus'* brigades. On the night of the 13th . . . agreeably to orders, I vacated my position and took up the line of march for Resaca. [*O.R.*, XXXVIII, pt. 3, p. 811.]

Report of Brig. Gen. John Newton, USA, Commanding Second Division, Fourth Army Corps, Army of the Cumberland

Sunday, May 8, Harker's brigade was ordered to ascend to the northern extremity of Rocky Face Ridge, the One hundred and twenty-fifth Ohio Volunteer Infantry . . . clearing the way as skirmishers, which being effectually done, the whole brigade ascended to the summit. The summit was a sharp ridge, never wider than the room occupied by four men abreast, and oftentimes so narrow and obstructed by boulders that men in single file could with difficulty climb over the obstacles. The enemy, protected by natural and artificial impediments, steadily resisted the advance of the brigade until dark, General Harker gaining about three-fourths of a mile of the crest. At night one piece of Battery M, First Illinois Artillery, was moved on the ridge, ready to open on the enemy's rock barricades in the morning. General Schofield having arrived on the ground mean time, one brigade of his army was moved on the crest, and took its place in General Harker's rear.

May 9, Schofield having withdrawn his troops from the ridge to make a demonstration with his whole corps in the valley on the east side of Rocky Face Ridge, General Harker opened with his piece of artillery at daybreak and charged the enemy, driving them gallantly until they found shelter behind their main line of works on the top of the ridge. The whole extent of the ridge occupied by us amounted to about a mile and three quarters.

From the ground thus gained the lines of the enemy on the east of Rocky Face could be distinctly seen. Their position was good and

Attack at Rocky Face Ridge (MOLLUS).

well fortified, running off at right angles with the general direction of Rocky Face. General Schofield having driven the enemy's skirmishers into their works in the valley, it was arranged that he should then attack while I attacked the enemy's works on the eastern slope of the ridge and on the top, General [George D.] Wagner's brigade being displayed on the eastern slope for this purpose. General Wagner, in advancing, found his farther progress impeded by an impassable ravine, on the opposite side of which the enemy had a line of entrenchments, receiving a heavy fire from the enemy in the mean time. The leading regiment of General Harker's brigade, without waiting for the partial success of the other attacks, prematurely advanced, and the column naturally followed. They carried the work immediately in front of them with heavy loss, marching by the flank, but found themselves confronted by another and stronger work on an eminence commanding the one they had taken. They held this position for some time, but farther progress being impossible, fell back somewhat, retaining about 100 yards of the ground they had gained. . . . This day's operations demonstrated the enemy's position on the slope and crest of the ridge to be impregnable. . . .

May 10, no change made except in the relative positions of the brigades. . . . Sharp picket firing all day.

May 11, no change except that Sherman's brigade relieved Wagner; picket firing all day.

May 12, General Schofield being withdrawn and sent toward the right, and the Fourth Corps forming the left flank of the army, Sherman's brigade, of my division, was left on the top of Rocky Face, the other brigades being withdrawn and placed in defensible positions on the flank of the army, General Stoneman's cavalry being also on my left to observe the enemy and cover the flank. The enemy moved out a heavy force, threatening our left . . . comprised of over twenty regiments of infantry and a large body of cavalry. General Stoneman was attacked, his pickets and front line being compelled to fall back. . . . I contracted my lines to get a better defense, and finding my force still insufficient called on General Wood for one brigade. . . . This brigade arrived promptly, with General Wood himself, and closed a gap in my line. The enemy, apparently satisfied with a demonstration merely, retired without attack. [*O.R.*, XXXVIII, pt. 1, pp. 291–293.]

•

Report of Maj. Gen. John M. Schofield, USA, Commanding Army of the Ohio

On the 9th we made a strong demonstration against the enemy's right as a diversion in favor of operations upon his rear through Snake Creek Gap. Early in the morning the troops moved into position across the valley east of Rocky Face, Judah on the right, with his flank resting at the foot of the mountain, [Brig. Gen. Jacob D.] Cox upon the left, and [Brig. Gen. Alvin P.] Hovey in reserve, covering the left. The corps advanced steadily during the day, driving the enemy's skirmishers and capturing several lines of barricades, and finally drove the enemy into their main works, pressed them closely, and occupied their attention until dark. During the afternoon General Hovey was sent with four regiments of his division to support General McCook's cavalry division, which was hotly engaged on our left, but did not find it necessary to bring his troops into action, and was recalled in the night. [O.R., XXXVIII, pt. 2, p. 510.]

Report of Brig. Gen. Jacob D. Cox, USA, Commanding Third Division, Army of the Ohio

We took position on the ridge running nearly north and south . . . covering the Varnell's Station road and the cross-roads leading to Ellidge's Mill and other points in rear, [Col. James W.] Reilly's brigade on the right, [Brig. Gen. Mahlon S.] Manson's on the left. . . . May 8, Reilly's brigade marched east to Kincannon's Cross-Roads and thence south one mile to Huffacre's, Manson's brigade taking position at Kincannon's, upon the northern continuation of Rocky Face Ridge, and the whole division being upon the left of the other divisions of the corps and upon the extreme left of the army.

May 9, advanced southeasterly to Burkels, on the Varnell's Station and Dalton road, and formed the division in line across the ridge immediately east of Rocky Face, the right connecting with Judah's division in the valley west of us, and the left, somewhat refused, covering the Dalton road, the front being covered with a heavy line of skirmishers.

The division advanced, keeping pace with Judah's division and preserving the alignment upon it, until the two divisions were swung forward at right angles to Rocky Face, and connecting with troops of the Fourth Corps immediately in front of the enemy's works, which extended across Rocky Face Ridge and the valleys and ridges east of it to Potato Hill. The whole march along the ridge in line was a difficult one from the nature of the ground, the formation being a rough, sharp, and very rocky backbone, with deep ravines cutting down to right and left, and the whole covered with timber and very dense undergrowth. The enemy's skirmishers were driven back nearly the whole distance, a lively running fight being kept up.

About the middle of the afternoon I received orders to make a demonstration with one regiment upon the works in my front, in order to assist an assault to be made by other troops on my right upon the enemy's position on the crest of Rocky Face. The one hundredth Ohio Volunteer Infantry, of Reilly's brigade (which had the right of the division), was ordered forward and pushed vigorously up to short musket-range of the fortifications in our front, driving the rebel skirmishers into the works, which were found to consist of a strong line of field fortifications for batteries on the higher points of ground, connected by a curtain of infantry trenches.

The advanced position thus taken was maintained under a very rapid fire of musketry and some artillery until about 8 p.m., when the regiment was withdrawn and the skirmish line re-established nearly in the former position. Occasional efforts were made by the enemy to drive back our left by artillery fire from Potato Hill, and a bickering skirmish fight was kept up along the whole line throughout the day.

May 10, at 8 a.m. orders were received to retire in line along the ridge we marched over in advance yesterday, then change front to the rear on right battalion, and go into position on the northern prolongation of Rocky Face, fronting eastward, allowing room for Hovey's division, which had been in reserve, to encamp in line between this division and that of General Judah. . . . The movement was made by the brigades with very satisfactory precision, although it was closely followed by the enemy's cavalry, who kept up an almost uninterrupted fight with our skirmish line, which covered the rear in the movement. [O.R., XXXVIII, pt. 2, pp. 674–675.]

Report of Maj. Gen. John M. Schofield, USA (continued)

The corps remained in position, confronting the enemy's works, until 8 a.m. on the 10th, when it withdrew slowly in line of battle and took position commanding the gaps north of Rocky Face. The enemy made no attempt to follow in force. This movement was a delicate and difficult one, owing to the character of the ground, the position and strength of the enemy, and our comparative isolation from the main army. I regarded it as a complete test of the quality of my troops, which I had not before had opportunity of seeing maneuver in the presence of the enemy, and gave me the fullest confidence in them and their commanders.

The Army of the Tennessee having occupied Snake Creek Gap, General Stoneman, who had just arrived with two brigades of cavalry, was left to operate, in conjunction with General Howard's corps, on the enemy's right, and I moved with the Twenty-third Corps to Villanow on the 12th, and on the morning of the 13th through Snake Creek Gap, leaving one brigade of Hovey's division to hold the western entrance of the gap. [O.R., XXXVIII, pt. 2, p. 510.]

5. THE FIGHT AT DUG GAP

Retrace your route back to U.S. Highway 41 by turning left onto
Poplar Springs Road and following it back to Willowdale Road. Turn
right onto Willowdale Road, cross under the interstate and over the
railroad tracks, and then turn right onto U.S. 41. Drive nearly 1.3 miles
on U.S. 41, moving into the left lane upon crossing Mill Creek, and
then turn left onto Old Lafayette Road. Drive about 0.6 mile on Old
Lafayette Road, and then turn left onto Mill Creek Road. Drive slightly
less than 5 miles on Mill Creek Road, and turn left onto Hurricane
Road just before you reach a church on your left. Follow this road
about 0.6 mile to a "Y" intersection, where you bear left onto Dug Gap
Battle Road. Follow this road slightly more than 1.3 miles to the top of
Dug Gap. Turn left into the parking lot for Dug Gap Battle Park at the
summit. If the parking lot is barricaded, there should still be room to
park safely between the barricade and the road. Walk uphill through
the parking lot and follow the asphalt path along the crest, away from
the road and the parking lot, until you come to the stone breastworks
and an overlook site constructed of railroad ties (about 150 yards).

STOP 5, DUG GAP

8–11 May 1864

*Narrative of Col. W. P. C. Breckinridge, CSA, Ninth
Kentucky Cavalry, Williams's Brigade, Hume's Division,
Cavalry Corps, Army of Tennessee*

The brigade of Kentucky cavalry was present at Dug Gap and
Snake Creek Gap, and . . . the regiment I commanded . . . was in
front at both places. . . .
The army lay behind an impassable ridge, through which, on its
left flank, were only two accessible gaps: Dug Gap, less than four miles
south-west from Dalton, on the main road from Dalton to Lafayette,
and perhaps six miles from Mill Creek Gap, and Snake Creek Gap,
some eighteen miles south from Mill Creek Gap. With these gaps

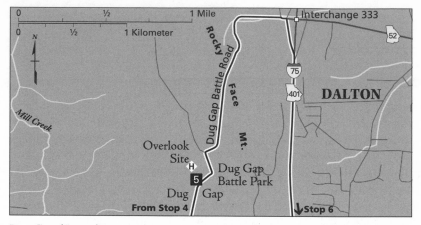

Dug Gap (Stop 5)

fortified, the left flank and rear of that army were absolutely safe, for while the Rocky-face and Chattooga ridges protected our flank, through these gaps we had access to attack the flank of the enemy if he attempted to make a march so far to the left and rear as to threaten our communication south of the Oostenaula or Coosa.

These gaps were capable of easy and impregnable fortification. Dug Gap was a mere road cut out of the mountain-side and really needed no breastworks, for the natural palisades and contour of the mountain rendered easy its defense by resolute men. Snake Creek Gap was a gorge apparently cut through the mountains by the creek that ran through it. It was a narrow defile . . . capable of impregnable defense.

These gaps were well known to both armies. Through them ran public roads and soldiers of both armies had marched through both. Late in February Dug Gap had been seized by an Indiana regiment and held until *Cleburne* retook it. . . . Neither of these gaps was fortified, and . . . when the campaign opened, Dug Gap was guarded by a small command of Arkansas troops under Colonel *[James A.] Williamson*, numbering perhaps 250, while Snake Creek Gap was left wholly unprotected. At Resaca, where the railroad crosses the Oostenaula, *Cantey's* brigade was held on the evening of the 7th of May, on its way from Rome to Dalton. . . .

On May 7th our cavalry was driven through Mill Creek Gap. On that night, after we had gone into camp, Colonel *Grigsby*, who commanded the Kentucky cavalry brigade, was ordered to send a regiment to the front of Dug Gap, to guard the approaches to it. In obedience to that order the 9th Kentucky Cavalry passed over Rocky Face Ridge, and near midnight bivouacked on Mill Creek, about a mile . . . in front of Dug Gap. Heavy picket lines were thrown out on all the roads leading down the valley. There were several of these roads, and scouts were sent to ascertain the movements of the enemy.

By daylight it was discovered that very large bodies of troops were moving down the valley on all the roads leading to the south. General McPherson had marched from Chattanooga to Rossville, thence . . . to Shipp's Gap and Villanow, where the road forks—one branch leading down the east foot of Taylor's Ridge, the other leading across toward Rocky Face; this road again forks—one branch leading through Dug Gap, the other down the valley to Snake Creek Gap. Until McPherson reached Villanow it was only a conjecture as to his course, and until the head of his column turned toward Snake Creek Gap his destination was uncertain.

His march was concealed by Hooker's corps of the Army of the Cumberland, which . . . marching from Ringgold via Nickajack Gap and Trickum, hid the flank movement of McPherson. . . . The possession of Dug Gap by Hooker not only would render Dalton untenable, but would make a retreat from Dalton by the line of the railroad extremely hazardous, and completely protect McPherson from attack on his left flank. With Hooker descending from Rocky Face on our left flank and rear, McPherson holding Resaca, Thomas, with the corps of Howard and Palmer, pushing to Dalton, and Schofield to his left, our army would have been in a perilous situation.

The march of Hooker and McPherson was discovered early on the morning of May 8th by the scouts of the 9th Kentucky Cavalry, and timely information was given that at least an attack on Dug Gap was certain, and that the columns on the march were very heavy and their movements were guarded by forces too large to be either resisted or developed by the detachments sent out by the 9th Kentucky. On this information the remainder of *Grigsby's* brigade was ordered to Dug Gap, and reached there none too soon. All possible delay to the march of Hooker's corps was made, but about 2 p.m. [Brig. Gen. John W.] Geary's division of that corps drove the 9th Kentucky across the creek and slowly up the mountain-side, until the regiment fell back in its proper position in the gap, where it found the brigade drawn in mere

"Geary's Assault on Dug Gap" (*Harper's Pictorial History of the Great Rebellion* [New York: Harper Bros., 1866–1868], 604).

skirmish-line along the edge of the mountain-side. As one-fourth of cavalry soldiers are detailed to hold the horses, I presume that we had about 800 of our brigade in the fight and 250 Arkansas troops; and this handful of men held that gap until nightfall. . . . Assault after assault was made from 3 o'clock until after dark, and each . . . was repulsed with loss. At first, in a mere spirit of exuberant fun, some of the men rolled stones down the mountain-side; but when the effect was noticed they were directed to use these means as part of our defense; great stones were rolled down on the supporting lines on the mountain-sides or at its foot; and as these boulders would go leaping, crashing, breaking off limbs, crushing down saplings, we fancied we could see the effect of the unexpected missiles. It also proved a valuable resource to us, for without them our ammunition would have given out; indeed it was about exhausted when the attack ceased. . . .

After nightfall *Granbury's* Texas brigade relieved us, but the assault was over. Hooker had failed in his part of the mission. That flank of our army was safe.

The importance of holding that gap was so manifest that Generals *Hardee* and *Cleburne,* with their staffs, galloped to the scene to encourage us by their presence and to aid Colonel *Grigsby* by their suggestions. . . . That command needed no encouragement. . . . Its officers and men knew that they were holding one of the doors to Dalton. [W. P. C. Breckinridge, "The Opening of the Atlanta Campaign," in Robert Underwood Johnson and Clarence Clough Buel, eds., *Battles and Leaders of the Civil War,* 4 vols. (New York: Century, 1888), vol. IV, pp. 278–279.]

Report of Brig. Gen. John W. Geary, USA, Commanding Second Division, Twentieth Army Corps, Army of the Cumberland

May 8, I received orders as follows:

March without delay to seize the gap in the Rocky Face Ridge called Babb's, and to establish yourself strongly at that point; take your two brigades and send word as soon as you are in position. Take no wagons and but few ambulances.

Having no map of the road or country, I took a citizen as guide and moved as ordered with my two brigades and two batteries of artillery at 11 a.m. The road taken was narrow and hilly, but was by several miles the most direct to the point designated, the distance by it being five miles.

On reaching Mill Creek Valley, at the foot of . . . Rocky Face Ridge, my skirmishers came upon the enemy's cavalry pickets near Babb's house. These retreated hastily across Mill Creek, pursued by my skirmishers, and made their way to the mountain crest by the only road—that leading to Dalton.

My preparations were immediately made for attacking the enemy, who were in plain sight along the crest of the mountain. . . . Its sides, steep, covered with forest, and corrugated with ridgy spurs and formations of rock, rise abruptly from the banks of Mill Creek, which flows along its base. . . . The banks of the creek are fringed with marshy thickets, and the creek itself is a sluggish, muddy stream with treacherous bottom. . . . The main road from La Fayette to Dalton crosses Mill Creek at Hall's Mill, thence winds up the steep ascent to an elevation of 800 feet from the valley, and there crosses over the ridge. This roadway has been cut out from the mountain side and through the palisades which crest the mountain, from which . . . comes the name of Dug Gap. Along the top, facing westward for miles on either side of the pass rise palisades of rock impossible to scale and to be passed only through a few narrow clefts filled with loose rocks and wide enough to admit five or six men abreast.

This summit I closely scanned while forming for the attack. On either side of the pass and along the crest . . . in addition to the natural strength of the position, were breast-works occupied by the enemy, but in what force could only be tested by attack. [Capt. James D.] McGill's (Pennsylvania) battery, 3-inch Rodman guns, was placed in position in the field near Babb's house, from which they could reach the crest with their fire, and the Fifth and Sixty-sixth Ohio Volunteers and One hundred and forty-seventh Pennsylvania Volunteers, of my First Brigade, were left as guard to the artillery. The One hundred and ninth Pennsylvania Volunteers and Thirty-third New Jersey Volunteers, of my Second Brigade, were both absent, the former as guard to the wagon train, the latter having been on picket duty.

With the rest of my command I crossed the creek in front of Babb's house at 3 p.m., and advanced the One hundred and nineteenth New York Volunteers, deployed as skirmishers, up the mountain, followed by [Col. Adolphus] Buschbeck's brigade on the right and [Col. Charles] Candy's on the left, each disposed in two lines of battle. Knapsacks had been unslung and piled before commencing the ascent.

Half way up the firing became lively. The enemy had posted skirmishers thickly across the steep face of the ridge, behind rocks, logs, and trees, and their fire was galling and destructive. Our skirmish lines, advancing rapidly, though they had to fairly clamber up the rough ascent, drove those opposed to them back with loss, and reached the foot of the palisades. Mean time my main lines pressed steadily forward under a severe musketry fire from the top of the palisades until the advanced regiments were halted to rest and form on the ground held by our skirmishers. The general line of advance had inclined at an angle toward the Dalton road and my extreme left was now across it. The atmosphere was hot and stifling, and the ascent was one of the greatest difficulty.

After a halt of fifteen minutes, the palisades were charged impetuously by portions of both brigades, Buschbeck's on the right and Candy's on both sides of the road. The attack was a most gallant one, officers and men rushing through the few narrow apertures or

Route of final Union assault on Dug Gap (Harold Nelson).

clambering the precipice. Many of them gained the crest, but were met by a tremendous fire from a second line of works which were invisible from below, and were shot down or compelled to jump back for their lives. Here hand-to-hand encounters took place, and stones as well as bullets became elements in the combat, the enemy rolling them over the precipice, endangering our troops below. Failing to hold the crest after two separate assaults, our front line was withdrawn about 150 yards and reformed in preparation for another effort.

Knowing that the enemy would hasten re-enforcements to the point attacked, I deemed it important to lose no time. One plan remained to be tried. My rifled battery (McGill's) had crossed the creek near Babb's house and taken position on a cleared knoll at the base of the ridge. By my order it now opened a steady and well-directed fire on the enemy's position. Under cover of this fire the Thirty-third New Jersey Volunteers, which had just arrived, was ordered to . . . attempt to gain the crest about half a mile to the right of the point of the previous attack, and at a place where the enemy did not show a strong force. In the meantime my main body was directed to keep the enemy in their front busily engaged and to support the movement promptly by again charging the crest in their front as soon as cheers from the Thirty-third New Jersey Volunteers should indicate their success on the enemy's flank.

The order was promptly executed, but it was found impossible by the Thirty-third . . . to gain the palisades at the point aimed at on account of their high, precipitous formations, and they were obliged to oblique a little to the left. There, finding a few narrow apertures, they rushed through where but two or three could climb abreast, and the rest of them reaching the crest their loud cheers were re-echoed along the lines.

At this signal the other regiments rushed again to the assault, and portions of the Twenty-eighth Pennsylvania Volunteers and One hundred and thirty-fourth and One hundred and fifty-fourth New York Volunteers again reached the summit, but it was impossible to hold it. So few at a time could clamber through the narrow clefts that the enemy overwhelmed them and forced them off the cliffs. During the several assaults to the right of the pass the Twenty-ninth Ohio Veteran Volunteers had fought heroically on the left of it, and having lost very heavily the Fifth and Sixty-sixth Ohio Volunteers had been brought up to its support.

It was now dusk, and official information was brought me from Colonel [David] Ireland, commanding my Third Brigade, that the movement on Snake Creek Gap was successful, and it was in full possession of the Army of the Tennessee. The object of my attack having been fully accomplished by securing the attention of the enemy while General McPherson's movement was made on Snake Creek Gap, I deemed further continuance of the action unnecessary and decided to withdraw to the foot of the mountain. Two sections of McGill's battery were brought across Mill Creek at Hall's Mill, and from a position at the foot of the ridge and on the left of the road they kept up a continuous fire on the enemy. The Fifth, Seventh, and Sixty-sixth Ohio Volunteers, which had not been seriously engaged, were so deployed as to cover the movement. Our dead and wounded were all removed to the field hospital, and my entire command was withdrawn and encamped . . . near Babb's house. . . . During the night breast-works were constructed encircling our encampment in an almost continuous line. . . . Casualties in battle . . . 49 killed, 257 wounded, 51 missing, total 357. [O.R., XXXVIII, pt. 2, pp. 114–117.]

Remnants of Confederate breastworks at Dug Gap
(Harold Nelson).

Report of Col. Adolphus Buschbeck, USA, Commanding Second Brigade, Second Division, Twentieth Army Corps, Army of the Cumberland

The ascent of the mountain was found very steep and arduous, requiring frequent halts to rest the men during the advance. The skirmish line of the One hundred and nineteenth New York Volunteers was strengthened by detachments from each regiment. The skirmishers were engaged in a desultory fire soon after beginning the assault, the enemy retiring until the line had reached to within 300 or 400 yards of the palisades of rock which form the ridge. Here the fire became general, engaging the whole line, the troops steadily advancing until the nature of the ground affording superior facilities for the ascent upon the extreme of the line the regiments diverged slightly to the right and left.

The One hundred and fifty-fourth New York Volunteers and One hundred and thirty-fourth New York Volunteers shortly after charged up the palisades and succeeded in planting their colors on the crest of the mountain; but few only could climb at a time, and the enemy, massing their force at the several points of attack, soon dislodged the brave heroes who had actually gained the very summit. The side of the mountain being so precipitous it was impossible to reform there, and the One hundred and fifty-fourth New York . . . Seventy-third Pennsylvania . . . and the Twenty-seventh Pennsylvania . . . were obliged to retire some distance from the ground held by them previous to the charge. The ground occupied by the One hundred and thirty-fourth New York . . . being better adapted for reforming, this regiment fell back about 100 paces.

After reforming, the One hundred and fifty-fourth New York, . . . Twenty-Seventh Pennsylvania, . . . and Seventy-third Pennsylvania . . . were moved to the support of the One hundred and thirty-fourth New York; . . . The One hundred and nineteenth New York . . . formed line to the left of that position. The Thirty-third New Jersey . . . having reported, was assigned a position in the rear of the One hundred and thirty-fourth New York. . . .

At this time orders were received to advance again, and, if possible, dislodge the enemy. For this purpose four companies of the Thirty-third New Jersey . . . were thrown to the left of the One hundred and thirty-fourth New York . . . to extend its line. The nature of the ground, as before, prevented much regularity of movements, but the officers and men rushed forward impetuously, determined to carry the heights, and so far succeeded that the greater part of the advance gained the crest, but the enemy having every advantage of position poured in a fire so destructive that after a brief struggle the line was again forced back to its last position. Here the several regiments held the ground, keeping up an irregular fire until about 7 o'clock, when, in obedience to orders received from the division commander, the several regiments retired to the base of the mountain. [*O.R.*, XXXVIII, pt. 2, pp. 203–204.]

Report of Capt. Thomas O'Connor, USA, Thirty-Third New Jersey Infantry, Second Brigade, Second Division, Twentieth Army Corps

The regiment was passed on to the front to strengthen and take part with the division engaged at . . . [Dug] Gap. The order was to move up the mountain and report to the brigade commander. Knapsacks were unslung and piled, and the regiment commenced to advance, but did not go far before another aide of the general commanding gave orders to keep well to the right, to advance in line of battle up the mountain, endeavor to carry the crest, and then, by changing front to the left, take the enemy in the flank and drive him toward our troops operating on the left.

The line advanced steadily under a moderately heavy skirmish fire, with skirmishers on the front and right flank, the enemy retreating before them. Steep, perpendicular rocks and inaccessible cliffs debarred our way, but the regiment was obliqued to the left, and with a rush succeeded in carrying the first tier of palisades. Here the line was reformed, forming connection with . . . the One hundred and thirty-fourth New York. Another order from the general commanding came to carry the point of the mountain. . . . Dispositions were at once made for the attack, and two large companies of the Thirty-third New Jersey . . . thrown out as skirmishers, one of them upon the flank. The storming party consisted of the One hundred and thirty-fourth New York and our companies of the Thirty-third New Jersey . . . the balance of the Thirty-third to act as circumstances required, either to check the enemy's pursuit in case of failure or to profit by success and push forward.

The order was given to advance, when, with a yell and rush, we charged up the side of the upper mountain. The enemy, at least two regiments strong, well screened and protected, met us with terrific volleys, but the brave men swerved not, and with shouts of defiance went to the top, only to halt again, however, under a steep, perpendicular palisade. A portion of the regiment on the left even clambered to the top of the hill and confronted on the highest level the breastworks of the enemy, but too few only could climb up at a time, and the enemy, in large force, soon dislodged these brave heroes, who had actually gained the very summit. Seeing that it was impossible to hold the top, the line was withdrawn about thirty paces and reformed, the enemy not daring to follow. We still held within fifty paces of the crest, when, toward dusk . . . the skirmish line was called in and the command withdrawn, the enemy following almost to the foot of the mountain. [*O.R.,* XXXVIII, pt. 2, pp. 226–227.]

Report of Surgeon H. Earnest Goodman, USA, Surgeon in Chief, Second Division, Twentieth Army Corps, Army of the Cumberland

Condition of command: Exhausted by long marches, day and night; roads made heavy by rain. Strength of command: Two brigades—officers 330; enlisted men, 4,363; only a part of which became engaged. Engagement lasted six hours. Made four charges up the ridge over large rocks and stones; enemy entrenched. Condition of supplies: Stimulants and surgical appliances in abundance, but only reached us two hours after engagement began; tents in the rear; dressings at first obtained from the numerous panniers. Field hospital established half a mile from foot of Taylor's Ridge and one mile from the enemy. Operations: Amputations (circular), 11; resections, 7. Water excellent and very abundant; food obtained from supply in ambulances; cattle captured and killed. Mode of removal of wounded: on blankets and stretchers to foot of mountain and in ambulance to hospital. Character of the fire: Musketry, continuous; range 20 to 300 yards. Subsequent disposition of wounded: Wounded removed next day . . . to Ringgold, Ga., a distance of twenty-five miles under the guidance of division ambulance officer and Assistant Surgeons. . . . Coffee prepared on the march from supplies in the ambulance boxes. . . . Anesthetics: Chloroform in all cases; no bad results. Casualties: Received in division hospital—wounded, 184; died during night, 7; while in transit, 1. [*O.R.,* XXXVIII, pt. 2, pp. 148–149.]

Report of Maj. Gen. Patrick R. Cleburne, CSA, Commanding Division, Hardee's Corps, Army of Tennessee

On the 7th . . . the enemy advanced, with heavy masses of infantry and other arms, toward Rocky Face Gap, near Dalton. . . . My division was at this time entrenched upon Mill Creek, on the middle Spring Place road. The next day . . . I was ordered to go with dispatch to Dug Gap . . . then being heavily attacked by Hooker's corps. I was to take [Brig. Gen. *Mark P.*] *Lowrey's* and *Granbury's* brigades. I arrived there after a rapid march, which was rendered very severe by the extreme heat of the summer and the steep acclivity of the ridge, about an hour before sundown. Reaching the gap in person, while my command was still at the foot of the ridge, I found the First and Second Arkansas Cavalry, dismounted, and *Grigsby's* brigade of Kentucky cavalry holding the position. They had gallantly repulsed every assault. The fight was still going on, and some anxiety was felt lest the overwhelming numbers of the enemy might carry the position before my command could ascend the hill. The Arkansans and Kentuckians held it firmly, however, until I placed *Lowrey* and *Granbury* in position, which was done by night-fall. With night the enemy remitted his attack, and everything was quiet.

On the morning of the 9th my pickets were advanced to the extreme base of the ridge on its west face. Many of the enemy's dead were found, and some wounded, who were brought in and cared for. A great many small-arms were collected and brought in also. The enemy did not attack during the day. His forces were plainly in view in the valley. Their numbers, however, could not be estimated, as the valley had only a small portion of cleared land.

At about 1 a.m. on the 10th I received orders . . . to move toward Resaca. Leaving Colonel *Williamson* with his Arkansas troops in the gap (*Grigsby* had been sent to Snake Creek Gap) I moved accordingly within a mile of . . . Resaca on the railroad. I remained here two or three hours, when I returned . . . to Dug Gap, arriving about sundown. My division was now together. Receiving orders during the night, I marched on the morning of the 11th, starting at 7 o'clock, upon the Sugar Valley road in the direction of Resaca.

This movement was rendered necessary by the untoward circumstances of Snake Creek Gap not being adequately occupied to resist the heavy force thrown against it, under the sagacious and enterprising McPherson. How this gap, which opened upon our rear and line of communication . . . was neglected I cannot imagine. General [William W.] Mackall, Johnston's chief of staff, told me it was the result of a flagrant disobedience of orders, by whom he did not say. Certainly the commanding general never could have failed to appreciate its importance. Its loss exposed us in the outset of the campaign to a terrible danger, and on the left forced us to retreat from a position where, if he adhered to his attack, we might have detained the enemy for months, destroying vast numbers of his men, perhaps prolonged the campaign until the wet season would have rendered operations in the field impracticable. As it was, if McPherson had hotly pressed his advantage, Sherman supporting him strongly with the bulk of his army, it is impossible to say what the enemy might not have achieved—more than probable a complete victory. But McPherson faltered and hung back, indeed after penetrating within a mile of Resaca he actually returned, because, as I understood, he was not supported, and feared if we turned back suddenly upon him from Dalton he would be cut off, as doubtless would have been the result.

After a few miles I camped for several hours. In the afternoon I resumed the march, and halted about sundown at a point where a new military road debauched into the Sugar Valley road, ten miles from Dalton. Determining upon a line of battle I camped for the night.

At 7 next morning, the 12th, the cavalry skirmishers in advance of me on the Sugar Valley road were driven in. Making my dispositions as promptly as possible, and more in detail than I had been able to do the evening before, I threw up breastworks and awaited the enemy, who was reported advancing in line of battle. He did not attack, however.

On the 13th I marched to Resaca and went into position on the crest of the ridge looking into a valley several hundred yards wide, formed by [Camp] Creek, which at this point was parallel with the railroad, and about a mile to the west of it. Here I covered myself with rifle pits—*Bate* on my right, *Cheatham* on my left. [O.R., XXXVIII, pt. 3, pp. 720–722.]

6. RESACA OVERVIEW

Resume driving in the same direction on Dug Gap Battle Road. After descending for about 1.3 miles, turn right onto Interstate 75, southbound. Drive south on I-75 to exit 320 (Resaca), about 12 miles. Leave the interstate at exit 320 and turn left onto Georgia State Highway 136. Follow this highway about 0.5 mile to a "T" intersection with a stop sign. Turn left onto U.S. 41. Drive about 0.3 mile, then turn left into the Resaca Baptist Church parking lot, which begins just beyond the highway guardrail on the left. Walk up the unimproved road that leaves the parking lot parallel to the highway, climbing to the cemetery by following the unimproved road about 200 yards as it circles up the hill behind the church. Position yourself so that you can look across the interstate.

Sherman's line of battle was along the wooded hills just beyond the interstate. There were few trees in the area at the time of the battle; the "bare hill" that features in many of the contemporary accounts is the hill now covered with hardwoods—two hills to the left of the hill that is bare today. Camp Creek flows between these hills and the interstate. You are standing on one of the low ridges that constituted the Confederate position. The Confederate line ran from the woods on your left through this position and continued to your right for about 400 yards before angling forward to cross the Interstate beyond the meadows on your right front.

STOP 6, RESACA

9–16 May 1864

OPERATIONS

As the bulk of his forces pressed against the Confederate defenses on Rocky Face, Sherman ordered Maj. Gen. James B. McPherson to march the Army of the Tennessee through Snake Creek Gap, secure the gap, and then to "make a bold attack on the enemy's flank or his railroad at any point between Tilton and Resaca."

Sherman wrote: "I hope the enemy will fight at Dalton, in which case he can have no force there that can interfere with you. But, should his

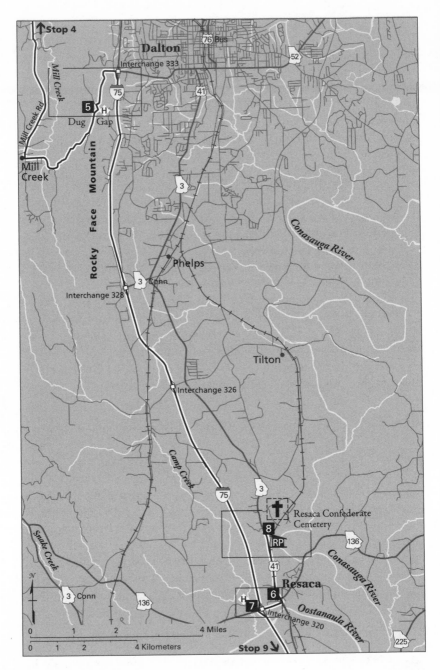

Dug Gap to Resaca

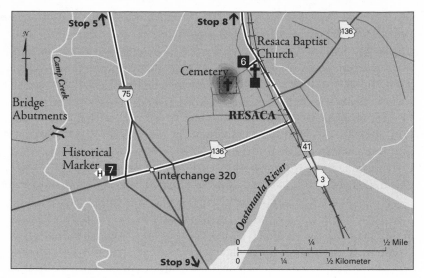

Resaca Overview (Stop 6)

policy be to fall back along his railroad, you will hit him in flank. . . by the most vigorous attack possible, as it may save us what we have most reason to apprehend—a slow pursuit, in which he gains strength as we lose it" [*O.R.*, XXXVIII, pt. 4, pp. 39–40].

McPherson's Army of the Tennessee (24,000) began the march on May 6 from Gordon's Mills via Villanow to Snake Creek Gap, and by May 9 his column had cleared the gap and was advancing toward Resaca, with Maj. Gen. G. M. Dodge's 16th Corps and some of Brig. Gen. Judson Kilpatrick's cavalry in the lead. General *Johnston* had anticipated such a move. To enhance his mobility he had already constructed or improved roads leading south from Dalton, and he had ordered defenses to be prepared at Resaca to guard the bridges across the Oostenaula River. On May 5 he ordered Brig. Gen. *James Cantey*, commanding in Rome, Georgia, to move his brigade from the Department of the Gulf by rail to Resaca; two days later he instructed Lt. Gen. *Leonidas Polk* to concentrate his corps from the Army of Mississippi at Rome, and on the 9th he notified *Polk* to bring his command to Resaca "as fast as possible." He also sent a brigade from the vicinity of Dalton, increasing Confederate strength in Resaca on May 9 to 4,000 men.

The first clash occurred when the Union advance guard of Dodge's 16th Corps, consisting of a regiment of mounted infantry and one of infantry, encountered Brig. Gen. S. W. Ferguson's Confederate cavalry brigade. A second Union brigade promptly joined the fight, and the Confederates fell back, skirmishing, to a ridge of high hills about three-fourths of a mile west of Resaca. Dodge pressed forward to the old Calhoun and Dalton crossroads, about a quarter of a mile from the new Confederate position. Leaving his Fourth Division to secure the crossroads, he sent the Second Division, commanded by Brig. Gen. John M. Corse, forward to attack Cantey's brigade of infantry on what then was known as "Bald Hill." (This hill, which today is heavily forested, overlooks the Oostenaula River and is not to be confused with the cleared hill about 0.4 mile to the north, where State Road 136 crosses before descending into the Camp Creek Valley.)

Corse soon captured Bald Hill, and the Confederates fell back across Camp Creek to the Resaca defenses. Later that afternoon Dodge received orders to send his Fourth Division to gain the railroad north of Resaca. His skirmishers had just reached a position from which they could command the railroad when McPherson ordered him to withdraw and return to the mouth of Snake Creek Gap, where he was to entrench and bring forward supplies. Dodge's men were out of provisions, and the several roads running south from Dalton would have exposed his left flank to enemy movements from that direction. "I had no cavalry except [Lt. Col. Jesse J.] Phillips' mounted men to feel out on the flanks," McPherson explained. "If I could have had a division of good cavalry I could have broken the railroad at some point."

For the next two days McPherson remained in his defensive position on the Resaca side of Snake Creek Gap. On May 10 Maj. Gen. Joseph Hooker's corps was ordered to reinforce McPherson, to be followed the next day by the rest of the Army of the Cumberland except for Maj. Gen. Oliver O. Howard's 4th Corps, which continued to hold the Union position at Buzzard Roost.

On the 13th Maj. Gen. John M. Schofield's Army of the Ohio also moved into Snake Creek Gap. Johnston used the time allowed by McPherson to concentrate his own forces at Resaca and to prepare the battlefield. On the 9th, when he first heard of McPherson's attempt against the railroad, he ordered Lt. Gen. John B. Hood's corps to the scene, and when he subsequently recalled Hood, after McPherson had withdrawn, he took the precaution of leaving two of Hood's three divisions near Tilton, about halfway between Dalton and Resaca, where they could be rushed to either

"Artillery Firing on the Railroad at Resaca" (*Harper's Pictorial History of the Great Rebellion* [New York: Harper Bros., 1866–1868], 605).

point if needed. On the 10th he sent a military engineer to lay out a line of works defending Resaca against an attack from the west, and during the next two days Maj. Gen. *William W. Loring's* division of *Polk's* corps arrived by train. *Polk* himself reported on the 11th, and *Johnston* promptly authorized him to call upon *Hood's* two divisions at Tilton if necessary. On the night of May 12, once assured that Sherman's army was indeed headed for Snake Creek Gap, *Johnston* ordered his artillery and remaining infantry to evacuate their positions and head for Resaca.

On the 13th McPherson moved forward again to attack Bald Hill, which the Confederates had reoccupied with Brig. Gen. *Thomas Scott's* brigade from *Loring's* division. The Confederates held the position until ordered back into the line of entrenchments behind Camp Creek. *Polk's* entire corps now occupied the Confederate left, its left flank anchored on the Oostenaula; Lt. Gen. *William J. Hardee's* corps held the center along the high ridge overlooking Camp Creek, and *Hood's* corps took position on the right, his line running eastward to a hill near the Conasauga River. There was "brisk skirmishing" all afternoon along *Polk's* line and in front of *Hardee's* left division.

The next morning Sherman's army "closed in," enveloping the Confederate lines from the north and west. Hooker's 20th Corps moved out the Resaca road to support McPherson's troops, while Maj. Gen. John M. Palmer's 14th Corps advanced along a parallel route a couple of miles to the north with orders to fight its way to the railroad. About noon, Palmer attacked, supported on his left by Schofield's Army of the Ohio, but in the hills bordering the railroad they encountered heavy resistance. Maj. Gen. George Thomas then directed Howard's 4th Corps, which had followed the Confederates from Dalton, to take position on Schofield's left.

The fighting here was "very severe," but Schofield and Howard drove the enemy back into his prepared positions. Palmer's subordinates were unaware of the presence of enemy breastworks and had no time to reconnoiter or even to adjust their lines before plunging into the boggy and open valley of Camp Creek, directly in front of *Cleburne's* position at the center of *Hardee's* line. Some of his units got tangled up with Schofield's troops and could not participate in the attack. Others managed to cross the creek but were forced back to the shelter of its miry banks, where they were pinned down until dark. The rest were withdrawn to higher ground, where they dug in.

The heaviest fighting was near the headwaters of Camp Creek, where late in the afternoon Brig. Gen. Jacob B. Cox's division of Schofield's Army of the Ohio drove the Confederates over rough and wooded ground into their works and carried the enemy's first line. Two divisions of Howard's 4th Corps later moved up to secure the position, opposite Maj. Gen. *Thomas C. Hindman's* division on the left of *Hood's* line. At 6 p.m., *Hood*, who held the right of the Confederate line, launched a fierce counterattack with his other two divisions. Holding with his left, *Hood* executed a left wheel that enabled his right to advance about two miles, overrunning a "round-topped hill" just east of the Dalton road that anchored the Union flank. Howard, however, had received timely warning from Maj. Gen. David Stanley, commanding the division in this sector. When he explained the situation to Thomas, the 20th Corps, which had been supporting McPherson, was sent behind the lines of Palmer, Schofield, and Howard to the extreme Union left. The lead division, under Brig. Gen. A. S. Williams, reached the vicinity of Nance Springs just in time to repel *Hood's* assault.

Only on the extreme right did Union attacks succeed. Here a brigade of Maj. Gen. Morgan L. Smith's division, 15th Corps, rushed forward and plunged across Camp Creek to seize rifle pits on a slight elevation about 500 yards in front of the main Confederate works. After fighting at close quarters, the Confederates fell back, their artillery opened fire, and a strong force counterattacked. Again the Confederates withdrew, and a second Union brigade forded the creek to help consolidate the position. Once more the Confederates attempted to regain their trenches. The fighting continued until dark, but McPherson's men held. Throughout the night the Union troops labored to dig rifle-pits, construct batteries, build bridges, and prepare the fords across Camp Creek, and by morning two divisions of the 15th Corps were well entrenched along the bridgehead.

Confederate earthworks with Resaca in the background (MOLLUS).

Sherman ordered the attacks to be resumed at daylight. He assumed—
in fact he hoped—that *Johnston* would attempt to retake the ground lost
the previous evening, for he planned to hold on his right while Howard
and Hooker attacked from the north, with Schofield moving around to
the extreme left of the line, near the Dalton and Resaca road, in support.
The two divisions on the left of Palmer's line would join in the attack once
Schofield had cleared their front; Palmer's other two divisions would remain on the defensive on the bluffs west of Camp Creek, connecting with
a division of the 16th Corps that now occupied Bald Hill. As the attack
drove the Confederates back into Resaca, McPherson's guns on Bald Hill
would bombard the bridges over the Oostenaula, making it "too hot for the
passage of troops."

The attack did not materialize as planned. Because the terrain on the
Union left was rough, hilly, and heavily wooded, and the commanders
knew nothing of the ground or the Confederate strength and defenses, it
took longer than anticipated to move the divisions of Maj. Gen. Dan Butterfield and Brig. Gen. John W. Geary to the area where Williams's division had stopped *Hood's* attack the night before. The configuration of the
terrain gave the Confederates "unusual facilities for cross firing and enfilading," and the Union brigades were forced to attack in columns without

adequate artillery support. The brunt of the attacks, first by Butterfield's division and then Geary's, was borne by Maj. Gen. *Carter Stevenson's* division. Union troops reoccupied the position lost by Stanley's division the previous evening and captured a battery on the "round-topped hill." In places they advanced to within thirty paces of *Stevenson's* defenses, but the Confederate line held.

To the west Howard's corps engaged in "heavy skirmishing" all day but never mounted a real attack, and no serious attempt was made to cross Camp Creek by Palmer's corps. Throughout the day Maj. Gen. John A. Logan's advance line east of Camp Creek poured steady fire, artillery as well as small arms, into the main Confederate works, while the guns on Bald Hill bombarded the town, the enemy's forts, and the bridges.

But the Confederates were not driven back into Resaca from the north as hoped, and there was no assault upon the town. In fact it was not necessary, for Sherman had already caused two pontoon bridges to be laid across the Oostenaula at Lay's Ferry, about three miles below Resaca, and during the day Brig. Gen. T. W. Sweeny's second division of the 16th Corps crossed the river. With the aid of two batteries on the northern bank, his troops beat back an attack by a portion of Maj. Gen. *William H. T. Walker's* division, of *Hardee's* corps, which was patrolling the railroad between Resaca and Calhoun. Once Sweeny's force had fortified the bridgehead, *Johnston* was in effect outflanked. This turn of events caused him to call off a projected attack by *Hood* and to cross the river that night. In the darkness he was unmolested by the Union guns on Bald Hill. By morning the Confederates were well on the way to Calhoun, having burned the bridges behind them.

On May 16 Sherman issued Special Field Orders No. 8, outlining the general plan for the next phase of the campaign.

Although *Johnston* at Resaca was outnumbered two to one, he had, to quote Sherman, "all the advantages of natural positions, of artificial forts and roads, and of concentrated action." Sherman's obvious weakness was his use of cavalry: although equal to the Confederate cavalry in numbers, Sherman assumed that his mounted arm was inferior—as indeed it was in leadership, if not in quality or numbers. Its main mission seems to have been to keep enemy cavalry away from his lifeline, the railroad. This may explain why Sherman failed to give his cavalry an independent role, but at Resaca it did not function well even in leading the advance.

One might also ask whether Sherman's plan to drive the Confederates into Resaca from the north was consistent with his hope of avoiding a slow

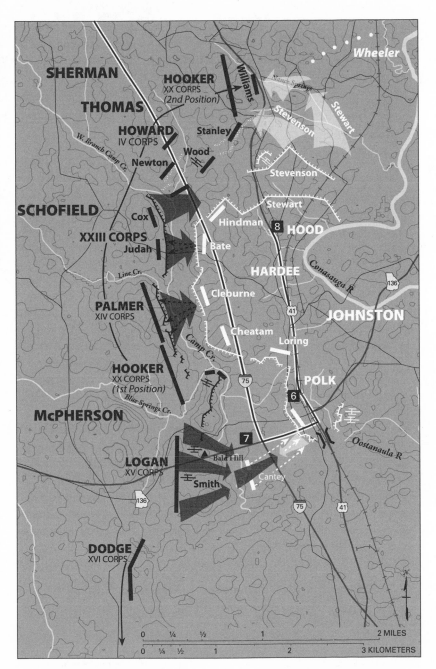

Union Attacks and Confederate Counterattacks at Resaca

pursuit as *Johnston* fell back on his line of communications, increasing his strength along the way. Two or three additional divisions thrown across the river to block the bridges from the south would have been more consistent with his operational goal, and troops were available for such a move.

Maj. Gen. William T. Sherman to Maj. Gen. H. W. Halleck, Washington, D.C., 10 May 1864

7 a.m. I am starting for the extreme front in Buzzard Roost Gap, and write this dispatch that you may understand. *Johnston* acts purely on the defensive. I am attacking him on his strongest fronts, viz., west and north, till McPherson breaks his line at Resaca, when I will swing around through Snake Creek Gap, and interpose between him and Georgia. I am not driving things too fast, because I want two columns of cavalry that are rapidly coming up to me from the rear, Stoneman on my left and Garrard on my right, both due today. Yesterday I pressed hard to prevent *Johnston* detaching against McPherson, but today I will be more easy, as I believe McPherson has destroyed Resaca, when he is ordered to fall back to the mouth of Snake Creek Gap and act against *Johnston's* flank when he does start. All are in good condition.

7.30 *p.m.* General McPherson reached Resaca, but found the place strongly fortified and guarded, and did not break the road. According to his instructions, he drew back to the *debouches* of the gorge, where he has a strong defensive position, and guards the only pass into the valley of the Oostenaula available to us. Buzzard Roost Gap . . . is naturally and artificially too strong to be attempted. I must feign on Buzzard Roost, but pass through Snake Creek Gap, and place myself between *Johnston* and Resaca, when we will have to fight it out. I am making the preliminary move. Certain that *Johnston* can make no detachments, I will be in no hurry. My cavalry is just approaching from Kentucky and Tennessee (detained by the difficulty of getting horses), and even now it is less than my minimum. [*O.R.*, XXXVIII, pt. 4, p. 111.]

Maj. Gen. William T. Sherman to Maj. Gen. George H. Thomas, USA, Commanding the Army of the Cumberland, 10 May 1864

I propose to leave hereabouts one of your corps, say Howard's, the cavalry of Colonel McCook, and the cavalry of General Stoneman to keep up the feint of a direct attack on Dalton through Buzzard Roost Gap as long as possible, and with all the remainder of the three armies to march . . . through Snake Creek Gap and to attack the enemy in force from that quarter. You may at once commence the necessary preparations and give orders that the force left here is to be under the command of the senior officer, who will strip his command light, sending all spare wagons to Ringgold; that the cars run daily to this point with daily supplies, but the main stores to be at Ringgold; that the cavalry watch well the passes north of Tunnel Hill and at Ray's Gap, and that in case the enemy detect the diminution of the force and attack, it gradually withdraw in the direction of Ringgold, but defend that point at all costs; that locomotive and construction train be kept here with orders and prepared if this retrograde movement be made necessary that the party shall take up at intervals rails, so as to make a repair train necessary to replace them; this that the enemy may not use the track to facilitate his movement in pursuit. . . .

The pass at Snake Creek is represented as very narrow. Please instruct a division to be there tomorrow provided with axes and spades so as to widen the road as to enable the passage of wagons, also to facilitate the march of troops by roads and paths outside the wagon track. General Stoneman will be at Varnell's tonight, and by tomorrow night all his command will be in, so that we will calculate all to go to Snake Creek and close up on General McPherson during the day after tomorrow. [*O.R.*, XXXVIII, pt. 4, pp. 113–114.]

Maj. Gen. William T. Sherman to Maj. Gen. James B. McPherson, USA, Commanding Army of the Tennessee, 10 May 1864, 10:30 a.m.

I regret beyond measure you did not break the railroad, however little, and close to Resaca, but I suppose it was impossible. We find in Buzzard Roost Gap an almost impassable obstacle; the spurs on either side run down to . . . Mill Creek, and all are escarped and rifle-pitted with batteries on the upper plateau. The ridge itself is very rocky. . . . I doubt if we can force a passage, but we may render it equally impassable to the enemy, and leaving a comparatively small force here can rapidly, and by night, if necessary, march through Snake Creek Gap and hold the point near Resaca, where the Dalton road comes in. I want you to select near the debouche a strong impregnable position . . . and fortify and strengthen it by fallen timber and rifle pits. I have sent one of Hooker's divisions to you; you should post them in support, with one regiment on the mountain to the east of the gap, not far from the letter "M" or "O" in the word "mountain" east of Villanow. This would prevent the occupation of this mountain, by which the pass would be made dangerous from sharpshooters. . . . Hold on a day or so and I will, as soon as all things are ready, come down. . . . In the mean time mask your own force as much as possible, but hold your ground and look well to secure the mountain range to the east and north. A single peak held by a regiment becomes a key to the whole range. I wish you to calculate to have ten days' supplies and to send your wagons to the rear, not to come up till the time expires or you order them. [*O.R.*, XXXVIII, pt. 4, pp. 125–127.]

Sherman to McPherson, 11 May 1864

You now have your 23,000, and Hooker is in close support, so that you can hold all *Joe Johnston's* army in check should he abandon Dalton. He can't afford to abandon Dalton for he has fixed it up so nice for us, and he observes we are close at hand waiting for him to quit. He cannot afford a detachment strong enough to fight you, as his army will not admit of it. Strengthen your position, fight anything that comes, and threaten the safety of the railroad all the time. But to tell the truth, I would rather he should stay in Dalton two more days, when he may find a larger party than he expects in an open field. At all events we can then choose our ground and he will be forced to move out of his trenches. I do not intend to put a column into Buzzard Roost Gap at present. See that you are in easy communication with me and all quarters. [*O.R.*, XXXVIII, pt. 4, pp. 138–139.]

Headquarters, Military Division of the Mississippi, in the Field, Snake Creek Gap, 12 May 1864

The object of the movement for tomorrow is to interpose between the enemy and Resaca, and to break his communications.

Major General McPherson will move his column directly on Resaca, occupying in force the hills on this side of Camp Creek, and his left extending along Camp Creek. He will prepare to advance a part of his force from his left to the railroad, and break it, and then fall back to his line.

Major General Thomas will follow close to General McPherson, and when he reaches a main road crossing the Resaca road, about two miles this side of the town, viz.: the Dalton and Calhoun road, he will turn to the left toward Dalton, prepared to deploy forward, and connect on his right with General McPherson's left, choosing strong positions to cover the movement on the railroad.

Major General Schofield will follow General Thomas, and at the first Dalton road, known as the Dalton and Rome road, will turn to the left and advance to abreast of General Thomas and connect with him. General Schofield will leave one brigade in Snake Creek Gap, about five miles east of Villanow, and the balance of the one division in General McPherson's entrenched camp at this point.

IV. The cavalry of General Garrard will picket all roads to our rear, and in case of being threatened from the north, will come into Snake Creek Gap and cover the rear of the army and the wagon train. The cavalry of General Kilpatrick will move south of the main road to Resaca, and be held in reserve near the forks of the road, and be subject to the orders of the Commander-in-Chief.

V. All trains will be brought in Snake Creek Gap, and be parked in convenient order off the road. Great care must be observed in keeping the road clear, and ambulances and wagons when not traveling the road must invariably turn out and leave all the road clear. Each army commander will leave his own wagon guards, and the men should leave their knapsacks in camp.

VI. The movement will begin at six (6) o'clock A.M. to-morrow.

By order of Major General W. T. Sherman [*Orders*, p. 241.]

Report of Maj. Gen. William T. Sherman, USA, Commanding Military Division of the Mississippi

The next day we moved against Resaca, General McPherson on the direct road, preceded by General Kilpatrick's cavalry. General Thomas to come up on his left, and General Schofield on his. General Kilpatrick met and drove the enemy's cavalry from a cross-road within two miles of Resaca, but received a wound which disabled him, and gave the command of his brigade to Colonel Eli Murray, who, according to his orders, wheeled out of the road, leaving General McPherson to pass.

General McPherson struck the enemy's infantry pickets near Resaca and drove them within their fortified lines, and occupied a ridge of bald hills, his right on the Oostenaula, about two miles below the railroad bridge, and his left abreast the town. General Thomas came up on his left facing Camp Creek, and General Schofield broke his way through the dense forest to General Thomas' left. Johnston had left Dalton and General Howard entered it and pressed his rear.

Nothing saved Johnston's army at Resaca but the impracticable nature of the country, which made the passage of troops across the valley almost impossible. This enabled his army to reach Resaca from Dalton along the comparatively good road, constructed beforehand partly from the topographical nature of the country and partly from the foresight of the rebel chief.

At all events, on the 14th of May, we found the rebel army in a strong position behind Camp Creek, occupying the forts at Resaca and his right on some high chestnut hills, to the north of the town. I at once ordered a pontoon bridge to be laid across the Oostenaula at Lay's Ferry, in the direction of Calhoun; a division of the Sixteenth Corps, commanded by General Sweeny, to cross and threaten Calhoun; also the cavalry division of General Garrard to move from . . . Villanow down toward Rome to cross the Oostenaula and break the railroad below Calhoun and above Kingston, if possible, and with the main army I pressed against Resaca at all points. [*O.R.*, XXXVIII, pt. 1, p. 64.]

Narrative of Gen. Joseph E. Johnston, CSA, Commanding Army of Tennessee

At night . . . on the 9th . . . Brigadier-General *Cantey* reported that he had been engaged at Resaca until dark with troops of the Army of the Tennessee, which was commanded by Major-General McPherson, and had held his ground. As intelligence of the arrival of that army in Snake Creek Gap had been received, Lieutenant-General *Hood* was ordered to move to Resaca immediately with three divisions—those of *Hindman*, *Cleburne*, and *Walker*.

On the 10th that officer reported that the enemy was retiring; and was recalled, but directed to leave *Cleburne's* and *Walker's* divisions near Tilton—one on each road. . . . At night reports were received from the scouts in observation near the south end of Rocky Face, to the effect that General McPherson's troops were entrenching their position in Snake Creek Gap. And on the 11th various reports were received indicating a general movement to their right by the Federal troops, as if to unite with those of McPherson.

On the same day, Brigadier-General *Cantey* again announced that a Federal army was approaching Resaca from the direction of Snake Creek Gap. But intelligence that Lieutenant General *Polk* had reached that point with *Loring's* division, prevented any immediate apprehension for the place. He was instructed to hold it with the troops then under his command there, and authorized to call *Cleburn[e]'s* and *Walker's* divisions to him, if necessary. They were within six miles. . . .

The Federal army, approaching Resaca on the Snake Creek Gap road, was met about a mile from the place by *Loring's* division, and held in check long enough to enable *Hardee's* and *Hood's* corps, then just arriving, to occupy their ground undisturbed. As the army was formed (in two lines), *Polk's* and *Hardee's* corps were west of the place and railroad, facing to the west; the former on the left, with its left resting on the Oostenaula. *Hood's* corps extended from *Hardee's* right across the railroad to the Connesauga [sic], facing to the northwest.

There was brisk skirmishing all the afternoon of May 13th on *Polk's* front, and that of *Hardee's* left division—*Cheatham's*. The [U.S.] Fourth Corps had been left in front of Mill Creek Gap, probably to prevent or delay the discovery by us of the withdrawal of the main body of the Federal army. Major General *Wheeler*, falling back before that corps, reached Tilton at three o'clock in the afternoon. He received instructions there to do every thing possible to prevent it from passing that point before nightfall to give Lieutenant General *Hood* time to dispose his corps carefully, and make other preparations to hold his ground. For this object his cavalry was re-enforced by *Brown's* brigade. These instructions were executed, and the enemy delayed until night—quite long enough for the object in view.

The skirmishers became engaged along our whole line early in the day (May 14th), beginning on the left. Those of *Polk's* corps, from some unaccountable mistake, abandoned their ground, which was regained only by great personal efforts on the part of their field officers. . . . A vigorous assault was made upon *Hindman's* division, but the assailants were handsomely repulsed. [*Military Operations*, pp. 306–310.]

TACTICS

Report of Maj. Gen. William W. Loring, CSA, Commanding Division, Army of Mississippi

Scott's brigade arrived at Resaca on the 10th of May, followed by [Brig. Gen. John] Adams on the 11th, and [Brig. Gen. Winfield S.] Featherston's brigade on the 12th. Myself and staff arrived with Adams on the 11th. The advance of McPherson's corps was reported, on my arrival, to be halted four miles west of Resaca. On the morning of the 13th the enemy resumed his advance upon Resaca, driving our cavalry slowly before him. Receiving orders to throw forward a brigade to check his advance, Scott's brigade was moved forward and took position in line on Bald Knob, about a mile west of town. About 1 p.m. the brigade became warmly engaged, and held the enemy in check three hours, and could have maintained its position longer, but was ordered to retire into our line of entrenchments. It drew off in perfect order and took position on the right of . . . Cantey's division. Adams' was drawn up on the right of Scott's, with Featherston's in rear as reserve. I ordered breast-works thrown up on both front and rear lines, which the men set about with great spirit and speedily accomplished. Bouanchaud's, Barry's, Cowan's, and Charpentier's batteries were placed in position on a high range of hills on line of Cantey's division. The losses occurring in the division after forming behind the intrenchments resulted from heavy shelling of the enemy and his sharpshooters, there being no heavy engagement on the part of the line it occupied. [O.R., XXXVIII, pt. 3, pp. 874–875.]

7. CAMP CREEK

Retrace your route by turning right onto U.S. 41, driving back to westbound GA 136, and turning right onto that highway. Drive just beyond the ramp you used to leave I-75 from the north and turn right into the crushed-rock parking lot with the state historical marker. Leave your car and face the historical marker with GA 136 on your left.

Camp Creek crosses the valley in front of you, and the abutments of an old bridge across the creek are visible about 300 yards in front of you to the right, just short of the tree line. Those abutments mark the route of the old road from Snake Creek Gap to Resaca.

The hill where Stop 6 is located should be clearly visible across the interstate to your right rear.

STOP 7, CAMP CREEK

9–14 May 1864

OPERATIONS

Report of Maj. Gen. Oliver O. Howard, USA, Commanding Army of the Tennessee

The plan of campaign contemplated that this army should turn the enemy's left flank at Dalton, while the other armies pushed more directly upon that place; whereupon, May 7, General McPherson moved his column toward Villanow, and halted for the night at a point west of Gordon's Springs Gap.

May 8, Major General Logan marched through this gap, whilst the rest of the command moved south as far as Villanow, and formed a junction with a brigade of cavalry under General Kilpatrick; encamped with the advance within seven miles of Resaca, near Snake Creek Gap. In final orders from this camp, General McPherson uses these words: "The object being to make a bold and rapid movement on the enemy's flank, or line of communication, all wagons and baggage of every kind will be left behind. . . ." With such a purpose the movement of the following day was ordered, "the command to pass through Snake Creek Gap in the direction of Resaca."

May 9, the column moved, General Dodge leading, at 5 a.m., preceded by a portion of General Kilpatrick's cavalry. The enemy's cavalry pickets were encountered on debauching from the gap at the eastern extremity. The command pushed on, the cavalry in advance, till within about three miles and a half of the town, when Kilpatrick encountered considerable infantry force, in charging which he was wounded and obliged to leave the field. . . .

Immediately upon the charge . . . General Dodge deployed his skirmishers under charge of Col. Patrick Burke, Sixty-sixth Illinois, who, with very little delay, gallantly drove back the rebel advance to the works around Resaca, and developed an artillery fire from his guns in position in the forts. In view of the enemy's works at several points, General McPherson deployed the Fifteenth Corps upon the right, and the Sixteenth Corps upon the left of the Resaca road, after which he pushed forward a division of General Dodge, with instructions to drive back the enemy and break the railroad. The best idea of his operations may be gained from General McPherson's letter of May 9, 10:30 p.m., to General Sherman. . . .

General Dodge's command moved up and skirmished with the enemy at Resaca this afternoon. While that was going on one company of mounted infantry succeeded in reaching the railroad near Tilton Station, but was forced to leave without damaging the track. They tore down a portion of the telegraph wire. The enemy have a strong position at Resaca naturally, and as far as we could see, have it pretty well fortified. They displayed considerable force, and opened on us with artillery. After skirmishing till nearly dark, and finding that I could not succeed in cutting the railroad before dark, or getting to it, I decided to withdraw the command and take up a position for the night between Sugar Valley and the entrance to the gap.

Here follow the reasons for retiring: first, the exposed position; second, General Dodge's command without rations. The general thought that if he had a division of good cavalry he could have broken the railroad at some point. General Garrard had just arrived at La Fayette, with horses fatigued and short of forage, and wished to remain there until his forage train came up from Chattanooga. The losses during the skirmish were 6 men killed and 30 wounded. . . . We captured 25 prisoners.

Shattered trees in the Confederate lines north of Resaca (George N. Barnard, MOLLUS).

Not having succeeded in getting upon the railroad, the command fell back to the intersection of the Dalton and Rome and Resaca roads, in Sugar Valley, taking up a strong position. Though the railroad had not been reached, still the mountain ridge . . . was passed. It seems that the rebel general had dispatched a brigade of cavalry at 10 p.m. of the night before, with orders to take possession of and hold Snake Creek Gap. He was a little too late.

May 10 and 11, a new position, nearer the gap and naturally stronger, was selected and occupied. On the 12th and 13th the lines were moved forward on the Resaca road to the cross-roads, two miles from the town.

As soon as the lines were formed, Major-General Logan pushed forward a strong skirmish line, driving the enemy before him. The enemy's skirmish fire was kept up, but he made no considerable stand till the advanced line had reached an open field. Beyond these fields, 700 or 800 yards distant, a ridge appeared, running nearly in a north and south direction. The enemy had taken position on his ridge, having artillery and infantry and slight barricades. General Logan placed some batteries of his command in position, and quickly silenced the enemy's guns. Immediately the main lines were moved forward and the ridge carried. As soon as the Fifteenth Corps had been formed, with the right across the Resaca road, one division of General Dodge's was brought up and deployed farther to the right. In this position the army entrenched; artillery was located bearing upon Resaca and the railroad bridge. When these guns opened in front of Generals Logan and Dodge, the effect upon the enemy was perceptible, and interruption of the railroad trains occasioned. This position, thus commanding the enemy's principal line of communication, rendered his stay at Resaca impossible unless he succeeded in dislodging our army.

During the 14th several demonstrations and feints were made by the command to keep the enemy from re-enforcing his right, where there was evidently a battle going on. [*O.R.*, XXXVIII, pt. 3, pp. 30–32.] [During the battle of Resaca Howard commanded the Fourth Corps; he was placed in command of the Army of the Tennessee after McPherson was killed on July 22 in the Battle of Atlanta.—*eds.*]

TACTICS

Report of Maj. Gen. John A. Logan, USA, Commanding Fifteenth Army Corps, Army of the Tennessee

On the morning of the 14th sharp skirmishing and heavy artillery exchanges were renewed. . . . The several brigades of [Brig. Gen. William] Harrow's division were removed from their positions on the left and stationed in rear of [Brig. Gen.] M[organ] L. Smith's and [Brig. Gen. Peter J.] Osterhaus' divisions as reserves. Appearances indicating that a severe battle was in progress upon the extreme left of our army, I caused a feint attack to be made, and continued for some time lively demonstrations to deter the enemy from sending re-enforcements from our front. General Osterhaus took advantage of the feint to attack the enemy's skirmishers in the heavily wooded valley near the road. This was done in the most gallant manner. The bridge over Camp Creek was carried, and the Twelfth Missouri Infantry thrown forward into the woods previously occupied by the enemy, thus forming a living tete-de-pont, which in the ensuing movement proved of great value.

Directly in front of M. L. Smith's division, and at a distance varying from one-half to three-quarters of a mile from it, a series of low, irregular hills extended from the Oostenaula due north as far as the

Resaca Road. They were occupied by the enemy in force, and were partially fortified. This position, if in our possession, would bring us within three-eighths of a mile of the enemy's nearest fort, and within half a mile of the railroad bridge, thus practically cutting the railroad.

To gain this position had been the work intended for the next day, and a number of bridges were to have been thrown over Camp Creek on the night of the 14th . . . to facilitate the passage of troops, but the continuous artillery and musketry fire on the left, and the necessity for us to make a further diversion, precipitated the movement, and at 5:30 p.m. of the 14th the assaulting column crossed Camp Creek as best they could, some over the bridge, others on logs, and others wading, with their arms and equipments held over their heads. The assaulting force consisted of Brig. Gen. Charles R. Woods' brigade, of the First Division . . . and Brig. Gen. Giles A. Smith's brigade, of the Second Division, on the right. Both brigades were formed in double lines, and in front and on the left of Woods' brigade the Twelfth Missouri Infantry, disposed as skirmishers, accompanied the assaulting columns. The average distance to the objective point was about one-third of a mile, over a marshy bottom, nearly clear of standing timber but full of fallen tree trunks and thickets and intersected with miry sloughs.

At ten minutes before 6 p.m. the advance sounded, and the lines of gallant men started at the double quick over the difficult ground, followed by the cheers of their fellow soldiers on the Camp Creek hills, and met by a storm of lead and iron from the enemy. The rebel infantry poured in from the hills in front a close, destructive, and well-directed fire. The artillery from their forts opened in one continuous roar. The direction of most of their artillery fire was at first diagonally across the lines, the angle growing less as the storming column advanced, until it nearly enfiladed them. Their practice was excellent, the bursting of shells directly over the devoted lines seemed continuous, but neither thicket, nor slough, nor shot, nor shell, distracted for a moment the attention of the stormers from their objective point. Lines temporarily disarranged were reorganized without slackening the speed, until, without firing a shot, they, at the point of the bayonet, planted their colors on the summits of the conquered hills.

Under the soldierly and efficient direction of their brigade commanders the troops were at once disposed in the most advantageous positions for holding the ground, and for protection from the artillery fire still furiously kept up. Pioneers and entrenching tools were sent over, and work was immediately commenced making rifle-pits. . . . The loss in my command was 102 killed, 512 wounded, and 14 missing; aggregate 628. We captured 92 prisoners. [*O.R.*, XXXVIII, pt. 3, pp. 92–93.]

Report of Brig. Gen. Morgan L. Smith, USA, Commanding Second Division, Fifteenth Army Corps, Army of the Tennessee

My division reached a high wooded hill about 400 yards in rear of Camp Creek, overlooking Resaca and the railroad bridge, about 4.30 pm. We found the ground along Camp Creek partially cleared, with all the dead trees, which were standing quite thick, on fire, to prevent their being used as cover for our skirmishers. I got my division in position on this hill under a heavy fire, and not without considerable loss. The enemy's guns were plainly visible as well as their colors in their main works. We rested here for the night, and prepared positions for our batteries, which were put in position before morning.

On the morning of the 14th heavy skirmishing commenced at daylight, and was continued until about noon, when I received General Logan's order to make a feigned attack on their works, as a movement of the enemy was apparent to mass his forces on our extreme left, and at about 4.30 o'clock I received his orders to send one of my brigades to storm a slight elevation across Camp Creek, and not more than 400 or 500 yards from the enemy's main works along the railroad, in conjunction with a brigade from the First Division. Knowing that this elevation was full of rifle-pits, and that Camp Creek could only be crossed at one or two points in my front, this looked like anything but a small contract.

The signal was given, and the First Brigade, General Giles A. Smith commanding, moved forward at double-quick, amidst a loud cheer from the whole division. The brigade having arrived at the creek, some crossed on logs, but the principal part waded, and found the water up to their waists. The enemy, evidently thinking the movement meant an assault on their main works, delivered a volley and retired from the hill, and immediately opened upon it with shell from four different batteries. General Smith reformed his brigade and moved rapidly to the brow of the hill, but before he could get his lines adjusted the shelling ceased, and a strong force of the enemy advanced

Remnants of Union earthworks west of Resaca (Harold Nelson).

to dislodge him from the hill. After a fight at close quarters of about three-quarters of an hour, the enemy gave way, or fell back to reform, and their shelling was resumed.

The second attack appeared to be an attempt to turn General Smith's right, and I received orders from General Logan in person to protect his right at all hazards with the Second Brigade. General [Joseph A. J.] Lightburn, commanding that brigade, responded nobly, and moved over or through the creek at the double-quick, some of his men being entirely immersed in crossing, and formed on General Smith's right, his own right resting near the Oostenaula River, and immediately opened fire. The enemy's assault continued until 8.10, when they gave way at all points. The division was entrenched at this place before morning.

Heavy skirmishing all day of the 15th, and soon after dark very heavy firing was heard on our extreme left; and, notwithstanding that did not indicate the evacuation of such a strongly fortified position, I ordered officers in command of skirmishers to feel forward all night, and press the enemy if he attempted to get away. [O.R., XXXVIII, pt. 3, p. 177.]

Report of Brig. Gen. Giles A. Smith, USA, Commanding First Brigade, Second Division, Fifteenth Army Corps, Army of the Tennessee

The skirmishers were all advanced until they reached the creek, and reported two or three places where logs or driftwood enabled them to cross. About 3 o'clock, in obedience to your order to show my force and make a diversion to prevent the enemy in our front from sending re-enforcements to our left, I advanced the One hundred and eleventh Illinois, the Fifty-seventh Ohio, and the Sixth Missouri Regiments to the creek, our skirmishers gaining some ground on its opposite bank. Although the high banks afforded partial cover to the men, still they were considerably exposed to the fire from the enemy from the hills in our front.

At 5 o'clock I received orders from you that the hills in our front . . . were to be carried, and that my brigade, with General Woods' brigade, of the First Division, were designated to make the assault. I accompanied General Logan to General Woods' quarters, where the final dispositions were made and the signal for starting agreed upon.

My line was formed as follows: The One hundred and eleventh Illinois . . . on the right; the Fifty-seventh Ohio . . . on the left; the Sixth Missouri . . . in the center; with the One hundred and twenty-seventh Illinois . . . and the One hundred and sixteenth Illinois . . . in reserve. Orders were given for the three regiments forming the advance line to cross the creek and form under the opposite bank preparatory to the general advance.

At 6 o'clock, General Woods having formed his brigade on my left, the whole moved forward and gained the crest of the hill, driving the enemy from the position, which was a rude breast-work of logs hastily thrown together. To extend my line farther to the right and prevent any flank movement from being attempted, I ordered up my two reserve regiments and placed them on my right, and also withdrew the Fifty-seventh Ohio from the hill they first ascended and placed them on the left of the One hundred and twenty-seventh Illinois, then occupying my extreme right.

I ordered the pioneer corps to report to Colonel [Americus V.] Rice [57th Ohio], who immediately set them to throwing up a slight work, and sent orders to Lieutenant-Colonel [Frank S.] Curtiss [127th Illinois] to have a few men from each company strengthen his log-work by throwing on such loose logs as lay close around, keeping the men prepared for an attack which I was momentarily expecting. In the mean time the skirmishers were well advanced, covering our whole front, and Lieutenant-Colonel Curtiss was directed to deploy a company on his right flank, and to support them with three companies to provide against any attack from that quarter.

These dispositions were scarcely made when our skirmishers were driven in, followed closely by the enemy, who had massed a large force in our front, and seemed determined to retake the position at all hazards. Colonel Rice . . . in whose immediate front they were advancing in column by regiments, opened a murderous fire on their closed columns, delivering his fire by rank, and with deadly effect. Lieutenant Colonel Curtiss . . . stationed on Colonel Rice's right, opened a crossfire on the same column; other portions of the left also delivered a well-directed fire on their right flank, notwithstanding which they had advanced to within thirty yards of our line before they were checked, and then only falling back to reform and renew the attack, threatening my right flank. They were again repulsed, and again rallied for another onset. I immediately dispatched an aide-de-camp to you for re-enforcements, but before reaching you, you had already discovered the danger and ordered General Lightburn's brigade to cross the creek and take position on my right, which he did at a double-quick and a cheer, that evidenced to my men that their right was no longer in danger. Another attack of the enemy was repulsed, and after some more desultory firing the enemy retired about 8 o'clock. . . . The danger for the night seemed to be over, and after disposing my forces properly, I deemed them sufficient to hold the position.

Sunday, the 15th, was occupied in strengthening our works and planting batteries commanding the greater portion of the enemy's works and the railroad bridge at Resaca. . . .

Of Col. A. V. Rice, Fifty-seventh Ohio Volunteers, I cannot speak in too high terms. It was his regiment against which the assaulting column of the enemy, composed of six or seven regiments in close column, was mainly directed. Colonel Rice awaited their near approach, without one man in his line faltering, and then delivered his fire by rank at the word of command, and with a coolness and precision seldom equaled by any troops. . . . The loss of my brigade was 2 commissioned officers and 21 enlisted men killed and 6 commissioned officers and 93 enlisted men wounded. [*O.R.*, XXXVIII, pt. 3, pp. 191–192.]

Resaca from Confederate earthworks (MOLLUS).

Report of Col. A. V. Rice, USA, Fifty-Seventh Ohio, First Brigade, Second Division, Fifteenth Army Corps, Army of the Tennessee

From 9.30 a.m., a furious battle raged on our left, with seeming doubtful results. At this time I received an order . . . to advance our skirmishers, with the rest of the brigade, across Camp Creek, 150 or 200 yards in front, and to advance our line of battle accordingly. This was promptly obeyed, charging across the open field with arms right shoulder shift, and at double-quick. The Fifty-seventh Ohio starting first, and the movement being so sudden, the enemy was somewhat surprised.

Resting here for a few moments, we again pushed forward our pickets through an almost impassable growth of wild roses, thorn, underbrush, and fallen timber to beyond a second creek or bayou. Our line of battle was immediately moved up through these heavy obstacles to easy supporting distance of the skirmish line, all the while under a sharp fire. The efficient manner that Lieutenant Stone conducted his skirmishers in these advances, and during the day, deserves mention.

Thus matters remained until 5.30 p.m., when we received orders to charge over the open field and to take and hold the hills 500 yards in our front. . . . Soon preparations were completed, and the bugle notes sounded "forward." With yells and shouts the enthusiastic troops went wildly over the field, under a terrible shower of lead, shot, and shell. I was instructed to hold my command at the foot of the hill to await further orders, but the war spirit so filled every breast that nothing was thought of but the occupation of the enemy's works on the crest of the hill; on and up the line of battle moved fearlessly and bravely. The enemy fled before us, and the gunners forsook their posts; the work was accomplished, and the position ours.

Just at this juncture I received an order from Brig. Gen. Giles A. Smith to withdraw my regiment, for now the left of our brigade lapped over and in front of General Woods' brigade, and to report with it to him 200 yards to the right, and at the base of the bald hill, which faced to the southeast. This was immediately done at double-quick and in good order, although the men sullenly left the rich prize of cannon they had captured to fall into other hands. At this moment the fighting was severe, and the whole heavens seemed to be split with bursting shells.

Under the immediate direction of General Giles A. Smith and staff, we advanced and occupied the brow of the bald hill. Company C . . . was now sent forward as skirmishers. Mean time the pioneer corps of the Second Division, which had promptly followed us with picks and spades, strengthened the line of rifle-pits facing the east just abandoned by the enemy. In a few moments, under the direction of General Giles A. Smith, I half wheeled the right wing of the regiment and advanced it to the line of works being constructed by the pioneers. Lieutenant-Colonel Mott brought up the left wing and formed a continuation of the line to the left.

Scarcely had the regiment got into position, when our skirmishers were driven back by overwhelming numbers. Immediately the right wing occupied the slight works constructed, the pioneers retiring, and now commenced to us the most critical and eventful portion of the fight. The sun was just setting; onward, and with a determination unequaled, came the enemy, charging us in three lines of battle, of *Loring's* division, with shouts and yells. Six or seven stand of colors were seen, and as many regiments were confronting us. We had just experienced the wild feeling of the assailing party; now breathless we stood awaiting the coming storm.

Capt. John W. Underwood skillfully conducted the skirmishers to the rear and placed them in their proper position, until which time the fire of the regiment was held, when, by command, the rear rank raised and delivered a most effective volley; this was followed by a volley from the front rank, and so on alternately, until the attacking force was hurled back. The enemy approached to within thirty or forty yards of our position. It was now growing dark, but nothing daunted by his failure, the enemy formed and charged again, and also a third time, only, however, to meet the fate of his first approach. A portion of the One hundred and sixteenth Illinois, fifty or sixty in number, was formed to the rear of our rear rank and did execution. The one hundred and twenty-seventh Illinois on the hill to our right delivered a left oblique with telling effect. My entire command was cool and collected and seemed determined to repel the foe or die at their posts. During the action General Smith sent five companies [of the] Thirty-fifth New Jersey Volunteers to our support, but there being no break in the line their services were not needed and were not used. The fighting closed about 8.30 p.m., when a beautiful moon shone brightly on the terrible scene of death, and the deep groans of the wounded and dying made us realize the horrors of war.

Immediately after the battle the pioneer corps . . . whose work no doubt saved many casualties in the regiment, with the assistance of heavy details from my regiment . . . went to entrenching, and before morning strong works were constructed, behind which we could have defied the enemy. The loss of the enemy must have been heavy. During the night most of his dead and wounded were taken away. In the morning blood, clothing, etc. told how terrible had been the slaughter . . .

On Sunday, May 15 . . . we were in line of battle at 3 a.m. At daylight . . . the skirmishers were advanced, but the whiz of bullets showed that the enemy was near. We remained in position behind the works, and all day long we lay in the trenches, with a heavy picket firing in front, with nothing to break the monotony save the rumor that a charge was expected from the rebels. After dark Companies B and G . . . relieved Companies E and K on the picket-line. At 11 p.m. a heavy attack was made on the left, which brought us in line of battle, but which proved only a cover for the retreat of the enemy. [O.R., XXXVIII, pt. 3, pp. 213–214.]

Report of Maj. Gen. George H. Thomas, USA, Commanding Army of the Cumberland

The concentration of the balance of the army in Snake Creek Gap having been completed by the night of the 12th, at 8 a.m. on the 13th Hooker's corps, preceded by Kilpatrick's cavalry, moved out on the Resaca road in support of McPherson's troops. . . . Palmer's corps moved out of Snake Creek Gap two miles northeast of Hooker, and then took a course parallel with the Resaca road, with orders to proceed as far as the railroad. On reaching the neighborhood of the railroad his skirmishers encountered those of the enemy strongly posted on the hills immediately west of the railroad, and continued a fierce skirmish with them until night-fall. . . .

About noon of the 14th Schofield's and Palmer's corps attacked the enemy's position on the hills bordering the railroad, meeting with very heavy resistance. General Schofield's left being threatened, and he having called on me for support, I directed Newton's division, of Howard's corps, which had just arrived from Dalton, to move to Schofield's assistance, and subsequently the whole of Howard's corps took post on the left of Schofield. During the afternoon Hooker's corps, which had been acting as support to General McPherson, was shifted to the left of Howard's command, and Williams' division reached the position assigned him just in time to meet and repel a fierce attack of the enemy who was endeavoring to turn Howard's left flank. McCook's division of cavalry took post on the left of Hooker to guard against any further attempt of the enemy in that direction. The fighting in Schofield's and Howard's front was very severe, but we drove the enemy from the hill he had occupied and forced him into his entrenchments beyond. [O.R., XXXVIII, pt. 1, p. 141.]

Report of Brig. Gen. Richard W. Johnson, USA, Commanding First Division, Fourteenth Army Corps, Army of the Cumberland

I found the enemy strongly posted and fortified on the hither slope and near the crest of a long, elevated ridge, their right slightly refused from the direction of my line. In front of their position was an open field of some 400 yards wide, sloping gradually down to a creek directly in my front. The general course of this creek in front of my line was nearly parallel to the enemy's works; the bottom was in some places miry with a considerable depth of water—in others quite the reverse, its crooked channel filled in some places with a dense underbrush, in others obstructed by fallen trees and drift. It afforded a serious obstacle to the advance of troops in line . . . as the land rose immediately from the creek in an abrupt bluff of nearly the same height as the enemy's position beyond, and then gradually sloped down again to the westward. With my skirmishers posted along the creek, I reformed my lines in the woods behind the slope, to the rear of it, and awaited instructions.

At about 11 a.m., I received notice from the major-general commanding corps that as soon as the left should get into position an assault would be made along the whole line. I was ordered to advance as soon as by the firing I should be warned of the movement of the troops on my immediate left.

Accordingly, about 11.30, heavy firing on the lines of Baird's division indicating that his troops were advancing, my two brigades moved forward, [Col. Benjamin F.] Scribner's having already, in anticipation of the movement, been brought up into close supporting distance. General Carlin, who lay very near the creek, . . . threw forward his skirmishers, driving those of the enemy within their works. No sooner had his first line emerged from the cover of the woods than the enemy—infantry and artillery—opened upon it with terrible effect. Notwithstanding this, however, Carlin pushed forward both lines beyond the creek and nearly half way across the open field. The passage of the creek had, however, sadly disordered his lines, and finding it impossible to reform them while advancing so rapidly as the emergency of occasion required, hopeless, moreover, of holding his position even if the assault should succeed, Carlin fell back to the cover of the creek, the eastern bank of which offered in some places all the protection of a well-constructed fortification. Here he remained, by my direction, all day, keeping up a desultory but effective fire in reply to the enemy's. [Brig. Gen. John H.] King's brigade, which lay considerably farther from the creek than Carlin's, did not advance so far, and, when it was seen that Carlin had suffered a repulse, halted.

Two 12-pounder guns of the enemy's in my front had opened upon our advance, and continued their fire subsequently, at intervals, with damaging effect. As soon as a practicable road could be found I brought forward two pieces of Captain [Hubert] Dilger's battery I, First Ohio Light Artillery, and caused them to be placed in position on the crest of the bluff overlooking the creek and near my center. The admirable practice of this section, conducted under the supervision of Captain Dilger in person, soon closed out the enemy's pieces, and was quite as annoying to them as theirs had been before to us. More than once their infantry, driven from their works by Dilger's shell, were shot down by my sharpshooters before they could gain the cover of the works in their rear. . . . In this affair General Carlin's brigade suffered severely, losing considerably over 200 in killed and wounded, this including many valuable officers. The loss in General King's brigade was comparatively light. [O.R., XXXVIII, pt. 1, pp. 521–522.]

Report of Brig. Gen. Absalom Baird, USA, Commanding Third Division, Fourteenth Army Corps, Army of the Cumberland

May 14, having received orders during the night from the major general commanding the corps to swing forward my entire line along with that of Brigadier General Johnson, his right being taken as the pivot, and to push on until the enemy was encountered, I put my troops in motion at daybreak. Colonel [Ferdinand] Van Derveer was on my right, formed in two lines, and Brigadier General [John B.] Turchin on the left, formed in the same manner. My right had moved some three-fourths of a mile, and the direction of our line was about due north and south, facing east, when I received another order . . . informing me that Major General Schofield, whose corps was then in line half a mile to my rear, with his right overlapping nearly the whole of my left brigade, was about to advance and charge the enemy's works, and directing me to move forward with him and assault at the same time.

I had not previously known that the enemy had works in our vicinity, nor was I then informed as to their position, their character, or the manner in which the attack was to be made. There was, of course, no time for a reconnaissance by me without neglecting to advance along with Major-General Schofield, as ordered. I had barely time to give the proper instructions to Brigadier General Turchin on my left, and was communicating the same to the right brigade, when the troops of Brigadier General Judah, on General Schofield's right, came up with my left. His front line passed through my rear line before mine began to advance, and, thus interlaced, both went forward together.

It was subsequently ascertained that the rebel line of works ran along the western slope of a ridge, which extended from near Resaca northward, on the west side of the railroad. A narrow valley, intersected along its length by a boggy creek, separated this from another ridge which lay parallel with and in front of our line. This our troops had to pass. It was covered for a space of nearly half a mile in width by so dense a growth of wood that an individual alone could make his way through it only with difficulty. It was utterly impossible in this thicket for a regiment, much less for a brigade commander, to see and control the two extremities of his command. Yet our line of battle worked through it and reached the crest overlooking the valley in as much order as could have been expected. From this position the rebel works could be distinctly seen, and could our men have been allowed to halt here, to reform and to readjust their lines, while an examination of the position should be made, better results might have ensued.

It would appear that Major-General Schofield's left, in open ground, did not encounter the same difficulties as his right, and, pressing forward, the impulsion was communicated along the line to his right, and carried my left brigade along with it. It was the affair of a moment, and before I could learn (at 300 yards' distance upon the right) of the condition of affairs, it was too late to stop the movement. Descending about 100 feet the almost vertical slope of the ridge, our men emerged into the open valley, and into direct view, at short range, of the rebel works, and immediately received a fire of artillery and musketry. The tried veterans of this division did not falter, but pushed forward until they had reached the creek. Few got beyond this. Many stuck under the miry banks of the stream, and the few isolated groups that got beyond, not being in sufficient force to sustain themselves, were soon driven back. It was at once apparent that this effort had failed and was at an end, and most of the men were withdrawn to the summit of the ridge to be reformed. A few, unable on account of the sharp fire from the rebel works to leave the banks of the creek, remained there until dark, doing valuable duty as sharpshooters. [O.R., XXXVIII, pt. 1, pp. 735–736.]

Report of Col. Moses B. Walker, USA, Commanding First Brigade, Third Division, Fourteenth Army Corps, Army of the Cumberland

The main portion of the lines rushed down the hill and charged toward the enemy's works, under a most murderous fire of canister and shell . . . as well as the musketry from their lines. Our lines suddenly found themselves confronted by a deep, narrow stream, with quicksand in places, and steep, muddy banks. The enemy's sharpshooters were posted here, but fled precipitately back to their works. . . . No assaulting column had been formed. The creek proved a bar to our advance. Our troops sprang into the creek and opened fire on the rebel lines, then within from seventy-five to one hundred yards of the enemy's works. This creek proved a protection to us and a source of great annoyance to the enemy, as we gained an enfilading fire upon one line of his works and quickly drove the troops out of this line. It then appearing that our troops had fallen back from the hills, and the number of men who gained a protection from the creek and remained there, being very small and very much exposed, Col. M. B. Walter . . . the ranking officer of the brigade present in the creek, ordered the men to fall back in single file, covering themselves the best way they could from the enemy's fire, and at the same time keeping as rapid a fire as possible from the creek, and making it difficult for the enemy to use his artillery, except from one battery, or to fire from his lines. . . . Our lines were quickly reformed in good order and posted on the first ridge in front of the rebel works. [O.R., XXXVIII, pt. 1, p. 759.]

Report of Maj. Gen. John M. Schofield, USA, Commanding Army of the Ohio

I moved with the Twenty-third Corps . . . on the morning of the 13th through Snake Creek Gap . . . and took position facing north, with my left resting on the slope of the mountain and my right connecting with the Fourteenth Corps. In the afternoon we advanced, in conjunction with the Fourteenth Corps, and rested for the night with our left, Cox's division, on the Rome and Dalton road, about a mile north of the [Snake Creek] Gap, Hovey's division being left at the gap.

The next morning Judah and Cox advanced upon the left of the Army of the Cumberland to the enemy's position on the head of Camp Creek, while a reconnaissance was sent toward Dalton to open communication with the Fourth Corps, which was in pursuit of the enemy, and which was soon found to be within supporting distance. The troops were then ordered to advance, develop fully the enemy's position, and attack. General Cox on the left, after driving the enemy's skirmishers some distance over very rough, wooded ground and into their works, reformed his troops, assaulted, and carried the enemy's first line. This attack was skillfully conducted and our loss was heavy. . . .

General Judah also ordered an assault, but it failed on account of natural obstacles, which rendered it impossible for the troops to reach the parapet in sufficient force. In spite of the most heroic efforts, this gallant division was compelled to retire with heavy loss. General Cox held the position he had carried until late in the afternoon, when he was relieved by troops of the Fourth Corps. Hovey's division was brought forward, and the next morning the corps moved to the extreme left on the Dalton and Resaca road, to support an attack to be made by the Twentieth Corps. [*O.R.*, XXXVIII, pt. 2, pp. 510–511.]

Report of Maj. Gen. Oliver O. Howard, USA, Commanding Fourth Army Corps, Army of the Cumberland

May 13 at 6 a.m., I received the report of the enemy having left [Dalton], and immediately ordered pursuit. . . . We pushed forward toward Resaca . . . skirmished with the enemy during the day, and encamped at dark about eight miles south of Dalton. Soon after we opened communication with the rest of the army before Resaca, happily finding that we were only one mile from General Schofield's left flank. Instructions were received from Major-General Thomas, at 5.15 on the morning of May 14, to wit:

> General: You will move your troops down the main roads toward Resaca until you form a junction with the rest of the army, when further orders will be given you. Report your approach when you get within sight of the troops in your front.
> Geo. H. Thomas Major-General, Commanding

These instructions were substantially the same as those I had already issued . . . during the night.

The general formation of General Sherman's army at this time was, as follows: The Army of the Tennessee, General McPherson on the right, with his right resting on the Oostenaula; center, General Thomas' command, excepting the Fourth Corps; and the left, General Schofield, on the Sugar Valley Road. The whole line faced easterly.

In obedience to the above order, General Newton, followed by General Wood, marched to the left of General Schofield, and General Stanley moved down the Tilton and Resaca road toward the enemy's extreme right. On reaching General Schofield we found him pushing his command toward the right and front. General Newton formed on his left. General Wood then changed direction so as to move on a Resaca road intermediate between Stanley and Newton.

The three columns were not at first connected, but very adroitly made their concentration in immediate contact with the enemy's line, having skirmished heavily in their respective fronts. By the advance movement the general line was shortened, so that a great part of Newton's division was reserved. Schofield's left carried a line of the enemy's works by assault, and immediately a portion of General Newton's division was pushed up, relieving more or less of Schofield's left center and holding every advantage gained.

Meanwhile a part of General Wood's division came up abreast of Newton's, driving the enemy from his rifle-pits, and secured the position, while General Stanley formed a junction on the extreme left, protecting his left flank by a brigade posted on the left of the Tilton and Resaca road.

The movements . . . were necessarily slowly executed from the nature of the country, which was exceedingly rough and covered for the most part with thick woods, besides the enemy disputed every inch of progress by his force already in position, meeting our advance with strong skirmish lines. The musketry firing during the day was quite heavy.

After our troops had been satisfactorily formed word came from General Stanley that the enemy was making a movement to turn his left flank. I saw General Thomas personally, representing the exact condition of things to him. He directed Major General Hooker to send a division to my extreme left. This was promptly done. This division (General Williams') arrived just in time. . . . The advance of the enemy was . . . effectually checked. . . . The casualties of the day were 400 killed and wounded in the corps. During the night good entrenchments were made along my entire front. [O.R., XXXVIII, pt. 1, pp. 189–190.]

8. ACTION NORTH OF RESACA

From Stop 7, turn left onto GA 136, pass over the interstate, and proceed to the "T" intersection. Turn left onto U.S. 41 and drive about 1.7 miles. On your right, just short of the road leading to the Confederate Cemetery, you will reach a roadside park with historical markers. Stop at the park and use the map display to assist in orientation.

STOP 8, NORTH OF RESACA

14–15 May 1864

Narrative of Maj. Gen. William T. Sherman, USA, Commanding Military Division of the Mississippi

During the 15th, without attempting to assault the fortified works, we pressed at all points, and the sound of cannon and musketry rose all day to the dignity of a battle. Toward evening McPherson moved his whole line of battle forward, till he had gained a ridge overlooking the town, from which his field artillery could reach the railroad bridge across the Oostenaula. The enemy made several attempts to drive him away, repeating the sallies several times, and extending them into the night, but in every instance he was repulsed with bloody loss.

Hooker's corps had also some heavy and handsome fighting that afternoon and night on the left, where the Dalton road entered the entrenchments, capturing a four-gun entrenched battery, with its men and guns; and generally all our men showed the finest fighting qualities.

Howard's corps had followed *Johnston* down from Dalton and was in line; Stoneman's division of cavalry had also got up, and was on the extreme left beyond the Oostenaula. [Sherman, *Memoirs*, II, pp. 35–36.]

Report of Maj. Gen. David S. Stanley, USA, Commanding First Division, Fourth Army Corps, Army of the Cumberland

On the morning of the 14th . . . the division advanced to within about two and a half miles of Resaca, driving in the skirmishers of the

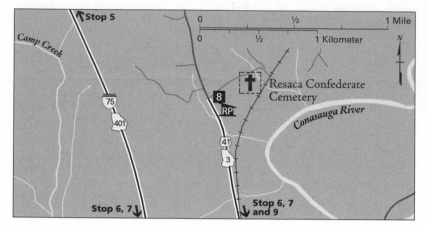

Action North of Resaca (Stop 8)

enemy; but as Wood's division, on our right, had not yet come up, and as firing was heard in rear of our right, the division was halted and directed to barricade. At 2 p.m. Wood advanced and made connection with the right of this division, and we advanced together until stopped by the heavy fire of artillery coming from the enemy's works. I received about this time an order to hold the Dalton road running by my left flank.

To do this I stationed [Maj. Gen. Charles] Cruft's brigade upon the left of the road, posting two of his regiments upon a round-topped hill about 100 yards from the road, and directing them to entrench themselves. These troops were not yet in position when the enemy was seen forming to attack them in flank, and word was at once sent the corps and department commanders of this fact. In the mean time [Capt. Peter] Simonson's battery, which had been advanced, was, as matter of caution, withdrawn and posted to sweep the open ground to the rear of the threatened brigade.

The attack came about an hour before sundown, and perpendicular to my line. The Thirty-first Indiana, stationed upon the round-topped hill, found itself fired into from three directions. They did the best they could under the circumstances; they got out of the way with such order as troops can hurrying through a thick brush. Directing their attack more to our rear than flank, the One hundred and first Ohio and Eighty-first Indiana were soon driven back, and the enemy was bursting exultingly upon the open field when Simonson opened on them with canister, which soon broke and dispersed that attack.

The enemy formed in the woods and attempted to cross the open field again, but met the same savage shower of canister.

Robertson's [in fact, Col. James S. Robinson's 3rd brigade of the First Division—eds.] brigade, of the Twentieth Corps, had also arrived and formed facing the attack. The broken regiments of the First Brigade had reformed near the battery, and the enemy was easily repulsed with very severe loss to him. The troops of the brigade did as well as could be expected, situated as they were. Attacked in flank, and greatly outnumbered, they could only get out of the way the best they could. Had it not been for the timely aid of the battery it would have gone hard with the brigade. Captain Simonson and the Fifth Indiana Battery deserve great praise; their conduct was splendid. The coming up of the Twentieth Corps was also timely, though, in my opinion, the fire of the battery was in itself adequate to the successful repulse of the enemy.

The night and the day following our lines were adjusted and strengthened, and a constant fire was kept up upon the enemy. The division was formed ready to follow up General Hooker's attack had he broken the enemy's line. Artillery firing was kept up during the night upon the rebel position. About 11 o'clock the rebels made a demonstration on our pickets, occasioning a general discharge of cannon and muskets along the whole line.

Soon after, early on the morning of the 16th, it was found the enemy had evacuated under cover of night. The loss of the division about Resaca, killed, wounded, and missing, amounted to 200. Early on the morning of the 16th the pursuit was commenced. [*O.R.*, XXXVIII, pt. 1, pp. 220–221.]

Report of Capt. Peter Simonson, USA, Fifth Indiana Battery, Chief of Artillery, First Division, Fourth Army Corps, Army of the Cumberland

On Saturday, the 14th, after our line had advanced to within a short distance of the enemy's works, a section of Battery B, Pennsylvania Volunteer Artillery, was placed in position in front of a 4-gun rebel battery and a hill to the left occupied by the enemy's infantry. The section only fired a few rounds, as they were entirely unprotected,

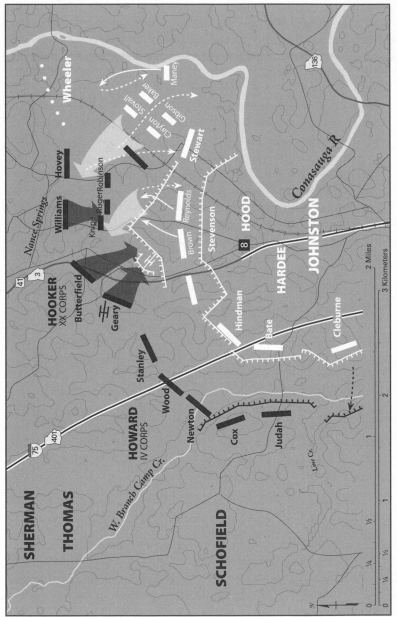

Action North of Resaca

Battle of Resaca, May 15, 1864; the attempt against General Hindman's position by a portion of the Army of the Cumberland (engraving by A. R. Waud in Joseph M. Brown, *The Mountain Campaigns in Georgia* [Buffalo: Matthews, Northrup Co., 1886] 23).

while all the troops of the enemy were under cover. General Stanley, receiving information that the enemy was massing his troops on our left, directed that both batteries should be placed in good positions, facing to the left, to check the enemy in case of our troops being repulsed. He designated to me a particular spot which the Fifth Indiana Battery should occupy.

Shortly afterward the left flank of the division was turned. I ordered the Fifth Indiana to open fire on the enemy, who were advancing in heavy force out of a thick woods, about 800 yards in front, which did not immediately check them as they advanced up the fields, driving our infantry back to and part of it in the rear of the battery, thus leaving the field clear in front and the enemy only about 400 yards distant. A very rapid fire of canister was opened on the advancing foe, which quickly cleared the field, the greater portion of the enemy's troops going into the woods toward our left.

The pieces were immediately turned by hand to the left, and spherical case and shell were used, canister being held in readiness in case they gained the hill on our immediate left. They soon appeared on this hill and opened with a heavy volley of musketry, shooting at least twenty feet above the battery. The regiments which were upon the right and left of the battery seeing themselves flanked by a heavy force, immediately withdrew. The distance to the top of the hill was 150 yards. The men themselves, without particular orders, double-shotted the pieces with canister, and maintained the most rapid firing possible. Some few of the rebels reached the road at the foot of the hill, within fifty yards of the battery, but the main body appeared to be greatly disconcerted by the firing, and although their officers could be seen and heard trying to urge them forward, they very quickly put the hill between themselves and the pieces.

They made one more endeavor to get over the hill more to our left, but were met in this attack at first by the fire of the battery with canister, and as they turned, by a volley from Robinson's brigade, of Williams' division, of General Hooker's corps . . . who immediately charged and drove them clear over the hill out of sight in great confusion. [*O.R.*, XXXVIII, pt. 1, pp. 488–489.]

Report of Brig. Gen. Alpheus S. Williams, USA, Commanding First Division, Twentieth Army Corps, Army of the Cumberland

On the morning of 14th of May . . . I massed the division in support of the Third Division, which was in line of battle in face of the enemy's forces before Resaca. About 4.30 p.m. I received orders to march my division as rapidly as possible to support the left of Stanley's division, Fourth Corps, which was heavily engaged some miles distant. I moved at once by the left flank, under guidance of a staff officer of Fourth Corps, and in about an hour and a half, without halts, reached the position designated . . . for deployment of the division.

This position was a wooded ridge facing and bordering a narrow cultivated valley of considerable length along the Dalton road, near the head of which were the defiles and steep hills held by the enemy for the defense of Resaca. Robinson's (Third) brigade deployed quickly along the left of this ridge, and the other brigades were ordered to prolong the line along the ridge south of a deep gorge which bisects it. In front of Robinson's brigade, Simonson's battery (Fifth Indiana), of Stanley's division, was in position looking toward Resaca, and supported by a detachment of that division. Scarcely was Robinson's brigade in line before numerous fugitives from our own troops came pouring in confusion over the open field in front, followed by the exultant enemy making confidently for the battery. After a fruitless effort with my staff officers to rally and organize the fugitives, I sent orders to them to clear the front, and rode back to bring forward Robinson's brigade.

At the brigade I found Lieutenant-Colonel Perkins, assistant adjutant-general, with orders to move at once to the open and support the battery. Robinson moved with great promptness down the steep wooded ridge side, crossing a difficult creek at the foot, and, changing front forward on his right regiment in good order, he opened in volley upon the astonished enemy. They fled in greater haste than they had advanced, and in fifteen minutes not a rebel gun was heard in the valley. Orders were sent to [Brig. Gen. Thomas H.] Ruger to advance his brigade so as to take the enemy in flank, but before it could be done they had fled. The division bivouacked for the night on the plain fronting toward Resaca. The brave and efficient conduct of Robinson's brigade in this affair served to create a strong confidence and good will between troops recently brought together from different corps in a new organization, a feeling closely cemented by the subsequent events and occurrences of the campaign.

May 15, the division was ordered to support Butterfield's and Geary's divisions, and marched at 12 o'clock. While on the march information was sent me by the major-general commanding corps that the enemy was threatening our left from the direction of the railroad, and I was ordered to cover and protect that flank. Facing by the left brought the division in line of battle, and in this formation I advanced it toward the menaced point, the brigades being in line according to numerical order.

The ground occupied by [Brig. Gen. Joseph F.] Knipe's (First) brigade, on the right, was very broken, trending off, however, toward the north in a ridge of slight elevation, running almost parallel with the railroad, partly through woods and partly through clearings. At a point where a road toward Green's Station from the Dalton road crosses the ridge there rises a considerable knoll or knob, upon which is a dwelling known as Scales' house. Ruger's (Second) brigade, extending from Knipe's left, reached and occupied this knoll, upon which slight breast-works were hastily thrown up. Two regiments of Robinson's brigade were deployed on the left of the knoll, where the ground sinks down into a timbered plain; three others of his regiments were held in reserve on the extreme left and one regiment placed in support of [Lt. Charles E.] Winegar's battery, which was with much difficulty put into position on a high hill, somewhat in our rear, but commanding much of our front. [Capt. John D.] Woodbury's light 12's were placed in the line near our left on ridges which commanded the approaches to what I regarded as the key to our position.

The enemy massed his forces in the woods near the railway, which was distant from 300 to 600 yards from the different portions of my line. Advancing under cover as far as practicable, he attacked the whole line with great vigor and apparent confidence. The attack was received with perfect steadiness and repulsed with signal failure. My line in no part was shaken or disturbed, and we literally had no skulkers.

The main efforts of the enemy were directed against the knoll heretofore mentioned, and were continued in that direction until near dark. The position was held at the close by two of Robinson's regiments, which had relieved Ruger's. The artillery of the division performed an important part in punishing and repulsing the enemy. I made no effort to pursue, as my orders were to cover and protect the left, and I was ignorant of the condition of affairs with the assaulting columns on the right; besides, the enemy's entrenchments, to which at each repulse he fell back, were but a few hundred yards in my front. It was evident, too, that the assaulting force (at least two divisions of *Hood's* corps) greatly outnumbered ours. [*O.R.,* XXXVIII, pt. 2, pp. 27–29.]

Brig. Gen. Alpheus S. Williams to His Daughter, *20 May 1864*

The fight ended about dusk and in the morning there was no enemy in front. I went out over the field in our front, not out of curiosity but to see what was in advance. There were scores of dead Rebels lying in the woods all along our front, and I confess a feeling of pity as I saw them. . . . Early in the war I had a curiosity to ride over a battlefield. Now I feel nothing but sorrow and compassion . . . especially when I see a "blue jacket" lying stretched in the attitude that nobody can mistake who has seen the dead on a battlefield. These "boys" have been so long with me that I feel as if a friend has fallen, though I recognize no face that I can recollect to have seen before. But I think of some sorrowful heart at home and . . . how sadly my heart sinks with the thought. . . . There is much that is beautiful as well as sad in these bloody events. I lost in this battle between four and five hundred killed and wounded. [M. Quaife, ed., *From the Cannon's Mouth: The Civil War Letters of General Alpheus S. Williams* (Detroit: Wayne State University Press, 1959), p. 309.]

HOOD'S ATTACK

Report of Lt. Gen. John B. Hood, CSA, Commanding Corps, Army of Tennessee

On arriving [at Resaca] I took position on the right of the army, *Hindman's* division on the left, *Stevenson* in the center, and *Stewart* on the right. On the 14th the enemy made repeated assaults on *Hindman's* left, but not in very heavy lines. *Walthall's* brigade, occupying the left of *Hindman's*, suffered severely from an enfilade fire of the enemy's artillery, himself and men displaying conspicuous valor throughout under very adverse circumstances. Brigadier-General [*William F.*] *Tucker*, commanding brigade in reserve, was severely wounded. [*O.R.*, XXXVIII, pt. 3, p. 761.]

Report of Brig. Gen. Edward C. Walthall, CSA, Commanding Brigade, Hindman's Division, Hood's Corps, Army of Tennessee

[At 2 p.m., May 12] I was directed to move . . . through Dalton on the Resaca road. About an hour after dark I was halted, and after resting several hours resumed the march in time to reach a point six miles north of Resaca, where my command had been on the 10th, about an hour before daylight. I remained here till about the middle of the day on the 13th, when I moved about two miles farther in the direction of Resaca, and formed line of battle facing northwest at a point indicated by the major-general commanding on the left of the road. At 6.30 o'clock in the evening I was directed by him to move to the left, and spent the night at a point where I was halted about dark by an order which he delivered to me in person.

Early on . . . the 14th, as directed by him, I moved about a mile farther to the left and occupied a position from which a brigade of Major-General *Bate's* division had just withdrawn. As soon as my line was formed, and I had thrown forward a skirmish line connecting with that on the right and left already established, I employed all the tools at my disposal in strengthening the earthworks left by the troops which had preceded me, and in cutting out the undergrowth in front. The Thirty-fourth Mississippi Regiment . . . occupied the right of my line, connecting with the left of [*Zachariah C.*] *Deas'* brigade; the Twenty-fourth and Twenty-seventh Mississippi Regiments (consolidated) . . . the center, and the Twenty-ninth and Thirtieth Mississippi Regiments (consolidated) . . . the left. Capt. *G. W. Reynolds,* with three companies of sharpshooters, previously selected from the several regiments of my command, and organized and drilled especially for such service, covered my front. *Tucker's* brigade was posted in my rear as support.

My command was the left brigade of Lieutenant-General *Hood's* corps, and on my left was [Brig. Gen. *Joseph H.*] *Lewis'* brigade, the right of Lieutenant-General *Hardee's*. Between . . . *Lewis'* right and the left of my entrenched line was [Maj. *Thomas R.*] *Hotchkiss'* battalion of artillery, behind which, under cover of the hill it was posted on, Colonel [*William F.*] *Brantly's* consolidated regiment was put in position, except the three right companies, which were put in the trenches, the major-general commanding having notified me that on my command the protection of this artillery would devolve. It was posted on a bare knob, the highest to be seen on the ridge along which the army line extended, and from it the line in either wing was slightly refused, conforming in its general direction to the course of the ridge, and forming an obtuse angle, of which it was the point.

Immediately in front of this elevation is an open field in a valley, about 300 yards in width, extending from the base of the ridge we occupied to that of a wooded hill beyond, and through it runs a small creek nearly parallel to the course of our trenches. This field extends some distance to the left of the high point the artillery was on, and on the right and opposite the position of my center and right regiments it is 600 or 800 yards wide, but between it and the position of those regiments there is a skirt of woods some 200 or 300 yards in width, very uneven, and thickly covered with undergrowth and timber. Beyond the field and running nearly parallel with that part of the battle line occupied by *Bate's* division, and about half a mile from it, is a thickly timbered ridge, as high as the point on which our batteries were posted.

About 11 a.m. the enemy's skirmish line encountered my own, but the latter held its ground, as directed, till forced back by a line of battle which advanced about 12. The artillery poured upon it a rapid and well-directed fire from the time it came in view, but it moved steadily forward till within 300 yards of my line, when, from both small-arms and artillery, it was subjected to a fire so deadly and destructive that it soon wavered, and then gave way in confusion.

In half an hour another line appeared and advanced under a similar fire, nearer than before, and until that part of it confronting the batteries was sheltered by means of a depression in the hill-side, within 150 yards of the guns. It was promptly dislodged by Colonel *Brantly,* who moved upon it with that part of his command not in the trenches, and at the same time the remainder of the line, which was in the woods opposite my right and center, yielded to the constant and steady fire of the troops occupying those positions, and the whole line fell back. It crossed the field in the wildest disorder, under a damaging fire from the artillery, which was admirably served.

As soon as the flying troops reached the hill beyond, a third line moved on us, but it was checked before advancing as far as either of the others had done, and fled before some parts of my command were able to discharge even a single volley. The enemy's sharpshooters, however, in large numbers secured themselves in the woods opposite my right and center, and so irregular and thickly wooded is the ground that it was found impossible to dislodge them. From these, and others posted in woods beyond the field in front of my left, a constant fire was kept up on my own line, as well as the batteries. The number of these sharpshooters in the woods nearest us was gradually increased by small bodies passing at irregular intervals rapidly across the open field to the cover of the woods. Many of them were enabled to shelter themselves behind some slight earth-works which had been constructed in front of the main earth-works which had been constructed in front of the main entrenched line, before I occupied it, for skirmishers. By reason of the unevenness of the ground, these were without the range of our artillery. Others found cover in a small ravine, and by sundown the force in the woods was almost as strong as a line of battle and very well-protected.

When the enemy made his first advance he employed his artillery, posted directly in our front, but with little effect; but soon after his third repulse he opened a furious fire from the ridge opposite *Bate's* division, which furnished him very fine positions for his guns, opposite my left and about three-quarters of a mile distant. The fire of both small-arms and artillery was kept up till 8.30 in the evening. During the afternoon a battery from *Martin's* battalion was sent to my line. After the firing ceased most of the night was spent in strengthening the works all along the line, for they had been materially damaged during the day.

About 5 o'clock on the morning of the 15th the firing was resumed, and was kept up incessantly during the entire day. In the night artillery had been concentrated on the point I occupied, and besides the small-arms, which were used without intermission, not less than thirty guns were vigorously employed against us, and with considerable effect. The guns on my left enfiladed the greater portion of my line of works, and the position would scarcely have been tenable but for the fact that its extreme left was its highest point, and in consequence furnished a partial protection for the remainder. The firing ceased about 8 p.m. My loss in killed was disproportionate to the number wounded, because most of the casualties were caused by artillery, and those men struck by balls from small-arms were in most cases shot in the head or upper part of the body while in the act of firing over the breast-works. When the engagement opened I had in line 1,158 men. Of this number 48 were killed and 116 wounded, and 5 of them mortally. . . .

Troops were never more severely tested than mine were in this battle, and none could have endured with more steadiness . . . the furious and continuous fire. . . . It is fitting . . . for me to attest the fearlessness and superior skill of both officers and men connected with the batteries along my line. They did their duty nobly and rendered most valuable service in a position of peculiar exposure, where unshaken they bore for two days a terrific converging fire from the enemy's guns advantageously posted. [*O.R.*, XXXVIII, pt. 3, pp. 795–797.]

Narrative of Lt. L. D. Young, CSA, Fourth Kentucky, Lewis's Brigade, Bate's Division, Hardee's Corps, Army of Tennessee

At Resaca was fought the first battle of magnitude in the celebrated Georgia Campaign. From then on there was not a day or night, yes, scarcely an hour, that we did not hear the crack of a rifle or roar of a cannon. To their music we slept, by their thunderings we were awakened and to the accompanying call of the bugle we responded on the morning of May 14 to engage in the death grapple with Sherman's well-clothed, well-fed and thoroughly rested veterans who moved against us in perfect step, with banners flying and bands playing, as though expecting to charm us.

When they had come within seventy-five or eighty yards, our lines opened a murderous fire from both infantry and double-shotted artillery. Having retired in disorder to their original position in the woods, they rallied and again moved to the attack to be met in the same manner and with similar results. Three times during the morning and early afternoon were these attacks made upon our lines. It was a veritable picnic for the Confederates, protected as we were by earthworks with clear and open ground in front. [L. D. Young, *Reminiscences of a Soldier of the Orphan Brigade* (Louisville, Ky.: Courier-Journal Job Printing Co., 1918), p. 81.]

Report of Maj. Gen. Carter L. Stevenson, CSA, Commanding Division, Hood's Corps, Army of Tennessee

On the night of the 13th . . . agreeably to orders, I vacated my position [Stop 4] and took up the line of march for Resaca. On the morning after my arrival near this place I took up position in two lines north of Resaca, and immediately upon the right of the Resaca and Dalton road. I was soon afterward ordered to connect with Major-General *Hindman*, on the left of the Resaca road, and for this purpose moved two regiments across the road. *Cumming* and *Brown* were in my front line, *Pettus* being the second line to the former and *Reynolds* to the latter. During the morning there were several attacks upon General *Hindman*, and in my front the sharpshooters of the enemy obtained positions which entirely enfiladed portions of *Cumming's* line. The men were sheltered as well as possible by such defenses as they could construct of logs and rails, but still suffered severely. The fire of these sharpshooters upon the artillery, some pieces of which were advanced in front of the line of General *Cumming*, was particularly destructive, and among the wounded was the brave Maj. *J. W. Johnston*, the battalion commander.

About 5 o'clock that evening, agreeably to orders, I commenced a movement to dislodge the enemy from the high point of the ridge some distance in front of General *Cumming. Brown* and his support (*Reynolds*) were directed to move out in front of their trenches and then swing around to the left. After the movement commenced General *Cumming* was also directed to wheel all of his brigade, which was to the right of the backbone of the ridge, to the left in front of his works, the regiment upon the crest being the pivot. I was much gratified by the gallantry with which the movement was made, and by the success which attended it. Too much praise cannot be awarded *Brown's* gallant brigade. . . . Late that night I received orders to retire from the position which I had taken, which was done.

The next morning I was ordered to retake it, which was accomplished without difficulty, the enemy not having reoccupied it. My command immediately went to work to construct defenses of logs and rails, and in a short time were quite well entrenched. During the course of the morning I received orders to place the artillery of my division in such a position as would enable it to drive off a battery that was annoying General *Hindman's* line. Before the necessary measures for the protection of the artillery could be taken, I received repeated and peremptory orders to open it upon the battery. . . . [Capt. *Maximillian Van Den*] *Corput's* battery was accordingly placed in position at the only available point, about eighty yards in front of General *Brown's* line.

It had hardly gotten into position when the enemy hotly engaged my skirmishers, driving them and pushing on the assault with great impetuosity. So quickly was all this done that it was impossible to remove the artillery before the enemy had effected a lodgment in the ravine in front of it, thus placing it in such a position that while the enemy were entirely unable to remove it, we were equally so, without driving off the enemy massed in the ravine beyond it, which would have been attended with great loss of life.

The assaults of the enemy were in heavy force and made with the utmost impetuosity, but were met with a cool, steady fire, which each time mowed down their ranks and drove them back, leaving the ground

Entrance to the Confederate Cemetery north of Resaca (Harold Nelson).

thickly covered in places with their dead. When *Brown's* brigade had nearly exhausted their ammunition I caused it to be relieved by *Reynolds'* brigade, upon which assaults were also made and repulsed with the same success. During the attack I ordered General *Pettus* up with three of his regiments, which had remained in our position of the day previous. My intention was to employ his force in attacking the enemy in front of the battery and remove it. A portion of *Gibson's* brigade, of *Stewart's* division, was also sent me, but was soon recalled. . . . During the day [Capt. *Charles E.*] *Fenner's* battery reported to me and rendered good service.

In the evening I received orders to move that portion of my force which was on the right of General *Cumming* out of the trenches, and cooperating with General *Stewart,* to swing around upon the enemy. At the moment that I received the order the enemy were making a heavy assault upon General *Reynolds,* and *Brown* had not yet replenished his ammunition. The orders, however, were peremptory, and the movement was attempted. The Fifty-fourth Virginia, on the right, leaped the trenches and rushed bravely upon the enemy, but found that there was no connection with General *Stewart's* left, and being thus unsupported were compelled to fall back before the rest of the brigade moved out. . . . The regiment in less than fifteen minutes lost above 100 officers and men.

That night I received orders to withdraw. . . . My last brigade had not marched 300 yards from the trenches before the enemy made an assault. Especial credit is due the skirmishers of *Brown's* brigade for their conduct in this affair.

As I have stated I covered the disputed battery with my fire in such a manner that it was utterly impossible for the enemy to remove it, and I knew that I could retake it at any time, but thought that it could be done with less loss of life at night, and therefore postponed my attack. When ordered to retire I represented the state of things to the general commanding, who decided to abandon the guns. [*O.R.*, XXXVIII, pt. 3, pp. 811–813.]

Report of Maj. Gen. Alexander P. Stewart, CSA, Commanding Division, Hood's Corps, Army of Tennessee

Thursday night (12th) we brought up the rear of the corps in retiring to Tilton. Friday night (13th) bivouacked along the railroad some three miles in advance of Resaca, and on Saturday morning (14th) took position in a line crossing the railroad, forming the right of the army, my right resting on the Connesauga [*sic*]. About 5 p.m., in compliance with the orders of the lieutenant-general commanding corps, I moved out along the railroad, formed in two lines parallel to the road, and advanced to attack the enemy's left. We moved forward a distance of one and a half to two miles, getting sight of the enemy's line near Union Church, which, however, hastily retired. By this time, owing to the eagerness of the men, the lines had become somewhat separated, and I halted to reform. In the meantime we were subjected to a heavy fire of artillery, which, however, caused but little or no loss. By the time the lines were reformed night had come on, and I deemed it imprudent to advance further. Toward midnight, under orders, we retired to our position in line.

On Sunday morning (15th) my line was advanced, the right of it half a mile and passing in front of Mr. Green's house, the left only a few hundred yards, and the position was soon entrenched. About 3 p.m. I received directions to advance and attack the enemy in my front at 4 o'clock, provided I had not myself been attacked by that time. Shortly previous to 4, information came to me of a heavy movement of the enemy to my front, which information was transmitted to the lieutenant-general commanding corps. My instructions were in advancing to gradually wheel toward the left, and I was notified that

Stevenson, on my left, would also advance. At 4 precisely *Clayton* on the left and *Stovall* on the right of the front line, were caused each to make a half wheel to the left to place them in the proper direction, and were also instructed to continue inclining by a slight wheel to the left in advancing. This . . . placed them in echelon, the object being to prevent my right, toward the river, from being turned. [Brig. Gen. *George E.*] *Maney's* brigade, which had reported to me, and a small body of cavalry under Colonel [*Daniel W.*] *Holman,* were directed to move out on the right, outflanking and covering *Stovall's* right. *Gibson* and *Baker* were brought forward and placed in position as supports to *Clayton* and *Stovall,* and the order to advance given.

The men moved forward with great spirit and determination and soon engaged the enemy. At this moment an order came by Lieutenant-Colonel *Cunningham* not to make the attack, which, however, had already commenced. We encountered the enemy in heavy force and protected by breast-works of logs. The ground over which a portion of *Stovall's* brigade passed was covered with a dense undergrowth and brush. Regiments in consequence became separated, and the brigade soon began to fall back. Hastening to it, and finding it impossible to reform it on the ground it occupied, it was suffered to fall back to its entrenched position, *Baker's* brigade retiring with it. *Clayton* being thus unsupported on the right, and *Stevenson's* division, on his left, not having advanced, also retired, and *Gibson* fell back by my order, as did *Maney.* . . . The attack would have been renewed but for the order received at the last moment countermanding it. . . .

During the retreat of the army at night the division remained in line of battle, crossing the railroad and Dalton and Resaca road, until the entire army had passed the bridges. The situation was perilous, and calculated to try the endurance of the men, as the enemy threatened an attack. They stood firm, however, and remained in position until about 3 o'clock in the morning, when we retired, in obedience to . . . orders. [*O.R.,* XXXVIII, pt. 3, pp. 817–818.]

Report of Capt. James A. Wemyss, CSA, Thirty-Sixth Alabama Infantry, Clayton's Brigade, Stewart's Division, Hood's Corps, Army of Tennessee

Went into line of battle at 8 a.m. on May 14; spent most of the day in erecting good breast-works. At 4 p.m. received orders to go forward, which was promptly done, to the skirmish line, from which we charged the enemy's heavy line behind breast-works; easily routed them and vigorously pursued until dark. The castaway guns, knapsacks, and blankets told too plainly of the terror and demoralization of the enemy, and what might have resulted in decisive advantage but for the approaching darkness. Resting quietly in distinct hearing of the enemy's orders and movements until 12 o'clock, we returned to our position behind the breast-works, sleeping until 7 o'clock on the 15th of May, when our orders were to move forward, which advanced our lines a few hundred yards, when we threw up breast-works and were soon under fire of the enemy's heavy line of skirmishers.

At 5 p.m. received orders to move forward, swinging around to the left and dressing to the right. This order was promptly obeyed, though under a deadly fire. After moving forward with the regiments of the brigade on our right a few paces were ordered to lie down. When again ordered to move forward the command promptly arose and moved under a tremendous volley, which mowed its ranks right and left until ordered the second time to lie down.

The second command to move forward was alike promptly obeyed by the thinned ranks, and persisted in, though without any support on our left, which was enfiladed by a murderous fire from the enemy in front of the brigade on our left. The wheel to the left by our regiment and brigade brought our left companies in front of the heavy line of the enemy behind strong works, in easy range, and under a fatal and scathing fire from our front and left flank. We were ordered to retire to our works, which was done in good order, some of the men on the left coming in over the breast-works of the brigade on our left.

This charge of but twenty-five minutes' duration resulted in heavy loss, our casualties being: Officers—killed 1; wounded mortally, 2; severely, 3; slightly, 3; total, 9. Enlisted men—killed, 13; wounded mortally, 9; severely, 26; slightly, 27; missing, 8; total, 83. Aggregate, 92.

May 15, at 12 o'clock at night, received orders to retire quietly; passing through Resaca at 1 o'clock, formed line of battle, protecting our rear and the bridge. Resuming our march at 2 a.m., crossing the bridge, by easy marches toward New Hope Church, passing and forming in line of battle at Adairsville and Cassville, reaching the bridge over the Etowah, crossing and burning it, resting, and recruiting two days, moving thence to the railroad; thence toward New Hope Church, where we went into line of battle from the march on the 25th of May. [O.R., XXXVIII, pt. 3, pp. 837–838.]

Report of Gen. Joseph E. Johnston, CSA, Commanding Army of Tennessee

On the 16th the enemy crossed the Oostenaula. Lieutenant-General *Hardee* skirmished with them successfully near Calhoun. The fact that a part of *Polk's* troops were still in the rear, and the great numerical superiority of the Federal army, made it expedient to risk battle only when position or some blunder on the part of the enemy might give us counterbalancing advantages. I therefore determined to fall back slowly until circumstances should put the chances of battle in our favor, keeping so near the U.S. army as to prevent its sending reinforcements to Grant, and hoping, by taking advantage of positions and opportunities, to reduce the odds against us by partial engagements. I also expected it to be materially reduced before the end of June by the expiration of the terms of service of many of the regiments which had not re-enlisted. . . . At Adairsville . . . on the 17th, *Polk's* cavalry, under Brigadier-General [*William H. (Red)*] *Jackson*, met the army, and *Hardee* after severe skirmishing checked the enemy. [*O.R.*, XXXVIII, pt. 3, p. 615.]

9. ADAIRSVILLE

You may wish to make a detour to see the Confederate Cemetery before proceeding to the next stop. Once you are ready to go to Stop 9, turn back onto U.S. 41 and head toward Resaca. Turn right on GA 136, pass over the interstate, and turn left onto I-75 southbound. Drive south on I-75 to exit 312 (approximately 7.5 miles). At that exit, turn right onto GA 53 toward Calhoun and drive about 0.9 mile to the intersection with U.S. 41, moving into the left lane as you approach that distance. Turn left onto U.S. 41 and drive slightly more than 5.2 miles to the intersection with Miller Ferry Road. Turn right here and drive 1.3 miles, then turn right on South Holcomb Road. Drive about 0.5 mile, and after you have passed a pond on your right, pull off onto the right shoulder to view the hillside.

On your right you will see a field in the foreground, the railroad, and another field beyond. The traces of Confederate earthworks are clearly visible in the distant field. Those lines blocked Union movement down the railroad from Calhoun, and the continuation of those lines beyond the crest blocked movement from the railroad southeast along Taylor Bridge Road to the highway from Calhoun to Adairsville.

STOP 9, OPERATIONS FROM RESACA TO ADAIRSVILLE

15–17 May 1864

Maj. Gen. William T. Sherman to Maj. Gen. H. W. Halleck, Washington, D.C., 15 May 1864

We have been fighting all day, pressing the enemy and gaining substantial advantage at all points. We will strengthen the line of circumvallation, so as to spare a larger force to operate across the Oostenaula, below Resaca. Two pontoon bridges are over at Lay's Ferry.

I cannot estimate our dead and wounded up to this hour, but it will not fall much short of 3,000. The cars now run down to within seven miles of us, and we have every facility to provide for the wounded. The troops fight well, and everything works smoothly. We intend to

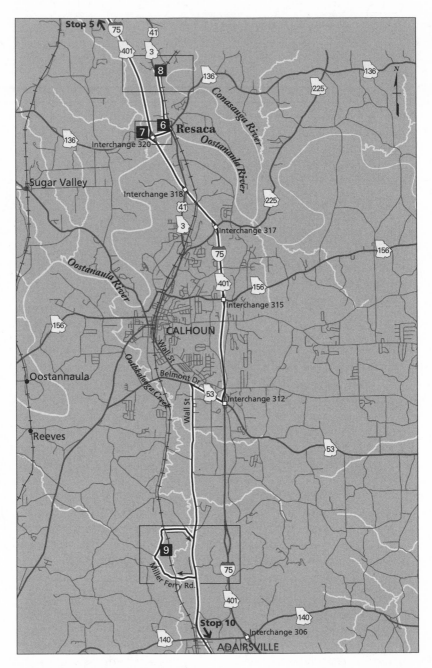

From Resaca to Adairsville

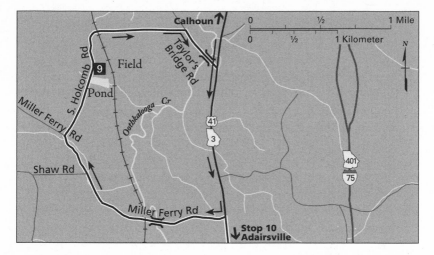

Confederate Defenses North of Adairsville (Stop 9)

fight *Joe Johnston* until he is satisfied, and I hope he will not attempt to escape. If he does, my bridges are down, and we will be after him. The country is mountainous and heavily wooded, giving the party on the defensive every advantage, and our losses result mostly from sharpshooters and ambush firing. [*O.R.*, XXXVIII, pt. 4, p. 189.]

Sherman to Halleck, 15 May 1864, a.m.

We are in possession of Resaca. It is a strongly fortified position, besides being a strong natural position. We saved the common road bridge, but the railroad bridge is burned. The railroad is good to this point, and our cars will run here today.

Our columns are now crossing the Oostenaula; General McPherson at Lay's Ferry, General Thomas here, and General Schofield about Newtown. We will pursue smartly to the Etowah. Generals Stoneman's and Garrard's cavalry are trying to get in rear of the enemy, and I hope will succeed.

Our difficulties will increase beyond the Etowah, but if *Johnston* will not fight us behind such works as we find here, I will fight him on any open ground he may stand at. All well and in high spirits. We have about 1,000 prisoners and 8 guns. [*O.R.*, XXXVIII, pt. 4, p. 201.]

Special Field Orders No. 8, Headquarters, Military Division of the Mississippi, Resaca, 16 May 1864

The enemy having retreated south, the following general plan will be pursued until he is beyond the Etowah River:

Major-General Thomas will pursue substantially by the line of the railroad to Kingston and Etowah bridge, keeping his forces well in hand at all times, but using two or three roads when available.

II. Major-General McPherson will move substantially by the Rome road, keeping up communications with the center.

III. Major-General Schofield will get over on the old Federal road from Spring Place to Cassville, or other road in that neighborhood.

IV. The repairs of the railroad and telegraph lines must be pushed forward with all possible rapidity, but troops must not wait for them. . . .

VIII. Major-General Thomas is charged with the duty of guarding all railroads to our rear, including all the country north of the Tennessee and the post and bridge at Decatur, Alabama, and Major-General McPherson may call forward to his army the effective corps and regiments now at and around Huntsville as soon as he can, leaving only small guards until they are relieved by detachments of the Army of the Cumberland. . . .

IX. Major General McPherson will collect a force of about 4,000 or 5,000 men out of the militia and garrisons of Paducah and Columbus, Ky., and place them at some suitable point on the Tennessee River, about Eastport, to serve as a threat to North Alabama and as a support to General Washburn's operations in Mississippi. [*O.R.*, XXXVIII, pt. 4, pp. 216–217.]

Journal, Fourth Army Corps, Army of the Cumberland, 16 May 1864

The crossing of the Oostenaula slow on account of bad condition of bridge. General Newton had the advance, then Wood, then Stanley. About one-half mile from Resaca heavy skirmishing with the enemy commenced, and our progress was therefore much impeded. We moved on the direct road from Resaca to Calhoun. Reached a point two miles from Resaca at 4.25 p.m., when we met a deserter, who informed us that the enemy was drawn up in line of battle, three brigades of infantry, one mile and a half from our left front. Instructed division commanders to watch well their left flank, to move part of their force as flankers along the railroad, and to move all of their artillery on the dirt road. Deserter further reported that . . . *Polk's corps moved on the road upon which we are marching, Hardee's on the road to our right, and Hood's on the road to our left.*

4.30 p.m., heard heavy firing off to our right, and in advance on our left, in the direction of McPherson's troops.

6.45 p.m. arrived at point within one-half mile of Calhoun. After heavy skirmish here, driving off regiment of infantry and rear guard of cavalry, went into camp to bivouac for the night. . . . The day was bright and warm; roads very dusty. Not much water on the road of today's march. Country rolling, covered with dense woods and undergrowth; occasional clearing; many ridges, but not high; very good road.

7 p.m. sent dispatch to Major-General Thomas, informing him of our arrival at this point. . . .

10 p.m., Colonel Hayes ordered to send up all our loaded wagons from Resaca tomorrow a.m., to follow the command. [*O.R.*, XXXVIII, pt. 1, p. 856.]

17 May 1864

Report of Maj. Gen. Oliver O. Howard, USA, Commanding Fourth Army Corps, Army of the Cumberland

Early on the 16th my corps led the pursuit along the direct road toward Kingston. Skirmishing occurred with the enemy's rear guard so as to make our progress slow.

The corps camped that night at Calhoun. My command, General Newton leading, continued the march next day, starting at 5 a.m., along the wagon road, except Wood's division, which moved on the right down the railroad. We had heavy skirmishing all day. The enemy's custom is, when retreating, to form his rear guard of cavalry with a section or battery of artillery, sometimes strengthened by infantry.

During this day's march the resistance was unusually great. He formed three lines, some half or three-quarters of a mile apart, and barricaded with rails, seeking the cover of woods with open fields in his front. As soon as we had succeeded in driving the first line it passed to the rear of the third, and in some new and favorable position made another line. However, as we moved in two columns, we were able to make considerable progress.

The resistance increased as we approached Adairsville. General Newton continued to deploy regiments as skirmishers till he had a large brigade engaged. General Wood, abreast of him, also skirmished heavily.

About 4 p.m. it was found that we had come upon the enemy's infantry in considerable force. Preparations were immediately made to assault and carry this position if possible, but it required time to bring up the troops and get them in readiness. General Thomas deeming it best, on account of the nearness of night, to make no formal attack, the movement already set on foot was postponed. Yet a real engagement was going on, since both parties continued to re-enforce the skirmish lines until they were tantamount to lines of battle. The enemy opened upon our column with artillery, to which our batteries replied with spirit. During the night the enemy withdrew. We found that he had taken up a strong position and had partially entrenched it, and that his whole army was present while the heavy skirmishing of the evening before was progressing. The casualties in my command at Adairsville were about 200 killed and wounded. [*O.R.*, XXXVIII, pt. 4, p. 191.]

Journal, Fourth Army Corps, Army of the Cumberland

May 17: Received no instructions in reference to today's march. Therefore started on the direct road to Kingston at 5.30 a.m., General Newton's division leading, then Wood's, then Stanley's. Wood's division moved on the railroad. . . .

Commenced to skirmish with the enemy as soon as we reached Calhoun. 7.30 a.m., the enemy opened fire upon our advance from two pieces of artillery. 7.30, sent word to General Wood to send two regiments to our left as far as advisable, as flankers, which was done. 7.45, sent a staff officer over to the Rome road to open communication with General McPherson. At 8.20 he returned, and reported that General McPherson was moving down said road about two miles to our right.

Owing to continued skirmishing with the enemy and occasional artillery firing, our advance was very slow. From 5.30 a.m. to 4 p.m. we only marched about eight miles, arriving at that time two and a half miles from Adairsville, with Newton's division moving on the

"Sherman's Army Entering Resaca" (*Harper's Pictorial History of the Great Rebellion* [New York: Harper Bros., 1866–1868], 606).

direct road. At about the same time the head of General Wood's column arrived three-fourths of a mile from Newton, on our right, on the railroad.

Here and at this time the enemy stubbornly resisted our advance, having now opposed to us infantry, cavalry, and artillery. At 4.20 p.m. General Wood reported that citizens from Adairsville had just informed him that there was a large force of the enemy's infantry in Adairsville. Commenced, after heavy skirmishing, to form a line of battle to drive the enemy from our front or to repulse any attack that he might make.

His line was formed running across and at right angles to the road leading to the town. On the right of the dirt road, running parallel to it and ending very nearly on the line of battle, was a low wooded ridge. On this rested the right of Newton's formation, which was a column by regiments, prepared for an assault. On the left of the road, extending through a wheat field and to the woods, rested his left, in two lines of battle. At 4.30 word was sent to General Wood to move upon the enemy at once from the position he occupied. This he could not do until he bridged a creek in his front, which could not be done before dark. At same time General Stanley was ordered up to cover Newton's left flank, as the enemy was moving around it.

During all of this time we had heavy skirmishing, and the enemy firing artillery on Newton. At 5.30, Stanley got into position, two brigades on the left of Newton, extending into the woods and holding a small hill therein, and the other brigade massed in the rear of Newton's left. At 6 p.m. assault was ordered to be made by General Newton, and was just about to be made when Major General Thomas, who had come up with Major General Sherman, stopped the movement, saying that it was too late in the evening to make it. The enemy kept up a steady fire along our line until dark, when it ceased.

7 p.m., General Wood reported his bridge finished, and, if General Howard would advise it, he would cross some troops over and assault the enemy, who, he said, was entrenched and was at Adairsville in force. General Howard replied, telling him to cross over and throw out [a] strong line of skirmishers to feel the enemy's position, but he would not advise a night attack. Wood's left was now not far from Newton's right.

The road we marched on was very good. The country . . . was rolling, and covered with dense woods and undergrowth, with occasional cultivated fields. It was admirably suited for the movements of the enemy's rear guard, he being able to make a stand, as he did, every few hundred yards. During the day we lost about 25 killed and 170 wounded. The first part of the day very warm; heavy storm from 2 p.m. to 4 p.m. The next day we found out that the greater part of *Johnston's* army had been in our front and that the enemy had well-constructed rifle-pits. [*O.R.*, XXXVIII, pt. 4, pp. 857–858.]

Itinerary, Hardee's Corps, Army of Tennessee

May 17, 1864. *Hardee's* corps retired slowly before the enemy about 1 a.m., leaving the cavalry to hold him in check. The rear of the army reached Adairsville, seven miles below, about noon. The enemy followed closely behind, and by 3 p.m. were skirmishing with our cavalry. They were hardly looked for so early, but by dint of great activity *Hardee's* corps was in position to confront them in good time, and again the now familiar popping of rifles was heard. The fighting at no time went beyond heavy skirmishing, which, on our part, was sustained by *Cheatham*, who occupied the front line.

When the firing ended at night we had not receded an inch any-where. At a council held at night it was decided to fall back to Cassville, fifteen miles south of Adairsville (in this council it was understood that General *Hardee* advocated giving battle in the position we then held in front of Adairsville, information having been received that McPherson's corps of the enemy were in the neighborhood of Rome and another had been sent to Virginia, which would give us greatly the advantage of the enemy, as we had our whole army massed at Adairs-ville), and orders were accordingly issued. At 12 p.m. our army was again in motion, passing through Kingston about 9 o'clock [on May 18] and arriving at camp near Cassville at about noon. [*O.R.*, XXXVIII, pt. 3, p. 704.]

Report of Maj. Gen. Joseph Wheeler, CSA, Commanding Cavalry Corps, Army of Tennessee

May 17, with *Kelly's* and [Col. *Thomas H.*] *Harrison's* divisions and [Brig. Gen. *John S.*] *Williams'* brigade, I resisted the enemy, who were advancing on the Calhoun road. They advanced with cavalry, infan-try, and artillery upon us, when we opened upon him with small-arms from behind our temporary rail breast-works and from two pieces of artillery, causing him to deploy his lines. Hearing that the enemy's cavalry was moving on the Tan-yard Ford road to gain my rear, I sent *Williams'* brigade on that road to reinforce that portion of General *Martin's* division on that road. By forming lines and fighting the en-emy at every favorable position we had forced the enemy to advance in line all day.

At about 3 o'clock I was obliged to retire to the position occupied by our infantry two miles south of Adairsville. The enemy moved around my left flank on the west side of the creek, which runs near and west of the Adairsville and Calhoun road. General *Kelly's* division was sent to oppose this force and prevent the enemy gaining our rear. *Cheatham's* division of infantry being formed in front of Adairsville, I formed *Martin's* division and *Williams'* brigade, dismounted, between *Cheatham's* division and General *Kelly's* command, and on a line with the infantry, with skirmishers deployed in front. Considerable skir-mishing was kept up until after dark, when I withdrew the main por-tion of my command to near the town to feed and rest the horses. [*O.R.*, XXXVIII, pt. 3, pp. 945–946.]

Report of Maj. Gen. Patrick R. Cleburne, CSA, Commanding Division, Hardee's Corps, Army of Tennessee

I arrived at Adairsville about daylight (17th), halting about two miles north of the town. About 3 p.m. the enemy appeared in some considerable force on the railroad, from Calhoun. *Cheatham* was placed in position on the crest of a ridge immediately confronting the enemy, his line crossing the railroad at right angles. My division was drawn up on the left of the road in two lines, in *Cheatham's* rear, about 800 yards distant—*Polk* and *Granbury* in the first line, *Govan* and *Lowrey* in the second. An open field, traversed by a creek with swampy margins, intervened between me and *Cheatham*; along my left ran a considerable creek.

Much attention was paid to my left flank. It was strengthened by rifle-pits, as also were my two lines. Skirmishers were disposed along the creek on my left, stretching down to *Cheatham's* left. A regiment of *Lowrey's* was thrown across the creek to my left for further protection to that flank: this force afterward gave place to *Bate*.

The enemy attacked *Cheatham*, but my division was not engaged. Soon after night I attended, at your [Lt. Gen. *Hardee's*] summons, at your headquarters, and received orders to retire. *Cheatham* was to lead; *Bate* to follow in half an hour; *Walker* in another half hour, and I to bring up the rear as soon as I could get to the road. Skirmishers were to be left in position until the corps had gone away. By some misunderstanding these skirmishers were withdrawn at 2 o'clock, and came in before my command had filed into the road, thus leaving nothing between me and the enemy. Fortunately, however, an impenetrable fog enveloped the army and covered our movements.

I reached Kingston during the early part of the 18th, and halted for some hours. Moving again, I marched until about 4 p.m. with three of my brigades to within two miles of Cassville. *Polk* was left in Kingston as a rear guard. The next morning, May 19, I went into position. [*O.R.*, XXXVIII, pt. 3, p. 723.]

Maj. Gen. William T. Sherman to Maj. Gen. George Thomas, USA, Commanding the Army of the Cumberland, 17 May 1864, in the Field near Adairsville

It is probable on reaching Adairsville in the early morning we will find that the enemy has retreated via Cassville. If such be the case

I want you to put your head of column after him as far as Cassville, when I will determine whether to continue the pursuit as far as Cartersville or let him go. I prefer he should divide between Rome and Cartersville, in which event you will march directly on Kingston. I will be with you in the morning, and only mention those points that you may instruct your leading division.

I wish you would put one of your boldest division commanders to lead tomorrow, and explain to him that General McPherson is close on his right and General Schofield on his left, and that two heavy columns of cavalry, Garrard's and Stoneman's, have orders to strike the road, the one between Kingston and Rome, and the other between Kingston and Cartersville. Instead of skirmishing only with the rear guard it should be attacked promptly by his whole division, deployed in whole or part, according to the ground, but it should be preceded by the usual skirmish line. A real battle tomorrow might save us much work at a later period. [O.R., XXXVIII, pt. 4, pp. 219–220.]

Maj. Gen. William T. Sherman to Maj. Gen. John M. Schofield, USA, Commanding the Army of the Ohio, Near Adairsville, 17 May 1864, 9 p.m.

I want your head of column up at the intersection of the roads about four miles east of Adairsville as early as possible, always with the standing order that if you hear the sounds of serious battle you turn toward it, otherwise shape your course toward Kingston. Thomas' head of column is against a pretty stubborn rear guard which fights at every point, and as he can present nothing but a head of column, the enemy delays us and saves the time he needs to remove his stores and army.

It may be tomorrow I will turn your column to Cassville and the railroad due south of Cassville, with a view to strike the flank of a retreating army; but unless you get such orders from me incline toward Kingston with your infantry, but send McCook's cavalry to Cassville and the railroad, giving him always your head of infantry as a *point d'appui* in case he encounter a very superior force; but tell McCook that it is all important to the cavalry arm to impress the enemy with a fear of him, as it will be an element of strength in our future operations. Kingston is our present objective point, and from there I will make new dispositions. [O.R., XXXVIII, pt. 4, pp. 222–223.]

Maj. Gen. William T. Sherman to Maj. Gen. James B. McPherson, USA, Commanding Army of the Tennessee, 17 May 1864, 6:15 p.m.

Direct your march early tomorrow to Adairsville and order the cavalry of Garrard and Murray to make a dash at the railroad between Rome and Kingston (if not already done) tonight. General Stoneman is on the other flank and will attempt the road between Kingston and the Etowah bridge. If not done tonight there will be no use in doing it at all. As I take it, the enemy is trying to make time to save his material from his army and from Rome. . . . We won't get into Adairsville tonight. [*O.R.*, XXXVIII, pt. 4, p. 227.]

Sherman to Schofield, 3.5 Miles from Kingston, 18 May 1864, 10:30 p.m.

I was in hopes you would be farther ahead by tonight, but the roads are not suited to one concentric movement on Kingston, and we must approach the game as near as the case admits of. All the signs continue of *Johnston's* having retreated on Kingston, and why he should lead to Kingston, if he designs to cover his trains to Carters- ville, I do not see. But it is probable he has sent to Allatoona all he can by [railroad] cars, and his wagons are escaping south of the Etowah by the bridge and fords near Kingston.

In any hypothesis our plan is right. All of General Thomas' com- mand will follow his trail straight, let it lead to the fords or toward Al- latoona. You must shape your course to support General Hooker and strike the line of the railway to his left. As soon as you can march in the morning, get up to General Hooker and act according to the devel- opments. If we can bring *Johnston* to battle this side of the Etowah we must do it, even at the hazard of beginning battle with but part of our forces. If you hear the sound of battle, direct your course so as to come up to the left of General Thomas' troops. If *Johnston* has got beyond the Etowah we will take two days to pick up fragments from Rome to Etowah. [*O.R.*, XXXVIII, pt. 4, p. 242.]

10. CASSVILLE

Continue driving in the same direction on South Holcomb Road. The road will curve to the right after about 0.3 mile and cross the railroad tracks. About 0.6 mile beyond the railroad crossing, the road intersects Taylor's Bridge Road at a "T" intersection with a stop sign. Turn right onto that road and drive about 0.3 mile to the stop sign at U.S. 41. Turn right onto U.S. 41. You will drive about 12 miles south on U.S. 41 before turning. Stay on the highway as it bypasses modern Adairsville and continue toward Cassville. The highway will cross a bridge just before your turn. After the bridge, turn left onto a road opposite a highway sign indicating Cassville. This is the old road to Cassville. Follow it about 0.9 mile into Cassville and turn left at the Cassville Grocery onto Cassville White Road. Follow this road about 0.6 mile as it curves out of town. Turn right in front of the state historical marker labeled "Confederate Dead," and turn left into the Cassville cemetery. Follow the one-way cemetery road to the top of the loop. Pull off to the side at an appropriate spot on the hilltop before the road begins to descend.

The Confederate defensive lines were constructed on this ridge. When you look back toward the north, you get a good perspective on the advantages General *Johnston* saw when he chose this position for making a stand against the advancing Union troops.

STOP 10, CASSVILLE CEMETERY

Narrative of Maj. Gen. William T. Sherman, USA, Commanding Military Division of the Mississippi

On the 17th, toward evening, the head of Thomas' column, Newton's division, encountered the rear guard of *Johnston's* army near Adairsville. I was near the head of column at the time, trying to get a view of the position of the enemy from an elevation in an open field. My party attracted the fire of a battery; a shell passed through a group of staff officers and burst just beyond, which scattered us promptly.

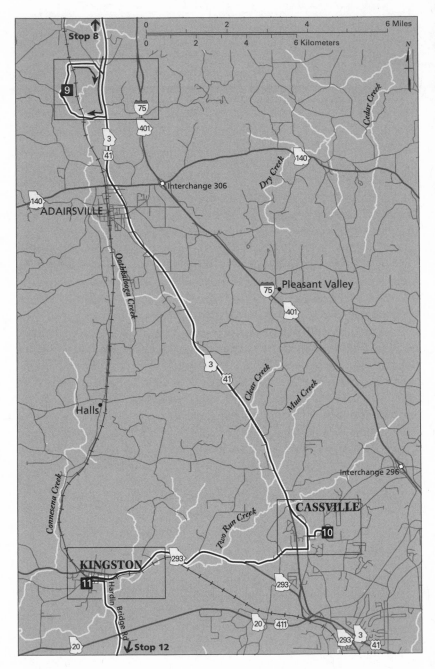

Adairsville to Kingston

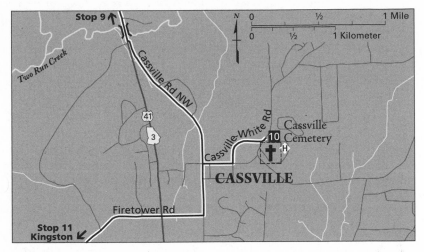

Cassville (Stop 10)

The next morning the enemy had disappeared, and our pursuit was continued to Kingston, which we reached during Sunday forenoon, the 19th.

From Resaca the railroad runs nearly due south, but at Kingston it makes junction with another railroad from Rome, and changes direction due east. At that time McPherson's head of column was about four miles to the west of Kingston, at a country place called 'Woodlawn'; Schofield and Hooker were on the direct roads leading from Newtown to Cassville, diagonal to the route followed by Thomas. Thomas's head of column, which had followed the country roads alongside of the railroad, was about four miles east of Kingston, toward Cassville, when about noon I got a message from him that he had found the enemy, drawn up in line of battle, on some extensive, open ground, about half-way between Kingston and Cassville, and that appearances indicated a willingness and preparation for battle.

Hurriedly sending orders to McPherson to resume the march, to hasten forward by roads leading to the south of Kingston, so as to leave for Thomas's troops and trains the use of the main road, and to come up on his right, I rode forward rapidly, over some rough gravel hills, and about six miles from Kingston found General Thomas, with his troops deployed; but he reported that the enemy had fallen back in echelon of divisions, steadily and in superb order, into Cassville.

I knew that the roads by which Generals Hooker and Schofield were approaching would lead them to a seminary near Cassville, and that it was all-important to secure the point of junction of these roads with the main road along which we were marching. Therefore I ordered General Thomas to push forward his deployed lines as rapidly as possible; and, as night was approaching, I ordered two field-batteries to close up at a gallop on some woods which lay between us and the town of Cassville. We could not see the town by reason of these woods, but a high range of hills just back of the town [*your present location*] was visible over the tree-tops. On these hills could be seen fresh-made parapets, and the movements of men, against whom I directed the artillery to fire at long range.

The stout resistance made by the enemy along our whole front of a couple of miles indicated a purpose to fight at Cassville; and, as the night was closing in General Thomas and I were together, along with our skirmish-lines near the seminary, on the edge of the town, where musket-bullets from the enemy were cutting the leaves of the trees pretty thickly about us. Either Thomas or I remarked that that was not the place for the two senior officers of a great army, and we personally went back to the battery, where we passed the night on the ground.

During the night I had reports from McPherson, Hooker, and Schofield. The former was about five miles to my right rear, near the "nitre-caves;" Schofield was about six miles north, and Hooker between us, within two miles. All were ordered to close down on Cassville at daylight, and to attack the enemy wherever found. [Sherman, *Memoirs*, II, pp. 37–38.]

Report of Gen. Joseph E. Johnston, CSA, Commanding Army of Tennessee

At Adairsville . . . on the 17th, *Polk's* cavalry, under Brigadier-General *Jackson*, met the army, and *Hardee* after severe skirmishing checked the enemy. At this point, on the 18th, *Polk's* and *Hood's* corps took the direct road to Cassville, *Hardee's* that by Kingston. About half the Federal army took each road.

[Maj. Gen. *Samuel G.*] *French's* division having joined *Polk's* corps on the 18th, on the morning of the 19th, when half the Federal army was near Kingston, the two corps at Cassville were ordered to advance against the troops that had followed them from Adairsville, *Hood's*

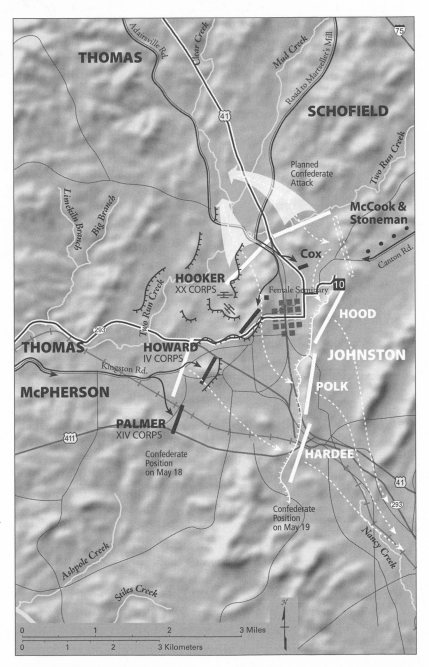

Opposing Lines and Confederate Plans at Cassville

leading on the right. When this corps had advanced some two miles one of his staff officers reported to Lieutenant-General *Hood* that the enemy was approaching on the Canton road in rear of the right of our original position. He drew back his troops and formed them across that road. When it was discovered that the officer was mistaken, the opportunity had passed, by the near approach of the two portions of the Federal army.

Expecting to be attacked I drew up the troops in what seemed to me an excellent position—a bold ridge immediately in rear of Cassville, with an open valley before it. The fire of the enemy's artillery commenced soon after the troops were formed, and continued until night. [*O.R.*, XXXVIII, pt. 3, pp. 615–616.]

19 May 1864

Journal of Operations of the Army of Tennessee, by Lt. T. B. Mackall, CSA, Aide-de-Camp to Brig. Gen. W. W. Mackall, Chief of Staff

May 18. Left headquarters beyond Adairsville about 4 a.m., *Hardee's* corps moved on Adairsville and Kingston road, *Hood's* and *Polk's* on Adairsville and Cassville. Reached creek near Cassville about 7.30 a.m.; got into camp 9.30 a.m.; no firing so far (just after breakfast). . . . *Hood* and *Hardee* and *Polk* at headquarters discussing over map plans for morning. Prisoner of Hooker's corps brought in; I questioned him. . . .

All appear in good spirits. Telegram received in afternoon . . . reporting enemy acknowledge loss of 45,000 and 31 generals in Virginia. General *Johnston* said Confederacy was as fixed an institution as England or France. Troops very much wearied by night marches; in good spirits and confident; press confident. Anxiety, however, to fight, particularly among officers, certain of whom thought good effect of Virginia and Louisiana news in raising gold in New York to 210 would be impaired by this retreat. Many thought Sherman would not fight— merely wanted to drive us across the Etowah and to occupy territory acquired and send reinforcements to Grant.

May 19. Moved out to attack enemy, but column reported advancing on Cartersville road; line changed; brisk skirmishing. General

[*Lawrence (Sul)*] *Ross* reports enemy throwing pontoons across Etowah at Wooley's bridge, and crossed a force—main force.

Line changed under fire. Brisk skirmishing in afternoon and toward evening to effect the change. New line principally along a ridge running nearly north and south, covering Cassville and Cass Station road and facing westwardly. The signal corps and General *Hardee* reported in afternoon that enemy in front of Cassville were moving toward Kingston, all advantageous to the designed attack on his left flank. An order was written about 7 or 8 a.m. thanking troops for patience, and telling them they would be led against enemy.

The text of the order referred to above was reproduced in the Official Records. It appears below (no number is included in the Official Records).

General Orders No.___, Headquarters, Army of Tennessee, CSA, Cassville, 19 May 1864

Soldiers of the Army of Tennessee, you have displayed the highest quality of the soldier—firmness in combat, patience under toil. By your courage and skill you have repulsed every assault of the enemy. By marches by day and by marches by night you have defeated every attempt upon your communications. Your communications are secured.

You will now turn and march to meet his advancing columns. Fully confiding in the conduct of the officers, the courage of the soldiers, I will lead you to battle. We may confidently trust that the Almighty Father will still reward the patriots' toils and bless the patriots' banners. Cheered by the success of our brothers in Virginia and beyond the Mississippi, our efforts will equal theirs. Strengthened by His support, those efforts will be crowned with the like glories. [*O.R.*, XXXVIII, pt. 4, p. 728.]

Journal of Operations of the Army of Tennessee, by Lt. T. B. Mackall (continued)

General *Johnston* rode over to General *Hood's* and then passing by general headquarters rode out Spring Place road, north of creek, with

Hood and *Polk* and *Hardee* to show the former where he was to form his line for attack. General *Mackall* rode from headquarters east of town to join him; found Generals *Johnston*, *Polk*, and *Hardee* returning ([Brig. Gen. *Claudius W.*] *Sears'* Mississippi brigade formed across the road). Riding back, all passed [Brig. Gen. *Francis M.*] *Cockrell's* Missouri brigade resting on road, and in town met *Hindman's* column, advance of *Hood's* corps, moving to take position on *Polk's* right. After a few moments in town rode rapidly back out Spring Place road; general saw *Hood* and returned to campground and dismounted; *Hood's* corps passing, *Polk's* troops shifting.

About this time—10.20 a.m.—a few discharges of artillery, on Adairsville and Cassville road, and in ten minutes report of artillery in eastern direction. General *Mackall*, who had ridden out to *Hood* with directions "to make quick work," sent word back by courier, who reported to me that "enemy in heavy force close to *Hood* on Canton road." I tell general, who says it can't be. ([Brig. Gen. *Frank C.*] *Armstrong* on that road reported none.) Called for map; said if that's so General *Hood* will have to fall back at once.

Presently General *Mackall* rode up at a rapid rate, spoke with general, who sent him back in haste, riding one of his horses. *Mason* went off on another; still firing had ceased; confusion in passing backward and forward of *Hood's* and *Polk's* troops. At this time could be heard officers all around reading orders to regiments and cheers of troops. Some regiments in field where headquarters were. *Polk* detains two of *Hood's* brigades, as *Hardee* on his left had not closed up a gap. Headquarters wagons sent beyond Cassville. Corps commanders and *Wheeler* arrive.

Instructions to change line. Generals *Johnston* and *Mackall* and *Polk* ride on high hill overlooking town and back from original line. New line marked out, and troops rapidly formed on it and along a ridge. Late in afternoon considerable skirmishing and artillery. Enemy's skirmishers occupied town. At one time confusion; wagons, artillery, and cavalry hasten back; noise, dust, and heat. Disorder checked; wagons made to halt. Consternation of citizens; many flee, leaving all; some take away few effects, some remain between hostile fires.

General *Mackall* and I remain several hours on roadside (Cassville and Cartersville road) . . . Governor *Harris* [of Tennessee, a volunteer aide] brings lunch. General *Johnston*, about 5 p.m. . . . rides down to *Hardee's*, leaving General *Mackall*; I remain. About 6 p.m. General

Mackall sets out to find our camp; meets the general and both go back to a field near road in rear of *Polk,* as skirmishing brisk. General *Johnston* tells Governor Harris he will be ready for and happy to receive enemy next day. *Wheeler* comes up; cavalry falls back behind Infantry. Dark ride to camp. By a muddy brook near General *Polk's* find supper ready and tents pitched. After supper General *Johnston* walks over to General *Polk.* . . . Soon General *Johnston* sends word by courier to send him two inspectors-general mounted; then one of *Polk's* staff officers brings word that all the staff must report mounted; I was directed to remain.

General *Mackall* returned to camping-place, where most all staff waited until about 2 a.m., when they rode to Cartersville, passing trains and artillery parked in field; all hurried off without regard to order. Reach Cartersville before day, troops come in after day. General *Johnston* comes up—all hurried over bridges, great confusion, caused by mixing trains and by trains which crossed first parking at river's edge and others winding around wrong roads; about 2,000 wagons crowded on bank. [*O.R.,* XXXVIII, pt. 3, pp. 982–984.]

Report of Gen Joseph E. Johnston, CSA (continued)

Soon after dark [on May 19] Lieutenant-Generals *Polk* and *Hood* together expressed to me decidedly the opinion formed upon the observation of the afternoon, that the Federal artillery would render their positions untenable the next day, and urged me to abandon the ground immediately and cross the Etowah. Lieutenant-General *Hardee,* whose position I thought the weakest, was confident that he could hold it.

The other two officers were so earnest, however, and so unwilling to depend on the ability of their corps to defend the ground, that I yielded, and the army crossed the Etowah on the 20th, a step which I have regretted ever since. [*O.R.,* XXXVIII, pt. 3, p. 616.]

There was no battle at Cassville except for a running "battle of the books," for in the coming years *Johnston* and *Hood* demonstrated greater animosity toward each other than they did toward the Yankees over what happened here. *Hood's* initial report mentions merely "some slight skirmishing" at Cassville [*O.R.,* XXXVIII, pt. 3, pp. 760–761], but in his final report of the campaign, written long after he had superseded *Johnston* in command of the Army of Tennessee, *Hood* boldly refuted his predecessor's version of events on May 19.

Report of Gen. John B. Hood, CSA, Commanding Army of Tennessee

After the army had arrived at Cassville I proposed to General *Johnston*, in the presence of Generals *Hardee* and *Polk*, to move back upon the enemy and attack him at or near Adairsville, urging as a reason that our three corps could move back, each upon a separate road, while the enemy had but one main road upon which he could approach that place. No conclusion was obtained. While Generals *Polk* and *Hardee* and myself were riding from General *Johnston's* headquarters the matter was further discussed; General *Polk* enthusiastically advocated, and General *Hardee* also favoring, the proposition. It was then suggested that we should return and still further urge the matter on General *Johnston*. We, however, concluded to delay till the morning.

The next morning while we were assembled at General *Johnston's* headquarters it was reported that the enemy was driving in the cavalry on the Adairsville road in front of *Polk's* position. *Polk's* corps was in line of battle, and my corps was in bivouac on his right. We all rode to the right of *Polk's* line, in front of my bivouac. *Hardee* soon left and went to his position, which was on the left, there being some report of the enemy in that direction. General *Johnston* said to me: "You can, if you desire, move your corps to the Canton road, and if Howard's corps is there you can attack it."

My troops were put in motion. At the head of the column I moved over to this road and found it in possession of our own dismounted cavalry, and no enemy there. While in motion a body of the enemy, which I supposed to be cavalry, made its appearance on the Canton road, in rear of the right of my original position. Major-General *Hindman* was then in that direction with his division to ascertain what force it was keeping the other two divisions in the vicinity of the Canton road. It was not a mistake (as General *Johnston* states) that the force appeared, as is shown from the fact that Major-General *Hindman* had men wounded from the small-arms and artillery fired from this body. [*O.R.,* XXXVIII, pt. 3, pp. 634–635.]

Writing long after the war, Maj. Gen. Oliver O. Howard suggested that "the force" that appeared to threaten *Hood's* right flank and rear on this occasion was Schofield's cavalry, under Stoneman, "which dismounted and acted as infantry," although he is mistaken in giving the date as May 18. If indeed it was Stoneman's cavalry that caused Hood to pull back on the following day, then Howard was correct in his assessment: "Stoneman deserved special recognition . . . for this good work" [*Autobiography of Oliver Otis Howard*, 2 vols. (New York: Baker and Taylor, 1907), vol. I, p. 532].

Report of Gen. John B. Hood (continued)

Maj. *James Hamilton*, of my staff, was sent to report to General *Johnston* the fact that the enemy had appeared on the Canton road. During Major *Hamilton's* absence Brigadier General *Mackall*, chief of staff, rode up in great haste and said that General *Johnston* directed that I should not separate myself so far from General *Polk*. I called his attention to where General *Polk's* right was resting, and informed him that I could easily form upon it, and orders were given to that effect, throwing back my right to look after this body, which turned out to be the enemy's cavalry.

Feeling that I had done all which General *Johnston* had given me liberty to do, I then rode to his headquarters, where General *Johnston* decided to take up his line on the ridge in rear of the one occupied by General *Polk,* a line which was enfiladed by heights, of which the enemy would at once possess himself, as was pointed out to General *Johnston* by Brigadier-General [*Francis A.*] *Shoup,* commanding the artillery. In a very short time thereafter the enemy placed his artillery on these heights and began to enfilade General *Polk's* line. Observing the effect upon the troops of this fire, I was convinced that the position was unsuited for defense. Accordingly, General *Polk* and myself said to General *Johnston* that our positions would prove untenable for defense, but that we were in as good position to advance upon the enemy as could be desired. We told him that if he did not intend to take the offensive he had better change our position. He accordingly ordered the army across the Etowah. [*O.R.*, XXXVIII, pt. 3, pp. 634–635.]

Upon reading *Hood's* report, *Johnston*—who had been superseded in command of the Army of Tennessee by *Hood,* and who was reappointed on February 23, 1865, to command of that army and the troops in the old Department of South Carolina, Georgia, and Florida—decided to prefer charges. Accordingly, on April 5, 1865, *Hood* was ordered to proceed to

Texas to await a court of inquiry. The war ended, however, before any official action could be taken.

Several months after the war, Sherman and Johnston had a chance meeting aboard a river steamer traveling from Memphis to Cairo. Sherman recorded the following.

> We were, of course, on the most friendly terms, and on our way up we talked over our battles again, played cards, and questioned each other as to particular parts of our mutual conduct of the game of war. I told *Johnston* that I had seen his order of preparation, in the nature of an address to his army, announcing his purpose . . . to accept battle at Cassville. *[Johnston* described how] . . . he had ridden over the ground, given to each corps commander his position, and orders to throw up parapets during the night, [and how] . . . *Hood* spoke of the ground assigned him as being enfiladed by our artillery, which *Johnston* disputed, when General *Polk* chimed in with the remark that General *Hood* was right. . . . General *Johnston* was surprised at this, for he understood General *Hood* to be one of those who professed to criticize his strategy, contending that instead of retreating, he should have risked a battle. General *Johnston* said he was provoked, accused them of having been in conference, with being beaten before battle, and added that he was unwilling to engage in a critical battle with an army so superior to his own in numbers, with two of his three corps commanders dissatisfied with the ground and positions assigned them. He then and there made up his mind to retreat still farther south [and] to put the Etowah River and the Allatoona range between us. [Sherman, *Memoirs*, II, 39–40.]

Five years later, when Sherman was visiting New Orleans, *Hood* called upon him to give *his* version of what had happened at Cassville. *Hood* claimed that he had argued against fighting the battle purely on the defensive and that he had asked permission to take his own corps and a portion of *Polk's* "to march rapidly to attack and overwhelm Schofield, who was known to be separated from Thomas by an interval of nearly five miles."

Hood said "he had then contended with *Johnston* for the 'offensive-defensive' game, instead of the 'pure defensive,' as proposed by *General Johnston*; and he said that it was at this time that *General Johnston* had taken offense, and that it was for this reason he had ordered the retreat that night" [Sherman, *Memoirs*, II, pp. 40–41].

Hood and Johnston both returned to the issue when writing their respective memoirs, and the facts (to borrow a phrase from Napoleon) seem destined to "remain in eternal litigation." Johnston cited letters from generals Hardee and Mackall to support his position, while Hood's evidence rested primarily on a document that, according to Professor Thomas Connelly, "was full of contradictions." In his authoritative history of the Army of Tennessee, Connelly concluded:

> Several people were at fault that night. Obviously Hood and Polk had arranged the conference beforehand, and had even attempted to accumulate some evidence of why they should not remain at Cassville. Hood was the more vocal of the two. The conference was somewhat reminiscent of Polk's old rump councils of war while Bragg was in command. Then, Polk and others had also made decisions without consulting the commander; the only difference was that in the former councils, the commanding general was absent during all deliberations.

Connelly faulted Johnston for making his decision "without consulting his second-in-command, Hardee," and Hardee recalled only that "when he expressed surprise at the retreat, Hood insisted the position could not be held" [Lawrence Connelly, *Autumn of Glory: The Army of Tennessee, 1862–1865* (Baton Rouge: Louisiana State University Press, 1971), pp. 350–352].

Narrative of Gen. Joseph E. Johnston, CSA, Commanding Army of Tennessee

Although the position was the best we had occupied, I yielded at last . . . and the position was abandoned before daybreak. The army was led to the Etowah, (near the railroad bridge), crossed it about noon, and bivouacked as near the river as was consistent with the comfort of the troops. The cavalry was placed in observation along the stream—Wheeler's above and Jackson's below the infantry.

Our loss in killed and wounded, not including the cavalry, from the commencement of the campaign to the passage of the Etowah, was, as shown by the report of the medical director of the army . . . 3,388 killed and wounded.

As the intervention of the river prevented close observation of the movements of the Federal army, Major-General *Wheeler* was directed to cross it on the 22d, five or six miles to our right, with all his troops not required for outpost duty, and move toward Cassville, to ascertain in what direction the Federal army was moving. He was instructed, also, to avail himself of all opportunities to inflict harm upon the enemy, by breaking the railroad and capturing or destroying trains and detachments.

He soon ascertained that the Federal army was moving westward, as if to cross the Etowah near Kingston. [*Military Operations*, pp. 324–326.]

Maj. Gen. William T. Sherman to Maj. Gen. H. W. Halleck, Washington, D.C., 19 May 1864

We entered Kingston this morning without opposition, and have pushed a column east as far as Cassville, skirmishing the latter part of the day with *Hardee's* corps. The enemy has retreated south of the Etowah. Tomorrow cars will move to this place, and I will replenish our stores and get ready for the Chattahoochee. The railroad passes through a range of hills at Allatoona, which is doubtless being prepared for us; but I have no intention of going through it. I apprehend more trouble from our long trains of wagons than from the fighting, though, of course, *Johnston* must fight hard for Atlanta. [*O.R.*, XXXVIII, pt. 4, p. 248.]

11. KINGSTON

Drive back down to the cemetery entrance and go straight ahead to return to Cassville on the same road you used to reach this site. Turn left at the Cassville Grocery and drive about 0.4 mile to Firetower Road. Turn right onto that road, follow it as it crosses U.S. 41, and stay on it for about 1.4 miles beyond that intersection until it terminates at Georgia Highway 293. Turn right onto that highway and follow it about 3.4 miles to Kingston. Turn left onto the first street on the edge of Kingston (Railroad Street), marked "Kingston Business District," paralleling the railroad tracks. Drive about 0.7 mile on this street, crossing Church Street at a stop sign and continuing through the business district. Then turn left to cross the railroad tracks at Johnson Street, drive one block, and turn right onto Main Street. Drive past the state historical marker for the Thomas V. B. Hargis House site and park in the lot on the right next to the ballfield. The text of the historical markers is of interest.

STOP 11, KINGSTON

20–24 May 1864

Narrative of Maj. Gen. William T. Sherman, USA, Commanding Military Division of the Mississippi

In early days (1844), when a lieutenant of the Third Artillery, I had been sent from Charleston, South Carolina, to Marietta, Georgia. . . . I had ridden the distance on horseback, and had noted well the topography of the country, especially that about Kennesaw, Allatoona, and the Etowah River.

I therefore knew that the Allatoona Pass was very strong, would be hard to force, and resolved not even to attempt it, but to turn the position, by moving from Kingston to Marietta via Dallas. . . . The country was very obscure, mostly in a state of nature, densely wooded, and with few roads. . . .

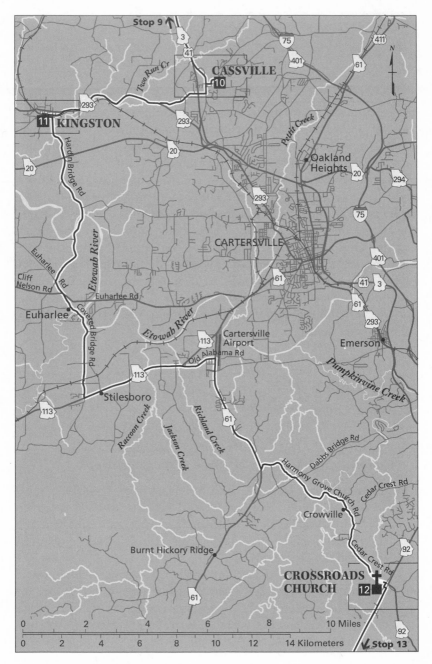

Cassville to Crossroads Church

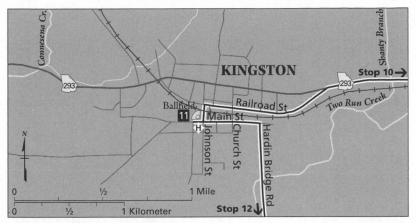

Kingston (Stop 11)

We crossed the Etowah by several bridges and fords, as many roads as possible, keeping up communication by crossroads or by couriers through the woods. I personally joined General Thomas, who had the centre, and was consequently the main column or "column of direction." The several columns followed generally the valley of the Euharlee, a tributary coming into the Etowah from the south, and gradually crossed over a ridge of mountains, parts of which had once been worked over for gold, and were consequently full of paths and unused wagon-roads or tracks.

A cavalry picket of the enemy at Burnt Hickory was captured, and had on his person an order from General *Johnston*, dated at Allatoona, which showed that he had detected my purpose of turning his position, and it accordingly became necessary to use great caution, lest some of the minor columns should fall into ambush, but, luckily, the enemy was not much more familiar with that part of the country than we were.

On the other side of the Allatoona range, the Pumpkin-Vine Creek, also a tributary of the Etowah, flowed north and west; Dallas, the point aimed at, was a small town on the . . . east side of this creek, and was the point of concentration of a great many roads that led in every direction. Its possession would be a threat to Marietta and Atlanta, but I could not then venture to attempt either, till I had regained the use of the railroad, at least as far down as its *debouche* from the Allatoona range of mountains. Therefore the movement was chiefly designed to compel *Johnston* to give up Allatoona.

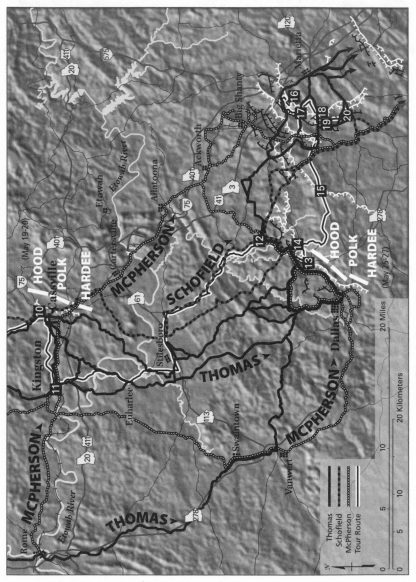

Movements, Major Positions, and Guidebook Stops: Kingston to Kennesaw Mountain

On the 25th all the columns were moving steadily on Dallas—
McPherson and Davis away off to the right, near Van Wert; Thomas
on the main road in the centre, with Hooker's Twentieth Corps ahead,
toward Dallas; and Schofield to the left rear. For the convenience of
march, Hooker had his three divisions on separate roads, all leading
toward Dallas, when, in the afternoon, as he approached a bridge
across Pumpkin-Vine Creek, he found it held by a cavalry force, which
was driven off, but the bridge was on fire. This fire was extinguished,
and Hooker's leading division (Geary's) followed the retreating cavalry on a road leading due east toward Marietta, instead of Dallas.
This leading division, about four miles out from the bridge, struck a
heavy force, which was moving down from Allatoona toward Dallas,
and a sharp battle ensued. I came up in person soon after, and as my
map showed that we were near an important cross-road called "New
Hope," from a Methodist meeting-house there of that name, I ordered
General Hooker to secure it if possible that night. [Sherman, *Memoirs*,
II, pp. 42–44.]

OPERATIONS

20–24 May 1864, Cassville to Cross-roads Church

Maj. Gen. W. T. Sherman to Maj. Gen. John M. Schofield,
USA, Commanding the Army of the Ohio, Kingston, 20
May 1864, 1:15 a.m.

My instructions for you to move toward Cassville Depot were
based on my theory or supposition that after reaching the "divide"
on Gravelly Plateau, roads would divide naturally, one set leading to
Kingston and one to Cassville Depot. Knowing that Hooker would take
one toward Kingston, I wanted you to take one toward Cassville, with
some rapidity of movement, to increase the chances of interposing
between Etowah bridge and the enemy's falling back before Thomas'
head of column.

Yesterday I was very anxious that Stoneman or yourself should
reach the road from Kingston to Etowah, for I saw by the singular
maneuvering of the enemy and the confusion of his wagon trains,
how uneasy he was to prevent our capturing a part of his forces. Had
10,000 men reached the railroad any time after 10 a.m. of yesterday,

Remnants of Confederate earthworks near New Hope Church (Harold Nelson).

we should have had a signal success; whereas now *Johnston* will encourage his men by his skillfully saving his army and baggage in the face of such odds.

I know the difficulties of the roads and country. . . . I did expect to catch a part of the army retreating before us, but I take it for granted that is now impossible, and therefore wish simply to be assured that he has crossed the Etowah, and that he there awaits our attack through the difficult pass at Allatoona.

I do not propose to follow him through that pass, but rather to turn south from here, leaving Allatoona to the north and east. I wish, therefore, that today, the 20th, you move so as to strike the railroad east of Cassville, and then turn east and push the enemy past Carters-ville and across Etowah, or Hightower, bridge. I left Thomas' head of column at dark on the skirts of the village of Cassville; he is ordered to support your attack. I have no doubt that the ground is very dif-ficult between Cassville and the bridge, and that you can alone push back any force of the enemy remaining this side of the bridge. . . . I will have the [railroad] cars into Kingston and Cassville today; shall replenish wagons and then on. [*O.R.,* XXXVIII, pt. 4, p. 266.]

Schofield to Sherman, 20 May 1864, 5:15 a.m.

The theory upon which your orders were based yesterday morn-ing was correct, except the supposition that Hooker would take the road toward Kingston; he sent only one division on that road while the other two took the Cassville road.

8.45 p.m. We reached the Etowah about sunset, driving the en-emy's rear guard of infantry and cavalry across the river. At dark no force could be seen but a few sharpshooters on the opposite bank. The rebels fired the railroad bridge about noon; it is entirely destroyed. They also set fire to the wagon bridge as soon as they had crossed, and it is now burning. The enemy's resistance was feeble and our loss quite small. The enemy appears to have but slight defensive works from this side of the river, but I will reconnoiter more thoroughly in the morn-ing. [*O.R.,* XXXVIII, pt. 4, 266–267]

Maj. Gen. William T. Sherman to Maj. Gen. H. W. Halleck, Washington, D.C., 20 May 1864

We have secured two good bridges and an excellent ford across the Etowah. Our cars are now arriving with stores. I give two days' rest to replenish and fit up. On the 23d I will cross the Etowah and move on Dallas. This will turn Allatoona Pass. If *Johnston* remains at Allatoona I shall move on Marietta; but, if he falls behind the Chattahoochee,

I will make for Sandtown and Campbellton, but feign at the railroad crossing. General Davis' division occupies Rome, and finds a good deal of provisions and plunder, fine iron-works and machinery. I have ordered the Seventeenth Corps, General Blair, to march from Decatur to Rome. My share of militia should be sent at once to cover our lines of communication. Notify General Grant that I will hold all of *Johnston's* army too busy to send anything against him. [*O.R.*, XXXVIII, pt. 4, p. 260.]

Maj. Gen. George Thomas, USA, Commanding the Army of the Cumberland, to Maj. Gen. William T. Sherman, 20 May 1864

I have just returned from a visit to Cassville. I found that the enemy had a very strong position there, and had commenced a series of very formidable breast-works and batteries. Our move upon them yesterday was so unexpected that I am inclined to think they were so demoralized that they dared not remain to contend with us today. . . .

I am very glad you concluded to rest today, as the men are very tired, but in most excellent spirits. We shall all be ready by tomorrow, if the trains can bring up sufficient forage and subsistence. [*O.R.*, XXXVIII, pt. 4, p. 263.]

Special Field Orders No. 9, Headquarters, Military Division of the Mississippi, 20 May 1864

I. Major-General Thomas will group his army in and around Cassville, Major-General Schofield his at or near Pettit's Creek or along Nancy's Creek, and Major-General McPherson his at Kingston and the fords and bridges across the Etowah in that vicinity.

II. Each army commander will use his cavalry and staff officers freely in the next two days in collecting information, making maps, etc., and in preparing for the next grand move, full details of which will in due season be made known.

III. The cars now run to our very camps. Each army commander will send to the rear all wounded and sick, as also all worthless men and idlers that have turned up on this march. He will then make provisions to subsist his command independent of the railroad for twenty days.

IV. The whole army must be ready to march by May 23, stripped for battle, but equipped and provided for twenty days. At the same time the wagon trains should rather be diminished than increased, as we can safely rely on getting much meat, and forage, and vegetables in the country to which we propose to go.

V. The ration will be for troops, one pound of bread, flour, or meal, beef on the hoof, two days' allowance of bacon per week, and sugar, coffee, and salt; four pounds of grain will be allowed each animal and no more. All else must be gathered in the country. Brigade quartermasters and commissaries will be instructed to forage and graze, but indiscriminate plunder must not be allowed. [*O.R.*, XXXVIII, pt. 4, pp. 271–272.]

Sherman to Halleck, Kingston, 21 May, 8:30 p.m. (received 11:40 p.m.)

Weather very hot and roads dusty. We, nevertheless, by morning will have all our wagons loaded and be ready for a twenty days' expedition. I will leave a good brigade at Rome—a strong, good point; about 1,000 men to cover this point, but will keep no stores here to tempt an enemy until I have placed my army about Marietta, when I will cause the railroad to be repaired up to that point. I regard Resaca as the stronghold of my line of operations till I reach the Chattahoochee.

I have ordered the Seventeenth Corps to march from Decatur to Rome, and to this point, to act in reserve until I call it forward. Returned veterans and regiments have more than replaced all losses and detachments, and we move tomorrow with full 80,000 fighting men.

General McPherson crosses the Etowah, at the mouth of Connasene Creek, on a bridge, and moves for Dallas, via Van Wert. General Thomas crosses by a bridge, four miles southeast of Kingston, and moves for Dallas, via Euharlee and Huntsville. General Schofield crosses near Etowah Cliffs, on pontoons, and takes position on Thomas' left.

I allow three days to have the army grouped about Dallas, whence I can strike Marietta, or the Chattahoochee according to developments. You may not hear from us in some days, but be assured we are not idle or thoughtless. [*O.R.*, XXXVIII, pt. 4, p. 274.]

Special Field Orders No. 11, Headquarters, Military Division of the Mississippi, Kingston, 22 May 1864

I. General McPherson will cause the Seventeenth Army Corps, Major General Blair commanding, to march from Decatur to Rome and Kingston, and will garrison Rome with a force of about 2,000 men until further orders. General Thomas will garrison Kingston with a small force, say 1,000 men, well covered by earth-works or stone buildings. Resaca will be held strong, and will be the depot of supplies until further notice. Such stores and provisions will be kept forward at Kingston and Rome as can be moved by the wagons or the troops present and no more.

II. The several armies will move punctually tomorrow morning, provided, as heretofore ordered, by separate roads, aiming to reach the positions hereinafter assigned them in the course of the third day, and in the meantime each wing communicating freely with the center by cross-roads.

The Army of the Cumberland will move on Dallas by Euharlee and Stilesborough, the division of General Jeff. C. Davis, now at Rome, marching direct for Dallas by Van Wert.

The Army of the Ohio will move for position on the left, via Richland Creek and Burnt Hickory or Huntsville.

The Army of the Tennessee will move, via Van Wert, to a position on the right at or near the head of Pumpkin Vine Creek, south of Dallas.

III. Marietta is the objective point, and the enemy is supposed to be in force at Allatoona, but with cavalry all along the line of the Etowah. Henceforth great caution must be exercised to cover and protect trains. [O.R., XXXVIII, pt. 4, pp. 288–289.]

Maj. Gen. William T. Sherman to Maj. Gen. Francis P. Blair, USA, Commanding Seventeenth Army Corps, Army of the Tennessee, 23 May 1864

We are now all in motion for the Chattahoochee. . . . Although you must move on Rome and Kingston by the direct road, still you can make believe you have designs on Gadsden and Talledega [a?]. Keep silent and the enemy will exaggerate your strength and purpose. *Johnston* has called to him all the infantry of the Southwest and also the cavalry of Mississippi, so you must watch out for them. [O.R., XXXVIII, pt. 4, p. 298.]

12. THE CONFEDERATE MOVE FROM THE ETOWAH RIVER

Return to Main Street and retrace it for approximately 0.3 mile until you reach the stop sign at Hardin Bridge Road. Turn right. After driving about 1.4 miles on Hardin Bridge Road, you will reach a traffic signal where it crosses U.S. 411/GA 20. Check your mileage there, cross the highway on the Hardin Bridge Road, and drive 4.6 miles beyond the intersection. You will cross the Etowah River during this drive.

At about 4.6 miles, you will come to the intersection with Euharlee Road. Turn left onto this road. Drive slightly more than 0.5 mile to a "Y"-shaped intersection and take the right fork onto Covered Bridge Road. Follow this road about 3.6 miles to the intersection with Georgia Highway 113. Turn left onto this highway. Drive about 3.4 miles, to the point where a secondary road enters from the right front as GA 113 curves left. Bear right onto the secondary road (Old Alabama Road) and follow it about 1.1 miles to the intersection with Georgia Highway 61. Check your mileage as you turn right onto that highway. Follow GA 61 about 4 miles, and then turn left onto Harmony Grove Church Road. After driving about 1.4 miles on this road you will cross the Dabbs Bridge Road. Continue another 1.3 miles to cross Pumpkinvine Creek. About 0.7 mile beyond the bridge, the road forks. Follow the right fork and drive an additional 1 mile to a "T" intersection with Cedar Crest Road. Turn right onto Cedar Crest and drive about 2.5 miles to Old Dallas-Acworth Road (about one block short of the stop sign on modern Georgia Highway 381). Turn right and stop in front of the Crossroads Church.

During the drive from Stop 11, the route parallels the move of Maj. Gen. John M. Schofield's Army of the Ohio. Most of the roads were in place in 1864, but the majority were little better than farm lanes. This stop brings us to one of the main routes used by Gen. *Joseph E. Johnston's* Army of Tennessee. Crossroads Church is adjacent to the old road—the modern highway is a "bypass" in this sector, but it still follows the old roadbed through much of its length as it carries today's traffic from the area around Allatoona and Ackworth to Dallas. Travelers continuing in the same direction you have been driving would arrive in Marietta, making this a significant crossroads in 1864.

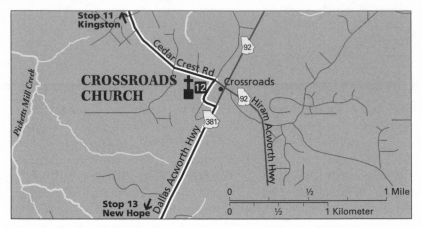

Crossroads Church (Stop 12)

STOP 12, CROSSROADS CHURCH

20–25 May, 1864

Journal of Operations, Army of Tennessee

20 May: Confusion, hurrying wagons and artillery across Etowah bridge. Supply train parked on plain on south side: two pontoon bridges, one wagon trestle bridge, one railroad bridge, wagons and artillery blocked up on road; trains mixed. Dust and heat, country rough and hilly, little water near railroad. . . . Wagons move toward Allatoona on two roads. After great delay trains removed out of range.

In afternoon headquarters established near Moore's house (*Hardee's* headquarters), near a crossing of railroad and lower Allatoona road, one mile and a half from Allatoona. Etowah Iron Works—most valuable machinery, teams, wagons, and negroes removed by G. W. Smith. Bridges burned in p.m. including railroad bridge by mistake.

Troops jaded, artillery and cavalry horses particularly; Georgia troops dropped off; all in pretty good spirits up to falling back from Cassville. Change of line not understood but thought all right, but night retreat after issuing general order impaired confidence; great alarm in county around. Troops think no stand to be made north of Chattahoochee, where supply train is sent. . . .

22 May: Enemy fortifying on both sides of river at Gillem's Bridge; their cavalry had gone out several miles to Stilesborough; inquired minutely about roads; said that today an army of 150,000 (?) strong would march out on Cedartown road to Atlanta; expected but little opposition, thinking this army utterly demoralized. . . . *Jackson's* division cavalry picketing river below as far as Rome; *Wheeler's* above as far as Canton. . . .

At 3.30 p.m. lieutenant generals and chief of artillery notified to have everything in readiness to move at moment's notice. . . . Guides obtained for country south of Etowah and west of railroad. Two bridges being built over Pumpkin Vine Creek, and road made, cutting off considerable distance in moving down river. Country hilly and rocky. Heat oppressive and road dusty. Many disloyal people in this section.

23 May: Heavy columns of dust and of infantry and wagons seen moving on north bank of Etowah toward our left. . . . *Ferguson* reported infantry having crossed. During day *Hardee* moved ten miles southwest, and *Polk* moved on road from Allatoona to Dallas. *Hood* still watching crossings near railroad. At night orders reiterated for *Hardee* to move to Dallas and Atlanta road, and *Polk* to do same and communicate. . . . [*Hardee*] was to take position near intersection of road on which he was, with Atlanta and Dallas road, and protect it, supported by General *Polk*. *Armstrong's* cavalry, in moving farther to left, strangely had fallen back to Burnt Hickory, leaving enemy's cavalry unobserved. *Armstrong* told of utmost importance to . . . observe enemy closely. Immediate information necessary. *Jackson's* [cavalry] commanders think main Yankee army west of our position, from Milam's Bridge to Rome. . . . *Wheeler* told to observe particularly what force could march directly from Cartersville on Allatoona.

24 May: (Near Moore's house, one mile and a half to Allatoona.) All ready to move to *Polk's* command. . . . All rode from headquarters near Bartow Furnace (near Moore's) to Powder Mill and Dallas Road, and camped at night on the road four miles from Dallas. *Hood* moved his troops by afternoon nearer Dallas from Etowah bridge, and headquartered where *Hardee's* had been the night before, at Doctor Smith's. *Hardee* at night camped in supporting distance of Dallas. *Polk* camped on Marietta and Dallas road.

In afternoon four of enemy's cavalry run into lines of a brigade at Dallas and carry off some of our men; not a gun loaded. *Jackson's* opinion that main army of enemy approaching Dallas and one corps

"Battle of Allatoona, Georgia, October 5, 1864." The message "Hold the fort, for I am coming!" signaled from Kennesaw Mountain to these heights, gave rise to the famous gospel hymn (engraving by A. R. Waud in Joseph M. Brown, *The Mountain Campaigns in Georgia* [Buffalo: Matthews, Northrup Co., 1886], 37).

and 2,500 cavalry going by Villa Rica. This information sent to *Hood*, who is told to move early in morning, that his advance may reach New Hope Church (on Allatoona and Dallas road) about four miles and a half from Robinson's, in order to guard against separation. *Polk* is to move up on Marietta and Dallas road to Robinson's. Join hands to be ready to fight. . . .

25 May. (5.30 p.m., at Robertson's house, four miles south of Dallas, near intersection of road from Marietta, Atlanta, and Allatoona to Dallas.) Half hour ago few discharges of artillery near New Hope Church, where *Hood* is, three miles distant. Prisoner says Hooker's corps is in front of him. General *Johnston* rode there an hour ago. We have been waiting here nearly all day. Few developments of enemy. Reports of their having crossed Pumpkin Vine Creek; citizens think moving around our left. All quiet in front of Dallas. This morning all

Allatoona Pass viewed from Confederate positions guarding the railroad bridge on the Etowah near Cassville (MOLLUS).

of *Hardee's* division in line. *Polk* got in wrong place. . . . *Stewart's* division repulsed Hooker's corps. [*O.R.*, XXXVIII, pt. 3, pp. 986–987.]

Narrative of Gen. Joseph E. Johnston, CSA, Commanding Army of Tennessee

Jackson had given information of General Sherman's march toward the bridges near Stilesboro, and of the crossing of the leading Federal troops there on the 23d. In consequence of this intelligence, Lieutenant-General *Hardee* was ordered to march that afternoon, by New Hope Church, to the road leading from Stilesboro, through Dallas, to Atlanta; and Lieutenant General *Polk* to move to the same road, by a route farther to the left. Lieutenant-General *Hood* was instructed to follow *Hardee* on the 24th. *Hardee's* corps reached the point designated to him that afternoon; *Polk's* was within four or five miles of it to the east, and *Hood's* within four miles of New Hope Church, on the road . . . from Allatoona. On the 25th the latter reached New Hope Church, early in the day. Intelligence was received from General *Jackson's* troops soon after that the Federal army was near—its right at

Dallas, and its line extending toward Allatoona. Lieutenant-General *Hood* was immediately instructed to form his corps parallel with the road by which he had marched, and west of it, with the centre opposite to the church; Lieutenant-General *Polk* to place his in line with it, on the left, and Lieutenant-General *Hardee* to occupy a ridge extending from the ground allotted to *Polk's* corps, across the road leading from Dallas toward Atlanta—his left division, *Bate's*, holding that road.

As soon as his troops were in position, Lieutenant General *Hood*, to "develop the enemy," sent forward Colonel *Bush Jones* with his regiment (the united Thirty-second and Fifty-eighth Alabama) and [Maj. *John E.*] *Austin's* sharpshooters, in all about three hundred men. After advancing about a mile, this detachment encountered Hooker's Twentieth corps. Having the written order of his corps commander to hold his ground after meeting the enemy, Colonel *Jones* resisted resolutely the attack of overwhelming Federal forces. But after a . . . fight . . . so gallant . . . that the commander of Hooker's leading division thought that he was engaged with a brigade, at least, he was . . . driven back to his division—*Stewart's*. [*Military Operations*, pp. 326–327.]

13. NEW HOPE CHURCH AND THE DALLAS LINE

From Crossroads Church, drive straight ahead to the next intersection (with Old Dallas-Acworth Extension) and turn left. Drive one block to the stop sign at the intersection with GA 381. Turn right onto this highway and drive about 4.1 miles to New Hope Baptist Church. Turn left onto Bobo Road and immediately left again onto Hosiery Mill Road to park in the lot beyond the church. Use the map at the historical markers to aid in orientation. In addition to the familiar Atlanta campaign orientation site, across Bobo Road there is a Confederate memorial site near reconstructed sections of Confederate breastworks.

OPERATIONS

When Sherman's army crossed the Etowah River on May 23, the Atlanta campaign entered a new phase. Previously his purpose had always been to turn or outflank *Johnston's* army by threatening the railroad in his rear. Now, with Allatoona Pass in the hands of the Confederates, he decided to leave the railroad and strike out cross-country for Marietta. With him were 80,000 fighting men and supplies in his wagons sufficient for twenty days. In three days he hoped to have his columns grouped about Dallas, from which point he could strike Marietta or the Chattahoochee "according to developments."

But even before Sherman's entire army had crossed the river, *Johnston*—acting on information from his cavalry—sent *Hardee's* corps to a road intersection about ten miles south of Dallas, with *Polk's* corps following along a parallel route to the left. On May 24, when his corps reached the Marietta road, *Hardee* was ordered northward to strike Union forces reportedly concentrating in that area. On the 25th, *Hood's* corps, which had been a day's march behind *Hardee*, reached the vicinity of New Hope Church, about five miles northeast of Dallas. As soon as his troops were in position—*Hindman's* division on the left, *Stewart* in the center near New Hope Church, and *Stevenson* on the right—*Hood* sent a regiment forward to make contact with the enemy, known to be moving steadily on Dallas. *Polk's* corps got into position on a commanding ridge between *Hood* and *Hardee* later that night.

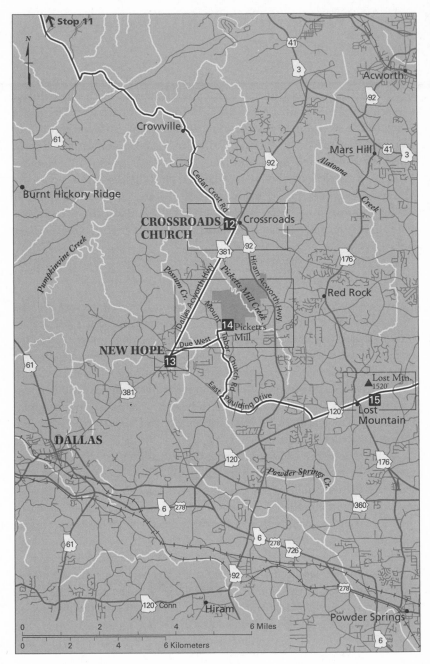

Crossroads Church to Lost Mountain

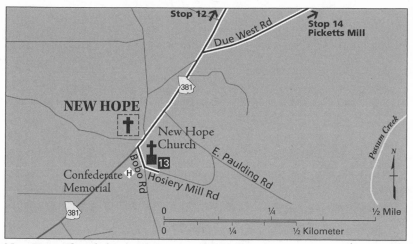

New Hope Church (Stop 13)

Sherman's army advanced in separate columns—McPherson's Army of the Tennessee off to the west, near Van Vert; Thomas's Army of the Cumberland in the center, along the main road to Dallas; and Schofield's Army of the Ohio to the left rear. Hooker's 20th Corps, of the Army of the Cumberland, was in the lead, his three divisions advancing on roughly parallel roads—Butterfield's division on the left, Geary in the center, and Williams to the right. From his cavalry preceding the infantry columns, Thomas learned on May 24 that Confederates were moving in the direction of Dallas and had already clashed with one of his cavalry divisions near Pumpkin Vine Creek.

Sherman had initially planned for Thomas to move straight on Dallas, but Confederate cavalry had burned the bridge across Pumpkin Vine Creek about three miles north of that important crossroad, and so he ordered Thomas to veer to the left and cross by a bridge a mile downstream that was still intact. Late on the morning of the 25th, Geary's division encountered a Confederate cavalry outpost near Owen's Mill, on Pumpkin Vine Creek. Brushing it aside, Geary's lead brigade, commanded by Col. Charles Candy, advanced another three miles and met two Alabama regiments under Col. *Bushrod Jones.* Supported by Geary's other two brigades, Candy attacked and drove the Confederates perhaps another mile to *Hood's* main line a short distance north of New Hope Church. Learning that *Hood's* entire corps was in his front, and that *Hardee's* corps was not far off, in the

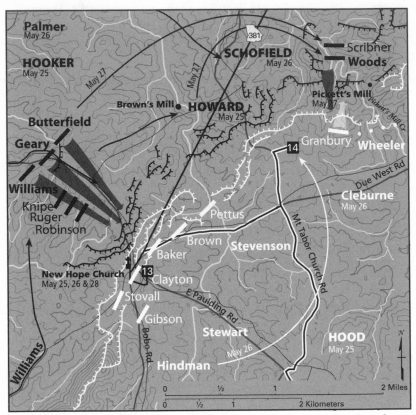

Positions, Movements, and Major Attacks around New Hope Church and Pickett's Mill

direction of Dallas, and aware that there were no supporting troops within five miles, Geary halted on a ridge in the woods and entrenched. Meanwhile, Hooker, the corps commander, ordered Butterfield and Williams to march their divisions to the scene.

By late afternoon both divisions had come up and massed for an attack, Williams to the right of Geary and Butterfield on his left. The terrain was intersected by small ravines and covered by dense woods with considerable underbrush. As Williams's division advanced in three lines, each a brigade front, the troops could scarcely see the main Confederate works, although they were exposed every step of the way to a continuous fire of canister and shrapnel. Geary's division and two of Butterfield's brigades also participated in this action against Maj. Gen. A. P. Stewart's division,

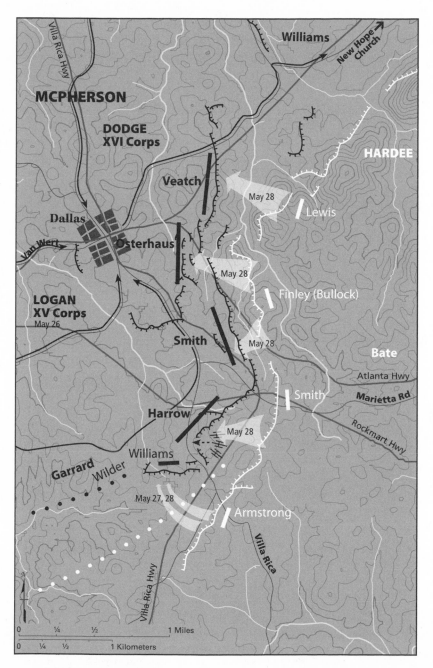

Positions and Major Attacks around Dallas

which held the center of *Hood's* line. Hooker's troops were repulsed at all points, although the leading line had penetrated to within twenty-five or thirty paces of the Confederate works before being forced to fall back and entrench. The Confederates here lost 300 to 400 men; Hooker reported losses of 1,665 in this action.

Breastworks were thrown up as fast as possible during the night. Howard's 4th Corps moved into position on Hooker's left during the night, prolonging the line beyond Brown's Mills, and the next morning the leading division of Palmer's 14th Corps reached the scene and was posted in reserve. By the night of the 26th, Schofield's Army of the Ohio arrived to extend Howard's line to the left. To meet this threat, *Hood* was forced to pull *Hindman's* division from the left of his line and move it around to the right.

For the next five days the fighting around New Hope Church, known to the men as "the hell hole," was incessant. Although little could be seen through the dense woods, the lines were so close to each other that the troops were constantly under fire. Even at night there would be gusts of artillery and small-arms fire, keeping the men of both armies constantly on the alert while detachments labored to strengthen the breastworks. In one rifle-pit alone twenty-one Union soldiers were picked off by Confederate sharpshooters in a single day. The Confederates, entrenched on higher ground, enjoyed the advantage of position, while Sherman's superior artillery and ability to maneuver were generally negated by the circumstances.

At first Sherman assumed that he had only *Hood's* corps in his front, and he ordered McPherson to move into Dallas, link up with Davis's division of Palmer's 14th Corps, and then move toward New Hope Church to hit *Hood's* left flank. As Logan's 15th Corps entered and moved south through Dallas on the Powder Springs road, however, it ran into *Hardee's* corps behind strong field works that extended across the Powder Springs and Marietta roads. McPherson's men threw up a line of works during the night. "I shall move against them in the morning," McPherson assured Sherman. "I will expect to hear of you on General Hooker's right before 10 a.m.," was the reply. But the next morning, May 27, Sherman ordered McPherson to use the Marietta road and edge toward Hooker's right flank. It would be more effective, he decided, to move around *Johnston's* right flank and place his concentrated army between the Confederates and the railroad.

Accordingly, on the 27th Hooker's and Howard's corps, supported by heavy artillery fire, pressed against *Hood*, while two divisions, one each

A section of the Confederate line near New Hope Church (MOLLUS).

from the 4th and the 14th corps, moved behind Schofield's line and then swung to the right to hit the exposed right flank of *Hood's* line. The day before, however, *Johnston* had transferred *Cleburne's* division from *Hardee's* line to the right of *Hood,* and as the Union divisions approached, *Cleburne* deployed quickly into line.

The ensuing battle at Pickett's Mill was the bloodiest thus far in the campaign. Sherman never mentioned the battle specifically in his official report: to him it was but another phase in a relentless effort to pry the enemy out of his fortified line that now stretched unbroken from Dallas to Pickett's Mill. As he reported the next morning to Maj. Gen. H. W. Halleck, the chief of staff in Washington: "I am gradually working round by the left to approach the railroad anywhere in front of Acworth. Country very densely wooded and broken. No roads of any consequence. We have had many sharp, severe encounters, but nothing decisive. Both sides duly cautious in the obscurity of the ambushed ground."

The final act in this phase of the campaign occurred at Dallas on May 28, when Maj. Gen. *William P. Bate's* division, on the left of *Hardee's* corps, stormed out of its trenches late in the afternoon to assault McPherson's force in his front. "Fortunately," Sherman noted, "our men had erected good breast-works, and gave the enemy a terrible and bloody repulse." Line after line advanced against the Union works. The fighting was fierce enough to convince Logan that *Hardee's* entire corps was involved. But everywhere the Union troops held, and in about two hours *Bate's* men fell back, leaving over 300 dead on the field. Although the attack did delay McPherson's efforts to disengage and reunite with the Army of the Cumberland near New Hope Church, as ordered, it affected only the timing, not the direction, of Sherman's next move.

On June 1 all three Union armies slid a few miles to the left. By June 4, Union cavalry occupied Allatoona Pass. With the bridges completed over the Etowah, Sherman was now in position to sidestep *Johnston*, link up with the railroad, and push on to Marietta and the Chattahoochee.

STOP 13, NEW HOPE CHURCH

25 May–1 June 1864

Report of Maj. Gen. George H. Thomas, USA, Commanding Army of the Cumberland

On the 25th the First Division of Cavalry (McCook's) moved on the road leading to Golgotha, preceding Butterfield's division, of the Twentieth Corps. The balance of General Hooker's command advanced on the road leading to Dallas running south of the one used by Butterfield's division. Howard's corps followed Hooker's, and in rear of Howard, Palmer's.

About 11 a.m. General Geary's division, of the Twentieth Corps, being in advance, came upon the enemy in considerable force at a point about four and a half miles from Dallas, the country on both sides of the road being thickly wooded and covered with undergrowth. Geary skirmished heavily with the enemy, slowly driving him, until Butterfield's and Williams' divisions came up and relieved Geary's troops. Soon after the arrival of Williams, about 3 p.m., the column was again put in motion, Williams' division in advance, and, although heavily engaged, drove the enemy steadily before it into his entrenchments. Our loss was heavy, but it is believed that the loss of the enemy was much greater.

Shortly after 3 p.m. the head of Howard's column got within supporting distance of Hooker's corps, and Newton's division was placed in position on Hooker's left about 6 p.m., and by morning the whole of Howard's corps was in position on the left of Hooker. The roads were so full of wagons that Palmer's [Fourteenth] corps could not get into position by night of the 25th, but on the morning of the 26th Johnson's division, of the Fourteenth Corps, was moved up to within a short distance of Hooker's and Howard's commands, and was posted in reserve.

McCook's division of cavalry met the enemy's cavalry on the road leading from Burnt Hickory to Marietta near its intersection with the lower Dallas and Allatoona road. McCook's troops skirmished heavily with the force opposing them, inflicting on them considerable loss and capturing 52 prisoners, from whom it was ascertained that the whole of *Wheeler's* cavalry was posted on the right of the rebel army. The left of General Howard's corps was swung around to the right, occupying a line of hills running nearly perpendicular to the line occupied by Hooker on the 25th, thereby threatening the enemy's right. The Twenty-third Army Corps, Major-General Schofield commanding, was posted on the left of my command . . . covering the road leading from Allatoona to Dallas, via New Hope Church. . . . In the meantime trains were brought up and rations and ammunition issued where practicable. Strong breast-works were thrown up all along the line, the men working cheerfully and prepared to resist any attack the enemy might see fit to make. [*O.R.*, XXXVIII, pt. 1, pp. 143–144.]

THE BATTLE BEGINS

Report of Brig. Gen. John W. Geary, USA, Commanding Second Division, Twentieth Army Corps, Army of the Cumberland

May 25, at 7 a.m. I marched with my command, taking the road to Dallas via bridge across Pumpkin Vine Creek at Owen's Mill. Williams' and Butterfield's divisions, moving respectively, by roads on my right and left, were to cross the creek by other bridges. . . . The major-general commanding corps and myself, with our staffs and escort, preceded the troops to the bridge at Owen's Mill, which we found burning. . . . While engaged in extinguishing the flames and repairing the bridge we were fired upon from the hill opposite. . . . A portion of Major-General Hooker's cavalry escort fording the creek, deployed and advanced . . . through the woods, driving before them a short distance . . . an outpost of twenty-five cavalrymen. My infantry soon came up, and the repairs to the bridge being finished by the pioneer corps, the entire division crossed; the Seventh Ohio Volunteers preceding, deployed as skirmishers, advanced rapidly in the direction of New Hope Church, Candy's brigade leading.

Near Hawkins' house, one and a half miles from the bridge, our skirmishers became heavily engaged with those of the enemy, and almost immediately a furious charge was made upon us. . . . Candy's brigade was deployed into line on the double-quick, and after a sharp engagement the charge was repulsed. The skirmish line was now reenforced and extended to the length of a mile by the Twenty-eighth Pennsylvania Volunteers. The remaining four regiments of Candy's brigade were deployed in line of battle, and, supported by my other two brigades, moved forward, attacking and driving steadily for half a mile a heavy force of *Hood's* corps. . . . From prisoners captured we learned that *Hood's* entire corps was in our front, and *Hardee's* not far off, in the direction of Dallas. My division was isolated, at least five miles from the nearest supporting troops, and had been sustaining a sharp conflict . . . for four hours. . . .

My command was, by order of the major-general commanding the corps (who was with me), halted and formed on a ridge in the woods, advantageous for defense, and a slight barricade of logs hastily thrown up. My skirmish lines were deployed to a still greater extent than before, and ordered to keep up an aggressive fire, the object being to deceive the enemy as to our weakness by a show of strength. During this halt a charge made by a brigade of the enemy in column upon that part of my skirmish line occupied by the Seventh Ohio . . . was handsomely repulsed. The skirmish line there formed nearly a right angle toward the enemy, who charged upon the center line, not seeing that [line] upon their flank. When the three regiments neared the angle they were met by a sharp fire in front and a heavy enfilading fire from their left flank, and retreated in hasty disorder and with considerable loss. [*O.R.*, XXXVIII, pt. 2, pp. 122–123.]

Report of Col. Bushrod Jones, CSA, Commanding Thirty-Second and Fifty-Eighth Alabama Infantry, Clayton's Brigade, Stewart's Division, Hood's Corps, Army of Tennessee

On the morning of the 25th, . . . while the brigade was halted near New Hope Church, my regiment was detached from the brigade, and I received orders to advance westwardly along a road which was indicated to me by Lieutenant *Mathes* of General *Stewart's* staff. After advancing a short distance, while halting to have a company of skirmishers deployed in my front, I was notified that my flanks would be protected by cavalry. Colonel *Cunningham*, of General *Hood's* staff, told me that General *Hood* wished me to advance along that road and drive the enemy back; that they were only mounted infantry and in small force. . . . In obedience to this order . . . I moved steadily forward, under a very light skirmish fire, for nearly a mile. Arrived at this point, the skirmishers of the enemy made a stubborn resistance. I halted my regiment, as the cavalry were driven back, uncovering my left flank, until *Austin's* battalion was deployed on my left. I received during this time several messages from Colonel *Jones*, commanding cavalry, that the enemy were advancing in line of battle and flanking me on the left. I requested Lieutenant *Mathes* to inform General *Stewart* that the enemy were in heavy force in my front, and that I had [advanced] as far as practicable with my force, then only 250 men.

An officer of General *Hood's* staff (a major) then rode up and read to me the written instructions of General *Hood* to the officers in front to press vigorously forward, make the enemy develop their strength, and then to hold the position. I was satisfied that the force advancing on me in line of battle was largely disproportionate to my own, and that I could make but a feeble resistance. My skirmishers were driven slowly back . . . contesting the ground bravely. *Austin's* skirmishers were driven back from my left, when I ordered my regiment to charge the advancing line of the enemy.

The charge was made with spirit and vigor, and broke the regiment in my front. As I ordered the charge *Austin's* skirmishers, who had been driven back about fifty yards, rallied and returned to the charge, but they were again soon repulsed. My regiment held a good position on the crest of a small hill, and poured a very heavy fire into the enemy for ten or fifteen minutes; but one regiment of the enemy that overlapped my right pressed forward, enfilading my right, as did also the line of battle extending several hundred yards beyond my left. I ordered a retreat barely in time to escape the capture of the entire regiment; but the losses in killed, wounded, and missing were again very heavy, being equal to the average losses of a heavy battle. Retreating in the best order practicable, I had most of my wounded brought off the field, and kept my command intact. . . .

I had advanced as far as I deemed practicable, and would have re-tired without engaging the enemy's line of battle if I had not received written and positive orders to hold my position. I thought the best means of holding it was to meet an attack by a counter attack. . . . My command behaved with rare and exemplary gallantry. . . . They charged with the courage of a forlorn hope and held their ground until ordered to retreat, and I believe that if I had resisted a few minutes longer my entire regiment would have been captured.

I reported in person to General *Stewart* immediately afterward my opinion as to the force and position of the enemy. I was ordered to report temporarily to General *Gibson,* and made a second advance over a part of the same ground without an engagement. Subsequently, about 4 p.m., I was ordered to report back to General *Clayton,* and was placed in reserve in rear of his line of breastworks. [*O.R.,* XXXVIII, pt. 3, pp. 843–844.]

Report of Brig. Gen. John W. Geary, USA (continued)

Orders had been sent . . . by the major-general commanding corps to Generals Butterfield and Williams to march their divisions to the point where mine was engaged. By 5 p.m. both had come up and massed, Williams on my right and Butterfield on my left and rear. Each division was quickly formed for attacks in columns by brigades, Williams leading, Butterfield next, my division as a reserve, and the corps advanced upon the enemy. In the advance Butterfield's brigades moved toward the flanks, leaving me in support of Williams, who had been heavily engaged, driving the enemy some distance.

I received orders to push forward and relieve his troops . . . be-tween 6 and 7 p.m. The movement . . . was made with great rapidity, through a dense woods, swept by a very heavy artillery and musketry fire. The discharges of canister and shell from the enemy were heavier than in any other battle of the campaign in which my command were engaged. The troops of General Williams' division were relieved by this movement, and [Col. George A.] Cobham [Jr.]'s brigade and portions of Candy's brigade engaged the enemy furiously at short range, driving him again until after dark, when my command was halted close un-der the enemy's batteries and entrenchments near New Hope Church. The night was intensely dark, and a very severe thunder-storm, with cold, pelting rain, added to the gloom. It was therefore impossible to form a regular line with the troops, and all the dispositions of them we could make was by the fitful flashes of lightning. Breast-works were thrown up as fast as possible during the night, and the dead and wounded were all cared for before morning. [*O.R.*, XXXVIII, pt. 2, pp. 122–124.]

THE "HELL HOLE"

Narrative of Brig. Gen. Alpheus S. Williams, USA, Commanding First Division, Twentieth Army Corps, Army of the Cumberland

May 25. My orders were to move in advance of Dallas and encamp to the right. I took a road leading south of the direct road; had rebuilt a bridge over Pumpkin Vine Creek, destroyed by the Rebels, and was within a mile of Dallas when an order came to me to countermarch and move back across the creek to the direct road to support Geary's division. He had met the enemy in force, and apprehended trouble. It was about 2 P.M., the day very hot, and my men much fatigued. Back I turned, and after a march of six miles or more came up with Butterfield and Geary's divisions occupying both sides of the direct route from Burnt Hickory to Dallas, four miles or more south of Pumpkin Vine Creek.

They were in dense woods with considerable underbrush and the ground full of small ravines enclosed in gently swelling hills, which evidently grew higher in front and [on which] was the entrenched line of the enemy. We could see but a few rods in front, but the constant rattle of the skirmish line showed that we had a stout enemy before us. I was ordered to the front with my division and told that I was to push forward and drive the enemy until I found out his force or chased him away from our front.

I formed in three lines of brigade front, the 3rd, Robinson's brigade, leading, next Ruger's, and last Knipe's. Two regiments were thrown forward as skirmishers. The bugles sounded the "forward" and on went the three lines in beautiful order, though the ground was broken, bushy, and covered with small stones. I followed just behind the leading line. We met the heavy supports of the Rebels in a few moments and the volleys of infantry firing became intense. Our lines never halted. As the opposition became intensified, I sounded the "double-quick" and all three lines pounded forward on the trot and the Rebels traveled back quite as quick. Soon we got within range of the enemy's artillery and they poured into us canister and shrapnel from all directions except the rear.

My front line, after advancing a mile and a half or more, brought up against the enemy's entrenched line. They had expended pretty much all their ammunition, sixty rounds per man. I sent forward the second line to relieve it, and they expended their ammunition, and Knipe's line was sent to replace it, and thus under continuous shot and shell we held the line close up to the enemy's entrenchments until my whole division had nearly expended its ammunition.

After dark we were relieved by troops of Geary's and Butterfield's divisions and I withdrew my division some three or four hundred yards to the rear. Rain began falling. I found the campfire of Gen. Newton, where I met many general officers. . . . Everybody congratulated me on the splendid manner my division made the advance. Gen. Hooker said to me, "it was the most magnificent sight of the war;" that in all his experience he has never seen anything so splendid. He has induced Dory Davis, the artist of Harper's, to make a sketch of it. . . . I lost about 800 men killed and wounded. . . .

We have been here now five days and have not advanced an inch beyond the point my division reached. On some points the troops sent to relieve us did not hold, and some of our dead lie there unburied. There is a constant rattle and has been all these five days on the skirmish line, and now and then tremendous volleys are poured in from one side or the other. Several batteries have been placed in the front in as favorable points as the woods and ground will admit. They occasionally join in the tumult of sounds.

On the 26th we opened with all our guns in position for three hours. I think Gen. Sherman intended to charge their lines. He probably came to the conclusion that the whole Rebel force, with strong reinforcements, were in front strongly posted and entrenched. Two nights ago they came out in some force to attack our position, not more than four hundred yards in front of where my division lies. There was a tremendous hubbub stirred up of infantry and artillery all along our front, extending for miles both ways. I had several men wounded by glancing balls. We have these affairs almost every night and there is not a minute of the twenty-four hours that popping is not going on. . . . I have been along the skirmish line several times. Little can be seen through the dense forest. On the extreme right of our corps, from a hill I can see a long line of entrenched hills. The Rebs. have evidently a strong place and I suppose have collected all their forces in the South to give us a final testing. . . . I suppose we shall move somewhere soon. It is a very tedious and worrying life as we are situated, for we are kept constantly on the *qui vive* ready for battle. Our rest, you can well fancy, is not of the most refreshing kind. We have had no mails since leaving Rossville. [Quaife, ed., *From the Cannon's Mouth*, pp. 312–314.]

Although the western armies frequently had resorted to earthworks to strengthen positions since the first operations around Tunnel Hill and Dalton, New Hope Church marks the first occasion on this campaign when opposing lines were in such close proximity that troops were almost constantly under fire. There was nothing new in the mere employment of entrenchments on the battlefield, for armies had constructed redoubts and fortified lines in the field long before the Civil War. The unique feature of Civil War entrenchments—and for the western armies it starts here—"lay in their habitual and almost universal use, and in their being constructed generally in the presence of the enemy, often under a musketry fire of an intensity and destructiveness never before known" [Maj. Arthur L. Wagner, "Hasty Entrenchments in the War of Secession," *Papers of the Military Historical Society of Massachusetts*. Vol. XIII, *Civil and Mexican Wars, 1861, 1846* (Boston: Military Historical Society of Massachusetts, 1913), pp. 130, 145].

After New Hope Church, both armies instinctively resorted to hasty entrenchments to increase their defensive power. In his *Memoirs* Sherman recalled:

> Very few of the battles . . . were fought as described in European text-books, viz., in great masses, in perfect order, manoeuvring by corps, divisions, and brigades. We were generally in a wooded county, and though our lines were deployed according to tactics, the men generally fought in strong skirmish lines, taking advantage of the shape of ground, and of every cover. We were generally the assailants, and in wooded and broken countries the "defensive" had a positive advantage . . . for they were always ready, had cover, and always knew the ground to their immediate front; whereas we . . . had to grope our way over unknown ground, and generally found a cleared field or prepared entanglements that held us for a time under a close and withering fire. . . .

When the enemy is entrenched, it becomes absolutely necessary to permit each brigade and division of the troops immediately opposed to throw up a corresponding trench for their own protection in case of a sudden sally. We invariably did this in all our recent campaigns, and it had no ill effect, though sometimes our troops were a little too slow in leaving their well-covered lines to assail the enemy in position. . . . Even our skirmishers were in the habit of rolling logs together, or of making a lunette of rails, with dirt in front, to cover their bodies. . . . On the "defensive" there is no doubt of the propriety of fortifying, but in the assailing army the general must watch closely to see that his men do not neglect an opportunity to drop his precautionary defenses, and act promptly on the "offensive" at every chance. [*Memoirs*, II, pp. 394, 396–397.]

A brigade commander in Geary's division describes in greater detail the nature of the fighting in the "trench warfare" that began along the New Hope Church and Dallas line during the closing days of May.

Report of Col. George A. Cobham, Jr., USA, Commanding Third Brigade, Second Division, Twentieth Army Corps, Army of the Cumberland

About 5 p.m. . . . I was ordered by General Geary to change front and advance in two lines to attack the enemy in front, who was now heavily engaged by the First and Third Divisions of the Twentieth Corps. I immediately ordered all detached regiments to be recalled (with the exception of the Seventy-eighth New York, which was left with the train as guard), formed line and advanced rapidly about one mile and a half through a thick wood to the front line of battle, where we relieved some troops of the First Division, and advancing on the enemy's lines, opened fire on them, receiving in return a severe and destructive fire of musketry and a heavy artillery fire of shell, grape, and canister from a battery in front of the right of our brigade front. Two regiments of the brigade . . . advanced on the battery . . . until within a short distance of the guns, pouring in a deadly and destructive fire on the gunners and their infantry supports.

The terrible discharges of grape and canister from the battery, which literally swept our men away, added to the severe fire from the enemy's infantry, prevented the capture of their guns. We, however, held the position to which we had advanced against such determined resistance until darkness put an end to the conflict and left us in possession of all the ground over which we had advanced during the day.

At 3 a.m. of the 26th . . . I extended my brigade line slightly to the right and relieved the line of skirmishers . . . (commanded by Colonel [Ezra A.] Carman, Thirteenth New Jersey Volunteers), and commenced building a substantial breast-work of logs, which was soon completed, although accomplished under a very annoying fire from the enemy's sharpshooters. . . . During the whole of this day the sharpshooters of the Sixtieth New York Volunteers held in check the enemy's battery, picking off the cannoneers, and effectually preventing the loading or using of the guns. . . . The sharpshooters on both sides kept up a severe and destructive fire during the day, the brigade being drawn up in one line and occupying the breast-works.

At 3 p.m., by direction of General Geary, my brigade moved to the left and formed connection with the Second Brigade, relieving a brigade of the Third Division, and formed in two lines, having a front of three regiments in the breast-works and three in the rear line. Every precaution was immediately taken to strengthen the breast-works in our front. I also caused small rifle-pits to be dug in front of the breast-works in such positions as to command the rebel works, and in these the sharpshooters were stationed and enabled to inflict a severe loss on the enemy while comparatively safe themselves.

May 27. Skirmishing commenced at daybreak along our front and continued incessantly until dark. Our sharpshooters were heavily reenforced and drove the enemy's sharpshooters within their first line of works with heavy loss. All the batteries along our front also opened fire on the enemy's works. . . . Strengthened our breastworks and dug small rifle-pits in front of this part of the line also, for sharpshooters. The loss on our part was quite heavy, but not near so great as that of the enemy during this day's fighting. On the morning of the 28th the enemy's batteries opened fire on our works with shell, grape, and canister-shot, which was kept up for about one hour with great rapidity. Our sharpshooters soon silenced their fire, however, by picking off the cannoneers while loading their guns. Sharp firing continued on both sides until about 10 a.m., when the enemy made a charge on our front line, but was speedily repulsed with loss and driven within their first line of works, our sharpshooters annoying them severely during the afternoon.

On the morning of the 29th skirmishing again commenced along our front and continued without interruption until dark; also during the whole of the 30th and 31st days of May and until 12.30 p.m. of June 1, when my brigade was relieved by a brigade of General Harrow's division, of the Fifteenth Army Corps, and retired from the trenches after eight days and nights of most severe duty, the men being constantly under fire, and engaged during a great part of each night in severe fatigue duty, building breast-works and digging rifle-pits, with but little opportunity for rest and poor facilities for cooking, which had to be done at all times amidst a shower of the enemy's balls and sometimes shells.

The behavior of the whole command during . . . these eight days was all that I could wish; all did their duty faithfully and well. Our position during the whole time was one of extreme difficulty and danger, requiring all . . . to be constantly on the alert to resist any attack during the day or to guard against surprise by night, which the extreme proximity of our lines to the enemy's works (consisting of two lines of strong breast-works defended by both artillery and infantry and a space of about 100 yards intervening) rendered extremely probable. [O.R., XXXVIII, pt. 2, pp. 279–280.]

Report of Lt. Gen. John B. Hood, CSA, Commanding Corps, Army of Tennessee

On the morning of the 25th, with my entire command, I arrived at New Hope Church. . . . About midday the enemy were reported advancing, when my line was formed, *Hindman* on the left, *Stewart* in the center, and *Stevenson* on the right. At 5 p.m. a very determined attack was made upon *Stewart*, extending along a very small portion of *Brown's* brigade, of *Stevenson's* division. The engagement continued actively until night closed in, the enemy being repeatedly and handsomely repulsed at all points. Thus Hooker's entire corps was driven back by three brigades of *Stewart's* division. . . . Too much praise cannot be awarded to the artillery, under the immediate direction of Colonel [*Robert F.*] *Beckham*, which did great execution in the enemy's ranks, and added much to their discomfiture.

On the morning of the 26th the enemy were found to [be] extending their left. *Hindman's* was withdrawn from my left and placed in position on the right, the enemy continuing to extend his left. Major-

General *Cleburne* with his division was ordered to report to me and was massed on *Hindman's* right.

On the morning of the 27th the enemy [were] known to be extending rapidly to their left, attempting to turn my right as they extended. *Cleburne* was deployed to meet them, and at 5.30 p.m. a very stubborn attack was made on his division extending to the right [near Pickett's Mill], where Major-General *Wheeler* with his cavalry dismounted was engaging them. The assault was continued with great determination upon both *Cleburne* and *Wheeler* until after night, but every attempt to break their lines was gallantly repulsed. About 10 o'clock at night Brigadier-General *Granbury*, with his brigade of Texans, made a dashing charge on the enemy, driving them from the field. . . . After the engagements around New Hope Church nothing of very great importance transpired while occupying that line. [*O.R.*, XXXVIII, pt. 3, pp. 761–762.]

Report of Maj. Gen. Alexander P. Stewart, CSA, Commanding Division, Hood's Corps, Army of Tennessee

On Wednesday evening, May 25, being in line of battle near New Hope Church—*Baker's* brigade on the right, *Clayton's* in the center, *Stovall's* on the left, *Gibson's* in reserve, except *Austin's* battalion, and the Sixteenth [Louisiana] under Colonel *Lewis*, who were in front as skirmishers—the enemy, after firing a few shells, advanced and attacked along my entire front. *Baker's* and *Clayton's* men had piled up a few logs; *Stovall's* Georgians were without any defense. The entire line received the attack with great steadiness and firmness, every man standing at his post. The fight began toward 5 o'clock and continued with great fury until after night. The enemy were repulsed at all points, and it is believed with heavy loss. . . .

Eldridge's battalion of artillery, consisting of [Capt. *Thomas J.*] *Stanford's*, [Capt. *McDonald*] *Oliver's*, and [Capt. *Charles E.*] *Fenner's* batteries, was admirably posted, well served, and did great execution. They had 43 men and 44 horses killed and wounded. Our position was such that the enemy's fire, which was very heavy, passed over the line to a great extent, which accounts for the fact that while so heavy a punishment was inflicted on the enemy, our own loss, between 300 and 400, was not greater.

The calm determination of the men during this engagement of two and a half or three hours was beyond all praise. The enemy's advance seemed to be in three lines of division front without artillery. No more persistent attack or determined resistance has anywhere been made. Not being allowed to advance and charge the enemy, we did not get possession of the ground occupied by the enemy, who entrenched, and during the two following days kept up a severe and galling skirmish fire, from which we suffered considerably, especially losing a number of valuable officers. During the 27th the Thirty-seventh Alabama . . . suffered severely from the fire of a battery, and with the Fifty-fourth [Alabama], who re-enforced it (both of *Baker's* brigade), is entitled to special mention for the fortitude with which they endured the ordeal. [*O.R.*, XXXVIII, pt. 3, p. 818.]

Report of Lt. Col. Alexander A. Greene, CSA, Commanding Thirty-Seventh Alabama Infantry, Baker's Brigade, Stewart's Division, Hood's Army Corps, Army of Tennessee

The command arrived at New Hope Church on the 25th day of May about noon, and was soon called into line of battle. The men threw up hasty works of old logs and fence rails. The enemy advanced about 4 p.m. and assaulted the position of General *Clayton*, whose right regiment was the next on my left. The enemy did not approach nearer immediately in my front than 150 paces, at which distance there was an eminence rather superior to the one on which my command was in line. This hill was densely covered with underbrush.

Here the enemy halted and remained until dark, firing above my line, which I am satisfied they did not see. The fire of my command was held during the entire engagement in order to get a fair aim at short range. My men were very eager to fire at the enemy to the left and in front of General *Clayton*, from which direction I had 6 men wounded, but promptly obeyed the order not to fire. My men spent the night in improving their works as much as could be done with a few dull axes.

The 26th passed off quietly. I discovered early in the night . . . that the enemy were placing a battery in position in front of my left wing, of which fact I immediately informed Brigadier-General *Baker* and Major-General *Stewart*, and proceeded to strengthen my works: but having only two picks and four shovels, much could not be done. The men, however, worked all night.

Early on the morning of the 27th . . . the enemy's battery of 20-pounder Parrott guns opened a furious fire of solid shot, shell, grape, and canister, but fired too high. This was continued until 11 a.m. About 4 p.m. the fire was again commenced and with terrible effect. One shell struck the top of my works and fell over and exploded, killing and wounding 4 men.

Finding that the enemy had gotten range of my line, I ordered my men to sharpshoot the battery, which was about 300 paces distant. After considerable firing I discovered that the aim of the enemy was not disturbed, although my men fired with a great deal of deliberation. Having only Austrian rifles in my command, I went to General *Baker* and asked for twenty men with Enfield rifles. These were sent me. In a few minutes the fire of the enemy was evidently agitated, as his missiles struck large trees immediately in front of his guns or passed high above our heads.

The fight lasted until nearly night, when the enemy ceased to fire. Although my men were subjected to a most terrible fire, had their works riddled by solid shot and shell, and had grape and canister poured through the breaches they had made, while many of them fell dead or frightfully wounded, and this at the hands of the enemy whom they could not reach, yet they gave no signs of wavering, and only two left their post unhurt. Almost all the suffering was sustained by four small companies, which did not number in the aggregate more than 100 men. My loss in this unequal contest was 56 men killed and wounded. Three men had their heads carried away, 1 had his right shoulder torn off, 1 had both hands carried away, and many had painful wounds in the head, and scarcely any man in the left wing of my regiment escaped unhurt. . . . My loss at New Hope Church, 25th and 27th of May, was 9 killed and 53 wounded. [*O.R.*, XXXVIII, pt. 3, pp. 848–849.]

ACTION AROUND DALLAS

There is little point in visiting Dallas, Georgia, where *Bate's* Confederate division assaulted McPherson's Fifteenth and Sixteenth Corps late in the afternoon of May 28. Much of the terrain is now developed, traffic is congested, and what remains of the old earthworks is on private property. But the hard soldiering in that sector should not be ignored.

Maj. Gen. James B. McPherson to Maj. Gen. William T. Sherman, 27 May 1864, 4 p.m.

We have forced the enemy back to his breast-works throughout nearly the whole extent of his lines and find him occupying a strong position extending apparently from the North Marietta, or New Hope Church, road, to across the Villa Rica road. Our lines are up within close musket range in many places and the enemy appear to be massing on our right. I cannot well work toward the left; certainly not until I get trains and everything out of the way, for as soon as I uncover this flank (the right), the enemy will be on it. [*O.R.*, XXXVIII, pt. 4, p. 327.]

Report of Maj. Gen. John A. Logan, USA, Commanding Fifteenth Army Corps, Army of the Tennessee

The command rested [near Kingston] until the morning of the 23d, by which time twenty days' supplies had been procured. On the 23d I moved nearly south, on Van Wert road, crossing the Etowah River at Wooley's Bridge, and camping at night on the Euharlee Creek, making a distance of eighteen miles. May 24, I marched through Van Wert toward Dallas, a distance of eight miles. May 25, advanced to Pumpkin Vine Creek, camping in line of battle.

Hearing heavy firing in the direction of Dallas, and learning from deserters and others that the enemy were near that place in heavy force, commanded by *Johnston* in person, I moved my command forward cautiously on the 26th, with a strong advance guard and flankers. General Dodge's command advanced on my left. The cavalry force, assisted by my artillery, having, after a spirited skirmish, driven away the enemy's light troops, which were confronting us, on the west side of Dallas, we entered and marched through the town, taking the Powder Springs road to the eastward.

At the distance of two miles beyond the town the enemy was found by our skirmishers in heavy force, occupying strong field-works. I caused their line to be felt of sharply, and by night had developed its general position, the general course of which was north-northeast and south-southwest, extending across the Powder Springs and Marietta roads, with their flanks well advanced.

I immediately placed my command in position, Harrow's division being on the right, extending just across the Villa Rica road, Morgan

L. Smith in the center, crossing the Marietta road, and Osterhaus on the left, connecting with General Dodge's command. Our right was afterward joined by the mounted infantry of [Col. John T.] Wilder's brigade. In this position I caused the most favorable line of works practicable to be thrown up during the night.

On the 27th heavy skirmishing and artillery firing was kept up during the entire day. In the afternoon a strong demonstration was made by the enemy upon General Harrow's front, which was checked promptly by his troops. The 28th opened with rapid skirmishing, which continued until 3.30 o'clock in the afternoon, when the enemy (afterward ascertained to be *Hardee's* entire command, estimated by prisoners to be 25,000) made determined assaults, in columns of regiments, on the most assailable positions along our entire front. The first assault was on Harrow, and was made directly down the line of the Villa Rica road, the weakest point in our whole position. The road there runs directly up the backbone of a ridge, which curved continuously to our right and constantly increased in height. It had been considered impracticable to carry our line far enough forward across this ridge to overcome this objectionable point, without weakening it too much elsewhere in thus adding to its length. The enemy at this point approached within 150 yards, without either being seen or exposed to our fire. His assault was made and with the utmost dash and confidence. Three guns of the First Iowa Battery, which had been run out on the skirmish line, were temporarily surrounded by the enemy. They cannot be said however, to have been in his possession, as the few who attempted to lay hands on them were shot down. The fighting at this point was close and deadly. As line upon line of the enemy debauched upon the open plateau, within eighty yards of our works, they were met by a front and flank fire from brave men, who stood unflinchingly to their guns, under the orders of their efficient officers. Colonel [Charles C.] Walcutt, commanding the brigade engaged, stood on the parapet, amid the storm of bullets, ruling the fight. Line after line was sent back broken to their works, and in half an hour the assault was over, their dead and wounded only occupying the ground on which they advanced.

The assault on [Brig. Gen. Morgan L.] Smith's division commenced a few minutes after that on Harrow, and that on Osterhaus a short time later still. The nature of the ground on these fronts being less favorable for the enemy than that on Harrow's front, they were repulsed very handsomely, and with great loss, though they held on for some time tenaciously, but uselessly. Their dead and severely wounded were mostly left on the field. The engagement, from first to last, lasted about one hour, our troops in many places following the enemy, in their retreat, to their works.

My losses were as follows. Killed, 30; wounded, 295; missing, 54; aggregate, 379. We captured 97 prisoners. The loss of the enemy was estimated at 2,000. We buried of the enemy's dead in my front over 300 bodies. [O.R., XXXVIII, pt. 3, pp. 95–96.]

Report of Brig. Gen. William Harrow, USA, Commanding Fourth Division, Fifteenth Army Corps, Army of the Tennessee

May 16, the division moved forward, by way of Kingston and Van Wert, arriving at Dallas on the 26th. Soon after passing through the town, the Second Division, then in advance, encountered the enemy's out-posts and, rapidly driving them back, took position in front of his main line. This division was placed in position on the right of the Second, and across the Dallas and Villa Rica road, the Third Brigade on the left, the Second in the center, and the First on the right, the First Brigade forming at nearly a right angle with the road, and being the extreme right of the Army of the Tennessee. On the 27th May the enemy attacked this command, directing the assault chiefly against the Second Brigade, with the evident purpose of dislodging them from their position resting on the crest of the ridge and crossing the Villa Rica road. The attack was made with much energy and persisted in for an hour, when it was abandoned, and the enemy retired, leaving his dead and wounded and 30 prisoners. During the night following the command strengthened their position by throwing up slight earth-works. On the 28th, our position remaining unchanged, Captain [Henry] Griffiths, chief of artillery, moved three guns 150 yards beyond my main line, where they were placed in position, and opened upon the enemy's works, 600 yards to the front.

Almost at the instant these guns commenced firing a second assault, in greater force and more obstinate than that of the day previous, was made upon the entire line of the Second Brigade, and upon the right of the Third and left of the First Brigade. The struggle was maintained with great spirit and determination on the part of the enemy for near two hours, and was met with unsurpassed gallantry, resulting in complete defeat to the enemy with severe loss, most of his dead and many of his wounded being left upon the field. . . .

At the first onset of the enemy Captain Griffiths, with the assistance of Captain Percy, Fifty-third Ohio Volunteers, at great personal hazard to themselves, withdrew the guns that had been placed in front of my lines.

On the morning of the 1st June the command moved from Dallas to New Hope Church, there relieving a division of the Twentieth Army Corps, taking their position in front of the enemy, and constructing works so near to his lines that during the night of the 4th June they were abandoned, a line of pickets being left to cover the evacuation. [O.R., XXXVIII, pt. 3, pp. 278–279.]

Report of Col. Reuben Williams, USA, Commanding First Brigade, Fourth Division, Fifteenth Army Corps, Army of the Tennessee

On May 27 was ordered forward, and moved up and took position on the extreme right of the army with two of my regiments (Twenty-sixth Illinois and One hundredth Indiana), leaving the other two (Ninetieth Illinois and Twelfth Indiana) with the train about a mile and a half in the rear. Here we constructed fortifications and threw out skirmishers, who immediately became engaged with the enemy, and the firing was very brisk.

One of the regiments left behind (the Twelfth Indiana) was ordered up and took position on the right, leaving the Ninetieth Illinois with the train. On May 28 the enemy drove in our skirmishers, following it up with a charge along our whole front in two lines of battle. They were repulsed with great slaughter, and retired in disorder to their entrenchments, leaving many of their dead and wounded in our hands, together with a number of prisoners who were unhurt.

On the evening of this day . . . I commenced withdrawing from the position on the right, and the Ninetieth Illinois Infantry, which had been brought up during the charge of the enemy, was ordered to commence the movement as soon as it became dark. I had successfully withdrawn my command, with the exception of my skirmish line, under the command of Major Johnson, when a fierce attack commenced on the Sixteenth Corps, and by your order I hastened back with my command, with the exception of the Ninetieth Illinois Infantry, and resumed my place in the line. I arrived just in time, as our skirmishers had already fallen back into the trenches so recently occupied by our main line. I pushed forward the skirmish line, and affairs assumed about the same aspect as before the withdrawal.

On June 1 I withdrew from the position held on the right at early dawn, moved through Dallas, and relieved a brigade of the Twentieth Corps at New Hope Church. Here the skirmishing was very severe, the enemy firing in many places from their main line of works. On the night of June 3 I advanced my main line of works so that the left of my brigade was not more than eighty rods from that of the enemy. The enemy evacuated their position the night of June 4. My command here captured 68 prisoners and 175 Enfield rifles. On the morning of June 5 began the march toward Acworth. [O.R., XXXVIII, pt. 3, p. 286.]

Report of Lt. Col. James Goodnow, USA, Commanding Twelfth Indiana Infantry Volunteers, First Brigade, Fourth Division, Fifteenth Army Corps, Army of the Tennessee

[At Kingston] the command was allowed a rest of two or three days, which proved of immense benefit to the nearly exhausted men. During our stay orders were received to carry forage sufficient for twenty days, and for the whole command to fit itself for an active campaign, and with view to leaving our railroad communications in the rear.

The necessary arrangements having been made I received marching orders on 23d May, at which time the march was continued in the direction of Dallas, at which place the advance came upon the enemy. On the 26th I was assigned my position in the line, which was the extreme right. I went in and secured my position, my right connecting with the cavalry division of General Garrard. I immediately sent forward a strong body of skirmishers, who found those of the enemy a few hundred yards in my front. The night was consumed in constructing a line of rifle-pits along my front, which were finished and occupied by the command at daylight on the morning of the 27th.

Nothing of interest transpired from this time until in the afternoon of the 28th. At about 2 p.m. of that day considerable firing was heard in the direction of my skirmishers, and in a few minutes thereafter my skirmish line was driven in, closely followed by a strong body of the enemy. As the enemy deployed from the woods and into an open field along my front, my fire was opened upon him. He pressed forward to within 200 yards of my works, where they attempted to reform their broken lines. The attempt proved unsuccessful, as they were so much exposed to my fire, and which eventually drove them from the field and into the cover of the woods in great disorder.

The action lasted about thirty minutes, and the enemy must have suffered severely. As to his actual loss I can only conjecture, as he continued to hold a portion of the ground, on which he must have lost heavily, with his skirmish line. My own loss was slight, having but 5 men wounded, the rifle-pits affording excellent protection to the men.

Skirmishing continued quite lively until 1st day of June, when, before daybreak of that day, the line upon the right was withdrawn, of which my command formed a part. After the withdrawal of the line was effected the command moved toward the center, where I, in obedience to orders, relieved some troops of General Hooker's command upon the front line. In this position I remained until the enemy evacuated his position in my front, my skirmishers capturing a number of prisoners on the morning of the evacuation. While I lay in this position I suffered severely on my skirmish line, losing 14 in killed and wounded; among the number were many of my most valuable men. The evacuation of the enemy from his position at New Hope Church, necessitated another movement on our part, which was ordered, and the command moved to Acworth. [O.R., XXXVIII, pt. 3, p. 303.]

14. PICKETT'S MILL

From the parking lot adjacent to the Atlanta Campaign bronze plaques, turn right onto Bobo Road. Drive to the stop sign on GA 381 and turn right. Drive about 0.2 mile and turn right onto Due West Road. After about 1.3 miles you will reach a stop sign at Mount Tabor Church Road. Turn left here and drive about 0.3 mile, where you will reach the entrance to Pickett's Mill Historic Site. Turn right onto the park road and drive about 0.5 mile to the Visitor Center. Take advantage of the programs there (a small fee will be charged for admission), and use the maps and trail guides for orientation. If you have time to hike one of the marked trails, they are worth the effort. The map in this volume suggests positions on the battlefield that can be reached using the blazed trails, but it should be supplemented by maps and advice available at the Visitor Center. If conditions do not favor a hike, take a position at the overlook behind the Visitor Center (Stop 14A), where you can get a sense of the Confederate lines and the ravines used by Union soldiers in their attack.

STOP 14A, PICKETT'S MILL OVERLOOK

OPERATIONS

On May 27, Hooker's and Howard's corps, supported by heavy artillery fire, pressed against *Hood*, while two divisions, one each from the 4th and the 14th corps, moved behind Schofield's line and then swung to the right to hit the exposed right flank of *Hood's* line. The day before, however, *Johnston* had transferred *Cleburne's* division from *Hardee's* line to the right of *Hood*, and as the Union divisions approached, *Cleburne* deployed quickly into line.

The ensuing battle at Pickett's Mill was the bloodiest thus far in the campaign. After struggling through dense forests and deep ravines and over difficult ridges for the better part of a day, Wood's division of the 4th Corps, in column of brigades, reached a point from which it was believed the column could strike the Confederate flank. At 4:30 P.M., the division moved forward to attack.

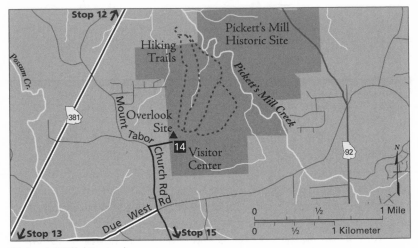

Pickett's Mill (Stop 14)

The next fifty minutes were easily the worst part of the day for the men of Brig. Gen. William B. Hazen's brigade. Everything went wrong. The first line, consisting of four understrength regiments, was hit by "a withering volley of musketry" from Brig. Gen. *H. B. Granbury's* brigade, which had moved into position behind a slight barricade on the extreme right of the Confederate line. About one-third of Hazen's first line fell before it had advanced twenty paces, yet the men pushed forward to within a few yards of *Granbury's* position. There Hazen's brigade halted, the men using whatever shelter they could find behind trees, logs, and dips in the ground.

The original concept was to have Hazen's second line close by to continue the momentum, but the thick woods had caused it to change direction to the left, and instead of reinforcing the first line it came into position along its left flank. Although there was but slight resistance in front, *Granbury's* men poured a heavy fire into the right flank of the second line, and it too was forced to halt and seek cover. The next brigade, which was to have moved forward in close support, attacked too late to restore momentum: Hazen's ammunition was exhausted, and Brig. Gen. *Mark P. Lowrey's* fresh Confederate brigade had moved into position where it could attack both flanks. Wood's third brigade likewise advanced in splendid style through a terrific fire, but with no greater success. Meanwhile, several hundred yards to the east, Col. Benjamin F. Scribner's brigade, from Brig. Gen. Richard W. Johnson's division of the 14th Corps, found its way blocked by *Wheeler's* dismounted cavalry, sheltered behind rude breastworks. Scribner never

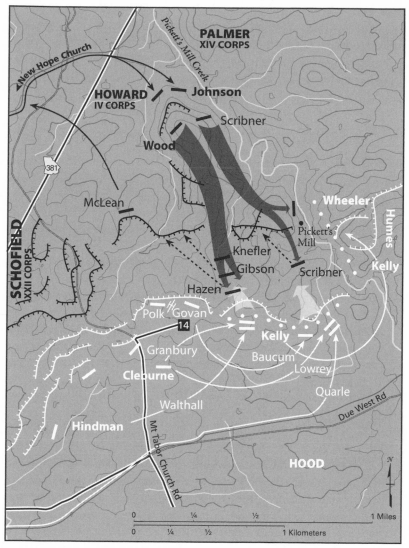

The Battle at Pickett's Mill

got forward far enough to align with Hazen, which then enabled *Lowrey's* brigade to fire into Hazen's left rear.

The fighting lasted well into the night, but the Confederate flank held firm. The Union troops withdrew in the dark and entrenched on a ridge farther to the right. Wood's division alone suffered about 1,400 casualties in what one Union officer described as "the crime at Pickett's Mill." *Cleburne* lost about 450 men killed and wounded.

Sherman never mentioned the battle specifically in his official report. To him it was but another phase in a relentless effort to pry the enemy out of his fortified line that now stretched unbroken from Dallas to Pickett's Mill.

Report of Maj. Gen. George H. Thomas, USA, Commanding Army of the Cumberland

On the 27th, in accordance with instructions given by the major general commanding the Military Division of the Mississippi, Hooker's and Howard's corps pressed the enemy, supported by considerable artillery firing. Wood's division, of Howard's corps, supported by Johnson's division, of Palmer's corps, was moved to the left of Schofield's line and swung around toward the right, attacking the enemy's right flank and driving him into his rifle-pits, with considerable loss, however, to our troops. Our men had to contend with an almost hidden foe, the ground being cut up into ravines and covered by a dense forest filled with undergrowth; but notwithstanding all the difficulties of the country both officers and men did their work nobly, and having assumed a position were not to be moved from it. [O.R., XXXVIII, pt. 1, p. 144.]

Report of Maj. Gen. Oliver O. Howard, USA, Commanding Fourth Army Corps, Army of the Cumberland

May 27, General Stanley moved to the left of General Newton and relieved General Wood's division preparatory to the latter making an assault on the enemy's line at a point which Major-General Sherman had designated. On a careful reconnaissance made by General Thomas and myself it was ascertained that the enemy were then prepared to bring a cross-fire of artillery and musketry upon the approaches to that position. Therefore I was directed to move General Wood farther to the left and beyond all troops and endeavor to strike the enemy's flank. Johnson's division of the Fourteenth Corps was sent to me as a support. . . . The Twenty-third Corps, Major-General Schofield commanding, was already in position on the left of the Fourth. Therefore I selected a field on the extreme left and rear of the Twenty-third

Corps, which was pretty well concealed from the enemy by intervening woods, and in this massed the troops, Wood's division on the right,
formed in a column of six lines deep, and General Johnson's on the
left, with a brigade front.

The advance from this position commenced at 11 a.m. and in an
easterly direction. The columns moved forward with very little interruption for nearly a mile. I thought we must have reached the enemy's
flank, whereupon General Wood wheeled his command toward the
right till he was faced nearly south. A brigade of the Twenty-third
Corps, [Brigadier] General [Nathaniel C.] McLean's, deployed so as to
form a junction with General Wood on his right.

The latter pressed forward his skirmishers till a large open field
was reached. Here it was discovered that the enemy's works were still
in our front. Immediately the skirmishers were withdrawn and the
column moved rapidly by the left flank at least another mile to the
eastward. The ground was carefully reconnoitered by General Wood
and myself. We still found a line of works to our right, but they did
not seem to cover General Wood's front, and they were new, the enemy still working hard upon them. I gave a little time for the troops
of Wood's division to rest, and for Johnson's to form a little retired
on . . . Wood's left.

From the position now occupied by the troops, woods more or
less open extended up to the enemy's apparent flank. A road skirted
the woods opposite our right, running perpendicular to the enemy's
lines. Another road ran obliquely toward the left and in rear of Johnson's position. McLean's brigade was sent to a place in full view of the
enemy's works, a little to the right of the point of attack, with a view to
attract the enemy's attention and draw his fire.

As soon as everything was in readiness, at about 5 p.m., General
Wood commenced his advance, Hazen's brigade leading. The entire
column marched briskly forward, driving in the enemy's skirmishers
and vigorously assaulting his main line. Complaint came immediately that the supporting column under General Johnson was not far
enough advanced. General Johnson was directed to push forward a
brigade to Hazen's left. He answered that he was doing so, and that it
would soon be in position.

General Wood became very heavily engaged, so as to necessitate
moving forward his supporting lines, and he found strong works in
his front, except, perhaps, opposite his two left regiments. Colonel

Scribner, who commanded General Johnson's advance brigade, finding his own left fired into from across Pickett's Mills creek, halted and
threw some troops across it for his own protection. This delay occurring at precisely the same time with Wood's assault was unfortunate,
for it enabled the enemy with his reserves to force back the left of
General Wood's line and bring an enfilading and reverse fire upon his
troops. Again by some mistake of orders, McLean's troops did not show
themselves to the enemy, nor open any fire to attract his attention on
General Wood's right, so that the enemy was able to pour a cross-fire
of artillery and musketry into his right flank.

Under these circumstances it soon became evident that the assault
had failed, and that the troops must be withdrawn with care in order
to bring off our wounded, and to prevent a successful sally of the enemy from his works. General Johnson formed his troops in rear of and
to the left of the entire position, while General Wood carefully withdrew his division and formed on a ridge farther to the right. General
McLean having been requested to push farther to the right in order to
make connection with the rest of the army, disregarded the request
and moved off at once by the road, leaving these two divisions isolated.
McLean alleged in excuse that his men were entirely without rations.

Our losses were very heavy, being upward of 1,400 killed,
wounded, and missing in General Wood's division alone. Though the
assault was repulsed, yet a position was secured near Pickett's Mills
of the greatest importance to the subsequent movements of the army,
and it has been subsequently ascertained that the enemy suffered im-
mensely in the action, and regarded it as the severest attack made during this eventful campaign. [O.R., XXXVIII, pt. 1, pp. 194–195.]

Narrative of Gen. Joseph E. Johnston, CSA, Commanding Army of Tennessee

The Federal troops extended their entrenched line so rapidly to
their left, that it was found necessary in the morning of the 27th to
transfer *Cleburne's* division of *Hardee's* corps to our right, where it was
formed on the prolongation of *Polk's* line. *Kelly's* cavalry, composed of
Allen's and [Col. *Moses W.*] *Hannon's* Alabama brigades, together less
than a thousand men, occupied the interval, of half a mile, between
Cleburne's right and Little Pumpkin Vine Creek. *Martin's* division (cavalry) guarded the road from Burnt Hickory to Marietta, two miles

farther to the right, and [Brig. Gen. *William Y. C.*] *Humes's* the interval between *Kelly's* and *Martin's* divisions.

Between five and six o'clock in the afternoon, *Kelly's* skirmishers were driven in by a body of Federal cavalry, whose advance was supported by the Fourth Corps. This advance was retarded by the resistance from *Kelly's* troops fighting on foot behind unconnected little heaps of loose stones. As soon as the noise of this contest revealed to Major-General *Cleburne* the maneuver to turn his right, he brought the right brigade of his second line, *Granbury's*, to *Kelly's* support; when the thin line of dismounted cavalry that had been bravely resisting masses of infantry gave place to the Texan brigade.

The Fourth Corps came on in deep order, and assailed the Texans with great vigor, receiving their close and accurate fire with . . . fortitude. . . . They had also to endure the fire of *Govan's* right, including two pieces of artillery on their right flank. At the same time *Kelly's* and a part of *Humes's* troops, directed by General *Wheeler*, met the Federal left, which was following the movement of the main body, and drove back the leading brigade. . . . The [Union] force continued to press forward . . . but [was] so delayed by the resistance of *Wheeler's* troops as to give time for the arrival . . . of the Eighth and Ninth Arkansas regiments under Colonel [*George F.*] *Baucum*, detached by General *Govan* to the assistance of the cavalry.

This little body met the . . . Federal troops as they were reaching the prolongation of *Granbury's* line, and charging gallantly, drove them back. . . . Before the Federal left could gather to overwhelm *Baucum* and his two regiments, *Lowrey's* brigade, hurried by General *Cleburne* from its position as left of his second line, came to join them, and the two, formed abreast of *Granbury's* brigade, stopped the [Union] advance . . . and successfully resisted . . . subsequent attacks. [*Military Operations*, pp. 329–332.]

General *Johnston* provided a clear image of Confederate advantages when he reflected on this battle in his essay for *Century Magazine's* "Century War Series." A brief quotation from that essay appears below.

Gen. *Joseph E. Johnston, Essay in* Century Magazine, *1888*

The Federal formation was so deep that its front did not equal that of our two brigades; consequently those troops were greatly exposed to our musketry—all but the leading troops being on a hillside facing us. They advanced until their first line was within 25 or 30 paces of ours, and fell back only after at least 700 men had fallen dead in their places. . . . Some time after nightfall the Confederates captured above two hundred prisoners in the hollow before them. [Joseph E. Johnston, "Opposing Sherman's Advance to Atlanta," in Robert Underwood Johnson and Clarence Clough Buel, eds., *Battles and Leaders of the Civil War,* 4 vols. (New York: Century, 1888), IV, pp. 269–270.]

Narrative of Lt. Gen. John B. Hood, CSA, Commanding Corps, Army of Tennessee

I was . . . on the right . . . [and] sent to [Gen. *Johnston*] for a good division, with the message that Howard's Corps was moving rapidly to turn my right flank, which was the right of the infantry of our Army; that I had extended my lines as far as possible. He sent *Cleburne's* Division to report to me. General *Cleburne* was given by me most explicit instructions in regard to the formation of his forces on the right of my corps. He was directed to place his troops in a column of brigades, in the rear of my immediate right, which was the right of *Hindman's* Division, with *Granbury's* brigade in rear of the column, so as to bring it on our extreme right when deployed into line. He was also instructed to allow the Federal cavalry to reconnoiter and find our right. Similar orders were given to our own cavalry.

As Howard's Corps advanced, *Cleburne* was directed to deploy quickly into line; the Federals thus came in contact with a solid line of infantry, in lieu of finding the open space on our flank, which existed at the time of the reconnaissance of the Federal cavalry.

I shall ever remember the enthusiasm and transport of the gallant *Cleburne* at the time of this . . . most brilliant affair of the whole campaign. [J. B. Hood, *Advance and Retreat* (New Orleans: Published for the Hood Orphan Memorial Fund, 1880), p. 117.]

Report of Maj. Gen. Joseph Wheeler, CSA, Commanding Cavalry Corps, Army of Tennessee

May 26, we moved from Acworth to join the main army, and took our position on its right on the Acworth and Dallas road. May 27, General *Cleburne's* division of infantry having been formed upon the right of our infantry line, placed portions of *Hannon's* and *Allen's* small cavalry brigades, of *Kelly's* division upon General *Cleburne's* right flank. They were dismounted, and entrenchments thrown up extending on the prolongation of General *Cleburne's* line for a distance of about 800 yards.

The enemy having during the morning and preceding day made several attacks upon the pickets on the Burnt Hickory road, I had placed General *Martin's* command in position to oppose the enemy, who were menacing that point, leaving a space of about two miles between General *Martin's* left and General *Kelly's* right, which was filled by a line of skirmishers from General *Humes'* command, which . . . was held in reserve to move to any point which might be attacked.

About 3 o'clock this line of skirmishers was driven in by a force of the enemy's cavalry advancing up Pumpkin Vine Creek by Widow Pickett's house. I immediately galloped to this point and found a squadron moving, by General *Humes'* direction, to re-enforce the picket. On arriving at the creek I soon observed that a considerable force of infantry was before us, and I directed General *Humes* to bring one brigade (dismounted) to that point, and to prolong his other brigade upon its right to fill the gap between said position and General *Martin's* left. These dispositions were made under a warm fire from the enemy.

At this moment I received information that General *Martin's* line was being attacked, and at the same time that *Granbury's* brigade of infantry was moving up to relieve General *Kelly,* whom I ordered to move to the right and close upon General *Humes.*

While making the movement, and before it was completed, the enemy moved a column up a ravine between *Kelly's* right and *Humes'* left. I ordered a regiment from *Humes* to oppose them, which was promptly placed in position, but finding it was warmly pressed, General *Humes* re-enforced it with another regiment from his command. While this movement was going on Hazen's Federal infantry brigade charged our line, but was repulsed by a counter-charge of *Humes'* and *Kelly's* commands.

My command captured 32 prisoners . . . whom they turned over to *Lowrey's* infantry brigade, which was just forming to their right to relieve General *Humes'* command. On the arrival of General *Lowrey's* brigade General *Humes* moved to the right in front of the temporary breast-works thrown up during the engagement. *Quarles'* brigade also reported to me during the fight, but too late to join in the action. . . .

I had but 822 men engaged, extending over the ground to such length as to enable me to form little more than a line of skirmishers. . . . We successfully thwarted this movement (to turn our right flank), holding this large force of the enemy in check until we were relieved by a division of our infantry, to whom we gave up our temporary breast-works, and then moved to the right to guard their right flank. But one infantry brigade (*Granbury's*) got into position before defeat of the enemy. The difficulty of maneuvering so thin a line in a thick woods under heavy fire will be appreciated. [*O.R.*, XXXVIII, pt. 3, pp. 948–949.]

Report of Maj. Gen. Patrick R. Cleburne, CSA, Commanding Division, Hardee's Corps, Army of Tennessee

About 2 or 3 o'clock of the afternoon of the 26th I arrived with my division on the extreme right of the then line of the army, when I was sent to support Major-General *Hindman*. At that point our lines, the general bearing of which was north and south, retired for a few yards to the east. In continuation of this retiring line I placed *Polk's* brigade (of my division) in and diagonally across it, upon a ridge en echelon by battalion to avoid an artillery enfilade from a neighboring position held by the enemy. Resting on *Polk's* right was placed *Hotchkiss'* artillery, consisting of four Napoleons, four Parrott guns, and four howitzers. Supporting *Hotchkiss* on the right was one regiment of *Govan's* [brigade], of my division. The remainder of my division was disposed in rear as a second line in support of *Hindman's* right brigades and my first line. Entrenchments were thrown up in the afternoon and night of the 26th and in the morning of the 27th. The position was in the main covered with trees and undergrowth, which served as a screen along our lines, concealed us, and were left standing as far as practicable for that purpose.

On the morning of the 27th, at about 7 o'clock, *Govan* was sent to the north front on a reconnaissance, with directions to swing to the left in his advance. From time to time, while engaged in this reconnaissance, *Govan* sent me word that the enemy was moving to the right— his own left. At 11 a.m., upon my order . . . *Govan* came in, leaving his skirmishers about three-quarters of a mile in front. I at once placed him on the right of *Polk*, where he covered himself in rifle-pits. About 4 p.m., hearing that the enemy infantry in line of battle were pressing the cavalry on my right (they had already driven in my skirmishers), I placed *Granbury* on *Govan's* right.

He had but just gotten into position and a dismounted cavalry force, in line behind a few disconnected heaps of stones loosely piled together, had passed behind him, when the enemy advanced. He showed himself first, having driven back my skirmishers, in the edge of an open field in front of *Govan*, about 400 yards across, where he halted and opened fire. From the point on the ridge where *Govan's* right and *Granbury's* left met, there made off a spur, which, at about 100 yards from it, turned sharply to the northeast, running then in a direction almost parallel with it and maintaining about an equal elevation. Between this spur and the parent ridge, beginning in front of *Granbury's* left, was a deep ravine, the side of which next to *Granbury* was very steep, with occasional benches of rock up to a line within thirty or forty yards of *Granbury's* men, where it flattened into a natural glacis. This glacis was well covered with well grown trees and in most places with thick undergrowth. Here was the brunt of the battle, the enemy advancing along this front in numerous and constantly reenforced lines.

His men displayed a courage worthy of an honorable cause, pressing in steady throngs within a few paces of our men, frequently exclaiming, "Ah! damn you, we have caught you without your logs now." *Granbury's* men, needing no logs, were awaiting them, and throughout awaited them with deliberate aim. The piles of his dead on this front, pronounced by the officers in this army who have seen most service to be greater than they had ever seen before, were a silent but sufficient eulogy upon *Granbury* and his noble Texans. In the great execution here done upon the enemy, *Govan* with his two right regiments, disdaining the enemy in his own front, who were somewhat removed, and [Capt. *Thomas J.*] *Key* with two pieces of artillery ran by hand upon my order to a convenient breach made in our breast-works, materially aided *Granbury* by a right-oblique fire which enfiladed the masses in his front. [O.R., XXXVIII, pt. 3, pp. 724–725.]

STOP 14B, BLUE LOOP TRAIL

If you can walk about a mile on well-marked trails, you can follow the "Blue Loop" trail from the Visitor Center to Station 9 for this stop. Station 9 will place you in the position where Brig. Gen. William B. Hazen formed his brigade for the attack. Trail blazes and markers will supplement the map in this guide to help you stay oriented.

Report of Brig. Gen. Thomas J. Wood, USA, Commanding Third Division, Fourth Army Corps, Army of the Cumberland

The morning of the 26th still found the enemy in our front. My division was early deployed into order of battle on the left of the Second Division, of the Fourth Corps. The day was spent . . . in very brilliant and successful maneuvering to determine the exact position of the enemy's entrenched line. To accomplish this it was necessary to drive in his light troops, who formed a screen to his position. The ground was in some parts difficult to maneuver on, and a deep stream had to be bridged, but the work was satisfactorily accomplished. . . .

Having satisfactorily defined the position of the enemy's entrenched line it was determined on . . . the 27th that it should be assaulted, and my division was selected for this arduous and dangerous task. A minute and critical examination of the enemy's entrenchments rendered it evident that a direct front attack would be of most doubtful success, and would certainly cost great sacrifice of life. Hence, it was determined to attempt to find the extreme right of the enemy's position, turn it, and attack him in flank. . . .

My division was moved entirely to the left of our line and formed, by order of Major-General Howard, commanding the corps, in six parallel lines, each brigade being formed in two lines. The order of the brigades in this grand column of attack was, first, the Second Brigade, Brigadier-General Hazen commanding; second, the First Brigade, Colonel [William H.] Gibson . . . commanding; third, the Third Brigade, Colonel [Frederick] Knefler . . . commanding. When all the dispositions were completed (and these required but a short space of time), the magnificent array moved forward.

For a mile the march was nearly due southward, through dense forests and the thickest jungle, a country whose surface was scarred by deep ravines and intersected by difficult ridges. But the movement of the column . . . was steadily onward. Having moved a mile southward and not having discovered any indication of the enemy, it was supposed we had passed entirely to the east of his extreme right.

On this hypothesis the column was wheeled to the right and advanced in nearly a westerly course. . . . The nature of the country was similar in all respects to that already described. After the movement had progressed nearly a mile and a half the flankers discovered that the column in wheeling to the right swung inside of the enemy's line. It was necessary, to gain the goal, to face to the left, file left, and by a flank movement conduct the column eastward and southward around the enemy's right flank. When all these movements, so well calculated to try the physical strength of the men, were concluded, and the point gained from which it was believed that the column could move directly on the enemy's flank, the day was well spent. It was nearly 4 p.m. The men had been on their feet since early daylight, and of course were much worn. The column was halted a few moments to readjust the lines, to give the men a brief breathing space, and to give the division which was to protect and cover the left flank of the column time to come up and take position.

At 4.30 p.m. precisely the order was given to attack, and the column with its front well covered moved forward. And never have troops marched to a deadly assault, under the most adverse circumstances, with more firmness, with more truly soldierly bearing, and with more distinguished gallantry. On, on, through the thickest jungle, over exceedingly rough and broken ground, and exposed to the sharpest direct and cross fire of musketry and artillery on both flanks, the leading brigade, the Second, moved (followed in close supporting distance by the other brigades) right up to the enemy's main line of works. Under the unwavering steadiness of the advance the fire from the enemy's line of works began to slacken and the troops behind those works first began perceptibly to waver and then to give way, and I have no hesitation in saying that so far as any opposition directly in front was concerned, though that was terrible enough, the enemy's strongly fortified position would have been forced. But the fire, particularly on the left flank of the column, which was at first only *en echarpe*, became, as the column advanced, enfilading, and finally took the first line of the column partially in reverse. It was from this fire that the supporting and covering division should have protected the assaulting column, but it failed to do so. Under such a fire no troops could maintain the vantage ground which had been gained, and the leading brigade, which had driven everything in its front, was compelled to fall back a short distance to secure its flanks, which were crumbling away under the severe fire by the irregularities of the ground. (It is proper to observe here that the brigade of the Twenty-third Corps which was ordered to take post so as to cover the right flank of the assaulting column by some mistake failed to get into a position to accomplish this purpose.) From the position taken by Hazen's brigade when it retired a short distance from the enemy's works it kept up a deadly fire, which was evidently very galling to the foe. The brigade was engaged about fifty minutes. It had expended the sixty rounds of ammunition taken into action on the men's persons; it had suffered terribly in killed and wounded, and the men were much exhausted by the furiousness of the assault. Consequently I ordered this brigade to be relieved by the First Brigade, Col. William H. Gibson . . . commanding.

I visited the battle-field of Pickett's Mills . . . twice after the evacuation of the enemy, and examined it closely. The numerous single graves and several lines of trenches (capable of containing from twenty-five to forty bodies) on the battlefield outside of the enemy's entrenchments explain where most of the 255 missing of that day went to. [O.R., XXXVIII, pt. 1, pp. 377–378, 387.]

In the following accounts of Hazen's brigade at Pickett's Mills, the terminology is confusing, for whenever Hazen and his subordinates use the word "battalion," the synonym for "regiment" on the drill ground, they refer in this instance to two linked regiments in a tactical formation. At the commencement of the campaign, Hazen had reorganized his brigade "for fighting, marching, and campaigning purposes" into four battalions of two regiments each. Obviously he did this so that his brigade, which in this campaign comprised nine regiments reduced by long service to less than two hundred men each, could still maneuver and function effectively as a unit in battle. For administrative purposes, these were sometimes called "demi-brigades," but in line of battle the word used was "battalion," the standard term in the drill manual.

Except for the U.S. Regular units and a small number of organizations that originally entered Confederate service as "battalions," the regiment was the standard tactical and administrative unit in both armies. But since both armies were maneuvered by drill manuals translated from the French, and because the battalion was the standard unit in the French army of that day, officers gave commands to "battalions" rather than to "regiments" in moving troops from column into line and through the various tactical evolutions—their only means of exercising command and control in battle. This probably was why Hazen called his amalgamated regiments "battalions."

Hazen's order dated May 5, 1864, further specified: "In action it is directed that volley-firing be that habitually employed either by wing, rank, or battalion; and in order to be perfectly prepared to execute these fires correctly, battalion commanders will exercise their commands in firing without cartridges at least once a day" [General W. B. Hazen, *A Narrative of Military Service* (Boston: Ticknor, 1885), p. 248].]

Narrative of Brig. Gen. William B. Hazen, USA, Commanding Second Brigade, Third Division, Fourth Army Corps, Army of the Cumberland

No attack could have been made in better form, nor persisted in with more determination; but as a column attack it was a failure. The several brigades, instead of striking in such rapid succession that each might benefit by the advantage gained by those before it, were put in at intervals of forty minutes. This resulted in separate attacks by detachments, with ample warning to the enemy to get ready and repair damage. Just as I was about to move, General Wood in my presence remarked to General Howard, "We will put in Hazen, and see what success he has."

This was a revelation to me, as it was evident there was to be no attack by column at all. The attack was made, however, with the belief on the part of the men that it was by column, which made the long interval before relief came seem inexcusable to many. [Hazen, *Narrative of Military Service*, p. 257.]

Report of Brig. Gen. William B. Hazen, USA, Commanding Second Brigade, Third Division, Fourth Corps, Army of the Cumberland

This brigade, in two lines, was then pushed forward to attack the enemy, the other troops not moving. After skirmishing about 800 yards, the front line came upon and immediately engaged the enemy, when one of the most desperate engagements of my experience ensued. The first line was composed of two battalions; the one on the right, commanded by Lieut. Col. R. L. Kimberly, Forty-first Ohio

Volunteers, was composed of his own regiment and the First Ohio Volunteer Infantry; the one on the left, by Col. O. H. Payne, One hundred and twenty-fourth Ohio Volunteers, composed of his own regiment and Ninety-third Ohio Volunteers. . . . The whole, under my own personal supervision, moved up within ten yards of the position in which the enemy was found in force. A slight irregularity in the ground gave a partial cover for our men.

The second line . . . moved with the first line. On account of the thick wood it had changed direction to the left, so as to come in position directly on the left flank of the first line. It found no works and but slight resistance in its front, but upon presenting its flank to the enemy in front of the leading battalions it received a fire from that direction which checked it.

My command had now lost 500 men in the attack and was powerless to push farther, although the enemy himself was partially broken. Believing our work well commenced, with certainty of the fullest success, I sent all of my staff in succession to bring forward the other lines of the column. In addition to these several members of regimental staffs were sent for the same purpose, some of whom were wounded while carrying the message. At last, forty minutes having elapsed since the beginning of the attack, the ammunition of my men being exhausted, and the enemy having been given time to bring forward a fresh brigade and attack strongly both my flanks, doubling them back, I was compelled to yield the ground, when I met for the first time the troops of the line in my rear, which was supposed, from the nature of the attack (in column), to have succeeded each other at short intervals.

I also found that Colonel Scribner's brigade, which was to have supported my left, was operating, not in conjunction with me, but with the brigade next in my rear, so that two rebel regiments found no difficulty in attacking the rear of my left battalion. . . . The Thirty-second Indiana, the first regiment I saw coming to my support, did so in detached fragments and not as a regiment. None of the other troops except about fifty men of the Forty-Ninth Ohio advanced as far as my lines during their desperate and unsupported battle. Colonel Payne, with a portion of his command [the two linked regiments on the left wing of the first line] held his position, quite at the front, until after dark when they were withdrawn.

It is due the brave brigade which I have commanded during the entire war . . . and which has been in the front of every battle of the Army of the Cumberland, to say that this battle of the 27th of May is its first and only unsuccessful effort during the war, and at this time, as its dead list will show, went at its work with an honest good will which deserved a better result. I shall ever believe its part bravely and well done. . . .

The brigade was put in position near where it fought, and during the night the enemy having permanently established its lines in our front, we remained here until the morning of June 5. [*O.R.*, XXXVIII, pt. 1, pp. 423–424.]

Report of Lt. Col. Robert L. Kimberly, USA, Forty-First Ohio Infantry, Commanding Regiment and "Demi-Brigade," Second Brigade, Third Division, Fourth Army Corps, Army of the Cumberland

At 4 the attack was made (this battalion having the right of the first line). This battalion moved through an open wood, the right flank passing along the side of an open field, across which, at a distance of 400 yards, were the enemy's works. A deep ravine was soon encountered, the opposite bank covered with an almost impenetrable undergrowth of oak. The skirmish line was stopped by the enemy's fire as it ascended from the ravine, and the battalion closed upon it. The line was here rectified and the ranks closed, when I ordered the charge.

The battalion had advanced hardly a half a dozen paces when it was struck by a withering volley of musketry from the thicket in front and from the right. The enemy's fire was sustained in greater severity than would be possible for a single line, and in advancing twenty paces nearly one-third of the battalion was stricken down. The line was within twenty-five paces of the slight barricade behind which the enemy's lines were posted, but it was impossible to carry the position, the line being too much broken and no shelter under which to reform. The battalion was held in this position, the men availing themselves of what shelter was offered by trees, logs, and the conformation of the ground, and opened a rapid fire upon the enemy, the effect of which could be plainly seen, while I dispatched a staff officer to hasten up the second line, hoping to be able with its aid to carry the position.

This officer . . . was shot while going back, and a second messenger was sent, but failed to find the proper officer or bring forward the second line.

In the mean time the enemy formed a regiment upon our right flank, and opened a battery from the same direction. Their fire was very severe, but the orders having been for an attack in column, I deemed it my duty to hold my battalion (the head of the column) as long as possible. Twice the enemy tried to charge from his works, but was stopped at the outset. Finally he closed upon our right, doubling it back. By strenuous efforts this was restored, but only to be again crushed by a more vigorous advance of the enemy, when, seeing it was impossible to hold the shattered line longer in this position, I ordered the battalion to fall back to the hill in rear.

This, except in the case of the three right companies, which the enemy nearly enveloped and pressed with great vigor, was effected in order, and without the loss of a man, but it was impossible to bring off all the wounded. A hundred yards in rear, the battalion in its retreat met one of the supporting brigades advancing, behind which it reformed, but was not engaged. The attack had continued for more than an hour and failed, but it was an honest effort to execute an order, without hesitating to calculate the chances of success, which all who took part in may be proud of. . . . I saw not a single instance of hesitancy when the order was given to charge, and if devoted gallantry could have won success the men would have had it. [O.R., XXXVIII, pt. 1, p. 435.]

Report of Col. Oliver Payne, USA, One Hundred and Twenty-Fourth Ohio Infantry, Commanding Regiment and "Demi-Brigade," Second Brigade, Third Division, Fourth Army Corps, Army of the Cumberland

At 4 p.m. the final attack was made. This battalion moved briskly forward through a thick woods, coming up with the skirmish line at the foot of a deep ravine, where it had been stopped by a rapid fire from the opposite hill, the sides of which were thickly covered with an almost impenetrable thicket and in many places were almost perpendicular. Here, stopping long enough to rectify the lines, I ordered them forward, the battalion gaining the hill, and had advanced a few yards from the crest to within about thirty paces of the enemy's works, when it was met with such a withering fire from the front and each flank that it was checked and compelled to find shelter behind the crest of the hill.

So rapid and close was the fire, that seeing that it would be impracticable to make another effort to carry the works with the battalion, now much depleted, I ordered the battalion to cover themselves as well as possible and hold the position, expecting every moment to be re-enforced by the second line. It not making its appearance, I sent an officer to find it and to communicate to the general commanding the brigade my position. Still the line did not come, and not until I had held the position for nearly an hour did any re-enforcements come up to the position the battalion occupied, and then only the left of one of the lines of the First Brigade, which indifferently lapped the right wing of my battalion, reached me in strength so weak that a feeble effort to advance beyond my position was easily repulsed.

Not hearing from the general, I now dispatched another officer to him for orders, but he, as well as the officer I had previously sent (I learned afterward) failed to find any one in authority. A little before dark the Ninety-third Ohio and Companies I and B, of the One hundred and twenty-fourth, seeing the left give way and supposing that the whole line had been ordered back, fell back with them, and reformed with the brigade which had been relieved and ordered to the rear.

Not receiving any order myself, I maintained my present position with the rest of my battalion until 7.30 o'clock; when it becoming quite dark, and feeling apprehensive that should the enemy make an offensive movement, the position could not be held, I started myself to report the situation, but had just reached the rear when the rebels suddenly and in large force attacked the battalion, which, seeing that it would be impossible to maintain their position, fell back before them into the new line already established. . . .

This attack, though unsuccessful, was made by the battalion with spirit and marked bravery, and I venture to say no more honest or bold attempt to carry the enemy's works has occurred during the campaign. Every officer and enlisted man in this battalion . . . behaved with great gallantry, and, if valor and heroism could have gained the point, would most assuredly have succeeded. At no time did the battalion become in the least disorganized, and had orders reached me at the same time the brigade received them to retire, the battalion could have withdrawn in order, bringing off all its wounded and dead; as it was, some were of necessity left on the field. [*O.R.*, XXXVIII, pt. 1, p. 442.]

THE SECOND WAVE

Report of Lt. Col. Ole C. Johnson, USA, Fifteenth Wisconsin Infantry, First Brigade, Third Division, Fourth Army Corps, Army of the Cumberland

About 4 p.m., General Hazen's brigade being repulsed, the front line of this brigade was ordered forward, closely followed by the Second. Our regiment in crossing a ravine was enfiladed by one of the enemy's batteries. Charging with a yell over the Second Brigade [Hazen], the regiment went so near to the enemy's breast-works that some of our men were killed within ten feet of them. Finding it impossible to dislodge the enemy, the regiment lay down about fifteen yards from their works, keeping up an effective musketry fire, Companies A and F firing at right oblique at a battery that was in position about sixty yards to the right, so as to enfilade our line of battle.

The firing from the enemy's musketry and artillery was very heavy, but we held our position until about 9 p.m., when we were ordered to fall back. In attempting to carry off our wounded the enemy charged on us and captured many of our men, including most of the wounded. About 11 p.m. the regiment was put in position some 300 yards to the right, on a ridge, and 200 yards from the enemy's works, where we fortified strongly. In this position we remained, constantly skirmishing with the enemy until he evacuated his position on the night of June 5. [*O.R.*, XXXVIII, pt. 1, pp. 418–419.]

THE THIRD WAVE

Report of Col. Frederick Knefler, USA, Commanding Third Brigade, Third Division, Fourth Army Corps, Army of the Cumberland

The brigade marched in support of the First Brigade . . . which was soon engaged with the enemy. The attack was so strongly resisted that it speedily necessitated the bringing of this brigade into action. In the advance the first line was completely enfiladed by the enemy's artillery, suffering severely.

The advance was made rapidly and in good order. After sustaining a murderous fire . . . it was thrown into disorder. The second line was then ordered forward. The advance was made in splendid style through a terrific fire; the crest of a deep ravine was reached in advance of the former line, which was stubbornly held against what appeared largely superior numbers of the enemy. A barricade was built of rails, which in a measure protected the line from the overwhelming fire of the enemy in front, but both flanks were exposed to a continual fire of musketry and artillery, the supports on both flanks having disappeared. . . .

A very heavy fire was kept up till dark, when ammunition began to fail and the men were compelled to have recourse to the cartridges of the dead and wounded. . . . Skirmishers were ordered to the front to guard against surprise. At 10 o'clock the order to withdraw was received. . . . All of a sudden, the enemy sallied from his works and made an assault upon the line, which was promptly and vigorously repulsed. The brigade then withdrew in good order . . . and fell back to the entrenched position of King's brigade, of the First Division, Fourteenth Army corps. . . .

The best possible disposition was made of the wounded who were in condition to be brought off the field. Many of the severely wounded, however, were left behind, owing to the impossibility of bringing ambulances to the scene of action, it being an almost impenetrable jungle, cut up by ravines, creeks and swamps, without roads or even paths, for vehicles of any description. [O.R., XXXVIII, pt. 1, pp. 447–448.]

STOP 14C, RED LOOP TRAIL

If you walked down the "Blue Loop" trail to Stop 14B, you can now continue your walk on the "Blue Loop" to the intersection with the "Red Loop" trail. Follow the blazes on the Red Loop uphill toward the Confederate positions until you reach Station 2. There you will find remnants of Confederate earthworks constructed after the repulse of the Union attacks.

Report of Maj. Gen. Patrick R. Cleburne, CSA (continued)

In front of a prolongation of *Granbury's* line and abutting upon his right was a field about 300 yards square. The enemy, driving back some cavalry, at this point advanced completely across the field and passed some forty or fifty yards in its rear. Here, however, they were confronted by the Eighth and Nineteenth Arkansas (consolidated), commanded by Colonel *Baucum*, hastily sent by *Govan* upon *Granbury's* request and representation of the exigency. In a sweeping charge *Baucum* drove the enemy from the ridge in his front, and with irresistible impetuosity forced him across the field and back into the woods, from which he had at first advanced. Here he fixed himself and kept up a heavy fire, aided by a deadly enfilade from the bottom of the ravine in front of *Granbury*. When *Baucum* was about to charge, *Lowrey*, of my division, who had been hastened up from his distant position upward of a mile and a half from my right as finally established, came into line, throwing his regiments in successively, as they unmasked themselves by their flank march. His arrival was most opportune, as the enemy was beginning to pour around *Baucum's* right. Colonel *Adams*, with the Thirty-third Alabama, which was the first of *Lowrey's* regiments to form into line, took position on *Baucum's* right and advanced with him, his seven left companies being in the field with *Baucum*, and his other four in the woods to the right. *Baucum* and *Adams*, finding themselves suffering from the enemy's direct and oblique fire, withdrew, passing over the open space of the field behind them. The right companies of *Adams*, which were in the woods, retired to a spur which rises from the easterly edge of the field about 200 yards from its southerly edge, where *Baucum's* and *Adams'* left companies rested. Here they halted. Captain *Dodson*, with fine judgment perceiving the importance of the position—it would have given the enemy an enfilading fire upon *Granbury*, which would have dislodged him— and making his company the basis of alignment for the remainder of *Lowrey's*, now coming into position.

This retrograde movement across the field was not attended with loss as might have been expected, the enemy not advancing as it was made. It was mistaken, however, for a repulse, and some of my staff officers hearing that my line had broken hastened forward *Quarles'* brigade, of *Stewart's* division, just then providentially sent up by General *Hood* to reestablish it. *Lowrey*, being under the same impression, detached his two right regiments (which had not been engaged) under Colonels [William H.] *Tison* and [Aaron B.] *Hardcastle*, and had them quickly formed in support of *Baucum* and *Adams*. The error, however, was soon discovered, and my line being ascertained to remain in its integrity, *Quarles'* brigade was conducted to the rear of *Lowrey*, and formed as a second line. The Fourth Louisiana, Colonel [*Samuel E.*] *Hunter,* finding itself opposite an interval between the two regiments of *Lowrey's* line (caused by *Baucum's* resting closer upon *Granbury* on his return from the advance, than he had done at first), under the immediate superintendence of General *Quarles,* advanced with great spirit into the field, halted, and delivered a very effective fire upon the enemy in his front. After some minutes *Quarles* withdrew this regiment and formed it behind the field, where they continued their fire across it. . . . During these movements the battle continued to rage on *Granbury's* front, and was met with unflagging spirit. About the time of *Quarles* getting into position night came on, when the combat lulled. For some hours afterward a desultory dropping fire, with short, vehement bursts of musketry, continued, the enemy lying in great numbers immediately in front of portions of my line, and so near it that their footsteps could be distinctly heard.

About 10 p.m. I ordered *Granbury* and *Lowrey* to push forward skirmishers and scouts to learn the state of things in their respective fronts. *Granbury,* finding it impossible to advance his skirmishers until he had cleared his front of the enemy lying up against it, with my consent, charged with his whole line, *Walthall,* with his brigade, from *Hindman's* division, whom I sent to his support, taking his place in the line as he stepped out of it. The Texans, their bayonets fixed, plunged into the darkness with a terrific yell, and with one bound were upon the enemy, but they met with no resistance. Surprised and panicstricken, many fled, escaping in the darkness, others surrendered and were brought into our lines. It needed but the brilliancy of this night attack to add luster to the achievements of *Granbury* and his brigade in the afternoon. . . .

My thanks are also due to General *Lowrey* for the coolness and skill which he exhibited in forming his line. His successive formation was the precise answer to the enemy's movement in extending his left to turn our right. Time was of the essence . . . and his movement was the quickest. His line was formed under heavy fire, on ground unknown to him and of the most difficult character, and the stern firmness with which he and his men and *Baucum's* regiment drove off the enemy and resisted his renewed attacks without doubt saved the right of the army, as *Granbury* had already done before.

During the progress of the battle much service was rendered by the rifle battery and two remaining howitzers of *Key's* battery, in position on *Polk's* right. They were trained in enfilade upon the enemy's reserves massed behind the hill in front of the spur we occupied. I regretted I did not have more guns for this service. I had sent the Napoleon guns to the right, where they were unable to find positions and so were useless.

Polk was not engaged, but it was a source of strength and confidence to the rest of the division to know that he had charge of the weakest and most delicate part of our line. . . .

My casualties in this battle were few. I had 85 killed, 363 wounded, carrying into the engagement 4,683 muskets. The enemy's losses were very heavy. The lowest estimate which can be made of his dead is 500. We captured 160 prisoners, who were sent to army headquarters, exclusive of 72 of his wounded carried to my field hospital. He could not have lost in all less than 3,000 killed and wounded. I took upward of 1,200 small arms. [*O.R.*, XXXVIII, pt. 3, pp. 724–726.]

The battle of Pickett's Mill also involved substantial fighting to the east of this position, where Scribner's brigade, from the accompanying Fourteenth Army Corps, encountered *Wheeler's* dismounted cavalry on the extreme right of the Confederate line.

THE CONFEDERATE RIGHT FLANK

Report of Col. Benjamin F. Scribner, USA, Commanding Third Brigade, First Division, Fourteenth Army Corps, Army of the Cumberland

Here, it was understood, rested the long-sought-for enemy's right, and dispositions were at once made to turn it. The ground was very broken, the [Pickett's Mill] Creek winding its tortuous way among the hills and a labyrinth of ravines, complicating the difficulties. Wood's brigades were each formed in two lines, making the division consist of six lines. After several slight modifications, I was finally ordered to form on the left of the center brigade (Gibson's) and advance with it to protect the left flank of the division. On the left of Wood flowed the creek, on the other side of which rose a ridge, cut by ravines and difficult of ascent. Skirmishers were thrown across the creek on the ridge, also to the front, and from the difficulty I would have in advancing from the prolongation of Wood's line, I determined to throw my left forward and strengthen the line when Wood advanced. Two regiments had hardly moved out when a sharp fire was opened by the skirmishers, which caused me to bring up the rest of the command by the flank to such a position as the nature of the ground would permit, so that they might come into their places in line as the front became extended as the column advanced.

It was about 5 o'clock in the evening when the column emerged from the wooded hill into an open wheat-field, across which we marched, ascended a wooded ridge; passing a mill and house we found the enemy in force, behind their ever-attending breast-works. Up to this time we had met with nothing but the enemy's skirmishers, who yielded stubbornly at our approach, but when Wood's leading brigade advanced into the open field a terrific fire was opened upon them. The line continued to advance under a galling fire of musketry and artillery.

It was soon found impracticable, however, to carry their works with our force, and dispositions were made by Wood to occupy the rising ground in the woods. This deployment placed me in the front line on the left of Knefler's brigade, which moved up into the edge of the field. The enemy, emboldened by his success . . . furiously assaulted the whole line; this was repeated several times and as often repulsed. They soon became more and more active upon my part of the line, and a movement to turn the left was discovered. Already a severe fire enfiladed the Thirty-seventh Indiana. The Twenty-first Ohio, First Wisconsin, and Thirty-eighth Indiana, who had been thrown across the creek, were swung forward, thereby clearing the hill and checking the enemy in this direction. . . .

The enemy, failing in their attempt to turn my left, renewed their attack upon my right. The Seventy-eighth Pennsylvania and Thirty-seventh Indiana were most exposed, and, with a persistency and heroism worthy of all praise, maintained their ground, expending sixty rounds of ammunition, and for four hours were hotly pressed. About 10 p.m., after a short lull in the battle, the enemy was discovered making preparations for a night attack. Ammunition was distributed from the surplus held by the second line. Breast-works of rails had been hastily thrown up, and every preparation to receive the assault. At length the yell of the enemy was heard. They came rushing and shouting like demons, and were received by a volley from our lines. After this a deep and ominous silence occurred. I soon observed that the troops on my right were falling back, and was soon left alone with my right exposed. . . . The Seventy-fourth Ohio was hastily brought up, and a strong skirmish line thrown out, with its right refused. . . .

We continued to hold the position. . . . At no time during the engagement did we yield ground. This was the state of affairs when I was ordered to retire my command. [*O.R.*, XXXVIII, pt. 1, pp. 595–596.]

Report of Maj. Gen. Joseph Wheeler, CSA, Commanding Cavalry Corps, Army of Tennessee

May 27, General *Cleburne's* division of infantry having been formed upon the right of our infantry line, I placed portions of *Hannon's* and *Allen's* small cavalry brigades, of *Kelly's* division, upon General *Cleburne's* right flank. They were dismounted, and entrenchments thrown up extending on the prolongation of General *Cleburne's* line for a distance of about 800 yards.

The enemy having during the morning and preceding day made several attacks upon the pickets on the Burnt Hickory road, I had placed General *Martin's* command in position to oppose the enemy, who were menacing that point, leaving a space of about two miles between General *Martin's* left an General *Kelly's* right, which was filled by a line of skirmishers from General *Humes'* command, which . . . was held in reserve to move to any point which might be attacked.

About 3 o'clock this line of skirmishers was driven in by a force of the enemy's cavalry advancing up Pumpkin Vine Creek by Widow Pickett's house. I immediately galloped to this point and found a squadron moving, by General *Humes'* direction, to re-enforce the picket. On arriving at the creek I soon observed that a considerable force of infantry was before us, and I directed General *Humes* to bring one brigade (dismounted) to that point, and to prolong his other brigade upon its right to fill the gap between said position and General *Martin's* left. These dispositions were made under a warm fire from the enemy.

At this moment I received information that General *Martin's* line was being attacked, and at the same time that *Granbury's* brigade of infantry was moving up to relieve General *Kelly*, whom I ordered to move to the right and close upon General *Humes*.

While making the movement, and before it was completed, the enemy moved a column up a ravine between *Kelly's* right and *Humes'* left. I ordered a regiment from *Humes* to oppose them, which was promptly placed in position, but finding it was warmly pressed,

General *Humes* re-enforced it with another regiment from his command. While this movement was going on Hazen's Federal infantry brigade charged our line, but was repulsed by a counter-charge of *Humes'* and *Kelly's* commands.

My command captured 32 prisoners . . . whom they turned over to *Lowrey's* infantry brigade, which was just forming to their right to relieve General *Humes'* command. On the arrival of General *Lowrey's* brigade General *Humes* moved to the right in front of the temporary breast-works thrown up during the engagement. *Quarles'* brigade also reported to me during the fight, but too late to join in the action.

I had but 822 men engaged, extending over the ground to such length as to enable me to form little more than a line of skirmishers. . . . We successfully thwarted this movement (to turn our right flank), holding this large force of the enemy in check until we were relieved by a division of our infantry, to whom we gave up our temporary breast-works, and then moved to the right to guard their right flank. But one infantry brigade (*Granbury's*) got into position before the defeat of the enemy. The difficulty of maneuvering so thin a line in a thick woods under a heavy fire will be appreciated. [*O.R.*, XXXVIII, pt. 3, pp. 948–949.]

SUMMARY OF THE BATTLE AND SUBSEQUENT ACTIONS

The best account by a participant in this battle comes from Lt. Ambrose G. Bierce, later a well-known journalist and short-story writer, who here served on Hazen's staff. His observations reveal much about the human dimension in Civil War combat.

Narrative of Lt. Ambrose G. Bierce, USA, Acting Topographical Engineer, Second Brigade, Third Division, Fourth Army Corps, Army of the Cumberland

[This] was the situation: a weak brigade of fifteen hundred men, with masses of idle troops behind in the character of audience, waiting for the word to march a quarter-mile up hill through almost impassable tangles of underwood, along and across precipitous ravines, and attack breastworks constructed at leisure. . . . True, we did not know all this, but if any man on that ground besides Wood and Howard expected a "walkover" his must have been a singularly hopeful disposition. As topographical engineer it had been my duty to make a hasty examination of the ground in front. In doing so I had pushed far enough forward through the forest to hear distinctly the murmur of the enemy awaiting us, and this had been duly reported; but from our lines nothing could be heard but the wind among the trees and the songs of birds. Some one said it was a pity to frighten them. . . . We laughed at that: men awaiting death on the battlefield laugh easily, though not infectiously.

The brigade was formed in four battalions, two in front and two in rear. This gave us a front of about two hundred yards. . . . We moved forward. In less than one minute the trim battalions had become simply a swarm of men struggling through the undergrowth of the forest, pushing and crowding. The front was irregularly serrated, the strongest and bravest in advance, the others following in fan-like formations, variable and inconstant, ever defining themselves anew.

For the first two hundred yards our course lay along the left bank of a small creek in a deep ravine, our left battalions sweeping along its steep slope. Then we came to the fork of the ravine. A part of us crossed below, the rest above, passing over both branches, the regiments inextricably intermingled, rendering all military formation impossible. The color-bearers kept well to the front with their flags, closely furled, aslant backward over their shoulders. Displayed, they would have been torn to rags by the boughs of the trees. Horses were all sent to the rear; the general and staff and all the field officers toiled along on foot as best they could. "We shall halt and form when we get out of this," said an aide-de-camp.

Suddenly there were a ringing rattle of musketry, the familiar hissing of bullets, and before us the interspaces of the forest were all blue with smoke, Hoarse, fierce yells broke out of a thousand throats. The forward fringe of brave and hardy assailants was arrested in its mutable extensions; the edge of our swarm grew dense and clearly defined as the foremost halted, and the rest pressed forward to align themselves beside them, all firing. The uproar was deafening; the air was sibilant with streams and sheets of missiles. In the steady, unvarying roar of small-arms the frequent shock of the cannon was rather felt than heard, but the gusts of grape which they blew into that populous wood were audible enough, screaming among the trees and cracking against their stems and branches. We had, of course, no artillery to reply.

Our brave color-bearers were now all in the forefront of battle in the open, for the enemy had cleared a space in front of his breastworks.

They held the colors erect, shook out their glories, waved them forward and back to keep them spread, for there was no wind. From where I stood, at the right of the line—we had "halted and formed," indeed—I could see six of our flags at one time. Occasionally one would go down, only to be instantly lifted by other hands. . . .

Early in my military experience I used to ask myself how it was that brave troops could retreat while still their courage was high. As long as a man is not disabled he can go forward; can it be anything but fear that makes him stop and finally retire? Are there signs by which he can infallibly know the struggle to be hopeless? In this engagement, as in others, my doubts were answered as to the fact; the explanation is still obscure.

In many instances . . . when hostile lines of infantry engage at close range and the assailants afterward retire, there was a "dead-line" beyond which no man advanced but to fall. Not a soul of them ever reached the enemy's front to be bayoneted or captured. It was a matter of the difference of three or four paces—too small a distance to affect the accuracy of aim. In these affairs no aim is taken at individual antagonists; the soldier delivers his fire at the thickest mass in his front. The fire is, of course, as deadly at twenty paces as at fifteen; at fifteen as at ten. Nevertheless, there is the "dead-line," with its well-defined edge of corpses—those of the bravest. Where both lines are fighting without cover—as in a charge met by a counter-charge—each has its "dead-line," and between the two is a clear space—neutral ground, devoid of dead, for the living cannot reach it to fall there.

I observed this phenomenon at Pickett's Mill. Standing at the right of the line I had an unobstructed view of the narrow, open space across which the two lines fought. It was dim with smoke, but not greatly obscured: the smoke rose and spread in sheets among the branches of the trees. Most of our men fought kneeling as they had fired, many of them behind trees, stones and whatever cover they could get, but there were considerable groups that stood. Occasionally one of these groups, which had endured the storm of missiles for moments without perceptible reduction, would push forward, moved by a common despair, and wholly detach itself from the line. In a second every man of the group would be down. There had been no visible movement of the enemy, no audible change in the awful, even roar of the firing—yet all were down. Frequently the dim figure of an individual soldier would be seen to spring away from his comrades, advancing alone toward that fateful interspace, with leveled bayonet. He got no farther than the farthest of his predecessors. Of the "hundreds of corpses within twenty paces of the Confederate line," I venture to say that a third were within fifteen paces, and not one within ten.

It is the perception—perhaps unconscious—of this inexplicable phenomenon that causes the still unharmed, still vigorous, and still courageous soldier to retire without having to come into actual contact with his foe. He sees, or feels, that he cannot. His bayonet is a useless weapon for slaughter; its purpose is a moral one. Its mandate exhausted, he sheathes it and trusts to the bullet. That failing, he retreats. He has done all that he could do with such appliances as he has.

No command to fall back was given, none could have been heard. Man by man, the survivors withdrew at will, sifting through the trees into the cover of the ravines, among the wounded who could drag themselves back; among the skulkers whom nothing could have dragged forward.

The left of our short line had fought at the corner of a cornfield, the fence along the right side of which was parallel to the direction of our retreat. As the disorganized groups fell back along this fence on the wooded side, they were attacked by a flanking force of the enemy moving through the field in a direction nearly parallel with what had been our front. This force, I infer from General *Johnston's* account, consisted of the brigade of General *Lowrey,* or two Arkansas regiments under Colonel *Baucum.* I had been sent by General Hazen to that point and arrived in time to witness this formidable movement. But already our retreating men, in obedience to their officers, their courage and their instinct of self-preservation, had formed along the fence and opened fire. The apparently slight advantage of the imperfect cover and the open range worked its customary miracle: the assault, a singularly spiritless one, considering the advantages it promised and that it was made by an organized and victorious force against a broken and retreating one, was checked. The assailants actually retired, and if they afterward renewed the movement they encountered none but our dead and wounded.

The battle, as a battle, was at an end, but there was still some slaughtering that it was possible to incur before nightfall; and as the wreck of our brigade drifted back through the forest we met the brigade (Gibson's) which, had the attack been made in column, as it should have been, would have been but five minutes behind our heels. . . . As it was, just forty-five minutes had elapsed, during which the enemy had destroyed us and was now ready to perform the same kindly office for our successors. . . .

Their losses were considerable, including several hundred prisoners taken from a sheltered place whence they did not care to rise and run. The entire loss was about fourteen hundred men, of whom nearly one-half fell killed and wounded in Hazen's brigade in less than thirty minutes of actual fighting. . . . I remember that we were all astonished at the uncommonly large proportion of dead to wounded— a consequence of the uncommonly close range at which most of the fighting was done.

For my commander and my friend, my master in the art of war, now unable to answer for himself [Brig. Gen. Hazen], let this fact answer: when he heard Wood say they would put him in and see what success he would have in defeating an army—when he saw Howard assent—he uttered never a word, rode to the head of his feeble brigade and patiently awaited the command to go. Only by a look which I knew how to read did he betray his sense of the criminal blunder. [Ambrose Bierce, "The Crime at Pickett's Mill," *Collected Works*, 12 vols. (New York: Neale, 1909–1912), vol. I, pp. 283–296.]

Bate's attack against the Union right on May 28 delayed McPherson's efforts to disengage and reunite with the Army of the Cumberland near New Hope Church, but it affected only the timing, not the direction, of Sherman's next move.

To move troops over the terrain around Pumpkin Vine Creek was an ordeal. Frequent delays made it difficult to achieve surprise and often gave the enemy time to extend his entrenchments. This is why Wood's attack failed at Pickett's Mill, and why, two days later, a similar attempt by *Hood* to get around the Union left flank near Pickett's Mill Creek never materialized. When *Hood* reached his objective he found Brig. Gen. Richard W. Johnson's division of the 14th Corps entrenching almost at right angles to the Union line. The Confederate plan was to have *Hood* roll up the Union left flank, with *Polk's* and *Hardee's* corps joining in successively. But when he saw Johnson's division entrenched where he had hoped to find an open flank, even the aggressive *Hood* thought better of attacking: he halted instead and asked *Johnston* for instructions. Such was the defensive capability of men behind earthworks.

In these battles *Johnston* continued either to anticipate Sherman's moves or to react quickly enough to utilize the terrain and the defensive power of earthworks to offset his opponent's advantage in numbers. He used his cavalry effectively not only to provide timely information, but as mobile firepower. Without *Wheeler's* dismounted troops to hold the right of the line at Pickett's Mill, Sherman's effort to turn *Johnston's* right flank might well have succeeded. Eventually the fighting along the Dallas–New Hope Church line convinced Sherman that the best way out of the impasse was not in the realm of tactics—attacking a flank—but of operations. On June 1 all three Union armies slid a few miles to their left. By June 4 Union cavalry occupied Allatoona Pass. With the bridges completed over the Etowah, Sherman was now in position to sidestep *Johnston*, link up with the railroad, and push on to Marietta and the Chattahoochee.

15. LOST MOUNTAIN

Return to your car. Drive back out to Mount Tabor Church Road using the park road and turn left. Check your mileage as you turn, and drive about 2.1 miles on Mount Tabor Church Road to a stop sign. Turn left onto East Paulding Drive. About 3.9 miles from Pickett's Mill you will cross GA 92. Continue on Paulding Drive. At about 4.8 miles from Pickett's Mill, turn left at the traffic light onto GA 120 East (Dallas Marietta Highway). Note your mileage. Drive about 1.7 miles on this road, crossing Lost Mountain Road en route. Turn right into Lost Mountain Park. Turn left on the first park road, and then turn right to park in the large parking lot. Position yourself so that you can look across the highway toward Lost Mountain.

STOP 15, LOST MOUNTAIN

OPERATIONS

Maj. Gen. William T. Sherman, Headquarters, Military Division of the Mississippi, in the Field Near Dallas, to Maj. Gen. H. W. Halleck, Washington, D.C., 2 June 1864

Yesterday General McPherson moved up from Dallas to the point in front of the enemy at New Hope Church, and Generals Schofield and Hooker were shifted to the extreme left. Today they pushed forward in a heavy rain and thunder storm, and have advanced about two miles toward Marietta. At the same time I sent General Stoneman's cavalry directly to Allatoona and General Garrard's cavalry to the western end of the pass. So our movement has secured to us that pass which was considered a formidable one. I have ordered the railroad to be repaired, and will gradually move across by the left of the railroad. The country is most difficult, being of dense undergrowth and short steep ridges of flinty stone. Thus far we have had no real battle, but one universal skirmish extending over a vast surface. [O.R., XXXVIII, pt. 4, p. 385.]

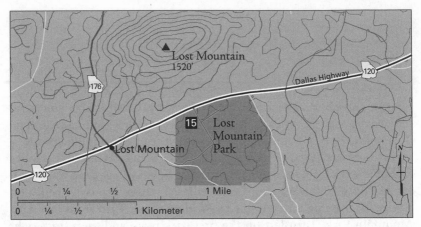

Lost Mountain (Stop 15)

During this move, both Union and Confederate commanders were hampered by rainy weather as well as difficult terrain. Sherman took advantage of the lull in active combat operations to tighten the administrative features of his army.

Special Field Orders No. 15, Headquarters, Military Division of the Mississippi, in the Field, 31 May 1864

In order to secure the rapid and efficient co-working of the Topographical Engineer Department of the Army in the field, and to avoid making surveys of any road by more than one officer, the following system will be adopted:

I. No Topographical Engineer shall be employed as an Aide-de-Camp, or in any other duty other than making purely military surveys. The selection of camps, location of picket lines and repairs of roads, are not to be imposed on them, but on Quartermasters and other Staff officers.

II. On a march they will survey the route of their commands. When the army comes to a permanent or temporary halt, they will report in person to the Chief Engineer of their respective Departments and make such special field surveys as may be assigned them, at all times complying with his orders and instructions. Their surveys will then be compiled, and maps will be sent to their chief, who will cause

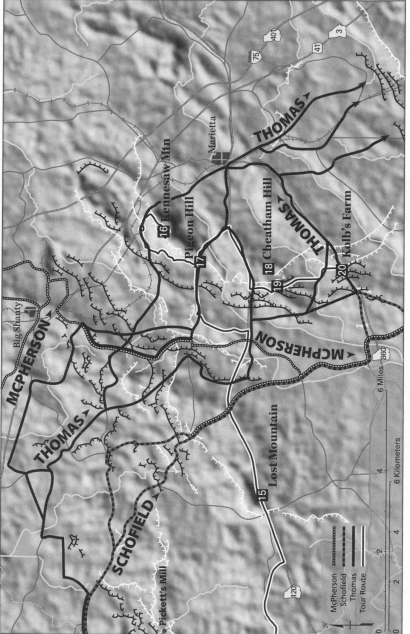

Movements, Positions, and Guidebook Stops: Pickett's Mill through Kennesaw Mountain

them to be consolidated and issued from time to time as the exigencies of the campaign will permit.

III. All Corps, Division and Brigade Commanders will assist their Topographical Engineers to work in harmony, and for the benefit of the whole army, and thus secure the data from which to compile, at the earliest possible moment, maps which are indispensably necessary to military movements, as in this manner only can all General officers receive the benefit of all military surveys. [*Orders,* p. 250.]

Special Field Orders No. 17, Headquarters, Military Division of the Mississippi, in the Field Near Dallas, 4 June 1864

The attention of the General commanding has been called to certain facts which had already attracted his own attention, and concerning which he orders:

I. In case of skirmish or battle the wounded must be brought off the field by musicians or non-combatants, distinguished by a badge of white cloth on the left arm. In no case, as long as firing continues, should an armed soldier abandon his comrades in battle to attend the wounded. See Par. 734, Army Regulations.

II. Hospitals are too far to the rear of their Corps or Divisions; they should be up as close as possible, and covered by the shape of the ground and not by distance. The Surgeons in charge are responsible that slight wounds or shirking be not the cause of detaining armed men about their hospitals. Each attendant should have at all times about his person the written authority which justifies his presence at the hospital, or in passing to and from the command to which the hospital belongs.

III. Shirking, skulking and straggling in time of danger are such high detestable crimes, that the General commanding would hardly presume them possible, were it not for his own observation, and the report that at this moment soldiers are found loafing in the cabins to the rear as far back as Kingston.

The only proper fate of such miscreants is that they be shot as common enemies to their profession and country; and all officers and privates sent to arrest them will shoot them without mercy on the slightest impudence or resistance.

"Lost Mountain at Sunrise" (*Harper's Pictorial History of the Great Rebellion*
[New York: Harper Bros., 1866–1868], 607).

By thus wandering to the rear they desert their fellows who ex-
pose themselves in battle in the full faith that all on the rolls are present, and they subject themselves to capture and exchange, to which
they have no title. It is hereby made the duty of every officer who
finds such skulkers to deliver them to any Provost Guard, regardless of
corps, to be employed in menial or hard work, such as repairing roads,
digging drains, sinks, etc. Officers, if found skulking, will be subject
to the same penalties as enlisted men, viz.: instant death or the hard-
est labor and treatment. Absentees not accounted for should always
be mustered as "deserters," to deprive them of their pay and bounties
reserved for honest soldiers.

IV. All will be styled skulkers who are found to the rear, absent
from their proper commands without written authority from their
proper commanders. Captains cannot give orders or passes beyond
their regimental limits, Colonels beyond brigade limits, Brigadiers beyond division limits, etc. The Commanding Generals of the three (3)
Departments alone can order officers or detachments with or without
wagons back to Kingston, or other general depots.

V. If unarmed soldiers are found on horses or mules at a distance
from their proper commands or trains, any Cavalry escort or patrol
will make prisoners of the men and appropriate the horses and mules
to the use of the Cavalry. Orderlies to General Officers on duty will be

easily recognized by bearing official orders or receipts for the same, but each General Officer should provide his orderlies with an official detail, to be carried with him.

Horses or mules sent for forage or to graze should be sent by detachments, with arms and military organization, when they will always be respected.

VI. Brigade and regimental commanders are the proper officers to keep their officers and men at their places. The Commanding General will, by his Inspectors and in person, give the matter a full attention, and when the time comes for reports on which to base claims for rewards and promotion, no officer having a loose, straggling command need expect any favor.

VII. The Commanding Generals of the three armies will make this order public, and at once organize guards and patrols to carry it into full effect. [*Orders*, pp. 251–253.]

When Union forces reached positions on the railroad south of Allatoona, General *Johnston* was forced to adjust his defensive line. Lost Mountain became the left flank of a new position that encompassed Pine Mountain, crossed the railroad south of Big Shanty (today's Kennesaw), and ended on Brush Mountain. General *Hardee's* corps held the left, *Polk* was in the center, where he was killed by a Union artillery shot on June 14, and *Hood* occupied the right.

On June 5, General Sherman reported on the situation to General Halleck, and he communicated his intent very clearly in a message to General Schofield on the same day. Writing in the evening on June 7, he gave General Halleck an excellent operational update, and he provided a more general overview of the situation in his *Memoirs*. Excerpts from these writings follow.

Sherman to Halleck, 5 June 1864

The enemy discovered us creeping around his right flank, abandoned his position and marched off last night. We captured about thirty of their pickets at daylight. General McPherson is moving today for Ackworth—General Thomas is on the direct Marietta road, and General Schofield is on the right. It has been raining hard for three days, and the roads are very heavy. The construction party is at work on the Etowah bridge and should repair it in five days, when I will move on to Marietta. I expect the enemy to fight us at Kennesaw Mountain, near Marietta, but I will not run head on his fortifications. An examination of his abandoned line here shows an immense line of works, all of which I have turned with less loss to ourselves than we have inflicted on him. The wheat fields of the country are our chief supply of forage, and we have in camp bread, meat, sugar, and coffee for many days, ample until the railroad will be complete to Ackworth. [*O.R.*, XXXVIII pt. 4, pp. 408–409.]

Sherman to Maj. Gen. John M. Schofield, USA, Commanding the Army of the Ohio, 5 June 1864

We can adjust our lines after reaching the ground. I prefer our lines not to be deployed too much, but held in masses at central points with connections from army to army made by skirmish lines. We being on the offensive should be prepared to move quick. When we reach our next position I will await Blair's arrival, replenish stores, make and fortify our depot at Allatoona, and then move on according to the point where *Johnston* selects for battle. I think he will oppose us lightly all the way to the Chattahoochee and defend that line with all his ability. Make your preparations and dispositions accordingly. This hard rain is unfortunate, but it is beyond our control. [*O.R.*, XXXVIII, pt. 4, pp. 413–414.]

Sherman to Halleck, 7 June 1864

I have been to Allatoona Pass, and I find it admirable for our purposes. It is the gate through the last, or most eastern, spur of the Alleghenies. It now becomes as useful to us as it was to the enemy, being easily defended from either direction. My left (General McPherson) now lies on the railroad in front of Acworth, seven miles southeast of Allatoona; center (General Thomas) three miles south, on main Marietta road; and right (General Schofield) two miles farther, a little refused. The cars now come to the Etowah River and we have sent back to replenish our supplies for a ten-days' move, to commence on Thursday, the 9th instant. Colonel [William W.] Wright reports it will take him ten days of which eight yet remain, to have cars come to Acworth. General Blair was at Kingston last night, and will be across the Etowah tonight, and will be up with us tomorrow. We have three

"Crest of Pine Mountain Where General Polk Fell" (*Harper's Pictorial History of the Great Rebellion* [New York: Harper Bros., 1866–1868], 607).

pontoon bridges at Etowah. I will leave a brigade in the pass covering the bridge and its eastern debouche, and have sent Captain Poe, U.S. Engineers, to lay out the work. The roads here into Georgia are large and good, and the country more open. The enemy is not in our immediate front, but his signals are seen on Lost Mountain and Kennesaw. I have had the cavalry at Allatoona Pass to get forage, but on the 9th will bring it forward. Colonel [Eli] Long's brigade is with Blair, and will re-enforce our cavalry by 2,000 horses. I send you by mail today copies of my orders up to date, with Atlanta papers of the 5th. [*O.R.*, XXXVIII, pt. 4, p. 428.]

Narrative of Maj. Gen. William T. Sherman

General Blair arrived in Ackworth on the 8th with his two divisions of the Seventeenth Corps—the same which had been on veteran furlough. . . . His effective strength, as reported, was nine thousand. These, with the new regiments and furloughed men who had joined early in the month of May, equaled our losses from battle, sickness, and by detachments; so that the three armies still aggregated about one hundred thousand effective men.

On the 10th of June the whole combined army moved forward six miles, to "Big Shanty," a station on the railroad, whence we had a good view of the enemy's position, which embraced three prominent Hills, known as Kennesaw, Pine Mountain, and Lost Mountain. On each of these hills the enemy had signal stations and fresh lines of parapets. Heavy masses of infantry could be distinctly seen with the naked eye, and it was manifest that *Johnston* had chosen his ground well, and with deliberation had prepared for battle; but his line was at least ten miles in extent—too long, in my judgment, to be held successfully by his force, then estimated at sixty thousand. As his position, however, gave him perfect view over our field, we had to proceed with due caution. McPherson had the left, following the railroad, which curved around the north base of Kennesaw; Thomas the center, obliqued to the right, deploying below Kennesaw and facing Pine Hill, and Schofield, somewhat refused, was on the general right, looking south toward Lost Mountain. . . . The rains continued to pour, and made our developments slow and dilatory, for there were no roads, and these had to be improvised by each division for its own supply-train from the depot at Big Shanty to the camps. Meantime each army was deploying carefully before the enemy, entrenching every camp, ready as against a sally. [Sherman, *Memoirs*, II, pp. 519–520.]

Sherman's orders for the move on June 10 were explicit. But the rain that delayed offensive operations gave him a chance to reflect on his generalship in a letter to his wife, Ellen, on June 12, after he received news that she had given birth to their son. Nevertheless, he prepared his offensive against an overstretched *Johnston*, who was struggling with political authorities as well as rain and losses. While Sherman was receiving veteran regiments fresh from furlough, *Johnston* was offered Georgia militia, which he initially relegated to guarding crossings on the Chattahoochee River.

Special Field Order No. 21, Headquarters, Military Division of the Mississippi, in the field, Ackworth, Georgia, 9 June 1864

The object will be to develop the enemy's position and strength, and to draw artillery fire from his entrenched works. This army will operate by heads of columns instead of deployed lines of battle, each column covering, its head and flanks with good advance and flanking skirmishers, and be prepared to deploy promptly, according to danger. Intrenched positions will not be attacked without orders. Each head of column will have a good battery of heavy rifled artillery, and should use it freely against rail and log barricades, and also to indicate the positions of the heads of columns. The flank columns will conform their motions to that of the center. Either column reaching a good military position should intrench it by leaving a brigade, but should not delay its advance. [*O.R.*, XXXVIII, pt. 4, p. 445.]

Sherman to His Wife, Ellen, 12 June 1864

You say that pending the important events now transpiring you cannot write. I feel so too. That it should have devolved on me to guide one of the two great armies on which may depend the fate of our People for the next hundred years I somewhat regret. Yet you know I have been drawn into it by a slow & gradual process which I could not avoid. Grant was forced into his position and I likewise. I think thus far I have played my game well. Had my plans been executed with the vim I contemplated I should have forced *Johnston* to fight the decisive Battle in the Oostenaula Valley between Dalton & Resaca, but McPherson was a little overcautious, and we cannot move vast armies of this size with the rapidity of thought or of smaller bodies. For the past ten days our movements have been vastly retarded by rains. It has rained hard all the time and today harder than ever, a steady cold rain. I am in an old house with a fire burning which is not uncomfortable. *Johnston* has 60,000 Infantry, 15,000 Cavalry and a good deal of militia. We must have a terrific Battle, and he wants to choose and fortify his ground. He also aims to break my roads to the Rear. I wish we could make an accumulation of stores some where near but the Railroad is tried to its utmost to supply our daily wants.

The Country is stripped of cattle, horses, hogs, and grain, but there are large fine fields of growing oats, wheat and corn, which our horses & mules devour as we advance. Thus far we have been well supplied, and I hope it will continue, though I expect to hear every day of *Forrest* breaking into Tennessee from some quarter. *Morgan* is in Kentucky but I attach little importance to him or his Raid, as we don't draw anything from Kentucky, and there are plenty of troops there to capture & destroy him. *Forrest* is a more dangerous man. I am in hopes that an expedition sent out from Memphis on Tupelo, about the 1st of June will give him full employment. I have also ordered A. J. Smith with the force he brought out of Red River to move against Mobile by way of diversion. *Johnston* is now between me and Marietta. As soon as these clouds and storms clear away I will study his position and determine to assault his Line or turn it and force him back of the Chattahoochee. As long as I press him close and prevent his sending anything to [Gen. *Robert E.*] *Lee* I fulfill my part of the Grand Plan. In the mean time Grant will give *Lee* all the fighting he wants until he is sick of the word. Every man in America should now be aroused, and all who will not help should be put in petticoats & deprived of the right to vote in the affairs of the after nation. I will telegraph you on all important occasions—Hoping you will soon be well & contented, I am as ever yrs. [Brooks D. Simpson and Jean V. Berlin, eds., *Sherman's Civil War: Collected Correspondence of William T. Sherman, 1860–1865* (Chapel Hill: University of North Carolina Press, 1999), pp. 646–647.]

As Sherman prepared his offensive against an overstretched *Johnston*, that general was struggling with political authorities as well as rain and losses. While Sherman was receiving veteran regiments fresh from furlough, *Johnston* was offered Georgia militia, which he initially relegated to guarding crossings on the Chattahoochee River. In the aftermath of General Grant's unsuccessful assault against *Lee's* forces at Cold Harbor, *Johnston* received a telegram from Gen. *Braxton Bragg* in Richmond. *Johnston* knew he could expect no help from Richmond, so he set out to generate a force that could be used to counterattack from strong positions in the region from Lost Mountain to Brushy Mountain. *Polk* agreed with *Hood's* estimate, but *Polk* died on June 14, before the plan could be executed. The renewed pressure of Sherman's attacks stymied Confederate efforts to generate a reserve that might be used to gain the initiative. Union attacks in the vicinity of Lost Mountain ultimately produced decisive tactical results.

Gen. Braxton Bragg, CSA, General in Chief, Richmond, to Gen. Joseph E. Johnston, 7 June 1864

I inclose you herewith copy of a note this morning addressed to the President, which will explain itself. The object is to place before him the real condition of affairs with you. I send a copy also to General *Lee*. The force in front of *Lee* in Virginia was composed of four corps, *Sedgwick, Hancock, Warren,* and *Burnside* commanding. Just now it is increased by about 12,000 men from Butler's force, under Baldy Smith. From this you will see the work on hand, and be able to judge better than I can what should be our policy. Grant has been so much crippled by his constant repulses (of which he sustained a very severe one yesterday) that I apprehend but little damage from him now. [*O.R.*, XXXVIII, pt. 4, p. 762.]

Enclosure to Gen. Joseph E. Johnston, Originally from Gen. Braxton Bragg to President Jefferson Davis, CSA, 4 June 1864

Mr. President: The condition of affairs in Georgia is daily becoming more serious, and though the enemy there has for a few days been quiet, I fear it is only to avail himself of heavy re-enforcements. The force under Sherman is composed as follows:

(1) Palmer's corps, (2) Howard's corps—Rosecrans' old army consolidated; (3) Hooker's corps—the two from Virginia consolidated; (4) Schofield's corps, from East Tennessee; (5) Logan's corps, F. P. Blair's, Dodge's division—McPherson's command. These have been joined by (6) A. J. Smith's corps (seventeenth), from Red River, and Maj. Gen. *S. D. Lee* reports another infantry corps (Sixteenth) from Red River now moving from Memphis, and that he had recalled the force ordered by him to *Johnston's* support to oppose its progress. Should all these forces concentrate on the Army of Tennessee we may well apprehend disaster. As the entire available force of the Confederacy is now concentrated with our two main armies, I see no solution of this difficulty but in victory over one of the enemy's armies before the combination can be fully perfected. [*O.R.*, XXXVIII, pt. 4, p. 762.]

Gen. Joseph E. Johnston, CSA, Commanding the Army of Tennessee, to Lt. Gen. Leonidas Polk, 13 June 1864

You will do me a favor by giving me the benefit of your opinion on the subject of the mode of occupying our entrenchments to the best advantage. It is important that we should keep in our works only the number of men necessary to hold them, that we may have a strong movable force. For the line you now occupy, how many men, on average, would be necessary for each hundred yards, and how many guns for the front? . . . General *Hood* has just written to me:

The distance from *Hindman's* right to *Stevenson's* left is about one mile and a half, and the position and works very strong. The strength can be increased by additional artillery; with this addition, I think, 5,000 men can hold it against any force of the enemy, and 6,000 would allow reserves at certain points on the line. [*O.R.*, XXXVIII, pt. 4, pp. 772–773.]

15–17 June 1864

Report of Brig. Gen. Milo S. Hascall, USA, Commanding Second Division, Twenty-Third Army Corps, Army of the Ohio

The very heavy rains which fell at this time prevented any active operations being undertaken, and during the 11th, 12th, 13th, and 14th nothing was done. On the 15th, as a part of the general demonstration along the line, the Second Brigade, Colonel [John R.] Bond, made a movement from the extreme right, which, with the strong demonstration made on the front, compelled a retrograde movement of the enemy, and Colonel [Joseph A.] Cooper, First Brigade, and Colonel [John Q.] McQuiston, Second Brigade, moved forward to take possession of the vacated works. Moving on, the enemy were found in still greater force, and in a better chosen position, with their left on the Lost Mountain. General Butterfield's division of the Twentieth Army Corps, becoming heavily engaged with the enemy, apparently near the angle of their line, the refused part of which was evidently in our front, Colonel Cooper with his brigade, was ordered to press forward, develop their position, and to make a diversion in his favor. The works were reached, but night came on, and the brigade was withdrawn. . . . On the 16th the command moved into position near the main works of the enemy, and in so doing, drove back the skirmishers of the brigade commanded by the rebel General *Mercer*. By dark the whole division had secured a strong position, very near the enemy's works, so near that our skirmishers were fired on from his main works. During the night of the 16th the enemy evacuated his works. On the morning of the 17th, at an early hour, the troops had possession of their works. Passing to the right, I formed my command on Lost Mountain. [*O.R.*, XXXVIII, pt. 2, pp. 568–569.]

*Report of Col. William Cross, USA, Third East Tennessee
Volunteer Infantry, First Brigade, Second Division,
Twenty-Third Army Corps, Army of the Ohio*

[On June 15th] I received directions to advance across an open
field to the enemy's works. I accordingly moved on the first line of
works and gained them without any fighting, except the part of my
regiment which was on skirmish line. I was then ordered to advance
and make a demonstration on their next line. I accordingly moved forward, the skirmishers driving the enemy, until I came in sight of his
second line of works. Just at night I received orders to fall back to the
position I occupied before making the demonstration of the second
line. Here I remained for the night and threw up works.

16th June, occupied same position till about 2 p.m., when I was
ordered to advance, my regiment being left of front line, over the same
ground I had the previous evening. After advancing about half the distance the skirmish line charged and drove the enemy. At about sunset
my regiment was ordered to the skirmish line, where I remained all
night.

17th June, this morning the enemy had left my front and I advanced and took possession of his works. [O.R., XXXVIII, pt. 2, pp.
600–601.]

16. KENNESAW MOUNTAIN OVERVIEW

Drive back to the park entrance and check your mileage. Turn right onto GA 120. Drive about 4.2 miles on this road, preparing for a left turn in the last mile. At the traffic light for Ridgeway Road, turn left. Drive about 1.3 miles on Ridgeway until you come to the traffic light for Burnt Hickory Road. Turn Right and drive about 1.2 miles. Turn left onto Old Mountain Road and drive about 1.4 miles. Turn right at the stop sign for Stilesboro Road and drive about 0.4 mile. Turn right to enter the Kennesaw Mountain National Battlefield Park Visitor Center parking lot. Park and use the Visitor Center for updated information on park programs.

Return to your car. Exit the parking lot at the rear onto Mountain Road. Drive to the parking lot at the north shoulder of the crest of Kennesaw Mountain. Park and use the National Park Service interpretive panel at the end of the parking lot for general orientation. Climb the steps to the overview platform, which gives excellent views to the west and north over ground covered by the two armies in May and June 1864. Then turn and follow the asphalt path to the crest. At the fork in the trail, follow the right-hand trail to the National Park Service interpretive panel, "The Atlanta Campaign." The round-trip walk from the parking lot is about 300 yards.

STOP 16, KENNESAW MOUNTAIN

17–27 June 1864

Report of Maj. Gen. William T. Sherman, USA, Commanding Military Division of the Mississippi

On the 9th of June our communications to the rear being secure and supplies ample, we moved forward to Big Shanty. Kennesaw, the bold and striking twin mountain, lay before us, with a high range of chestnut hills trending off to the northeast, terminating to our view in another peak called Brush Mountain. To our right was a smaller hill, called Pine Mountain, and beyond it in the distance, Lost Mountain.

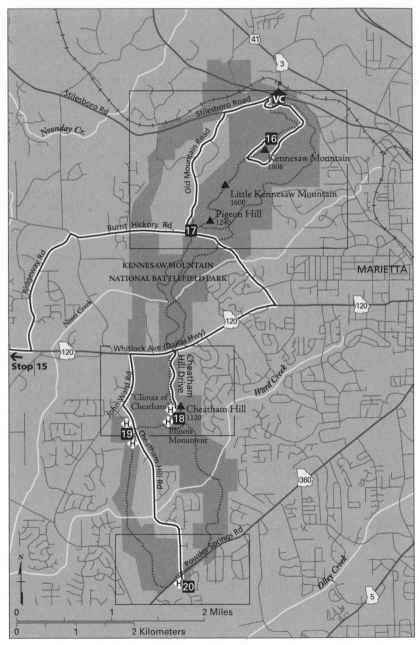

Kennesaw Mountain and Kolb's Farm (Stops 16 and 17)

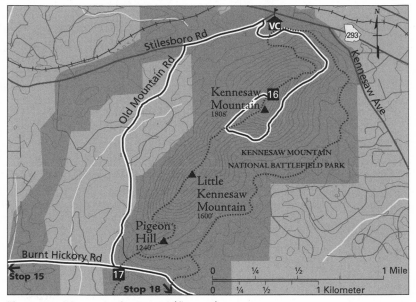

Kennesaw Mountain Overview (Stop 16)

All these, though linked in a continuous chain, present a sharp, coni-cal appearance, prominent in the vast landscape that presents itself from any of the hills that abound in that region. Kennesaw, Pine Mountain, and Lost Mountain form a triangle. Pine Mountain the apex, and Kennesaw and Lost Mountain the base, covering perfectly the town of Marietta, and the railroad back to the Chattahoochee. On each of these peaks the enemy had his signal station, the summits were crowned with batteries, and the spurs were alive with men busy in felling trees, digging pits, and preparing for the grand struggle im-pending. The scene was enchanting; too beautiful to be disturbed by the harsh clamor of war, but the Chattahoochee lay beyond, and I had to reach it. On approaching close to the enemy, I found him occupying a line full twelve miles long, more than he could hold with his force. General McPherson was ordered to move toward Marietta, his right on the railroad, General Thomas on Kennesaw and Pine Mountain, and General Schofield off toward Lost Mountain; General Garrard's cavalry on the left, and General Stoneman on the right, and General McCook looking to our rear and communications. Our depot was at Big Shanty.

By the 11th of June our lines were closed up, and we made dispositions to break the line between Kennesaw and Pine Mountains. General Hooker was on its right and front, General Howard on its left and front, and General Palmer between it and the railroad. During a sharp cannonading from General Howard's right, or General Hooker's left, General *Polk* was killed on the 14th, and on the morning of the 15th Pine Mountain was found abandoned by the enemy. Generals Thomas and Schofield advanced and found him again strongly entrenched along the line of rugged hills connecting Kennesaw and Lost Mountain. At the same time General McPherson advanced his line, gaining substantial advantage on the left. Pushing our operations on the center as vigorously as the nature of the ground would permit, I had again ordered an assault on the center, when, on the 17th, the enemy abandoned Lost Mountain and the long line of admirable breast-works connecting it with Kennesaw. We continued to press at all points, skirmishing in dense forests of timber and across most difficult ravines, until we found him again, strongly posted and entrenched, with Kennesaw as his salient, his right wing thrown back so as to cover Marietta, and his left behind Noyes' Creek, covering his railroad back to the Chattahoochee. This enabled him to contract his lines and strengthen them accordingly. From Kennesaw he could look down upon our camps and observe every movement, and his batteries thundered away, but did us but little harm on account of their extreme height, the shot and shell passing harmlessly over our heads, as we lay close up against his mountain town. During our operations about Kennesaw the weather was villainously bad, the rain fell almost continually for three weeks, rendering our narrow wooded roads mere mud gullies, so that a general movement would have been impossible, but our men daily worked closer and closer to the entrenched foe, and kept up an incessant picket-firing galling to him. Every opportunity was taken to advance our general lines closer and closer to the enemy—General McPherson watching the enemy on Kennesaw and working his left forward; General Thomas swinging, as it were, on a grand left wheel, his left on Kennesaw, connecting with General McPherson, and General Schofield all the time working to the south and east, along the Sandtown road.

On the 22d, as General Hooker had advanced his line, with General Schofield on his right, the enemy (*Hood's* corps with detachments from the others) suddenly sallied and attacked. The blow fell mostly

Battle of Kennesaw Mountain (engraving by A. R. Waud in Joseph M. Brown, *The Mountain Campaigns in Georgia* [Buffalo: Matthews, Northrup Co., 1886], frontispiece).

on General Williams' division, of General Hooker's corps, and a brigade of General Hascall's division, of General Schofield's army. The ground was comparatively open, and although the enemy drove in the skirmish line and an advanced regiment of General Schofield sent out purposely to hold him in check until some preparations could be completed for his reception, yet when he reached our line of battle, he received a terrible repulse, leaving his dead, wounded, and many prisoners in our hands. This is known as the affair of the Kolb House. Although inviting the enemy at all times to commit such mistakes, I could not hope for him to repeat them after the example of Dallas and the Kolb House, and upon studying the ground I had no alternative in my turn but to assault his lines or turn his position. Either course had its difficulties and dangers, and I perceived that the enemy and our own officers had settled down into a conviction that I would not assault fortified lines. All looked to me to outflank.

An army to be efficient must not settle down to a single mode of offense, but must be prepared to execute any plan which promises success. I wanted, therefore, for the moral effect to make a successful assault against the enemy behind his breast-works, and resolved to attempt it at that point where success would give the largest fruits of victory. The general point selected was the left center, because if I could push a strong head of column through at that point by pushing it boldly and rapidly two and one-half miles, it would reach a railroad below Marietta, cut off the enemy's right and center from its line of re- treat, and then by turning on either part it could be overwhelmed and destroyed. Therefore, on the 24th of June, I ordered that an assault should be made at two points south of Kennesaw on the 27th, giving three days' notice for preparation and reconnaissance, one to be made near Little Kennesaw by General McPherson's troops, and the other about a mile farther south by general Thomas' troops. The hour was fixed and all the details given in Field Orders No. 28, of June 24. [O.R., XXXVIII, pt. 1, pp. 67–68.]

Maj. Gen. William T. Sherman to Maj. Gen. H. W. Halleck, Washington, D.C., 21 June 1864, 1 p.m. (Received 22 June 1864, 11 a.m.)

This is the nineteenth day of rain, and the prospect of clear weather as far off as ever. The roads are impassable, and fields and woods become quagmires after a few wagons have crossed, yet we are at work all the time. The left flank is across Noonday and the right across Noyes' Creek. The enemy hold Kennesaw, a conical mountain, with Marietta behind it, and has retired his flank to cover that town and his railroad. I am all ready to attack the moment weather and roads will permit troops and artillery to move with anything like life. [O.R., XXXVIII, pt. 4, p. 544.]

Sherman to Halleck, 23 June 1864, 9:30 p.m. (Received 24 June 1864, 4:20 p.m.)

We continue to press forward, operating on the principle of an advance against fortified positions. The whole country is one vast fort, and Johnston must have full fifty miles of connected trenches, with abatis and finished batteries. We gain ground daily, fighting all the time. On the 21st General Stanley gained a position near the southeast of Kennesaw, from which the enemy attempted in vain to drive him, and the same day General T. J. Wood's division took a hill, which the

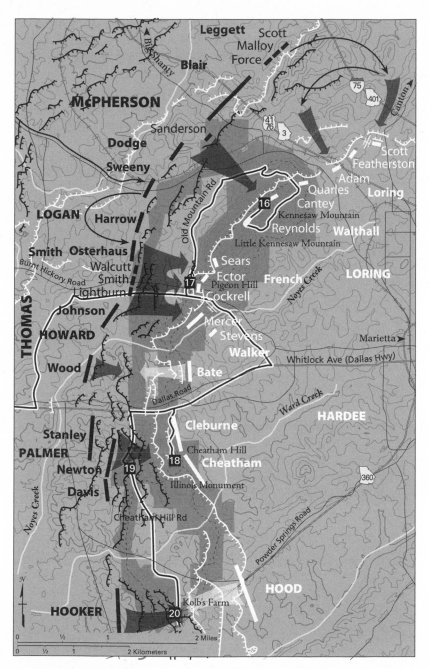

The Battles of Kolb's Farm and Kennesaw Mountain

enemy assaulted three times at night without success, leaving more than 100 dead on the ground. Yesterday the extreme right (Hooker and Schofield) advanced on the Powder Springs road to within three miles of Marietta. The enemy made a strong effort to drive them away, but failed signally, leaving more than 200 dead on the field. Our lines are now in close contact and the fighting incessant, with a good deal of artillery. As fast as we gain one position the enemy has another all ready, but I think he will soon have to let go Kennesaw, which is the key to the whole country. The weather is now better, and the roads are drying up fast. Our losses are light, and, notwithstanding the repeated breaks of the road to our rear, supplies are ample. [*O.R.*, XXXVIII, pt. 4, p. 573.]

Maj. Gen. George H. Thomas, USA, Commanding Army of the Cumberland, Near Kennesaw Mountain, 24 June 1864, 9:15 a.m., to Maj. Gen. William T. Sherman

I have been along the line this morning, and find that the enemy's entrenchments in front of Howard and Palmer are very strong. The troops are also much fatigued in consequence of the continuous operations of the last three or four days. Howard's and Palmer's fronts are now so much extended that it will be exceedingly difficult for them to mass a sufficient number of men to make an effective move on any point. If Schofield and Hooker were moved up on the Powder Springs and Marietta road it would contract our lines and enable us to strengthen them. I have just heard from General E. M. McCook, who was ordered to send a reconnaissance, in the direction of Powder Springs yesterday. He reports no enemy in Powder Springs, but all on south side of Noyes' Creek. [*O.R.*, XXXVIII, pt. 4, p. 581.]

Sherman to Thomas, 24 June 1864

Your note is received. Schofield reports he can't go ahead for the enemy and his entrenchments, and is far out-flanked. I suppose the enemy, with his smaller force, intends to surround us. But I propose to study the ground well, and the day after tomorrow break through, after letting him develop his line as much as possible and attenuate. According to Blair his right is now at Roswell Factory, and according to Schofield his left is more than a mile to his right, across Olley's

Federal artillery emplacements near the base of Little Kennesaw Mountain
(George N. Barnard, MOLLUS).

Creek; so our best chance is to break through. I am just making orders
on this subject, which I wish kept to army commanders for the present. Railroad and telegraph again broken between Dalton and Tunnel
Hill. McPherson had a column one mile and a half to his left front on
the Bell's Ferry road, and is now feeling Kennesaw. Hooker and Schofield will advance along the Powder Springs road as soon as they come.
[O.R., XXXVIII, pt. 4, p. 582.]

Special Field Orders No. 28, Headquarters, Military Division of the Mississippi, Near Kennesaw Mountain, 24 June 1864

The army commanders will make full reconnaissances and preparations to attack the enemy in force on the 27th instant, at 8 a.m. precisely. The commanding general will be on Signal Hill, and will have
telegraphic communication with all the army commanders.

I. Major-General Thomas will assault the enemy at any point near
his center, to be selected by himself, and will make any changes in

his troops necessary by night, so as not to attract the attention of the enemy.

II. Major-General McPherson will feign by a movement of his cavalry and one division of infantry on his extreme left, approaching Marietta from the north, and using artillery freely, but will make his real attack at a point south and west of Kennesaw.

III. Major-General Schofield will feel well to his extreme right and threaten that flank of the enemy with artillery and display, but attack some one point of the enemy's line as near the Marietta and Powder Springs road as he can with prospect of success.

IV. All commanders will maintain reserve and secrecy even from their staff officers, but make all the proper preparations and reconnaissances. When troops are to be shifted to accomplish this attack the movement will be made at night. At the time of the general attack the skirmisher at the base of Kennesaw will take advantage of it to gain, if possible, the summit and hold it.

V. Each attacking column will endeavor to break a single point of the enemy's line, and make a secure lodgment beyond, and be prepared for following it up toward Marietta and the railroad in case of success. [O.R., XXXVIII, pt. 4, p. 588.]

Sherman to Halleck, 25 June 1864, 8 p.m. (Received 10 p.m.)

I have nothing new to report. Constant skirmishing and cannonading. I am making some changes in the disposition of our men, with a view to attack the enemy's left center. I shall aim to make him stretch his line until he weakens it and then break through. *Johnston* has made repeated attempts to break our road to the rear, and has succeeded in two instances, which were promptly repaired. General Steedman, at Chattanooga, reports that General Pillow approached from the south with 3,000 men, but was met at La Fayette by Colonel Watkins and repulsed. Full details not yet received. I think the arrangements to protect our rear are ample as against any probable danger. [O.R., XXXVIII, pt. 4, p. 589.]

Sherman to Thomas, 25 June 1864

On my visit to Schofield I found that the enemy had strengthened his works across the Powder Springs road very much, having made embrasures for three complete batteries, all bearing on Powder Springs road. Line extends as far as can be seen to the right, mostly in timber and partly in open ground. The enemy is also on his right flank on the other side of Olley's Creek. I have ordered him tomorrow, Sunday, to move a brigade of infantry and all of Stoneman's cavalry down the Sandtown road and effect a crossing of Olley's Creek on the Sandtown road; at the same time to use artillery pretty freely against the enemy where seen from Cox's present position, which is about two miles above the Sandtown road. My object is tomorrow to attract to that flank as large a force of the enemy as possible, and thereby weaken his center and right. [*O.R.*, XXXVIII, pt. 4, p. 589.]

Maj. Gen. John M. Schofield, USA, Commanding Army of the Ohio, to Brig. Gen. Jacob D. Cox, Commanding Third Division, Twenty-Third Army Corps, 26 June 1864

To carry out fully General Sherman's plans it will be necessary for you to make a strong demonstration this afternoon in addition to that to be made by Colonel Reilly. It might be made a short distance this side of the Sandtown road, or near your present right, or even through the strip of woods near Hascall's right. Such a demonstration made today and continued until dark will be far more valuable than one made tomorrow morning. A brigade and a battery will doubtless be sufficient force, its real strength being concealed from the enemy. Hascall will also open with his artillery on the right. [*O.R.*, XXXVIII, pt. 4, p. 599.]

Maj. Gen. John M. Schofield to Brig. Gen. Milo S. Hascall, USA, Commanding Second Division, Twenty-Third Army Corps, 26 June 1864, 12:15 p.m.

You may open with your artillery on your right about 2 or 3 o'clock this afternoon, and keep up the firing at intervals until dark. Let the fire be directed mainly toward the enemy's extreme left and toward any force which can be seen in front of Cox, who is going to make a demonstration across the Olley Creek at some point between your right and the Sandtown road, where Reilly now is. The object is not to attack the force in your front, but to compel the enemy to reinforce his extreme left, even afar around as the Sandtown road, where he now has some infantry and artillery. [*O.R.*, XXXVIII, pt. 4, p. 599.]

While General Sherman was using the Army of the Ohio to encourage General *Johnston* to extend and strengthen his left before Sherman attacked near the Confederate center, his adversary was informing Richmond of the problems he faced and seeking help.

Gen. Joseph E. Johnston, CSA, Commanding Army of Tennessee, to Gen. Braxton Bragg, General in Chief, Richmond, 27 June 1864

I have endeavored by my telegrams to keep you informed of the course of military events in this department. I have not been able, however, in that brief style of correspondence to explain the mode of operating by which we have been pressed back so gradually but continually. I informed the Government, through Brigadier-General *Pendleton*, that Sherman's army was more than double that under my command. I could not prevent such superior forces from turning the position at Dalton, under cover of Rocky Face Ridge, by Snake Creek [Gap]; so that Dalton was necessarily abandoned. The entrenched position of the enemy before Resaca also threatened our communications. The attempt to hold that place would have compromised the army. It was, therefore, abandoned also.

In falling back from that point I intended to take advantage of the first good position to give battle, but found none capable of giving us such advantage as our inferior numbers required, or, indeed, any. In this way we crossed the Etowah. A few days after the Federal army also crossed that river more than a day's march below the railroad bridge. On May 24 we found it entrenched near Dallas, and our own was placed between it and Atlanta. By his engineering operations (rendered easy by superior numbers and the character of the country, which is densely wooded) the enemy has pressed us back to a position the right of which is about two miles north of Marietta. The left was at first due west from the town, the extent of the line being five miles. The usual gradual extension of the enemy's entrenched line to his right southwardly has compelled us to lengthen ours on the same side at least three miles.

Since May 7 in almost daily skirmishes and the attacks upon different points of our lines (which have been reported to you by telegraph), we have lost about 9,000 men in killed and wounded. Long and cold, wet weather, which ended five days ago, produced a great deal of sickness. Our superior officers think that we have inflicted a loss on the enemy treble our own, as our men have almost always fought under cover or under favorable circumstances, The Federal army has received no other reinforcements, I believe, than Blair's troops, estimated at from 5,000 to 7,000, and garrison and bridge guards relieved by 100-days' men.

I have been unable so far to stop the enemy's progress by gradual approaches on account of his numerous army and the character of the country, which is favorable to that method. Our best mode of operating against it would be to use strong parties of cavalry to cut his railroad communications. Our own cavalry is so weak compared with that of the Federal army that I have been unable to do it. If you can employ cavalry in that way quickly great benefit must result from it—probably Sherman's speedy discomfiture. [*O.R.*, XXXVIII, pt. 4, pp. 795–796.]

General Sherman's pressure on both Confederate flanks held the bulk of General *Johnston's* cavalry in place and set the stage for the planned attacks against the Confederate center on June 27.

TACTICS

As envisioned in Special Field Order Number 28, the Union forces that would have been visible from this observation site on June 27 were only engaged in holding attacks. Their activity was sufficient to prevent Confederate commanders from shifting forces to strengthen points chosen for the main attacks—had that been necessary—and contributed to the Confederate impression of a decisive victory at all points in the line.

Report of Maj. Gen. Edward C. Walthall, CSA, Commanding Division, Loring's Corps, Army of Tennessee

[On June 27] the division occupied a position in the line with its right resting on the Marietta and Big Shanty road, extending to the left up the Big Kennesaw Mountain and down its western declivity into the gorge between it and the Little Kennesaw, with the brigades in the following order from right to left: *Quarles'*, *Cantey's*, *Reynolds'*, the first commanded by Brig. Gen. *William A. Quarles*, the second by Col. *E. A. O'Neal*, and the last by Brig. Gen. *D. H. Reynolds*. At about 9 a.m., while I was proceeding to the top of the Big Kennesaw Mountain, accompanied by General *Quarles* and two of my staff, the enemy commenced quite a brisk cannonade across the eastern slope and top of the mountain, which continuing some hour or more, he commenced an advance of his infantry in my front. From the rugged character of the ground and the thickness of the undergrowth in front of my skirmish line, much of which runs along a bench of the mountain, the alignment of the enemy was so broken on reaching it that it was impossible to decide clearly whether he advanced with a line of battle or only with a very thick line of skirmishers strongly supported, except in front of General *Quarles'* brigade, where from the top of the mountain a line of battle of the enemy was clearly seen to approach. This fact, coupled with the double cross-fire from the right and left of his regiment, deployed as skirmishers, directed against the enemy, may explain the greater loss supposed to have been inflicted on the enemy at this point than elsewhere.

The firing from commands both to my right and left could be distinctly heard from the top of the mountain and indicated a very general advance. Between 11 and 12 o'clock a report was made to me that a portion of General *Reynolds'* skirmish line had given back. I immediately ordered General *Reynolds* to re-establish it unless a line of battle of the enemy should be occupying it or intervening between him and it. General *Reynolds* reported to me in less than an hour that his line had been restored without loss or difficulty.

The lines of General *Quarles* and Colonel *O'Neal* were assaulted at the same time, but held their ground firmly, inflicting a heavy loss on the enemy without sustaining a corresponding loss. General *Reynolds* estimates the enemy's loss in his front at 50 killed and wounded.

Maj. *S. L. Knox*, commanding the First Alabama Regiment on skirmish line in front of *Quarles'* brigade, reports that the enemy came within thirty yards of his line at almost all points, and that some 28 got into our pits, of whom 16 were captured. The rest, seeing that it was only a skirmish line into which they had run, sought safety in flight, but were mostly killed or wounded. Major *Knox* estimates the enemy's loss at 300 killed and wounded.

Colonel *O'Neal* reports the enemy's supposed loss in his front at 30 killed and wounded. [O.R., XXXVIII, pt. 3, pp. 922–923.]

Report of Brig. Gen. William A. Quarles, CSA, Commanding Brigade, Walthall's Division, Loring's Corps, Army of Tennessee

During the action I had a position on the mountain side above the field in which the fight occurred, and hence could see the whole line.

The enemy first advanced his sharpshooters, then a heavy line of skirmishers, and directly in rear of these a line of battle. Indeed, the force was so heavy that I had no idea my picket-line could resist it without re-enforcement, and placed two regiments in readiness to be advanced as soon as I observed the least wavering in my line. This, however, did not occur, and to the First Alabama is due the whole credit of the most brilliant affair it has ever been my fortune to witness.

The steady, well-directed fire of the men drove the enemy back on the right. Moving, however, by the right flank to a point on my left where they had cover, they concentrated in three lines of battle. Major *Knox* re-enforced his left with his whole reserve, and without giving ground at any point repelled several obstinate and daring assaults. The Federal officers with great gallantry endeavored to bring their men up to a last and final charge, but succeeded only on the right, where the effort was as feeble as it was abortive. I am satisfied Major *Knox* underestimates the number of the enemy's killed and wounded. At one point, some distance, but in easy range of my line, the enemy was compelled to uncover his line in advancing across a clear field. It was here we had a cross-fire on them, which was so destructive that their line always broke and retired in confusion. In Major *Knox's* estimate he only includes what he could see from his line and counted nearby, because he could not reach the clear field where so many fell. Captain Wakefield, the Federal prisoner captured, told me that their chief loss was at this point. I therefore think it is safe to estimate the enemy's loss at 500 in killed, wounded, and prisoners. [*O.R.*, XXXVIII, pt. 3, pp. 929–930.]

Report of Maj. Samuel L. Knox, CSA, Commanding First Alabama Infantry, Quarles's Brigade, Walthall's Division, Loring's Corps, Army of Tennessee

Immediately after dark on the evening of the 26th instant I was placed on picket with the right wing of my regiment, numbering 188 effective men. About 10 a.m. on the 27th instant the enemy, having already shelled our works very severely, threw forward a very heavy line of skirmishers, moving up at double-quick against my whole line. They advanced but a short distance against my right, which rested in an open field, before a destructive fire forced them to oblique to the right, thus massing their whole force into a very dense line of battle in front of about one company and a half, on my left center. Their extreme right obliqued to the left in a similar manner. By directing the fire of my right companies, however, to the left oblique and the left to the right oblique, I brought my whole strength to bear upon them. At most points of that portion of the line immediately pressed the enemy only succeeded in getting within twenty or twenty-five yards of the works; at other points they came within ten feet; at one or two points they leaped into the pits, thinking they had carried them, but were forced to surrender. They attempted to form within thirty yards of the works, but found it impossible. About the time we had succeeded in checking their front line, they were attempting to form a line of battle in the rear of the first and about 150 yards in our front, under cover of a slight sassafras hedge. A rapid and well-directed fire from the three right companies of my line soon resulted in confusing and dislodging this line. I am informed by officers, who from Kennesaw Mountain had a better point for observation, that the enemy formed another line still in rear of this, rather under cover of their own advance works, but of this I had no knowledge at the time, and hence did not inform the brigadier-general commanding, nor call for re-enforcements.

After the most careful reconnaissance possible I am convinced the loss of the enemy in killed and wounded in front of my line was not less than 300. Other officers estimate that at least 100 were killed. We captured 18 prisoners.

We lost 1 sergeant killed and 5 privates slightly wounded. Two of the latter did not leave the works. [*O.R.*, XXXVIII, pt. 3, pp. 933–934.]

The report of the Union brigade commander responsible for the holding attack against Brig. Gen. *Quarles's* line agrees with few particulars of the action and cites much lower casualty figures.

Report of Col. William L. Sanderson, Commanding First Brigade, Fourth Division, Seventeenth Army Corps, Army of the Tennessee

In obedience to orders I moved at 8 a.m. on the enemy's lines with four companies each of the Fifty-third Indiana and Twenty-third Indiana and Twelfth Wisconsin, and two companies of the Thirty-second Illinois Infantry in advance, under command of Major Ferguson, Twenty-third Indiana, and Major Vestal, Fifty-third Indiana, the companies of the Fifty-third Indiana (A, D, I, and B) occupying the right of the line and connecting with the line of the Sixteenth Army

Corps. The enemy's skirmishers were soon encountered and driven back to their rifle pits, where three regiments of the rebels were held in reserve and so completely concealed by bushes and undergrowth as to be unperceived by our men. The enemy evidently expected to capture the entire line, as they did not fire until our men reached in some instances the parapet of their works, when they opened a murderous fire of musketry, compelling our men to fall back with a loss of 65 killed, wounded, and missing.

The reconnaissance developed the fact that on the mountain in our immediate front the enemy had several lines of strong works defended by a very heavy force. [*O.R.*, XXXVIII, pt. 3, pp. 586–587.]

If you walked to the crest you should return to the parking lot for good views to the east-northeast, where Confederates easily held their prepared defensive positions against secondary Union attacks probing for weaknesses.

Report of Brig. Gen. Winfield S. Featherston, CSA, Commanding Loring's Division, Loring's Corps, Army of Tennessee

[On the 27th] the division formed a line of battle running in a northeastern direction from the Big Shanty and Marietta road, at the base of Kennesaw Mountain, to a point between the Bell's Ferry and Canton roads, and were posted as follows: *Scott's* brigade on the right, *Featherston's* in the center, and *Adams'* on the left. Each brigade had some 600 yards in its front on the skirmish line one full regiment, making in the aggregate about 1,100 or 1,200 in front of the division.

About 10 a.m. the enemy advanced in force against the skirmishers of General *Scott*, on the Bell's Ferry road. They came in one line of skirmishers and three lines of battle. Our whole skirmish line was well entrenched, and General *Scott's* skirmish regiment (Twelfth Louisiana, under command of Colonel [*Noel L.*] *Nelson*) held their position against this overwhelming force until the enemy had advanced to within twenty-five or thirty yards of their rifle pits. They poured into the advancing columns repeated volleys of minie-balls, which thinned their ranks and caused them to falter, but did not check them. In this advance the enemy sustained a heavy loss. Colonel *Nelson* finally withdrew his regiment and fell back to the main line of battle in good order. This regiment not only did good service in inflicting heavy loss upon the enemy but displayed great coolness, courage, and determination during the entire engagement. The skirmish line having been driven in, and the enemy having advanced to within 250 or 300 yards of our main works, a concentrated converging fire was directed upon their position by our artillery. Cowan's and Bouanchaud's batteries, of Major [John D.] Myrick's battalion, and [Minor W.] Havis', of Colonel [James H.] Hallonquist's regiment, and one of Lieutenant-Colonel [Felix H.] Robertson's batteries, of General Wheeler's command, poured into the enemy for the space of one hour a most galling and destructive fire. The artillery was ably and skillfully served, and so terrible was the fire and severe its results that the enemy retired before it, leaving some of their dead upon the field unburied and hastily burying others.

This advance of the enemy in force and in three lines of battle was evidently made with the intent and for the purpose of attacking our forces in the main line of battle. At the same time this advance was made on General Scott's front the enemy also made their appearance with infantry and artillery in front of General Wheeler's command, on the right of this division. General Scott's skirmishers resumed their original position in front of the brigade after the firing of the artillery had ceased, about 4 p.m. At the same time the enemy advanced upon General Scott's skirmish line, three of his regiments made their appearance in front of the line of skirmishers of Featherston's brigade. His line of skirmishers was composed of the First Mississippi Battalion of Sharpshooters, commanded by Major [James M.] Stigler, and the Third Mississippi Regiment, Major Dyer commanding. The three regiments of the enemy made their appearance on the right of the line, passing through a field and going in the direction of the Bell's Ferry road. They came within easy range of Stigler's battalion, when a destructive fire was poured into them, which caused them to fall back and oblique to the right, bearing from the field several of their dead and wounded. The line of skirmishers before this brigade held their position during the day, except on the right, where they were ordered to fall back some distance to guard against flank movement by the enemy after Scott's pickets had been driven in.

About 4 p.m. the enemy advanced upon this line of skirmishers on the left and center with a heavy line to within sixty yards of our line. They were met by a galling fire in their advance until they were repulsed in great confusion. Their loss is supposed to be very heavy as they had no protection except the undergrowth. A brisk fire was kept up on this line during the evening, and both the battalion and Third Mississippi Regiment acted with great coolness, courage, and determination.

The skirmish line of Brigadier-General *Adams* consisted of the Sixth Mississippi Regiment, under the command of Col. *Robert Lowry.* About 8 a.m. the enemy charged upon the extreme left of his line, and at the same time advanced upon the line of General *Quarles,* which connected with that of General *Adams* on his left. The enemy was handsomely repulsed on the left of General *Adams'* skirmish line, and from the position our line held it was enabled to cross-fire with two companies upon the enemy moving upon General *Quarles.* Major *Borden,* who commanded on the left of Colonel *Lowry's* regiment, reports that he thinks he drove in some 15 or 20 of the enemy to General *Quarles* line, where they surrendered. It appeared that after getting to a certain distance in General *Quarles'* line they were unable to get back because of the heavy cross-fire of the two left companies. They made an effort, were driven back, and then surrendered. About 10 a.m. the enemy made a charge on Colonel *Lowry* with a heavy, close line of skirmishers, supported by a strong reserve immediately in rear. They charged rapidly, shouting, etc., and were permitted to get in about 150 paces, when a heavy fire was opened upon them and kept up until they got in some seventy yards of the skirmish line, where they wavered, broke, and fled in much confusion. In this advance as well as retreat, they received a severe punishment.

Our whole loss during the engagement was 5 killed and 14 wounded; that of the enemy could not have fallen short of several hundred. [*O.R.,* XXXVIII, pt. 3, pp. 878–880.]

Report of Brig. Gen. Mortimer D. Leggett, USA, Commanding Third Division, Seventeenth Corps, Army of the Tennessee

[On June 27th] I moved my division to the left and to the front into line of battle, the left resting on a hill about 100 yards from the Bell's Ferry road, and connecting by a line of skirmishers with the cavalry division, General Garrard, which was refused on my left.

During the night previous I advanced my pickets, and made a road from my camp to the place where I formed my line of battle, a distance of nearly one mile. The character of the ground over which

I was obliged to pass to get into line was rocky hills, densely wooded. I placed a battery of regulation guns, Company H, First Michigan, in position on my extreme left, where they were in full view of the rebel works. My order of formation was a double line, with skirmishers in front, the First Brigade, Brig. Gen. M. F. Force commanding, on the right; the Second Brigade, Col. R. K. Scott commanding, on the left; and the Third Brigade, Col. A. G. Malloy commanding, in the center.

At 8 a.m. I moved forward, and met the enemy in considerable force at once, but drove them rapidly into their main works, and took possession of their advanced works, across the whole front of my division. Being enfiladed by sharpshooters upon hills to my right and also at the left, I reduced my formation to a single line, and thereby extended my front. At this point we were brought under a cross-fire from three rebel batteries, one on our left, one in front, and one on our right. We held this position for two hours, it not being possible to advance farther without entering their main works, which we could not have held with so small a force and both our flanks so greatly exposed.

I was then directed to withdraw my division and make another demonstration farther to the right, which I did, but the position was such that but one brigade, the Second, became actively engaged. We were here met by a heavy infantry force, and could make but little advance.

The design of my operations being to hold the force in my front from being taken to oppose our right wing, where the real attack was to be made, I think we fully accomplished our object, for I am informed that we not only held those who were in our front in the morning, but caused them to be largely re-enforced during the day.

The casualties of the day were, killed, 10; wounded, 76. [O.R., XXXVIII, pt. 3, p. 563.]

17. PIGEON HILL

Drive back down Mountain Road, proceed through the Visitor Center parking lot, and turn left onto Stilesboro Road. Drive about 0.4 mile and turn left onto Old Mountain Road. After about 1.4 miles, you will reach a stop sign at the intersection with Burnt Hickory Road. Turn left and immediately park on the right side of the road in the designated parking area. Walk back down the hill and turn left into the field at the gate; use the National Park Service interpretive panel for orientation.

STOP 17, PIGEON HILL

27 June 1864

Stop 16 was on the highest part of Kennesaw Mountain. The peak of Little Kennesaw Mountain is about half a mile southwest of that summit, and the top of Pigeon Hill is about half a mile south of Little Kennesaw. As you face uphill and look across Burnt Hickory Road, you are looking toward Pigeon Hill.

Confederate defenses in the Pigeon Hill sector were part of Maj. Gen. *William W. Loring's* responsibility. *Loring* had been given temporary command of General *Polk's* corps when *Polk* was killed by Union artillery fire on June 14. At that time, *Hood's* corps had been on the Confederate left, but *Johnston* shifted *Hood* to the right flank on June 21, sensing that Sherman might attempt another move away from the railroad and around the Confederate left. General *Wheeler's* Confederate cavalry division then occupied *Hood's* positions, and *Loring's* corps extended from just east of the railroad, along the top of the Kennesaw peaks, and over Pigeon Hill. Maj. Gen. *Samuel G. French's* division held the left flank of *Loring's* sector, with Brig. Gen. *Francis M. Cockrell's* Missouri Brigade assigned the left-most position on Pigeon Hill. Burnt Hickory Road was on the left flank of *Loring's* corps, so the ground on this side of the road was defended by Lt. Gen. *William J. Hardee's* corps. Maj. Gen. *William H. T. Walker's* division had responsibility for the right of his line, and *Walker* placed Brig. Gen. *Hugh Mercer's* Georgia brigade on his right with Brig. Gen. *Clement H. Stevens's* Georgia

Brigade in division reserve nearby. Confederate artillery was positioned to fire across the open field, covering the link between the two corps and interdicting the Burnt Hickory Road.

Union forces in this area were adjusted in accordance with General Sherman's orders.

THE PLAN

Special Field Orders No. 51, Headquarters, Department of the Tennessee and Army of the Tennessee, Near Kennesaw Mountain, 26 June 1864

In order to carry out Special Field Orders, No. 28, Military Division of the Mississippi . . . corps commanders will make the following dispositions:

First. Maj. Gen. G. M. Dodge will direct Brigadier-General Sweeny to move his division (with the exception of one regiment to remain on picket and provost-guard duty at Big Shanty) at 2 p.m. down the main Marietta road and relieve the division of Brigadier-General Osterhaus.

Second. Maj. Gen. John A. Logan will cause the divisions of Brigadier-Generals Osterhaus and Morgan L. Smith, on being relieved this afternoon, the 26th instant, to fall back quietly, under cover of the woods, to a position where they will be screened from view of the enemy on Kennesaw Mountain, and they will remain there until dark, when they will move to the right and occupy substantially the position on the right of Brigadier-General Harrow's division now held by Brigadier-General Baird's division, Fourteenth Army Corps. As soon as these divisions arrive on the ground the attacking columns should be organized, and should consist of at least four brigades, the remaining troops of the divisions to hold a line and constitute a reserve to reinforce any column which may be successful in breaking the enemy's lines or cover its retreat in case of reverse. The points of attack will be selected after further reconnaissance, and will be designated in time.

Third. Maj. Gen. F. P. Blair, Jr., will cause Brigadier-General [Walter Q.] Gresham's division to stretch out to the right this afternoon, the troops to move under cover of the woods and hills and relieve the division of Brig. Gen. M. L. Smith. Tomorrow morning, the 27th instant, at 6 o'clock, he will move Brigadier-General Leggett's division in the direction of Marietta from our extreme left, and, in connection with

Brigadier-General Garrard's cavalry, feign an attack on the enemy's works covering Marietta on the northeast, using artillery freely. This movement, though intended as a feint, should be vigorous, and the advance should not be stopped by a line of the enemy's skirmishers, the object being to prevent the enemy from sending reinforcements to oppose our center and right where the real attack will be made.

Fourth. Brigadier-General Garrard, commanding cavalry division, will move with his whole command at 6 a.m. on the 27th instant, and cooperate with Maj. Gen. F. P. Blair in the movement on our left, and attending to the enemy's cavalry.

Fifth. The skirmishers of Generals Blair and Dodge will press forward and those on Kennesaw Mountain will gain the summit if possible, and hold it until reinforcements can reach them. The roads leading from Marietta to Acworth and Burnt Hickory, which will be covered by [Brig. Gen. James] Veatch's and Gresham's divisions, must be held at all hazard, and Generals Blair and Dodge must understand that they have to rely upon themselves and not expect reinforcements from the right, as all our troops will probably be engaged in that quarter.

Sixth. All the artillery in position will remain where it is until the result of this movement is determined. As little change as possible should be made in the appearance of things along our line, and the movements made with as much caution and as little noise as possible.

Seventh. The pioneer corps of the respective divisions will follow the assaulting columns, in charge of the engineer officer of the division, prepared to secure by rifle-pits, etc., any vantage points gained. [*O.R.*, XXXVIII, pt. 4, pp. 605–606.]

Special Field Orders No. 33, Headquarters, Fifteenth Army Corps, Near Kennesaw Mountain, 26 June 1864

I. Brig. Gen. Morgan L. Smith's and Brigadier-General Osterhaus' commands will occupy tonight the line of works now occupied by General Baird's division, in equal proportion. General Morgan L. Smith will have the right of the line and Brig. Gen. P. J. Osterhaus the left (or center of the corps), with his left resting on the right of Brigadier-General Harrow's command. A staff officer from each command will be sent at once to ascertain positively the best roads to the position and determine the points precisely at which the troops will be placed in position.

II. Special Field Orders, No. 51, from department headquarters . . . are so changed by direction from department headquarters that there will be but one assaulting column at 8 o'clock tomorrow morning. Brigadier-General Osterhaus will move with his division, except artillery, after dark and relieve Brigadier-General Baird's division of the Fourteenth Corps on the right of Brigadier-General Harrow. Brig. Gen. M. L. Smith will move his division tonight, and form them under cover in rear of Brigadier-General Harrow's right and center brigades. His division, with Colonel Walcutt's brigade, of the Fourth Division, will form the assaulting column, under command of Brig. Gen. M. L. Smith, and will make the assault at the point to be indicated by Captain [Chauncey B.] Reese [Chief Engineer of the Department], of General McPherson's staff. Generals Osterhaus and Harrow will press forward skirmishers and engage the enemy during the assault vigorously, and be ready to reinforce General Smith or take any advantage of any success that may be gained at any time.

III. Brigadier-General Harrow will extend his line so as to relieve Colonel Walcutt's brigade, and direct him to report to Brig. Gen. M. L. Smith, commanding Second Division, for orders, upon General Smith's arrival with his command in rear of his present position. [*O.R.*, XXXVIII, pt. 4, p. 606.]

TACTICAL EXECUTION OF THE PLAN

Report of Maj. Gen. John A. Logan, USA, Commanding Fifteenth Corps, Army of the Tennessee

In pursuance of instructions, I organized the division of Brig. Gen. M. L. Smith, consisting of Brig. Gen. J. A. J. Lightburn's and Brig. Gen. Giles A. Smith's brigades, and Col. C. C. Walcutt's brigade, of the Fourth Division, General Harrow commanding, into an assaulting column, under command of General M. L. Smith, with orders to be ready at 8 o'clock precisely, on the morning of the 27th, to assault the enemy's works on the south and west slope of Little Kennesaw Mountain. The column for assault being formed, I directed it at 8 o'clock precisely to move forward. Immediately after uncovering themselves, they became engaged. The advance was continued in two lines, steadily, in the face of a destructive fire from three batteries of about twelve pieces, throwing shot and shell, and from a musketry fire from the sharpshooters of the enemy, situated below the enemy's

"The Rifle Pits before Kennesaw" (engraving by A. R. Waud in Joseph
M. Brown, *The Mountain Campaigns in Georgia* [Buffalo, N.Y.: Matthews,
Northrup Co., 1886], 40).

first line of rifle-pits and also from the rifle-pits. After a most stubborn
and destructive resistance, my attacking column succeeded in taking
and holding two lines of the enemy's rifle pits, and advanced toward
the succeeding works of the enemy, situated just below the crest of
the mountain. It soon became evident that the works could not be
approached by assault, on account of a steep declivity of rocks twenty
and twenty-five feet in height, and the nature of the ground, which
was of the most rugged and craggy character, exposing at times small
bodies of my troops to the concentrated fire of the enemy. After vainly
attempting to carry the works for some time, and finding that so many
gallant men were being uselessly slain, I ordered them to retire to the
last line of works captured, and placed them in a defensible condition
of occupancy. The pioneer corps of the command were at once sent to
General Smith for this purpose. No less than seven commanding officers of regiments were killed or disabled in this assault.

In this assault we captured 87 prisoners, including 3 commissioned officers. My casualties were 80 killed, 506 wounded, 17 missing. [*O.R.*, XXXVIII, pt. 3, p. 99.]

Report of Brig. Gen. Morgan L. Smith, USA, Commanding Second Division, Fifteenth Corps

In accordance with General Logan's order, I withdrew my division from its position to the left of the mountain after dark on the night of the 26th instant, and massed it opposite the extreme right of the mountain and a hill, which is a continuation of the same, to the right. This hill was the objective point of the assault, and my division and Colonel Walcutt's brigade of General Harrow's division, was designated as the assaulting column, and 8 a.m. of the 27th the hour to advance. General Lightburn, commanding Second Brigade, of about 2,000 muskets, was directed to form in two lines and assault through a little orchard, about 400 yards to the right of the hill, and to advance as soon as he heard a brisk fire on the left. General Giles A. Smith, commanding First Brigade, of about the same strength, was directed to move at the same time in two lines directly on the hill. Colonel Walcutt, commanding the brigade of General Harrow's division, of about 1,500 muskets, was directed to move directly for the gorge where the hill joins on to the mountain, lapping the mountain and the left of the hill, feel into the gorge as far as possible, and capture the works in his front. As the enemy could not depress their artillery sufficiently to fire on him, he was ordered to advance first, and the opening of the enemy's fire upon him was the signal for the other two brigades to advance. The line moved about 8 o'clock. It advanced steadily, with a strong line of skirmishers, but owing to the extreme density of the underbrush it was impossible for the skirmishers to keep in front of their lines. Found the enemy's line of rifle-pits about 400 yards from their main works, and killed or captured most of their skirmishers. After passing a deep, swampy ravine, the line fixed bayonets, advancing, moved steadily and rapidly for the enemy's works, amidst a shower of shot and shell. Officers and men fell thick and fast. In addition to the steepness of the ascent, trees had been felled and brush and rocks piled in such a manner as to make it impossible to advance with any regularity. Officers and men still pushed forward. Reinforcements of the enemy were seen coming in from the right and left. Within about thirty feet of the enemy's main works the line staggered and sought cover as best they could behind logs and rocks. General Lightburn, on the right, pressed on through a swamp, where officers and men sank to their knees, and a very dense thicket, but on account of an enfilading fire, was unable to get nearer than 150 yards of the orchard and the works beyond. He, however, by coming suddenly out of the thicket and swamp, killed and wounded quite a number of the enemy.

Colonel Walcutt, commanding the brigade from General Harrow's division, moved forward promptly toward the gorge, encountered the enemy's rifle-pits; captured about 50 prisoners; found the gorge perfectly impassable on account of the rocky and precipitous entrance. [O.R., XXXVIII, pt. 3, p. 178.]

Report of Brig. Gen. Charles C. Walcutt, USA, Commanding Second Brigade, Fourth Division, Fifteenth Corps

By direction of General Smith, my brigade was placed on the left, and ordered to lead the assault, my column to assail the enemy's works commanding the gorge between the two mountains. At 7 a.m. on the 27th I moved to near the left of General Osterhaus, and formed my brigade in two lines, with the Forty-sixth Ohio (Spencer Rifles) deployed in two lines as skirmishers. At 8:15 a.m. I sounded the "advance." A column never charged more gallantly or with greater determination. The enemy opened upon me at once with artillery from the mountain and a heavy musketry fire from their skirmishers, who were strongly intrenched. The latter, however, were nearly all killed, wounded, or captured. The main works of the enemy were found to be in a very formidable position on the crest of a gorge, having a steep ascent covered by a heavy abatis. After repeated attempts to reach the enemy's works had been made and failed, it being impossible to force our way through the tangled brush under so terrific a fire, the line was withdrawn and intrenched on the crest of the gorge opposite the one occupied by the enemy. In this assault the officers and men behaved most gallantly, many nearly reached the enemy's works, but it was useless. A line never struggled harder to succeed, but it was not in human power. My loss was severe; 246 killed and wounded. [O.R., XXXVIII, pt. 3, p. 318.]

Report of Brig. Gen. Giles A. Smith, USA, Commanding
First Brigade, Second Division, Fifteenth Army Corps,
Army of the Tennessee

Early on Monday morning, the 27th, our assaulting column was formed, consisting of three brigades. My brigade, in the center, was formed in two lines, as follows: The Fifty-seventh Ohio, Colonel Rice, on the right; the One hundred and eleventh Illinois, Colonel Martin, on the left; the One hundred and sixteenth Illinois, Captain Windsor, in the center, in front. The second line was composed of the Sixth Missouri, Lieutenant-Colonel Van Deusen; the One hundred and twenty-seventh Illinois, Captain Little; the Fifty-fifth Illinois, Captain Augustin, in the order named, from right to left. General Lightburn's brigade was on my right, and Colonel Walcutt's brigade, of the Fourth Division, on my left. My line of battle was formed about 100 yards in front of our works, then occupied by the First and Fourth Divisions of the Fifteenth Corps, and immediately in rear of their picket-lines.

The position of the enemy works to be assaulted was a ridge or hill on the right of Kennesaw Mountain, Colonel Walcutt's brigade to enter the gorge or ravine between the mountain and hill, his right to overlap the left of the hill and his left to extend over a portion of the mountain. General Lightburn's objective point was a ridge farther to my right about 800 or 1,000 yards. The ground was wooded, with thick underbrush in many places, and held by the enemy's skirmisher. Nothing further of the ground was known, and very little of the enemy's position, except what could be seen from a high point in our lines over the tops of the trees.

The movement commenced at 8 o'clock. The enemy's skirmishers were steadily driven back, leaving some dead and wounded on the field. The ground over which my line of battle advanced proved even worse than was anticipated. A part of the way was low swampy ground, and so densely covered with underbrush as to compel the men to crawl almost on their hands and knees through the tangled vines. These difficulties were finally overcome, and the open ground in front of the enemy's works gained. The hill was steep and rugged, covered with fallen trees, precipitous rocks, and abatis, rendering an advance in line of battle utterly impossible. The works, a little below the crest of the hill, were very formidable, and filled with men, completely commanding the whole slope of the hill, and, from the nature of the ground, being enabled in many places to pour in a cross-fire that no troops could withstand. My command moved gallantly up the ascent, making their way independently as best they could over all obstructions, some nearly gaining the works, but only to be shot down as they arrived. Our loss, particularly in officers, was very heavy. . . . To gain any portion of their works seemed impossible. The ground gained was mostly held until dark, when the picket-line was established in the edge of the woods, and the men withdrawn from the side of the hill. Our pickets were soon after relieved by the First Division, and my brigade ordered to occupy the camp of the previous night.

Losses: 4 officers and 20 men killed, 6 officers and 122 men wounded, and 2 men missing; total, 154. [O.R., XXXVIII, pt. 3, pp. 193–195.]

Report of Brig. Gen. Joseph A. J. Lightburn, USA, Commanding Second Brigade, Second Division, Fifteenth Army Corps, Army of the Tennessee

Pursuant to orders, I marched from my bivouac at 7:30 a.m., formed in two lines in rear of a battery in Brigadier-General Osterhaus' lines, and at ten minutes past 8 moved forward. My advance was a part of the way through an open field under a raking fire of artillery obliquely on my right and left, also a musketry fire from the same directions. After passing through this open field, crossing a small stream into low ground covered with underbrush and interwoven with vines, through which I advanced a distance of 150 yards to another open field in my front and immediately in front of the enemy's main works. The edge of this field was occupied by the enemy with a heavy entrenched skirmish line, which I could not see until the front line was within twenty paces of it. A few volleys were fired, and my men dashed forward with clubbed muskets and succeeded in carrying this work, and advanced 150 yards into the open field. Finding this position exposed to a complete flank fire of artillery from the left and musketry from the right, the line fell back under cover, of the woods, where I remained with my command until after dark, when, by order, I withdrew to the bivouac left in the morning.

During the advance my officers did all that could be done, but the underbrush through which we advanced was so thick that it was impossible to preserve a line; the consequence was the entire line was broken (this accounts for the heavy loss in officers), which was impossible to reform in the woods, on account of the thick underbrush, or in the open field in front, on account of the raking fire to which they were exposed. Some regiments fell back and reformed in the open field in the rear, only to be broken again in advancing. I, however, reformed the line as well as I could under the circumstances, and held my position, pursuant to orders, under a heavy fire.

My casualties are as follows: Commissioned officers—killed, 2; wounded, 13; Enlisted men—killed, 16; wounded, 140. Total, 171. [O.R., XXXVIII, pt. 3, pp. 221–222.]

Report of Lt. Col. George H. Hildt, USA, Commanding Thirtieth Ohio Infantry, Second Brigade, Second Division, Fifteenth Army Corps, Army of the Tennessee

June 27, moved at 8 a.m. to the south point of Kennesaw Mountain, where we threw out a company of skirmishers and passed over our works. . . . Moving, as soon as all were over, by the right flank a short distance, then forward, guide right, to the thicket, across a small stream, met considerable fire, both of artillery and musketry, but the losses were small. Formed line in the thicket, and drove the enemy from a rifle-pit near its edge, capturing a few prisoners. Moved forward again to the crest, at which point we received a heavy fire from their works. We halted and returned it for a few minutes, when the Eighty third Indiana, on our right, moved back to the thicket, and we fell back to the line of rebel pits, a short distance in advance, bringing Lieutenant White, killed, and Lieutenant McIntyre, seriously wounded.

At this point we were enfiladed by the enemy's artillery. Captain Chamberlain had his head taken off by a percussion shell, which exploded afterward, taking off both his arms. Capt. E. Warner, wounded in foot, besides a number of non-commissioned officers and men. We again fell back across the run to the edge of the thicket in front of our works, where their fire was more destructive than before, a shot passing through a color-corporal, tearing both arms of the color-sergeant and both legs of another corporal, and pieces wounding men in all parts of the line in the process of being formed.

An order was then given to fall back to our line of works by small squads and reform, which was done without any serious loss. An hour afterward an order was received from General Lightburn, commanding brigade, to return to our position in the thicket, which we did without loss, and remained until 9 o'clock, when we were relieved, and returned to the camp left in the morning.

A short time before sundown a tremendous artillery fire passed over us both ways from the enemy's batteries and our own, but as few shots were directed at the thicket we suffered but little. [*O.R.,* XXXVIII, pt. 3, pp. 208–209.]

Confederate accounts can be appreciated from this site, but a much greater understanding of the strength of this defensive position can be achieved by a short walk up to the remains of some of the earthworks that protected *Cockrell's* Missouri Brigade.

EXCURSION: PIGEON HILL TRAIL

Cross Burnt Hickory Road at the crosswalk. Climb the path about 200 yards past the first line of Confederate earthworks to the National Park Service interpretive panel on the right. These well-preserved positions are worth the short climb.

Report of Maj. Gen. Samuel G. French, CSA, Commanding Division, Loring's [Polk's] Corps, Army of Tennessee

[On June 27] between the hours of 8 and 9 a.m., the enemy in my front and that portion of Major-General *Walker's* front, on my left, were seen forming in lines of battle behind their entrenchments, and at the same time their batteries opened on my line with all their guns. Soon after the enemy's line of skirmishers rose from their works and were followed by two lines of infantry. They were soon seen to be in an almost hand-to-hand conflict with the skirmishers on General *Walker's* right, and after a short but spirited contest most of those skirmishers appeared to have been killed or captured. Soon after my skirmishers in General *Cockrell's* front were forced from their pits on the right of the road by an attack in front and on their left and rear, and many were killed and captured. From my position on the west extremity of the mountain I could see but little of my line to the left in the woods, but observing the enemy in force on the right of *Walker's* front, I directed the artillery to be run down to the west end of the Kennesaw Mountain, and it opened on the enemy to the south of the road in *Walker's* front with such effect that they were driven back.

In the mean time the enemy on the right of the road and in my front advanced and attacked the line of entrenchments occupied by Brig. Gen. F. M. *Cockrell*, commanding the Missouri brigade, and a portion of the left of the line occupied by General *Sears'* brigade, and after a spirited contest of an hour were signally repulsed with severe loss. The killed of the enemy that fell nearest our lines were left on the field. So severe and continuous was the cannonading that the volleys of musketry could scarcely be heard at all on the line. My impression is that my artillery, almost enfilading the lines of the enemy on the left of the Marietta road, drove them back, and thus frustrated the attack intended on General *Walker's* right. General *Cockrell* sent an officer to inform the brigade commander on my left that we were being hotly pressed by the enemy, but from some cause the artillery that could command my front in part was not fired. . . .

Our loss . . . was pretty severe, being 17 killed, 92 wounded, and 77 missing; total 186. The enemy's loss is not known, but by those who had the best opportunity to observe, it is computed at 500. [*O.R.*, XXX-VIII, pt. 3, pp. 900–901.]

Report of Brig. Gen. Francis M. Cockrell, CSA, Commanding Brigade, French's Division, Loring's Corps, Army of Tennessee

[A]bout 8 a.m. to-day a very heavy line of skirmishers, closely followed by two lines of battle advanced into the skirt of timber in front of the open field at the foot and South of Kennesaw Mountain, just south of the road leading from Marietta, and drove in the extreme right of the line of skirmishers resting on the northwestern corner of the said open field, and immediately began to press back the left flank of my skirmishers, which rested in the bottom just north of the road. All the reserves of my skirmish line were thrown out to protect my left flank, and the enemy's skirmishers were held in check until the lines of battle closely following closed in upon them. When this was done the enemy rapidly drove back my left and center, passing along the base of Kennesaw Mountain in front of my main line. The companies on the right of my skirmish line were holding the enemy in check in their immediate front, but the enemy advanced so rapidly against and in rear of my left that before Lieutenant-Colonel *Carter*, commanding skirmishers, ordered the right of the line to fall back the enemy had gained their rear and they were thus exposed to a double fire, and in falling back were compelled to pass through the enemy's lines, and many thus fell into their hands.

Lt. *Samuel Ross*, a most gallant officer, and 41 men are now missing, many of whom are known to be either killed or wounded. My skirmishers fought very stubbornly and were pressed back up the gorge on the right, followed by the enemy at the distance of thirty to forty paces. The enemy appeared in force on the west edge of the open field on my left, but were quickly driven back into the woods by a few volleys from the left of my main line. They also appeared in force at the base of the mountain in front of my left regiment, but were easily kept back in the woods. In front of Colonel [*James*] *McCown's* regiment, the second from my left, they made an assault in force and succeeded in getting within twenty-five paces of the works, and by secreting themselves behind rocks and other shelter held this position for fifteen or twenty minutes, and were distinctly heard by my officers in the main line to give the command "fix bayonets." They advanced up the gorge along the line as far as my right, and succeeded in gaining the spur of the main mountain in front of my right and on General *Sears'* left at a point higher up than my main line, and for some time had a plunging fire on my works. All attempts on my line were handsomely repulsed with loss to them.

The bodies of 1 lieutenant-colonel, 1 captain, 1 lieutenant, and some 30 soldiers of the enemy were left dead in my front, and so close to my lines that they could not be carried off. A number of their wounded also fell into our hands, and 1 or 2 prisoners.

My loss in the engagement has been 10 killed, 2 mortally wounded, 27 severely, 28 slightly, and 42 missing, as before stated, making an aggregate of 109. [*O.R.*, XXXVIII, pt. 3, pp. 914–915.]

Report of Maj. George S. Storrs, CSA, Commanding Artillery Battalion, Loring's Corps, Army of Tennessee

Soon after sunrise [on 27 June] [Capt. *Henry*] *Guibor's* and [Capt. *John J.*] *Ward's* batteries and one of [Capt. *James*] *Hoskins'* guns, on Kennesaw Mountain, opened a fire on a column of infantry, supposed to be a brigade, passing to the left. About the same time the guns on the west slope of the mountain and Burnt Hickory Road, composed of *Hoskins'* section of 10-pounder Parrotts, [Capt. *Richard*] *Bellamy's* 10-pounder Parrot battery, and [Capt. *Charles L.*] *Lumsden's* battery of Napoleons under the immediate command of Captain *Hoskins*, opened on a body of infantry which appeared behind the enemy's line of works.

At about 9 o'clock from the top of the mountain I heard rapid musketry firing on our left, and soon perceived the enemy driving in our skirmishers on and to the left of the Burnt Hickory road. I opened on them as soon as possible with a section of *Ward's* battery, but they soon came so near to the base of the mountain that the guns could not be depressed enough to reach them. I at the same time brought a gun from *Guibor's* battery around on the left brow of the mountain and opened a very effective fire with shell. A large body of the enemy when repulsed halted in a wood on the west of the Burnt Hickory road, in front of General *Walker's* right, within easy range of the gun, which kept up a rapid and accurate fire for some two hours, driving large numbers, if not all of them, back to their main works. One shell exploded directly in their line while they were for a short time in the open field, and a great many in the woods to which they had retired. They were evidently much demoralized by this fire, as those who went from the woods to their works were going at their utmost speed.

Their loss was heavy. Many litters were seen carried out of this place, and ambulances were running to a point in rear of this for several hours afterward.

The guns on the left, under Captain *Hoskins,* could see the enemy but a short time, but did good execution while they were in sight. The enemy's advancing lines could not be seen in front of Kennesaw, nor by any means distinguished from our own, so that guns bearing in that direction were not used. [*O.R.,* XXXVIII, pt. 3, pp. 968–969.]

Even though Union accounts confirm the accuracy of *Storrs's* report, surviving messages indicate that Confederate commanders encountered difficulty in coordinating their defense against a Union attack aimed at the junction between two corps.

27 June 1864

ON KENNESAW MOUNTAIN

French to Cockrell, 10 a.m.

Can I shell the woods in your front? I will do so, and when I stop, try and retake your skirmish line. Send me word when you can do it. [*O.R.,* XXXVIII, pt. 4, pp. 798–799.]

Cockrell to French

You can easily shell the woods in my front. Two heavy lines of skirmishers and one line of battle advanced against my skirmishers and were held in check until flanked on the left. The enemy kept pressing around my left. After my skirmishers withdrew the enemy came to the foot of my hill and were quickly driven back by my line in my works. The enemy occupy the woods in the edge of the open field on my left and the bottom in my front, and I understand are a portion of the way up the mountain in *Sears'* front. I can't advance my skirmishers until General *Mercer* on my left and General *Sears* on my right advance and protect my flanks, as my line is a curve, each flank thrown back. [*O.R.*, XXXVIII, pt. 4, pp. 798–799.]

French to Maj. Gen. William H. T. Walker, 2 p.m.

I have shelled your front as far as my guns can reach, and have driven out much of the force of the enemy. I have repelled the assault but cannot advance my skirmishers without your cooperation. I beg you to send an officer to confer with General *Cockrell* to advance our lines. The enemy in my front fills the woods, and could be shelled by your artillery. General *Cockrell* begs cooperation in advancing his skirmishers. Will you please send an officer to see General *Cockrell* at once, and oblige me? [*O.R.*, XXXVIII, pt. 4, pp. 798–799.]

Walker to French

My skirmishers are about 250 yards in my front now. I think, general, from a communication I have just read from you to General *Loring* about my skirmishers, that you are laboring under a great misapprehension. I understand your skirmishers are in your intrenchments; mine are 250 yards in front of mine. [*O.R.*, XXXVIII, pt. 4, pp. 798–799.]

Walker to French

I have just sent a staff officer, Major *Williams* (of *Mercer's* staff), to General *Cockrell*. To advance my skirmishers now, who are 250 yards in front of my line, yours being in your intrenchments, (if I am correctly informed), exposes them to an open fire in a field, which after they have crossed they meet a line of battle which they gallantly fought with today, being clubbed and bayoneted in the pits, owing, they say, to the enemy having passed their right flank, where your skirmishers were supposed to be. [*O.R.*, XXXVIII, pt. 4, pp. 798–799.]

18. THE DEFENSE OF CHEATHAM HILL

Resume driving in the same direction as before on Burnt Hickory Road for about 1.1 miles, passing through the traffic signal on Polk Street before coming to the traffic signal at Whitlock Avenue (Dallas Highway). Turn right onto this road, following the National Park Service sign for Cheatham Hill/Kolb Farm. Drive about 1.1 mile and turn left onto Cheatham Hill Drive. Follow this road about 0.7 mile to the parking area at its end. Use the National Park Service interpretive panel at the end of the parking lot ("Climax of Cheatham") for orientation. Then follow the trail to the Illinois Monument, stopping near the National Park Service interpretive panel "The Dead Angle" and looking down across the field toward the Federal lines.

STOP 18, CHEATHAM HILL

27 June–2 July 1864

Stops 18 and 19 are linked. Today there is no good vantage point from the Union lines for views of this critical defensive position. The material presented at this stop gives a short overview of the Confederate defense. The more detailed material covering the Union plan and its execution is presented in the next chapter, but some readers may choose to consult it while on this dramatic site.

Narrative of Lt. Thomas H. Maney, CSA, Company B, First Tennessee Volunteer Infantry Regiment, Maney's Tennessee Brigade, Cheatham's Division, Hardee's Army Corps, Army of Tennessee

Two or three days before the place was selected [by the Union for their attack] we were supplied with shovels and picks and told to go into the ground. We built what we imagined to be good works out of rock and dirt; but we reckoned without our host, for on the 25th the enemy moved a battery up on a hill about 800 yards from our line, opened a terrific cannonade, and ruined our works. We had to endure

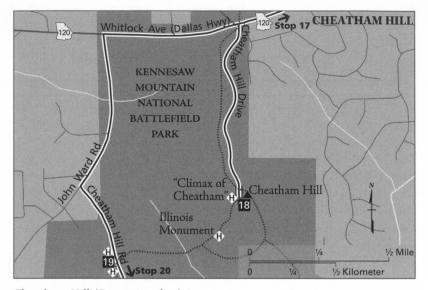

Cheatham Hill (Stops 18 and 19)

it and wait for night, promising ourselves if we were spared until then we would do better. And we kept our promises, for I suppose the works are standing to this day. We put head logs on the works, planted chevaux-de-frise in front, and laid down to rest and wait them to come on, which they did on the 27th. . . .

Stand we must and stand we did. Some of the enemy were killed in our works. The battle lasted nearly an hour. The enemy fell back below the crest of the hill and commenced fortifying, for they had been at work while fighting us. And it was then we discovered that our works were too far beyond the crest of the hill for us to successfully defend them. [T. H. Maney, "Battle of the Dead Angle on Kennesaw Line," *Confederate Veteran* 11 (April 1903), pp. 159–160.]

Narrative of Capt. W. J. McMurray, CSA, Twentieth Tennessee Volunteer Infantry Regiment, Maney's Tennessee Brigade, Cheatham's Division, Hardee's Army Corps, Army of Tennessee

[T]he main and direct assault fell on *Cheatham's* Tennessee division and the left of *Cleburne's* of *Hardee's* Corps, although the assaulting lines that were more or less engaged were ten miles long. Sherman's assaulting column at this point was . . . seven lines deep, numbering not less than 35,000 men while the Confederates had engaged all of *Cheatham's* division, about 4,000, and about 2,000 of *Cleburne's*—a total of 6,000.

The lines of the two armies at this point were close together, so when the Yankees were formed and moved forward the action began at close range. The Yankees were seven lines deep and led by gallant officers; they came forward with a rush like a great cloud of Egyptian flies. Their front lines began to melt from their first step, but onward they came over their dead and dying. Their front lines had now grown thin, and began to recoil; their real lines pushed on in this mad vortex of human destruction. As this great blue wave was about to reach the earthworks of this Spartan band, a Rebel yell of defiance rolled heavenward that said to the other portion of the Confederate line that the immortal *Cheatham* and the tenacious *Cleburne* were here to do or die. *Maney's* Brigade held the salient, which was the deadliest point on the line. It was defended by *Maney's* Brigade of Tennesseeans, commanded by Colonel *F. M. Walker* of the 19th Tennessee, and nobly did they sustain the fighting reputation of the Volunteer State. [W. J. McMurray, *History of the Twentieth Tennessee Volunteer Infantry Regiment* (Nashville, 1904), pp. 316–317.]

Diary of Private Robert D. Smith, CSA, Second Tennessee Volunteer Infantry Regiment, Polk's Brigade, Cleburne's Division, Hardee's Army Corps, Army of Tennessee

June 27. At about 10 a.m. the enemy charged our works. They had two lines of skirmishers and three lines of battle in front of our brigade and seven lines of battle in front of *Cheatham's* Division. We only had four brigades engaged: *Maney's* and *Vaughn's* of *Cheatham's* Division, *Polk's* and *Lowrey's* of *Cleburne's* Division. The enemy came within five feet of our breastworks and the slaughter was terrific as our troops literally mowed them down. We lost only 12 killed and wounded in our brigade. The enemy could not stand the steady fire of our troops and in a few moments fell back to their breastworks except in front of *Maney's* brigade, where it is reported they are fortifying within 50 yards of our lines.

About half an hour after the charge, our brigade stopped skirmishing and called the enemy to stop and come out and get their dead and wounded that were in the woods, as the heavy firing had set the dry leaves on fire and wounded were in danger of being burnt up; during the armistice I succeeded in getting 90 rifles from the field, 7 of them were Henry's patent (16 shooters). . . . [O]ur brigade captured 40 Yankees . . . they were a hard looking set of men. [*Confederate Diary of Robert D. Smith,* transcribed by Jill K. Garrett (Columbia, Tenn., 1997), p. 142.]

Narrative of Private Sam R. Watkins, CSA, Company H, First Tennessee Volunteer Infantry Regiment, Maney's Tennessee Brigade, Cheatham's Division, Hardee's Army Corps, Army of Tennessee

The First and Twenty-seventh Tennessee Regiments will ever remember the battle of "Dead Angle," which was fought June 27th, on the Kennesaw line, near Marietta, Georgia. It was one of the hottest and longest days of the year, and one of the most desperate and determinedly resisted battles fought during the whole war. Our regiment was stationed on an angle, a little spur of the mountain, or rather promontory of a range of hills, extending far out beyond the main line of battle, and was subject to the enfilading fire of forty pieces of artillery of the Federal batteries. It seemed fun for the guns of the whole Yankee army to play upon this point. We would work hard every night to strengthen our breastworks, and the very next day they would be torn down smooth with the ground by solid shots and shells from the guns of the enemy. Even the little trees and bushes which had been left for shade were cut down as so much stubble. For more than a week this constant firing had been kept up against this salient point. In the meantime, the skirmishing in the valley below resembled the sounds made by ten thousand wood-choppers.

Well, on the fatal morning of June 27th, the sun rose clear and cloudless, the heavens seemed made of brass, and the earth of iron, and as the sun began to mount toward the zenith, everything became quiet, and no sound was heard save a peckerwood on a neighboring tree, tapping on its old trunk, trying to find a worm for his dinner. We all knew it was but the dead calm that precedes the storm. On the distant hills we could plainly see officers dashing about hither and thither, and the Stars and Stripes moving to and fro, and we knew the Federals were making preparations for the mighty contest. We could hear but the rumbling sound of heavy guns, and the distant tread of a

Fighting at the Dead Angle, from a drawing by a Confederate participant (anonymous engraving in Joseph M. Brown, *The Mountain Campaigns in Georgia*, 2d ed. [Buffalo: Matthews, Northrup Co., 1890], 40).

marching army, as a faint roar of the coming storm, which was soon to break the ominous silence with the sound of conflict, such as was scarcely ever before heard on this earth. It seemed that the arch-angel of Death stood and looked on with outstretched wings, while all the earth was silent, when all at once a hundred guns from the Federal line opened upon us, and for more than an hour they poured their solid and chain shot, grape and shrapnel right upon this salient point, defended by our regiment alone, when, all of a sudden, our pickets jumped into our works and reported the Yankees advancing, and almost at the same time a solid line of blue coats came up the hill. I discharged my gun, and happening to look up, there was the beautiful flag of the Stars and Stripes flaunting right in my face, and I heard *John Branch*, of the Rock City Guards, commanded by Captain *W. D. Kelly*, who were next to Company H, say, "Look at that Yankee flag; shoot that fellow; snatch that flag out of his hand!" My pen is unable to describe the scene of carnage and death that ensued in the next two hours. Column after column of Federal soldiers were crowded upon that line, and by referring to the history of the war you will find they were massed in column forty columns deep; in fact, the whole force of the Yankee army was hurled against this point, but no sooner would a regiment mount our works than they were shot down or surrendered, and soon we had every "gopher hole" full of Yankee prisoners. Yet still the Yankees came. It seemed impossible to check the onslaught, but every man was true to his trust, and seemed to think that at that moment the whole responsibility of the Confederate government was rested upon his shoulders. Talk about other battles, victories, shouts, cheers, and triumphs, but in comparison with this day's fight, all others dwarf into insignificance. The sun beaming down on our uncovered heads, the thermometer being one hundred and ten degrees in the shade, and a solid line of blazing fire right from the muzzles of the Yankee guns being poured right into our very faces, singeing our hair and clothes, the hot blood of our dead and wounded spurting on us, the blinding smoke and stifling atmosphere filling our eyes and mouths, and the awful concussion causing the blood to gush out of our noses and ears, and above all, the roar of battle, made it a perfect pandemonium. Afterward I heard a soldier express himself by saying that he thought "Hell had broke loose in Georgia, sure enough."

I have heard men say that if they ever killed a Yankee during the war they were not aware of it. I am satisfied that on this memorable day, every man in our regiment killed from one score to four score, yea, five score men. I mean from twenty to one hundred each. All that was necessary was to load and shoot. In fact, I will ever think that the reason they did not capture our works was the impossibility of their living men passing over the bodies of their dead. The ground was piled up with one solid mass of dead and wounded Yankees. I learned afterwards from the burying squad that in some places they were piled up like cord wood, twelve deep.

After they were time and time again beaten back, they at last were enabled to fortify a line under the crest of the hill, only thirty yards from us, and they immediately commenced to excavate the earth with the purpose of blowing up our line.

We remained here three days after the battle. In the meantime the woods had taken fire, and during the nights and days of all that time continued to burn, and at all times, every hour of day and night, you could hear the shrieks and screams of the poor fellows who were left on the field, and a stench, so sickening as to nauseate the whole of both armies, arose from the decaying bodies of the dead left lying on the field.

On the third morning the Yankees raised a white flag, asked an armistice to bury their dead, not for any respect either army had for the dead, but to get rid of the sickening stench. I get sick now when I happen to think about it. Long and deep trenches were dug, and hooks made from bayonets crooked for the purpose, and all the dead were dragged and thrown pell mell into these trenches. Nothing was allowed to be taken off the dead, and finely dressed officers, with gold watch chains dangling over their vests, were thrown into the ditches. During the whole day both armies were hard at work, burying the Federal dead.

Every member of the First and Twenty-seventh Tennessee Regiments deserves a wreath of imperishable fame, and a warm place in the hearts of their countrymen, for their gallant and heroic valor at the battle of Dead Angle. No man distinguished himself above another. All did their duty, and the glory of one is but the glory and just tribute of the others.

After we had abandoned the line, and on coming to a little stream of water, I undressed for the purpose of bathing, and after undressing found my arm all battered and bruised and bloodshot from my wrist to my shoulder, and as sore as a blister. I had shot one hundred and twenty times that day. My gun became so hot that frequently the powder would flash before I could ram home the ball, and I had frequently to exchange my gun for that of a dead comrade.

Colonel *H. R. Field* was loading and shooting the same as any private in the ranks when he fell off the skid from which he was shooting right over my shoulder, shot through the head. I laid him down in the trench, and he said, "Well, they have got me at last, but I have killed fifteen of them; turn about is fair play, I reckon." But Colonel *Field* was not killed—only wounded, and one side paralyzed. Captain *Joe P. Lee,* Captain *Mack Campbell,* Lieutenant *T. H. Maney,* and other officers of the regiment, threw rocks and beat them in their faces with sticks. The Yankees did the same. The rocks came in upon us like a perfect hail storm, and the Yankees seemed very obstate, and in no hurry to get away from our front, and we had to keep up the firing and shooting them down in self-defense. They seemed to walk up and take death as coolly as if they were automatic or wooden men, and our boys did not shoot for the fun of the thing. It was, verily, a life and death grapple, and the least flicker on our part, would have been sure death to all. We could not be reinforced on account of our position, and we had to stand up to the rack, fodder or no fodder.

When the Yankees fell back, and the firing ceased, I never saw so many broken down and exhausted men in my life. I was as sick as a horse, and as wet with blood and sweat as I could be, and many of our men were vomiting with excessive fatigue, over-exhaustion, and sunstroke; our tongues were parched and cracked for water, and our faces blackened with powder and smoke, and our dead and wounded were piled indiscriminately in the trenches. There was not a single man in the company who was not wounded, or had holes shot through his hat and clothing. Captain *Beasley* was killed, and nearly all his company killed and wounded. The Rock City Guards were almost piled in heaps and so was our company. [Sam R. Watkins, *"Co. Aytch": A Sideshow of the Big Show* (Jackson, Tenn.: Bell Wiley, 1952), pp. 156–159.]

19. THOMAS'S ATTACK

Reverse your route on Cheatham Hill Drive and return to the intersection with Dallas Highway. Turn left onto that road and drive about 0.4 mile to John Ward Road, which is further identified with a National Park Service sign for Kolb Farm. Turn left onto John Hardy Road. Drive about 0.6 mile and turn left onto Cheatham Hill Road, following the sign for Kolb Farm. Drive about 0.2 mile on Cheatham Hill and turn right into the parking lot. Park and position yourself in front of the National Park Service interpretive panel ("Sherman's Command Post") between the two state historical markers.

As you look beyond the National Park Service interpretive panel, you are facing the "Dead Angle" on Cheatham Hill. The distance between these two points is approximately 0.4 mile. Your present position is in the area where Col. Daniel McCook's Third Brigade, Second Division, Fourteenth Army Corps, formed for the attack. Col. John G. Mitchell's Second Brigade of that same division was about 200 yards to your right.

The attack columns of the Fourth Army Corps were well to your left, with an interval of about 300 yards between McCook's left flank and their right-most column (Harker's).

EXCURSION

Everything that follows can be read in this assembly area, but part of the Union line of attack is accessible. Cross Cheatham Hill Road at the crosswalk and follow the path across Activity Area 3 into the woods on the forward slope. Union earthworks dug after the failed assault on Cheatham Hill are visible in the woods. For another view of the Dead Angle, cross the footbridge and walk to the edge of the field below the Illinois Monument. (The leaf-covered clay soil on the steep slope approaching the creek is slippery when wet. Use caution, especially if wearing smooth-soled shoes.)

STOP 19, CHEATHAM HILL

26 June 1864

THE PLAN

Special Field Orders, Headquarters, Department of the Cumberland, in the Field Near Kennesaw Mountain

In accordance with Special Field Orders, No. 28, from headquarters Military Division of the Mississippi, dated: "In the field, near Kennesaw Mountain, June 24, 1864," the following will be the order for the operations of the Army of the Cumberland tomorrow:

I. The corps of Major-General Howard will assault the enemy's intrenchments at some point near the left of General Stanley's and Davis' divisions, which will be selected by General Howard after a careful reconnaissance. He will support his attack by such dispositions of his artillery as, in his judgment, is best calculated to insure success.

II. Major-General Palmer will, with his column on the right of General Howard's, cooperate with the latter by carrying the enemy's works immediately in his front. The batteries of Generals Baird's and Davis' divisions will remain as presently posted until the contemplated movement is made. General King's division will occupy its present position, but hold itself in readiness to follow up any advantage gained by the other troops.

III. Major General Hooker will support General Palmer on the latter's right, with as much of his force as he can draw from his lines, selecting positions for his artillery best calculated to enfilade the enemy's works to his left and on General Palmer's front. In supporting General Palmer's movement General Hooker will watch carefully his own right flank, and be prepared to meet any demonstration of the enemy upon it.

IV. The troops must get into position as early as possible and commence the movement at 8 a.m. tomorrow, precisely. All the troops will be ready to follow up with promptness any success which may be gained. [O.R., XXXVIII, pt. 4, pp. 602–603.]

Special Orders No. 98, Headquarters, Fourth Army Corps, Near Kennesaw Mountain

I. In pursuance of instructions from headquarters Army of the Cumberland, an attack will be made upon the enemy tomorrow at

Colonel William H. Martin, commanding 1st and 15th Arkansas, observes
Federal aidmen removing wounded from the path of a brushfire during a
truce, June 27, 1864 (engraving by A. R. Waud in Joseph M. Brown, *The
Mountain Campaigns in Georgia*, 2d ed. [Buffalo, N.Y.: Matthews, Northrup
Co., 1890], 42).

8 a.m. by this corps in conjunction with the Fourteenth Corps. The
points of attack selected are near the present position of Colonel [Wil-
liam] Grose's brigade.

II. General Newton will lead the assault, being prepared to cover
his own left.

III. Major-General Stanley will retain one of his brigades in position extending from General Palmer's left to the ravine, and will be
prepared, with his other two brigades well in hand, to follow closely
General Newton's movement.

IV. General Wood will occupy his present front and extend to
the ravine on his right with one brigade, while he will hold his other
two brigades in readiness to follow up the movement of the attacking
column.

V. The points for massing the troops of Generals Stanley's and
Wood's divisions will be pointed out in the morning.

General Newton will commence his movement for the attack at sunrise, keeping his troops as well concealed from the enemy's view as possible. [*O.R.*, pt. 4, p. 603.]

Orders, Headquarters, Twentieth Corps

In execution of special field orders, headquarters Department of the Cumberland, June 26, 1864, General Geary will advance his skirmishers and take possession of the woods in his immediate front and, if possible, the small house to the left, now occupied by the rebel pickets. When this is done, he will advance his division and establish it in the woods and out of sight, if practicable, of the rebels. General Williams will advance the left of his picket-line and keep up connection of General Geary's division. General Williams will detach a brigade to establish itself along the whole line now occupied by General Geary's division, and General Butterfield will send one brigade to hold the right of General Williams' line—the right of this brigade resting on the Powder Springs road. Under the chief of artillery of the corps not less than four batteries will be put in position at points already designated near the left of the line now held by the corps. The changes in the position of the infantry will be made before daylight tomorrow morning, and all should be in their places on or before that hour. The artillery should be in position by or before 7 a.m. All the troops will be held in readiness to march at the shortest notice and will spring to the assistance of those on the right or left, if necessary, without waiting for orders. [*O.R.*, XXXVIII, pt. 4, pp. 603–604.]

TACTICS

Report of Maj. Gen. George H. Thomas, USA, Commanding Army of the Cumberland

June 25, Davis' division, of Palmer's corps, being on line extreme left of my army, was relieved by troops from General McPherson's army, and moved to a position in reserve, behind the right of Howard's line. This change was effected after dark, and by daylight on the 26th Davis' troops had reached the position assigned them. Baird's division, of Palmer's corps (being relieved by troops from the Army of the Tennessee), was also withdrawn from its position in line in front of Kennesaw Mountain and moved during the night of the 26th to a position in reserve near that occupied by Davis' troops.

June 27, at 8 a.m., the enemy's works were assaulted at two points, one in front of Newton's division, of Howard's corps, and the other in front of Davis' division, of Palmer's corps, Davis having relieved the right division (Stanley's) of General Howard's line. Stanley moved his command a short distance to the left, and acted as a support to Newton's division in its assault upon the works, Wood's division being in reserve. Davis' assault was supported by Baird's division, of Palmer's corps, on the right, and Hooker's whole corps was held in readiness to support the movement of Palmer's and Howard's commands.

Although the troops were enabled to drive the enemy into his main works and reached that point with their main line, they were unable to carry the positions on account of the heavy fire of musketry and canister brought to bear upon them at short range, but held the ground gained. Our loss was 1,580 killed, wounded, and missing, some of our men being shot while on the parapets of the enemy's works. We took 130 prisoners. General Davis immediately commenced fortifying his advanced position at the distance of about seventy-five yards from the enemy's fortifications, covering the working parties with such a heavy and well-directed fire of musketry that the enemy could not molest them in their operations. About midnight on the 29th the enemy attacked Davis, overwhelming his skirmishers and driving them back, when they rallied and drove the rebels back again to their works. During the 29th and 30th all remained comparatively quiet along the line, the skirmishers in the most advanced positions only exchanging occasional shots with the enemy. [O.R., XXXVIII, pt. 1, p. 151.]

Report of Maj. Gen. Oliver O. Howard, USA, Commanding Fourth Army Corps, Army of the Cumberland

June 27, in General Thomas' special field orders, of June 26, I was required to assault the enemy's works at some point near the left of General Stanley's division. General Palmer, with his column on my right, was directed to carry the enemy's works in his front. The whole movement was to take place at 8 a.m. After a careful examination of the ground, I found only two points where the troops could have a reasonable cover in Stanley's front, and decided to make two columns of attack. Brigadier-General Harker led one column and General Wagner another, while [Brigadier] General [Nathan] Kimball moved in support in echelon with Wagner's brigade. These columns each had a regimental division front [By specifying this formation, General Howard put the attacking brigades into narrow, deep columns. A "regimental division front" put two companies abreast. Each company had two ranks, and there were ten companies in a regiment, so the regimental column was ten ranks deep. Had the regiments been at full strength, the frontage of each brigade would have been about 50 yards, but these columns would have been much narrower—probably 25 yards or less. Since the brigades each employed three regiments in their columns, the brigade columns were 30 ranks deep.—*eds.*], and were separated by about 100 yards interval. The whole front was covered by a strong line of skirmishers. Such troops of Stanley's and Wood's as were free to move were massed in support. The artillery of the corps was so placed as to bring a heavy fire on the points of attack. General Palmer's arrangements were made simultaneous with mine. The artillery opened from all points and continued firing for about fifteen minutes. At a preconcerted signal the columns pushed rapidly forward, driving in the enemy's skirmishers, and were not checked until they reached the entanglements in front of the enemy's works. At this place the artillery and infantry fire became so galling that the advance was stopped. General Harker is reported to have made a second advance, when he received the wound which caused his death. Some of his men succeeded in reaching the enemy's works, but failed to secure a lodgment. As soon as it became evident that the enemy's intrenchments could not be carried by assault the command was directed to resume its former position.

Our losses were very heavy, particularly in valuable officers. I call special attention to the report of Brigadier-General Newton of this attack, and to his opinion as to the causes of its being unsuccessful. My experience is that a line of works thoroughly constructed, with the front well covered with abatis and other entanglements, well manned with infantry, whether with our own or that of the enemy, cannot be carried by direct assault. The exceptions are where some one of the above conditions is wanting or where the defenders are taken by surprise. The strength of such a line is, of course, increased by well-arranged batteries. Notwithstanding the probabilities against success, it is sometimes necessary to assault strong works, as has occurred in several instances during the present campaign.

From June 28 to July 2, inclusive, preparations were made and partially executed for resting the left of the entire army opposite the southern extremity of Little Kennesaw, so as to extend the right and turn the enemy's left flank. The enemy, doubtless perceiving these movements, evacuated his position in our front on the night of the 2d. [*O.R.*, XXXVIII, pt. 1, p. 199.]

Report of Brig. Gen. John Newton, USA, Commanding Second Division, Fourth Army Corps, Army of the Cumberland

June 27, my division was ordered to assault the enemy's lines before Kennesaw, in front of the position held by General Stanley's division. The formation prescribed by General Howard was in two columns, composed of divisions closed in mass. Accordingly, General Harker's brigade was formed on the right in one column in mass. General Wagner's and General Kimball's on the left in one column closed in mass. The columns were preceded by a strong line of skirmishers, under command of Colonel [Emerson] Opdyke. . . . At about 9 a.m. the skirmishers advanced, gallantly driving the enemy's pickets into the works, the columns immediately following them. General Harker's brigade advanced through dense undergrowth, through the slashing and abatis made by the enemy, in the face of their fire, to the foot of their works, but were unable to get in, and fell back a short distance. General Wagner's brigade passed through similar obstacles, and were compelled to stop their advance a short distance from the enemy's works. General Harker then attempted another advance, and in the act this gallant and distinguished officer was killed. After a short respite General Kimball's brigade was ordered to advance. It moved to the front gallantly to the foot of the enemy's works, when his command was retired. It having been demonstrated that the enemy's works were too strong to be taken, the division was withdrawn, leaving our pickets in the captured rifle-pits, where they were afterward relieved by General Stanley's division.

Apart from the strength of the enemy's lines, and the numerous obstacles which they had accumulated in front of their works, our want of success is in a great degree to be attributed to the thickets and undergrowth, which effectually broke up the formation of our columns and deprived that formation of the momentum which was expected of it. Beside the enemy's musketry our troops were exposed to a heavy fire of canister and case-shot. . . .

The loss of the division in the assault was 654 killed and wounded. [*O.R.*, XXXVIII, pt. 1, pp. 295–296.]

Report of Brig. Gen. Luther P. Bradley, USA, Commanding Third Brigade, Second Division, Fourth Army Corps, Army of the Cumberland

On the morning of the 27th the brigade moved out at 6 a.m. and formed in column of attack in front of Stanley's division; between 9 and 10 were ordered forward to assault and carry the enemy's works in our front. The brigade advanced steadily and attacked with spirit but found the works too strong for them. After a short and sharp fight, and the loss of a large number of officers and men, the brigade was retired by me, bringing off most of our wounded. General Harker, the very gallant commander of the brigade, was shot in the endeavor to carry the men up to a second charge. The brigade retired to its position behind the works, where it remained without material change until July 2. [*O.R.*, XXXVIII, pt. 1, p. 355.]

Report of Lt. Col. David H. Moore, USA, Commanding 125th Ohio Infantry Regiment, Third Brigade, Second Division, Fourth Army Corps, Army of the Cumberland

June 27, it having been determined to charge the enemy's works to the right of Kennesaw Mountain, the Third Brigade was designated to form one of the charging columns to assault the enemy in front of works occupied by the extreme right of Fourth Army Corps. Colonel Opdyke, in charge of the skirmish line for the division, selected the One hundred and twenty-fifth for skirmishers, ordering that it should push ahead at all hazards, scaling the enemy works with the head of the column, in case the charge was successful, or protecting the rear if repulsed. I deployed the regiment in rear of our works, at intervals of four feet, placing Major Bruff in charge of the right wing, while I directed the movements of the left. Between our main works and those of the enemy there was an interval of not to exceed 400 paces. Fifty paces in front, and running nearly parallel to our works, was a ravine, which was the only place between the lines where men were not exposed to fire from the enemy's main works. At the sound of the bugle, fifteen minutes before 10 a.m. the line sprung over the works and moved forward in quick time without firing. We passed the enemy's advance pits, capturing almost his entire line of pickets, and sent them to the rear in charge of wounded men, or without guard when there were not wounded men at hand, as I would not spare well men from the ranks.

As the line advanced beyond the enemy's rifle-pits it was exposed to a more withering fire, but it moved forward in splendid style till it encountered the abatis in front of his main works, when I halted and lay down to await the charging column. The head of the column no sooner reached the abatis than it, too, was unable to stand the fire, and the men immediately threw themselves flat on the ground; all attempts to again rally them were unsuccessful, although several men struggled through the dense abatis and were cut down while climbing the outer slope of the enemy's works. There was no concerted action, and after maintaining its position fully fifteen minutes the column was forced to fall back. The One hundred and twenty-fifth retired to the pits occupied by the enemy during the morning, and held them half an hour after the column had withdrawn, and until after relieved by fresh troops. The entire loss of the regiment during the engagement amounted to 1 officer killed, 2 mortally wounded, and 8 officers more or less severely wounded; 6 men killed, 8 mortally wounded, and 33 men more or less severely wounded. [*O.R.*, XXXVIII, pt. 1, pp. 370–371.]

Report of Brig. Gen. George D. Wagner, USA, Commanding Second Brigade, Second Division, Fourth Army Corps, Army of the Cumberland

[On the 27th] I moved my command to the rear of the outer line of works occupied by Colonel Grose's brigade of General Stanley's division, and massed them in column by division, left in front. . . . General Harker's brigade was formed on my right, leaving sufficient interval to admit my deploying to the right, and forming connection with his left. General Kimball was formed to my left and rear. At a given signal the skirmishers on my front moved forward, and soon became heavily engaged, and soon thereafter my entire command moved up to and scaled our outer line of works. As soon as the head of my column began crossing our works the enemy opened a terrific and deadly fire of artillery and musketry from their main line of works, but, nothing daunted, the column moved forward, charging the works of the enemy, unmindful of the terrific havoc in their ranks. After repeated efforts of both officers and men to get to the enemy's works, the same being defended by heavy lines of abatis, as well as by artillery and infantry, the command fell back for shelter to a ravine close to the enemy's works, and deployed into line. About this time I received an order to the effect that General Kimball's brigade would charge in conjunction with mine, and I directed the regiments in my brigade to move forward with those of his. The commands moved forward simultaneously, but met with such a terrific fire from the enemy that they were compelled to fall back. In falling back a heavy fire was poured into the right flank of my command, giving evidence that the troops on my right had failed to effect a lodgment in the enemy's works, and had fallen back to our main line of works, and that the enemy were coming out of their works and striking me on the flank. After my command was repulsed in the last charge they fell back to the main line, and I received orders to return to the camp I had left in the morning, relieving those of General Wood's troops who had relieved me. My losses in this assault were 4 commissioned officers and 35 enlisted men killed, and 11 commissioned officers and 165 enlisted men wounded. [O.R., XXXVIII, pt. 1, pp. 335–336.]

Report of Lt. Col. Willis Blanch, USA, Commanding Fifty-Seventh Indiana Infantry, Second Brigade, Second Division, Fourth Army Corps, Army of the Cumberland

[On the 27th I was ordered] to deploy my entire regiment as skirmishers and at a signal advance the line, when I would be followed by the assaulting columns. The deployment was made, the signal given, and we moved, drawing as we did so a very heavy fire from both the main line of works and rifle-pits of the enemy. In a short time after becoming engaged I was overtaken by the assaulting columns, and during the remainder of the battle my regiment operated with and as a part of this, the deployment, however, remaining complete. I remained on skirmish line after the assault had been abandoned until nearly nightfall. [O.R., XXXVIII, pt. 1, p. 348.]

Report of Brig. Gen. Nathan Kimball, USA, Commanding First Brigade, Second Division, Fourth Army Corps, Army of the Cumberland

On the 27th . . . my command was formed in close column by divisions, right in front, to support the Second and Third Brigades in an assault upon the enemy's works. My position was on the left, and retired from that occupied by General Wagner's brigade, at the time the assault commenced. At 9 a.m., General Wagner having advanced to near the enemy's rifle-pits, and then been checked, [I] was ordered to advance my command and take the works, if possible.

My column was immediately in motion, advancing with fixed bayonets, Col. W. W. Barrett, of the Forty-fourth Illinois Infantry, in immediate charge of the right wing, and the Seventy-fourth Illinois Infantry, under command of Lieut. Col. James B. Kerr, in the front. The column pushed forward, under thick undergrowth of brush to the edge of the woods, within seventy yards of the enemy's abatis, where the Seventy-fourth Illinois deployed and rushed forward. From the time of starting until it reached the edge of the woods, the head of my column was exposed to canister from the enemy's batteries, and upon debauching from the woods and deploying, was swept away by it and the murderous fire of the enemy's riflemen. Still those of the regiment who did not fall pressed forward and reached the parapet of the enemy's works. . . . At the time the second regiment, the Eighty-eighth Illinois Infantry, was about to deploy, [the division commander's] order to halt and remain where I was reached me. The halt was made, Wagner's brigade was withdrawn, and I was ordered to fall back behind our works, which movement was accomplished without confusion, under a most terrific fire from the enemy. My loss in this action was 194 killed, wounded, and missing, nearly all of whom were from the Seventy-fourth, Eighty-eighth, and Forty-fourth Illinois Regiments and neither of which numbered 160 men. The loss of officers in my command in this action was in remarkable disproportion to that of enlisted men, being one to six. . . . Many of my dead and wounded were between the enemy's abatis and their works, and were left there until the evening of the 28th, when they were recovered through an arrangement made for that purpose by Major Sabin, of the Forty-fourth Illinois Infantry, my Brigade officer of the day, and Lieutenant-Colonel

Martin, of Arkansas, the officer of the day for the enemy in our front. [*O.R.*, XXXVIII, pt. 1, p. 304.]

Report of Lt. Col. Porter C. Olson, USA, Commanding Thirty-Sixth Illinois Infantry Volunteer Regiment, First Brigade, Second Division, Fourth Army Corps, Army of the Cumberland

The Thirty-sixth Illinois formed part of the force ordered to storm the enemy's works on the morning of the 27th of June. Previous to the charge the regiment was advanced to support the skirmish line. When the charge was made the regiment moved forward with the main force. That the enemy's works were not carried it seems to me was not the fault of either officers or men. It was simply an impossibility on our part of the line.

The fortifications on our front consisted of heavy earth-works, deep moat, and intricate abatis. In addition to strong lines of infantry opposed to us, our entire front was swept by discharges of grape and canister. The regiment behaved in the most gallant manner. Our losses in the charge were heavy, comprising about 33 per cent of the officers and men present for duty. [*O.R.*, XXXVIII, pt. 1, p. 314.]

Report of Maj. Arthur MacArthur, Jr., USA, Commanding Twenty-Fourth Wisconsin Volunteers, First Brigade, Second Division, Fourth Army Corps, Army of the Cumberland

[On the 27th] I formed my regiment on the First Division, right in front, and directly in rear of the Eighty-eighth Illinois. About 8:30 the formation was complete, and the advance ordered; the ground passed over was covered with fallen timber, forming an almost impassable abatis; the men, however, advanced most admirably. Having advanced three-fourths of the distance between my own and the enemy's works, I was ordered to halt. The head of the column had reached the enemy's works and on account of our halting began to retire in some confusion, this was communicated to some extent to the men that were somewhat retired, but was quickly quieted. I remained in this position exposed to a most galling fire of artillery and infantry for half an hour, unable to reply on account of the formation. After it had been sufficiently demonstrated that we could not occupy the enemy's works,

I was ordered to retire with my command. I marched the regiment back to the position occupied before the assault. [*O.R.*, XXXVIII, pt. 1, p. 329.]

Report of Maj. Gen. Jefferson C. Davis, USA, Commanding Second Division, Fourteenth Army Corps, Army of the Cumberland

My command . . . bivouacked during the 26th in rear of General Stanley's division, of the Fourth Corps, preparatory to storming the enemy's works at some point near that place on the following morning. Being informed by Major-General Thomas of the distinguished duty for which my division had been designated, in company with Generals Stanley, [John M.] Brannan, and Baird, I made a thorough reconnaissance of the enemy's works and selected the point of attack.

The point selected was immediately in front of [Brigadier] General [Walter C.] Whitaker's brigade, of Stanley's division, of the Fourth Corps. The enemy's works here conforming to a projecting point in the ridge, upon which his works were built, presented a salient angle, and, in the absence of abatis, fallen timber, and other obstructions which generally confront their works, this point seemed the most assailable. Early on the morning of the 27th the brigade commanders accompanied me to the ground and familiarized selves with it. McCook's and Mitchell's brigades had been designated for this conspicuous duty, and at 8 o'clock were massed in an open field in rear of our breastworks (now occupied by Morgan's brigade as a reserve), some 600 yards from the point to be carried. No place nearer the enemy's line could the troops be massed without receiving the enemy's fire, both of infantry and artillery. The ground to be passed over was exceedingly rocky and rough, and a considerable part of it covered with forest trees, interspersed with undergrowth.

The signal was given a little before 9 o'clock, and the troops, following the example of their admired leaders, bounded over our own works, in the face of the enemy's fire, and rushed gallantly for the enemy, meeting and disregarding with great coolness the heavy fire, both of artillery and infantry, to which they were subjected, until the enemy's works were reached. Here, owing to exhaustion, produced by the too rapid execution of the movement, the exceeding rough ground, and the excessive heat, the troops failed to leap and carry the works to which their noble daring and impetuous valor had carried them. McCook had fallen, dangerously wounded, and [Col. Oscar F.] Harmon, next in rank, had assumed command, but fell immediately. [Col. Caleb J.] Dilworth, the next senior in rank, promptly took command of the brigade, and with great personal gallantry held his command to the fierce contest now being fought so near the works that a number of both officers and men were killed and wounded at the trenches. Mitchell's brigade, moving in column parallel with McCook's, received and returned the fire with the same impetuosity and invincible determination, but failed, from the same cause, to carry the works.

The position of the troops at this juncture was one of extreme solicitude and presented a problem of some difficulty of solution. To retire, and thus receive the full effect of the enemy's unrestrained fire, now considerably diminished in severity by the effect of our own, was sure to incur an additional loss. A renewal of the assault in the present exhausted condition of the troops was exceedingly hazardous. Under the circumstances, after a thorough examination of the ground and the enemy's works, I reported to Major-General Thomas, and recommended that the position be held and the troops entrenched where they were.

This he ordered to be done, and entrenching implements were immediately furnished to the troops, and both brigades threw up works a few yards from and nearly parallel to those of the enemy. This was done under fire so severe that at times it might almost be termed a general engagement. Works thrown up under such circumstances were of necessity of rude character, but sufficed to protect the men until night, during which the whole command entrenched itself in excellent works. During the succeeding six days the position was held, the troops sleeping on their arms at night. Details were kept engaged in throwing up new works where-ever an advanced line could be established, until the morning of the 3d of July, when it was discovered that the enemy had abandoned the position.

The assault failed in its immediate object, but the courage and discipline exhibited by the troops in the attacks, the determined manner in which they clung to the works afterward, and the noble physical endurance displayed by them during the six days and nights, have never been exceeded in modern soldiery.

Casualties of the division: 131 killed, 625 wounded, 68 missing, for a total of 824. [O.R., XXXVIII, pt. 1, pp. 632–633, 637.]

Report of Col. John G. Mitchell, USA, Commanding
Second Brigade, Second Division, Fourteenth Army Corps,
Army of the Cumberland

June 27, received orders to assault the enemy's works at 8 a.m. The ground over which the assaulting column was to pass was hilly, with thick belts of trees interspersed, while the valleys were low and marshy. The distance to be passed was little less than one-half mile. The Thirty-fourth Illinois was deployed as skirmishers, and ordered to advance to the enemy's main works. The assaulting force was formed in column of regiments, the One hundred and thirteenth Ohio in advance, my brigade on the right of Colonel McCook's and the extreme right of the line.

The signal was given, and the line sprang from the trenches at 8:30 a.m. The enemy's skirmishers were all killed or captured, the first line of rifle-pits taken, and the column passed to the last thin belt of trees separating us from the main works. As the column reached this point the fire which had before been very heavy, now became terrific. [The brigade] was subjected to an enfilading fire of artillery and musketry. Still the column moved on, the summit of the hill was gained, the works were reached, but we could not pass them. A few of my men did get through the dense abatis, succeeded in scaling the works, and are now held as prisoners, but no continuous line could have done so. We fell back until covered by the crest of the hill, and with bayonets and tin cups threw up a line of works within forty paces of the enemy.

Our failure to succeed in this assault is owing to the following facts: First, the distance to be passed was too great; second, the excessive heat; third, inadequate support on right flank. Our loss was very heavy, especially in the two regiments in the front line, the One hundred and twenty-first Ohio having deployed, as was ordered, to the right the moment the One hundred and thirteenth Ohio reached the works; these two regiments lost nearly one-half of their force.

June 28, 29, and 30, July 1 and 2, no material change in position. Continued to advance my lines by a system of gradual approaches, keeping up constant firing; were much annoyed by the enemy's sharpshooters. July 3, at 2 a.m. the enemy evacuated his works. [*O.R.*, XXXVIII, pt. 1, p. 680.]

Report of Capt. Toland Jones, USA, Commanding 113th Ohio Infantry Regiment, Second Brigade, Second Division, Fourteenth Army Corps, Army of the Cumberland

[On the 27th of June] we received orders at daylight to be prepared to storm the enemy's works in our front. The brigade was formed and in position by 9 o'clock, the Thirty-fourth Illinois being deployed as skirmishers, and the One hundred and thirteenth leading the main force. At the signal for the advance, the whole line sprang forward at the double-quick. The skirmish pits of the enemy were passed over, when we proceeded through thick woods up one hill and down across a small creek. Owing to the rough nature of the ground, the lines were not kept in as perfect order as desirable, but every man moved forward with ardor and the highest courage.

When crossing the creek we found before us a hill of some size, at the summit of which were the main works of the enemy. Our skirmish support having fallen back, our regiment advanced up, exposed to the full fire of the enemy. It was not until we had advanced half way up the hill that the enemy poured into our ranks his heaviest fire. Our left was then in close proximity to a salient angle in the hostile works, toward which Colonel McCook's brigade was charging with his entire line. The firing then became most terrific. The rebels opening up with two batteries upon either flank and delivering from the left a most galling musketry fire. The men, however, advanced without faltering, the One hundred and twenty-first taking position on our right. We found before us a heavy abatis work and the enemy's line heavily fortified and defended with all the appliances of the most skillful engineering. We charged rapidly forward, and our men falling by scores, until the left had nearly reached the works, some of the men falling immediately upon them. At this time Lieutenant Colonel Warner was severely wounded, and the brigade on our left was forced to retire. The order was given to fall back, which was done with perfect coolness, and position taken back of our supports in the rear, and entrenchments rapidly thrown up under fire. . . . It is sufficient evidence of the nature of the contest to say that in a space of not over twenty minutes the regiment lost 153 men. Of the 19 commissioned officers who went into the charge 10 were killed or wounded. Although the assault was not successful, still a most important advantage was gained, and we had the melancholy satisfaction of knowing that we failed only because we attempted impossibilities. 28th remained in same position, within stone's throw of the rebel works, and heavy firing from the main lines. . . . 29th and 30th, and 1st and 2nd of July, no material change in position, but continued heavy skirmishing, with an occasional casualty. 3rd, the enemy evacuated his works at night, we following through Marietta, came upon him again and again entrenched. [O.R., XXXVIII, pt. 1, pp. 697–698.]

Report of Colonel Henry B. Banning, USA, Commanding 121st Ohio Infantry, Second Brigade, Second Division, Fourteenth Army Corps

On the morning of the 26th the regiment was relieved before day and moved to the right, where it rested with the brigade, in the rear of the first line, until the morning of the 27th. On the morning of the 27th of June, in accordance with orders, I held my command ready to move at day-light. Leaving the sick to guard the knapsacks, tents, and cooking utensils, which I had been ordered to leave behind, we moved out and formed, the Second Brigade being on the right of the line that was to storm the enemy's works. The formation was a column of regiments closed in mass. Our column was four regiments deep. In the front line was the One hundred and thirteenth Ohio; just behind the One hundred and thirteenth was the One hundred and twenty-first Ohio; next was the Ninety-eighth Ohio, and next was the Seventy-eighth Illinois, while the Thirty-fourth Illinois was deployed as skirmishers in front of the column.

My orders were to overlap the One hundred and thirteenth Ohio two companies to my right, making the right guide of my third company the guide of my regiment, which I ordered to cover the right guide of the regiment in front, and ordered the two right companies to guide left. [In the drill book, "cover" means to take alignment with respect to the direction of movement by remaining directly behind the designated individual. The individual designated as Company Guide sets both direction and pace for the company on the march. Soldiers within the formation keep their lateral alignment by looking to the Guide. In this instance, the eight companies to the left of the designated Guide were ordered to "Guide right" while the other two companies were ordered to "Guide left." Thus a single individual, taking his cue from the lead regiment, provided the moving reference point for his regiment's march in line of battle.—*eds.*] The other regiments, I understood, were to form in echelon, guiding and overlapping in like manner. I was also instructed to deploy my regiment to the right when I struck the enemy; that my left would probably strike an angle in the enemy's works, and that I would have to wheel my regiment to the left, and that I would be supported on my right by the regiments in my rear.

I deployed my regiment as I raised the hill in front of the enemy's works, and uncovering the angle at the very point at which I had been advised I would find it, I started my regiment upon a left wheel, my left already resting well up toward the enemy's works. The enemy still was reserving his fire, and continued to do so until my command got close up to his ditches on the right, when he opened upon my single line with grape and canister from both flanks and a full line of small-arms from my front.

On the left, from the first volley from the enemy, the captain of Company B was mortally wounded, the captain of Company G was shot dead; the captain of Company E was shot through the ankle and carried from the field, from which wound he has since died, while the major who was in charge of the left received three mortal wounds, from which he died before he could be taken from the field. Company I had lost 29 out of 56 men she took into action. Their commander, Captain Robinson, was wounded in the knee, and the only commissioned officer now on the left, while most of the sergeants were either killed or wounded. In Company B all of them were either killed or wounded.

The enemy now opened another battery from an angle in his works on my right. On this flank I was entirely without support. Believing it would be impossible to carry the strong position of the enemy with my now weak and thin line, I closed my regiment to the right and withdrew some twenty paces to the rear, and had my command to lie down, where the formation of the ground offered some protection, and where I would be prepared for any counter-charge the enemy might make, ordering my men to keep a constant fire on the enemy to keep him inside his trenches and prevent him from getting possession of my wounded. Having made these dispositions, I sent a written statement of my position to Colonel Mitchell, commanding the brigade, who sent me orders to refuse my right and hold and intrench it if I could do it without too great a sacrifice. Leaving one-half of my men on the line to keep up the fire, with the other half I built a line of earthworks in the rear of the line under cover of the woods, refusing my right, and at night-fall withdrew my line behind my earthworks.

Having my line thus made safe and secure, my next care was for my dead and wounded. Many of them had lain in the hot sun all day without even water to moisten their parched lips, but they were so situated that it was impossible for me to remove them or get them any assistance whatever. Every effort to go to the wounded during the day on my left resulted in either the killing or wounding of those who attempted to go to their relief.

In the engagement I lost 3 officers killed and 3 wounded, 15 non-commissioned officers and privates killed and 123 wounded. Two of them, who were wounded in the outside ditch of the enemy's works, were captured. The loss was a severe one to my command. How much we damaged the enemy I do not know, but my opinion is their loss was small, as they fought behind heavy earth-works.

We fought the flower of the Southern army, being *Cheatham's* division, of *Hardee's* corps. We succeeded in making a lodgment so close up to their works as to compel them to evacuate four days afterward. On the night of the 28th the enemy, growing uneasy about the tenacity with which we held on to our position so close to their works, charged us and attempted to drive us away. We repulsed him with the small loss of 5 men wounded. On the night of the 2d of July the enemy, having discovered that we were building a new parallel still closer to his lines, evacuated all his earth-works and forts and withdrew beyond the town of Marietta to a prepared line of heavy works near the Chattahoochee River. [*O.R.*, XXXVIII, pt. 1, pp. 703–704.]

Report of Lt. Col. John S. Pearce, USA, Commanding Ninety-Eighth Ohio Infantry Regiment, Second Brigade, Second Division, Fourteenth Army Corps, Army of the Cumberland

On the morning of the 27th the regiment constituted the third line in the brigade column that was to charge the enemy's works. At 9 o'clock the charge was made at the double-quick. It was the full distance of three-fourths of a mile from the place where the column was formed to the enemy's works. The column advanced amidst a perfect shower of canister and bullets to within a few yards of the enemy's lines, but so strong was their position that their front lines were compelled to give way and came back hurriedly through the two rear lines, carrying with them Companies G and B of the regiment. Those two companies, however were soon in position and intrenching, along with the balance of the regiment which held the ground it occupied at the time it was ordered to halt and lie down. . . . Allow me to say that, in my opinion, the officers and especially the men could not possibly have conducted themselves more gallantly than they did on that occasion. . . .

As soon as the regiment lay down, they commenced with their bayonets to dig, and their hands, spoons, and tin mess-pans to construct earth-works for their protection and defense. Never did men labor with more patience and undaunted bravery than did the musket-bearers of the Ninety-eighth Regiment on that occasion. There, under one of the heaviest fires, both of canister and ball, during this campaign, did they erect a work in one hour which afforded them much protection. Now they could raise their heads from the ground with some safety, where before it was almost sure death to take your face out of the dust. . . . The regiment at night used the pick, spade, rails, and logs, and before morning of the following day had strong works erected within seventy-five yards of the enemy.

We remained in the trenches until the night of the 30th, when we were relieved by the Thirty-fourth Illinois Regiment. [O.R., XXXVIII, pt. 1, pp. 692–693.]

Report of Lt. Col. James W. Langley, USA, Commanding Third Brigade, Second Division, Fourteenth Army Corps, Army of the Cumberland

On the morning of the 27th of June, [the Brigade] was disposed in order of battle as follows: Eighty-fifth Illinois, commanded by Colonel Dilworth, deployed as skirmishers, with lines of battle composed of— first, the One hundred and twenty-fifth Illinois; second, the Eighty-sixth Illinois; third, Twenty-second Indiana; fourth, Fifty-second Ohio. These dispositions were made in an open field little more than one-half mile from the works to be stormed. The Second Brigade was formed on the right, and General Harker's brigade, Fourth Corps, on the left.

At a few minutes before 9 the command, "Forward!" was given, and responded to by the brave men of the brigade with the will and determination to succeed where success is possible. The movement began at quick time, and continued in this for nearly one-third the distance, when it was changed to double-quick. The lines moved with marked precision until they reached the foot of an abrupt hill, where they encountered a marshy creek lined on either side with shrubs and thickly matted vines. The command relieved itself as rapidly and orderly as possible from this confusion, and, turning its face to the enemy, rushed forward across an open field extending to within fifteen rods of the point of attack; here it entered a skirt of light timber, and from this point also commenced an ascent of the ground. On and up the brave men rushed, with their gallant leader at their head, until some of them reached the base of the enemy's parapet. Nothing daunted, they struggled to scale the works. In their efforts to do this some were knocked down with stones and clubs hurled at them by the enemy.

Here the gallant Colonel McCook fell, mortally wounded, while present with and cheering his men on. Shot and stoned down, completely exhausted by the length and impetuosity of the charge, the brave men reformed their lines a few steps in the rear and partially under the crest of the hill. While this was being done Col. O. F. Harmon, of the One hundred and twenty-fifth Illinois, left the command of the regiment to Major Lee and placed himself at the head of the brigade; but hardly did he enjoy this command five minutes, when a musket-shot from the enemy pierced his heart, and in a few moments his remains were borne from the field. Col. O. J. Dilworth then assumed command, leaving the command of the Eighty-fifth Illinois to Major Rider. After adjusting his lines to his satisfaction, he ordered works to be constructed, which was hastily done, and the front line of which did not exceed sixty yards from the enemy's strong line of works.

The loss to the brigade in this bloody contest was 410 killed and wounded, nearly all of which occurred within the short space of twenty minutes. These casualties fell heaviest upon the One hundred and twenty-fifth Illinois and Fifty-second Ohio. By 3 p.m. of this day the men were well sheltered behind their new lines of works and were confronting the enemy as sharpshooters. . . . After the confusion of the battle was over, the brigade was disposed thus: The Eighty-fifth Illinois on the right, connecting with the Second Brigade; the Twenty-second Indiana on the left, connecting with General Harker's brigade; the One hundred and twenty-fifth Illinois in the center, and the Eighty-sixth Illinois and Fifty-second Ohio in reserve, the lines remaining the same until the morning of the 28th, when the One hundred and twenty-fifth was relieved by the Eighty-sixth Illinois; that in turn was relieved on the morning of the 29th by the Fifty-second Ohio.

On this day a cessation of hostilities was effected and arrangements made under flag of truce by which the dead between the lines were removed or buried. On the 30th a new line of works was constructed within from five to seven rods of the enemy's line. From this position our sharpshooters did excellent service, many of them using an invention called the refracting sight. [This was a small mirror held by a wire behind the rear sight and angled so that a soldier could rest his piece on the parapet, sight and fire on the enemy position without exposing himself.—*eds.*] The testimony in favor of the use of this sight at short range was abundant. The brigade did duty here until morning of the 3d of July, the enemy having abandoned their works. [*O.R.*, XXXVIII, pt. 1, pp. 710–711.]

Report of Lt. Col. Allen L. Fahnestock, USA, Commanding Eighty-Sixth Illinois Infantry Regiment, Third Brigade, Second Division, Fourteenth Army Corps, Army of the Cumberland

Early on [June 27] I received orders to be ready to move at sunrise, leaving camp and garrison equipage behind. A charge on the rebel center had been ordered. At about 8 a.m. our gallant and brave colonel (Dan. McCook) formed his brigade, my regiment in the second line. The signal guns soon pealed forth their thunder, and in a moment thousands of brave soldiers stood ready to advance on the traitorous foe. The charge was gallantly led, but the works proved too strong to be carried. In this charge my regiment lost 4 commissioned officers wounded . . . 27 enlisted men killed, 56 wounded, and 11 captured, all wounded except 3. But notwithstanding the rebel works were not carried, the charging column was not repulsed, for it maintained the position gained and fortified from twenty-five to sixty yards from the rebel works. My regiment, with the brigade, remained within twenty-five yards of the rebel works, keeping up an incessant fire until they fell back, on the night of July 2. During the six days we lay so close to the rebel works my regiment lost [an] additional 2 enlisted men killed and 8 wounded. [*O.R.*, XXXVIII, pt. 1, p. 721.]

COMMANDERS' ASSESSMENTS

Since General Sherman was in telegraphic communication with his army commanders, a few messages survived for inclusion in the *Official Record*. These messages help us understand the nature of the reports he received and the guidance he issued while the battle was under way.

27 June 1864

Thomas to Sherman, 10:45 a.m.

Yours received. General Harker's brigade advanced to within twenty paces of the enemy's breastworks and was repulsed with canister at that range, General Harker losing an arm. General Wagner's brigade, of Newton's division, supporting General Harker, was so severely handled that it is compelled to reorganize. Colonel Mitchell's brigade, of Davis' division, captured one line of rebel breast-works, which they still hold. McCook's brigade was also very severely handled, nearly every colonel being killed or wounded. Colonel McCook wounded. It is compelled to fall back and reorganize. The troops are all too much exhausted to advance, but we hold all we have gained. [*O.R.*, XXXVIII, pt. 4, pp. 608–609.]

Sherman to Thomas, 11:45 a.m.

McPherson's column reached near the top of the hill through very tangled brush, but was repulsed. It is found almost impossible to deploy, but they still hold the ground. I wish you to study well the position, and if it be possible to break the line do it; it is easier now than it will be hereafter. Hold fast all you make. I hear Leggett's guns well behind the mountain. [*O.R.*, XXXVIII, pt. 4, p. 609.]

Sherman to Thomas, 1:30 p.m.

McPherson and Schofield are at a dead-lock. Do you think you can carry any part of the enemy's line today? McPherson's men are up to the abatis and can't move without the direct assault. I will order the assault if you think you can succeed at any point. Schofield has one division close up on the Powder Springs road, and the other across Olley's Creek, about two miles to his right and rear. [O.R., XXXVIII, pt. 4, p. 609.]

Thomas to Sherman, 1:40 p.m.

Davis' two brigades are now within sixty yards of the enemy's intrenchments. Davis reports that he does not think he can carry the works by assault on account of the steepness of the hill, but he can hold his position, put in one or two batteries tonight, and probably drive them out tomorrow morning. General Howard reports the same. Their works are from six to seven feet high and nine feet thick. In front of Howard they have a very strong abatis. Davis' loss in officers has been very heavy. Nearly all the field officers in McCook's brigade, with McCook, have been killed or wounded. From what the officers tell me I do not think we can carry the works by assault at this point today, but they can be approached by saps [A sap is "the extension of a trench to a point beneath an enemy's fortifications" (Merriam-Webster's Collegiate Dictionary, 11th ed.).—eds.] and the enemy driven out. [O.R., XXXVIII, pt. 4, p. 609.]

Sherman to Thomas, 2:25 p.m.

Secure what advantageous ground you have gained; but is there anything in the enemy's present position that if we should approach by regular saps he could not make a dozen new parapets before one sap is completed? Does the nature of the ground warrant the time necessary for regular approaches? [O.R., XXXVIII, pt. 4, p. 610.]

Thomas to Sherman

Your dispatch of 2:25 received. We still hold all the ground we have gained and the division commanders report their ability to hold it. They also report the enemy's works exceedingly strong; in fact, so strong that they cannot be carried by assault except by immense sacrifice, even if they can be carried at all. I think, therefore, the best chance is to approach them by regular saps, and if we can find a favorable position to batter them down. We have already lost heavily today without gaining any material advantage; one or two more such assaults would use up this army. [*O.R.*, XXXVIII, pt. 4, p. 610.]

Sherman to Thomas, 4:10 p.m.

Schofield has gained the crossing of Olley's Creek on the Sandtown road; the only advantage of the day. You may order all ground of value gained today to be secured and prepare batteries in the manner proposed by Davis. I doubt if we can resort to regular approaches. [*O.R.*, XXXVIII, pt. 4, p. 610.]

Sherman to Thomas

What is your estimate of loss today? McPherson's is about 500. He took 100 prisoners. [*O.R.*, XXXVIII, pt. 4, p. 610.]

Thomas to Sherman, 6 p.m.

The assault of the enemy's works in my front was well arranged, and the officers and men went to their work with the greatest coolness and gallantry. The failure to carry them is due only to the strength of the works and to the fact that they were well manned, thereby enabling the enemy to hold them securely against the assault. We have lost nearly 2,000 officers and men, among them two brigade commanders, General Harker, commanding a brigade in Newton's division, and Colonel Dan McCook, commanding a brigade in Jeff Davis' division, both reported to be mortally wounded, besides some 6 or 8 field officers killed. Both General Harker and Colonel McCook were wounded on the enemy's breast-works, and all say had they not been wounded we would have driven the enemy from his works, Both Generals Howard and Palmer think they can find favorable positions on their lines for placing batteries for enfilading the enemy's works. We took between 90 and 100 prisoners. [*O.R.*, XXXVIII, pt. 4, pp. 610–611.]

Sherman to Thomas

Let your troops fortify as close up to the enemy as possible. Get good positions for artillery, and group your command as conveniently as you can by corps and divisions, keeping reserves. Schofield has the

Sandtown road within eleven miles of the Chattahoochee, and we could move by that flank. The questions of supplies will be the only one. I regret beyond measure the loss of two such young and dashing officers as Harker and Dan McCook. McPherson lost 2 or 3 of his young and dashing officers, which is apt to be the case in unsuccessful assaults. Had we broken the line today it would have been most decisive, but as it is our loss is small, compared with some from the East. It should not in the least discourage us. At times assaults are necessary and inevitable. At Arkansas Post we succeeded; at Vicksburg we failed. I do not think our loss today greater than *Johnston's* when he attacked Hooker and Schofield the first day we occupied our present ground. [*O.R.*, XXXVIII, pt. 4, p. 611.]

20. KOLB'S FARM

Note your mileage and resume driving in the same direction on Cheatham Hill Road. After about 0.7 mile you will pass a state historical marker for Kolb's Farm. Continue driving in the same direction until you reach the traffic light at Powder Springs Road (about 1.6 miles from the parking area at Stop 19). Go straight across that road and immediately turn right to park in the small parking area. Use the National Park Service interpretive panel ("Battle of Kolb's Farm, June 22, 1864") and the state historical markers for orientation.

The first heavy engagement between Union and Confederate forces around Kennesaw Mountain occurred on June 22, 1864, when General Hood's corps moved around to the Confederate left flank and immediately attacked Union forces moving forward on the Powder Springs Road. That attack was repulsed, but it seems to have been one of the factors that led General Sherman to decide upon the frontal attacks of June 27. As we have seen, Sherman tried to improve the prospects for the success of those attacks by demonstrating against the Confederate left.

Given the physical strength of the Confederate defenses at the points chosen for the attacks, we can only wonder whether any demonstration the Union might have devised could have sufficiently weakened the Confederate center. But the limited Union attacks by Schofield's Army of the Ohio against the Confederate left flank on June 27 resulted in some significant gains. Sherman immediately began to explore the possibilities of moving around this flank. After resupplying his army and adjusting his deployments, he made that move on July 3, forcing Johnston to abandon his strong position on Kennesaw Mountain and withdraw to fortifications that had been prepared in advance to give him a defensible bridgehead on the Chattahoochee River.

For many of the soldiers engaged around Kolb's Farm on June 22, these machinations at higher levels resulted in ten days of "continuous operations" as they struggled for advantage in a sector recognized by higher commanders on both sides as critical to the outcome of the campaign.

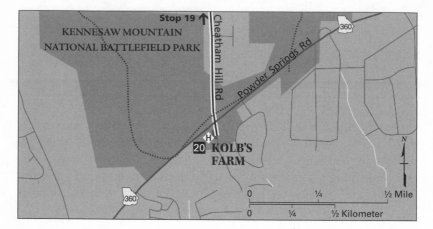

Kolb's Farm (Stop 20)

STOP 20, KOLB'S FARM

22 June–3 July 1864

THE BATTLE OF KOLB'S FARM

Report of Maj. Gen. William T. Sherman, USA, Commanding Military Division of the Mississippi

On the 22nd, as General Hooker had advanced his line, with General Schofield on his right, the enemy (*Hood's* corps with detachments from the others) suddenly sallied and attacked. The blow fell mostly on General Williams' division, of General Hooker's corps, and a brigade of General Hascall's division, of General Schofield's army. The ground was comparatively open, and although the enemy drove in the skirmish line and an advanced regiment of General Schofield sent out purposely to hold him in check until some preparations could be completed for his reception, yet when he reached our line of battle he received a terrible repulse, leaving his dead, wounded, and many prisoners in our hands. This is known as the affair of the Kolb House. Although inviting the enemy at all times to commit such mistakes, I could not hope for him to repeat them after the example of Dallas and Kolb House, and upon studying the ground I had no alternative but to assault his lines or turn his position. [*O.R.*, XXXVIII, pt. 1, p. 68.]

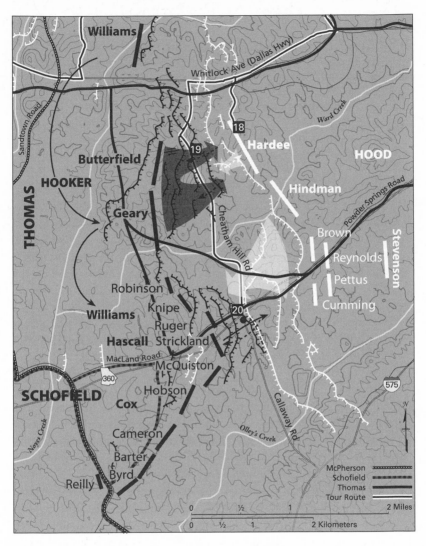

Positions and Attacks—Cheatham Hill and Kolb's Farm

ACTION NORTH OF THE POWDER SPRINGS ROAD

Initial Report of Maj. Gen. Joseph E. Hooker, USA, Commanding Twentieth Corps, Army of the Cumberland, Near Kolb's House, 22 June 1864, 12 p.m.

I have the honor to report that the operations of the Twentieth Corps commenced with throwing forward Geary's division and driving away the rebels from some commanding heights about a mile in advance of my center. When this was accomplished batteries were posted to sweep the ground to the left to enable Butterfield to advance about the same distance and take possession of some wooded heights, which were held by the enemy, as it was believed that the possession of them would give us command of the Dallas and Marietta road, and that in rear of the enemy in front of the Fourth Corps. Meanwhile Williams threw forward his right flank, driving the enemy before him, step by step, between two and three miles to the Kolb house, on the Powder Springs and Marietta road, his left connecting with Geary. This was the position of the corps at 2 o'clock. Soon after Hascall's division, of the Twenty-third Corps, came up on the Powder Springs road, and as it was yet early an effort was made to push the right still farther forward on the last-named road, as it was thought some advantage would be gained by establishing ourselves on some high ground beyond. General Knipe threw forward a force on the road, and also skirmishers on the left, while Major-General Schofield advanced a similar column from the Twenty-third Corps on the right. Before advancing far they encountered the enemy in force, and in order to gain time to establish our lines and batteries the advanced troops were instructed to make a resolute defense, and only abandon their position when overcome by superior numbers. About 4:30 p.m. the enemy had deployed his lines and commenced throwing his masses forward with great violence on our right and center, which was madly persisted in until after sundown. As often as he made his assaults he was spiritedly repulsed, sometimes with his columns hopelessly broken and demoralized. Our artillery did splendid execution among them. At this hour I have no means of estimating his loss or my own. The enemy's must be severe; ours inconsiderable for the number of men engaged and the heavy blow they gave to the enemy. After his troops were routed it was my desire to pursue, but the smallness of my force available for the service would not justify the movement. The conduct of the troops throughout the day was sublime. [*O.R.*, XXXVIII, pt. 2, pp. 14–15.]

Report of Brig. Gen. John W. Geary, USA, Commanding Second Division, Twentieth Army Corps, Army of the Cumberland

June 22, at 3 o'clock in the morning Cobham's party drove the rebels from a high hill one mile in front of the main line of the division. Early in the morning I moved the command forward upon the hill gained by my skirmishers. I at once set to work fortifying my new position, which was upon an important and commanding ridge, completely developing to our view the disposition of the enemy. Perceiving the great importance of the place, I immediately communicated its capture to Major-General Hooker, who came in person. He directed me to hold the place at every hazard. I at once set about reversing the enemy's works and throwing up such others as were necessary to cover my whole command in [a] single line, including the artillery. Whilst in this position the enemy opened a tremendous cannonade which was not permitted to interrupt the prosecution of the work. From prisoners captured by my advanced posts I learned that *Hood's* and *Hardee's* corps were massed at no great distance in my front. This was also communicated to the major-general commanding corps, who without delay advanced Butterfield's division to the ridge on my left and Williams' to a corresponding ridge on my right, but separated by a deep ravine and low ground. Skirmishing, almost amounting to battle, continued during the morning, our lines gaining ground. My works were scarcely completed when, to close a gap between me and Williams, I ordered the Second Brigade to extend still farther to the right, reaching to the ravine before mentioned, posting in this new line on a small knoll the Thirteenth New York Battery, the ground in front consisting of cleared fields with gradual slope. The brigade had scarcely extended to the position designated when a furious attack burst upon Williams, driving in his pickets and engaging his main body. The pickets of the First Division being driven in, the flank of my line was completely exposed, which the enemy attacked furiously, taking advantage of the cover afforded by the houses in the vicinity. The line maintained its position, keeping up a constant and heavy fire. The enemy contented himself with assaulting my skirmishers, not attacking my main line. At the moment of the attack my artillery opened upon the charging column of the enemy and continued with great effect during the entire fight, completely enfilading the rebel ranks and literally sweeping them down. After repeated attempts to carry Williams' works the enemy retired repulsed, their retreat harassed by the fire from my own and Williams' batteries, my position on the surrounding hills enabling me to pour a concentrated fire upon the enemy, sweeping with great effect the ravine in which they had sought refuge. . . . The losses of the enemy under the fearful cannonade were heavy. From the appearance of the field, and from the statements by prisoners, I estimate their losses between 2,000 and 3,000. [O.R., XXXVIII, pt. 2, pp. 132–133.]

Report of Capt. Henry Bundy, USA, Commanding Thirteenth New York Independent Battery, Second Division, Twentieth Army Corps, Army of the Cumberland

On the 22nd one section of the battery, under command of Lieutenant Muller, was ordered forward to a position on Kolb's farm, on the left of the First Division. From this position the section opened a rapid and effective fire upon the enemy's columns as they advanced to retake a position just occupied by the First Division. Here, while directing the fire of this section, Captain William Wheeler, then commander of the battery and chief of artillery of the Second Division, was instantly killed by one of the enemy's sharpshooters. The remainder of the battery joined this section while the enemy was being repulsed, and aided in throwing a few shells into their retreating and disordered columns. Works were thrown up here and we occupied them until the morning of the 27th. [O.R., XXXVIII, pt. 2, p. 481.]

Report of Brig. Gen. Alpheus S. Williams, USA, Commanding First Division, Twentieth Corps, Army of the Cumberland

On June 21st, after reconnoitering to my front, sent out two regiments, under Colonel [William] Hawley, Third Wisconsin Volunteers, and took possession with small loss of an important hill in direction of Kolb's farm. The enemy made fruitless efforts to regain it.

June 22, I advanced the division, preceded by a strong skirmish line, especially on the right and on to the left of the Powder Springs and Marietta road. The division was massed by brigades in the woods, the right near the Powder Springs road at Kolb's house, Ruger's brigade on the right, Knipe's in the center, and Robinson's on the left. In front of Knipe was an open elevated plateau with a deep gully along its front, beyond which the ground rose gently to the woods occupied by the rebel picket reserves in strong rifle-pits 500 or 600 yards distant. Robinson occupied a hill about 200 yards to the rear and left of Knipe, placing his brigade in echelon to Knipe's. He had before him an open [area] of at least 1,000 yards and extending to the low ground in front of Geary on my left, from whom I was separated by a swampy ravine. Ruger had thick woods in his front, except the ground for two regiments on Knipe's right. Soon after arriving on this ground I strengthened my skirmishers by an additional regiment, and drove back the enemy's pickets to the woods in our front, where his reserves were strongly intrenched, not far from his main works. I placed Winegar's battery (3-inch rifles) in front of Robinson's brigade, and Woodbury's (light 12-pounders) in front of Knipe's brigade, positions that commanded all the open ground in front. About 3 p.m., hearing there were credible rumors of an attack, I reported in person to the major general commanding the corps at Kolb's house, and received orders to deploy my division in one line and throw up breast-works without delay.

The information seemed reliable that the whole of *Hood's* corps was advancing to attack us. I had barely reached the left of my line (conveying the orders in person to each brigade commander as I returned from the corps headquarters) before the peculiar yell of the rebel mass was heard as they emerged from the woods and dashed forward toward our line. The heaviest columns were directly in front of Woodbury's battery, and in three lines. He swept them fearfully with canister from those effective guns, and rolled them into a confused mass. A few volleys from Knipe's brigade and the two left regiments (the Thirteenth New Jersey and One hundred and fiftieth New York) of Ruger's brigade speedily compelled those who were not driven back into the woods to take shelter in the deep ravine, and a dense clump of wood and underbrush on Knipe's front and left.

While this was transpiring, a very heavy column came rapidly from the woods into the open on our extreme left, and were brought to a stand-still by the first shell from Winegar's battery exploding in its front division. A few additional rounds taking effect in the midst of the column threw the whole mass into confusion, and it broke in the utmost disorder for the woods. No further attempt was made to attack this part of my line. In the mean time the forces of the enemy which had taken shelter in the ravines, and others which had got up under cover, attempted to take advantage of the woods on Knipe's left front to turn that flank. The Sixty-first Ohio, of Robinson's brigade, was sent to re-enforce that part of the line, and Winegar was ordered to open with canister and case-shot along the ravine and through the woods. The punishment to the enemy must have been very severe. He at once discontinued his movements and relapsed into silence. It was now quite dark and under cover of darkness the enemy withdrew his troops, carrying away during the night many of his dead and most of his wounded. He left, however, in our front abundant proofs of his severe loss, which was acknowledged by the rebel journals of Atlanta to have exceeded 1,000 men.

Our losses in this engagement did not exceed 130 men, including some 19 reported missing in action, who were captured by the sudden rush on my Sixty-first Ohio Volunteers. . . . The division remained in the same position in front of the enemy's works until 2nd of July. [*O.R.*, XXXVIII. pt. 2, pp. 31–32.]

Report of Lt. James C. Rogers, USA, Commanding 123rd New York Volunteer Infantry Regiment, First Brigade, First Division, Twentieth Army Corps, Army of the Cumberland

June 21, built a line of breast-works.

June 22, at 8 a.m. moved out in front of the works and deployed the whole regiment as skirmishers, covering the front of the division, and immediately advanced, driving the rebel skirmishers back more than a mile upon their main force, which was discovered to be hard at work throwing up fortifications. In this advance the Powder Springs and Marietta and the Sandtown and Marietta roads were uncovered. While the rest of the division was getting into line and entrenching this regiment held its position without relief or support, in the face of a constant and galling fire from a much superior force, until 5 p.m., when the rebel artillery opened, and *Stevenson's* division, in three lines of battle, advanced rapidly out of the woods. It then fell slowly back to the main line of battle, posted on a slight eminence some distance in rear. Here the advancing columns of the enemy were met by murderous volleys of musketry, grape, and canister, and after enduring an hour of fruitless slaughter they were driven with heavy loss and in confusion and disorder back to their fortifications. [*O.R.*, XXXVIII, pt. 2, p. 49.]

Narrative of Corporal Rice C. Bull, USA, Company D, 123rd New York Volunteer Infantry Regiment, First Brigade, First Division, Twentieth Army Corps, Army of the Cumberland

On the evening of the 21st we were notified to be ready for an early start in the morning. Our ammunition boxes were to be full and we were to carry ten extra cartridges in reserve. Fortunately we had a good night's rest, and by six o'clock were packed, had our breakfast of pork, hardtack, and coffee, and were ready to move. It was a bright morning, with little air stirring and all the signs for a hot day. Our 1st and 2nd Divisions were at the front in line of battle with the 3rd Division in reserve. From early morning everything indicated a movement by our right flank of the Army. Ordnance wagons and ambulance trains were well in front, guns in the batteries were ready for their horses that were feeding near-by, couriers and staff officers were busy carrying orders. It was fully nine o'clock before everything was ready and the order to advance given. Our Regiment was taken from the line to act as skirmishers for the entire Division. We marched by the right flank to the outer posts which were about a half mile in advance of our battle line and near where our pickets were posted. There we deployed right and left, relieving the pickets who returned to their commands.

We spread ten feet apart, deploying the entire Regiment. As we were in heavily wooded forest, it took time to complete the work. At ten-thirty we were ready for the signal but it was nearly eleven before the bugle rang out "forward." We then moved through the underbrush, slowly and cautiously feeling the way as we knew we were near the enemy. In less than a half hour we ran into their picket line and firing began. For some distance we drove them through the woods, they retiring slowly and contesting every foot of the way. By noon we had forced them through the forest into a large clearing which was east of the woods.

This open space was a large plantation owned by a man named [Kolb]. It had been cleared in the usual way used in north Georgia; by girdling the big trees and then leaving them to die, and in time decay. There were many of these trees still standing and their dead limbs pointing in every direction made a weird appearance. The fields in which the plantation was divided were hilly and cut with ravines; this made it an ideal place for skirmishing for the side that was on the defensive. Where we came out of the timber we were on quite an elevation, the cleared lands descending for at least a mile; then there was another forest gradually rising to another range of hills, beyond which ran the railroad to Atlanta. As we advanced through the open country the Johnnies held to every protected spot as long as they could. They clung to every hill and ravine until our men on the right and left advanced so far as to endanger their capture then they would crawl back to the next hill or ravine. While this was going on we were using every protection there was to give us cover. One looking lengthwise of our line would have seen men behind trees and stumps, others lying flat on the ground behind some hummock, and many in the little gullies and ravines. From twelve-thirty in the afternoon we continued the skirmish in the open field; the sun was shining brightly and it was terribly hot but in the excitement we did not notice this. By this time we had forced them back to the woods beyond the clearing; there we saw a line of rifle pits that were well protected from our fire. When they dropped into the pits they gave us a big yell; which was saying, "Now get us if you can." In front of their breastworks and about a hundred yards from them was a ravine running for a long distance parallel to their line. On our last rush we were ordered to take the ravine. To get there we were in the open and while we covered the ground in record time, we lost several men. It was now four in the afternoon and we were as close as we could get to the rifle pits with a skirmish line. For more than an hour we remained in the ravine and the firing was lively as we waited for the battle line to come up. . . .

[A courier] brought orders for a forward movement of our Regimental skirmish line; Colonel Rogers at once gave orders for an advance. On our left this was impossible unless supported by the main line; our thin skirmish lines were as close as they could get. The right of our line was better protected by trees and bushes and could make some advance. The left half of our Company was in the ravine with no cover between them and the rifle pits. Captain Anderson divided the

Company, leaving the left half with Lieutenant Quinn; the rest of the men proceeded to the right. I was near the center of the Company and he directed me to go with him. In front of us was a farmhouse with the usual outbuildings of a plantation. These were nearly surrounded by a peach orchard and other trees; this was the protection that screened us as we advanced. A short distance beyond the buildings was a forest, running in nearly a straight line with the one in which the enemy's skirmishers were located on our left. We found as we advanced that the ravine which we had occupied ran diagonally to the left after entering the woods and the enemy skirmish line followed the ridge on the east side of the ravine thus running off in an angle from the line we had been forcing back all day. We moved cautiously into the woods. There was at that time no firing on our immediate front but we halted on the west side of the ravine and took cover behind the large trees. The ravine was filled with trees and underbrush; and from where we were descended about seventy-five feet to a dry stream in the bottom and then up the other side to the same level we were on. Our advance was so quiet that the enemy on the other side of the ravine, not more than two hundred feet from us, did not know we were there.

At first it was very still but soon we heard voices beyond the opposite hill. As we silently waited the noise increased in volume. I could hear men marching, the giving of orders in a low voice, the neighing of horses, and further back, bugle calls. I told O'Connor, who was . . . with me, to remain quietly behind his tree and listen; and not to fire unless they advanced. I would go back and report to Captain Anderson. I found Colonel Rogers with the Captain. After I had told them what I had heard, the Colonel went back with me and heard what was going on himself. He at once saw what the Confederates were preparing to do. Before leaving me he said, "They are massing troops and will probably attack. In case they advance have the men fire and then fall back."

During the afternoon the battle line had moved up very slowly, waiting, it was said, for Schofield's 23rd Corps to come to the right of our 20th to protect its flank when the advance was made. For some reason there was a delay on the part of the 23rd in arriving at their position and it was nearly three in the afternoon before the line advanced. Then our troops in line of battle moved in to the open field and halted near its center where there was quite an elevation. Our 1st Division was located along the ridge, and the 2nd upon our left farther back. By this time it was nearly four o'clock, and as it seemed as though there would be no further advance during that afternoon, the men began to build breastworks a half mile back of our skirmish line but on much higher ground.

When the Colonel left us, we remained quietly on our post listening. There was no question what was going on in our front. The enemy was massing troops very rapidly and we could hear every movement as this went on. When the Johnnies came in we noted the warning commands of their officers, the orders to halt, front, dress, etc., orders familiar to us. The massing of a division cannot be made under any conditions in less than an hour and it was fully five o'clock before their work was completed and they were ready to advance. To us on the skirmish line who were waiting for them to move it seemed as though they would never start. Our guns were cocked and we were ready to fire at sight of them.

Shortly after five a bugle sounded "forward," then we heard low commands given by their officers, followed by the rustle of many feet, as they marched through the under-brush. They had not far to go before they reached the crest of the hill on the opposite side of the ravine where we could see them. They came without skirmishers which meant an attack in force. We fired and dropped back through the woods and plantation grounds and into the open field over which we would have to retreat for nearly a half mile to reach our battle line on the hill. The men there were working with pick and shovel, as men will work whose lives depend on constructing barricades to stop bullets. Back of them we saw our batteries being wheeled into place. Everything was being done that could be for the fight that was coming.

The Rebel line advanced rapidly for they were in light marching order. We skirmishers were loaded with our full equipment, knapsacks, etc. This made it harder for us to retreat than for them to follow. When we reached the [Kolb] buildings we halted long enough to load our guns but the enemy were so close we continued to run, with them calling on us to surrender. As soon as they were in front of the buildings they commenced firing on us as we retreated. As their bullets would strike in the sand around us, little fountains of dust would rise two feet in the air. On our way back on the run we came to a knoll and halted on the crest long enough to fire our last volley; then we started for our line, every man for himself.

By this time the enemy were in view of our forces; and several of our batteries opened fire with shot and shell; we were in their line of fire and for a time in as much danger from them as the enemy, so we tried to file off to the right and left out of range. Winded, we made a last effort and struggled through our lines. Everyone fell to the ground exhausted, and many were in a dead faint. We had lost forty-eight men killed and wounded. . . .

The attack was made by *Hood's* Corps and lasted until after eight that night. There were three or four charges, all unsuccessful and with great loss to the enemy. The farthest advance on our line as measured by the dead was within two hundred feet. Fighting in defense behind our works our Division only lost two hundred and fifty men, of whom forty-eight were from our own skirmish line. The enemy's loss in killed and wounded was some twelve hundred. Many of their wounded and a few unwounded prisoners were taken. From them, it was learned that the attack was made by *Hindman's* and *Stevenson's* Divisions of *Hood's* Corps, with *Hood* in direct command.

On the 23rd, our Regiment remained as we were behind the line until the afternoon, so I had an opportunity to look around and see what had happened during the battle. Our artillery had been effective, as it could sweep the entire field over which the enemy charged. In the afternoon a new line was laid out for the infantry halfway between the hill where the battle had been fought and the [Kolb] farmhouse. In the new line our Regiment was placed on the extreme left of the Division, in the open field over which we had skirmished the day before. When we reached this position we commenced to fortify our line. At this time the enemy was about a mile east of us behind heavy works; our location was some three miles southwest of Marietta and as we looked toward the northeast, the two peaks of Kennesaw stood plainly in view. At night the mountains were lighted by the artillery fire from the lines that ran along the side of the hills. We remained in this place until the 3rd of July. Nothing startling happened in our immediate front. [K. Jack Bauer, ed., *Soldiering: The Civil War Diary of Rice C. Bull* (Novato, Calif.: Presidio Press, 1977), pp. 128–135.]

Report of Maj. Gen. Carter L. Stevenson, CSA, Commanding Stevenson's Division, Hood's Corps, Army of Tennessee

My division had for one or two days previous to the 22d of June been lying in reserve on the extreme left of the infantry of the army, about three miles from Marietta, on the Powder Springs road. About

12 m. I moved the command farther from Marietta and halted it at
Mount Zion Church. The enemy, as I moved forward, were driving
in the cavalry. About 2.30 p.m. I was directed to take position on the
left of General *Hindman's* division, about half a mile in advance of the
church. I at once advanced my skirmishers, and, driving those of the
enemy, established my line under fire of his artillery. *Brown's* and *Cumming's* brigades formed the first line, *Reynolds'* and *Pettus'* the second.
The men hastily constructed breast-works of logs and rails.

Soon afterwards I received orders to advance from my position
and drive the enemy on the road toward Manning's Mill. The divi-
sion of General *Hindman* was also directed to advance on my right.
I placed General *Cumming* in charge of the first line—*Brown's* and
Cumming's brigades, commanded by Cols. E. C. Cook (Thirty-second
Tennessee) and E. P. *Watkins* (Fifty-sixth Georgia), respectively, and
General *Pettus* in charge of the second line—*Reynolds'* and *Pettus'*
brigades, commanded by Cols. R. O. *Trigg* (Fifty-fourth Virginia) and
O. M. *Shelley* (Thirtieth Alabama), respectively. A good deal of time
was occupied in getting and giving instructions and making the neces-
sary preparations.

About 5 p.m. we advanced and soon struck the enemy, driving him
quickly before us from his advanced works, which consisted of one
line of logs and rail works complete, and one partially constructed.
The fire under which this was done was exceedingly heavy, and the
artillery of the enemy, which was massed in large force and admirably posted, was served with a rapidity and fatal precision which could
not be surpassed. The nature of the ground over which we passed was
most unfavorable to such a movement—the two right brigades moved
for much of the way over open fields, the two left through dense undergrowth. The line thus became more irregular and broken every
moment, and when the two right brigades had driven the enemy into
their main works the line was so much broken and mixed up that, although the men were in good spirits and perfectly willing to make the
attempt, it was not deemed practicable to carry the works by assault.

The commands were halted and the best possible line, under the
circumstances, formed. *Brown's* and *Trigg's* (*Reynolds'*) brigades lay in
a swampy ravine within pistol-shot of the enemy's works. The other
brigades held the road on their left. The dead and wounded were all
removed to the rear, and after holding our position for several hours,
in compliance with the orders of General *Hood*, the division returned

to its old position. With perhaps some few exceptions the conduct of the troops was highly creditable.

My loss was heavy—807 killed and wounded. [*O.R.*, XXXVIII, pt. 3, pp. 814–815.]

ACTION SOUTH OF THE POWDER SPRINGS ROAD

Report of Maj. Gen. John M. Schofield, USA, Commanding Army of the Ohio

[On the 22nd] General Hascall moved toward Marietta and connected with the right of Twentieth Corps at Kolb's. While reconnoitering with General Hooker, with a view to advancing our troops to a more desirable position, we discovered that the enemy was advancing in heavy force to attack us; our troops were therefore ordered to intrench the position they then held as rapidly as possible, while the Fourteenth Kentucky, of General Hascall's division, which was covering the reconnaissance, was ordered to hold the enemy in check to gain time for the troops to prepare for defense. This gallant regiment detained the enemy an hour and a half, and only retired to the main line when ordered to do so, contesting stubbornly every foot of ground. The enemy now advanced in mass in front of General Hascall and General Hooker's right, but was quickly repulsed with heavy loss by the fire of our infantry and artillery in position. [*O.R.*, XXXVIII, pt. 2, p. 513.]

Report of Brig. Gen. Milo S. Hascall, USA, Commanding Second Division, Twenty-Third Army Corps, Army of the Ohio

On the 22d my command was in motion. Crossed Noyes' Creek and, leaving General Cox on the Sandtown road to my right, moved down on a road to the left to the Powder Springs and Marietta road, near Kolb's school-house, where I went into position on the right of General Hooker, covering the two roads.

My skirmish line, supported by the Fourteenth Kentucky, Colonel [George W.] Gallup, was ordered forward to gain and hold a ridge that was desired for a new position. The brigades commanded by Colonels [Silas A.] Strickland, McQuiston, and [William E.] Hobson were put in position, and at once began throwing up works. Colonel Gallup, in the mean time, advancing promptly, captured a number of prisoners, who reported a rebel corps as having just come from the right and as preparing to attack us. Having gained the ridge, he built a light barricade, when the enemy in force (portions of *Stevenson's* division) advanced and attempted to drive him back. Three times they advanced, and at each advance strengthening their lines, but each time they were repulsed. I had ordered Colonel Gallup to retire to the main line with his regiment if he was hard pressed, but he remained in his position, until finding the attack a determined one, I ordered him peremptorily to fall back to the main line.

The works were but partially constructed. Captain [Joseph C.] Shields [commanding 19th Ohio Light Battery] and Captain [Byron D.] Paddock [commanding 1st Michigan Light Battery] were placed in position, and every one prepared for a stubborn resistance. The regiment came back slowly and in good order. When they had reached the works the artillery opened their fire, and in a short time the woods and ridge in our front was cleared of the enemy, the shell and case-shot sweeping every one from the front. The infantry, though, became sharply engaged before the enemy retired.

The enemy carried off his wounded, and, it may be, some of his dead. In front of the line defended by Colonel Gallup 57 dead rebels were found. The cross-fire from General Hooker's and from my batteries proved very destructive, as was afterward shown. On the 23d, in conjunction with General Hooker's troops, I moved forward and occupied the ridge fought for the day before. [*O.R.*, XXXVIII, pt. 2, p. 569.]

Report of Col. George W. Gallup, Fourteenth Kentucky Infantry, Third Brigade, Second Division, Twenty-Third Army Corps, Army of the Ohio

About 12 o'clock on the 22d instant, the brigade having taken its position in the front, I was ordered by Col. S. A. Strickland to take my regiment and advance in line of battle to the front, my left resting on the Marietta road, and ascertain if the enemy were in force in our front, and if so, to develop their lines, go as far as I could consistently, and when obliged to stop and assume the defensive, to hold my position as long as possible. Companies A and G were deployed as skirmishers. Advancing across an open field some 300 yards, we received the fire of a strong line of the enemy skirmishers, who had the woods. Lieut. W. H. C. Brown, with Company A of the skirmish line, charged the woods with fixed bayonets, and captured six groups of five each of the enemy's skirmishers (all who were in his front). Steadily advancing, I passed the first skirt of woods, crossed a field, and to the edge of the next woods, where the skirmishers reported a heavy force of the enemy in line of battle in my immediate front, some 800 yards distant.

Reporting this force to General Hascall, commanding division, I received orders to construct a barricade and hold my position, if possible. The One hundred and twenty-third New York held the line on my left, while one-half of my regiment was constructing barricades. The enemy advanced in three lines deep. Hastily forming, we awaited the approach of the enemy. At this point the One hundred and twenty-third New York was forced to give way to the right, and a portion ran over the Fourteenth Kentucky, who were lying on the ground. The enemy approached reluctantly and in much disorder, resembling a mob more than they did soldiery. The first line came within thirty feet before we fired. At the first volley deliberately delivered, the enemy was thrown into confusion and gave way, firing a heavy volley, not a shot of which took effect. We then advanced to the works we had partially constructed and were in readiness to receive the enemy's second advance.

We held our position and the enemy in our front until they had possession of our left flank and were firing an enfilading fire into the regiment. Immediately, on seeing this, ordered the regiment to break from the left by companies, changing front to the left and fight in retreat. We were pressed back to the next skirt of woods, and there reformed, and then gave way, as we were obliged to. When driven from this second position I ordered the left to retire on the brigade in our rear, and with four companies of the right wing I took position under the crest of a ridge, which I held until ordered to retire by the general commanding the division.

My loss was 1 lieutenant and 7 privates killed, 52 wounded (4 mortally), among them 1 captain and 1 lieutenant. The enemy's loss was 69 found dead on the field, 1 wounded (brought off), and 36 prisoners, besides the wounded. [*O.R.*, XXXVIII, pt. 2, p. 655.]

SUBSEQUENT ACTION ON THE UNION RIGHT FLANK

Special Field Orders No. 36, Headquarters, Army of the Ohio, 26 June 1864

. . . IV. In accordance with the general plan of operations for tomorrow, the 27th instant, General Cox will resume at daylight his demonstration across Olley's Creek. He will first endeavor to secure the crossing of Olley's Creek on the Sandtown road by turning the enemy's present position or otherwise, as may be found practicable, and gain possession of the commanding ground on the main ridge beyond the Creek. He will then, if practicable, move along the ridge substantially toward the railroad, and make a strong demonstration upon the left of the enemy's main infantry line, keeping his own left near the open fields along the valley of Olley's Creek. The position gained on the Sandtown road beyond Olley's Creek will be held by the dismounted men of General Stoneman's command, and, if necessary, by an additional force from General Cox's division.

General Stoneman's mounted force will cover General Cox's right during his operations. The primary object of this movement is to occupy as large a force of the enemy as practicable as a diversion in favor of the real attack to be made elsewhere. General Cox will, however, take advantage of any success he may gain, or of the weakness of the enemy to turn his left and sweep the line in front of General Hascall's right.

General Hascall will open his guns at 6 a.m. upon the enemy's lines in front, and keep up a continuous and steady fire until after the real attack shall be made at other points of the line. He will hold his division in readiness to press forward and gain the enemy's works if the diversion by General Cox on his right, or the attack of General Thomas on his left shall create a favorable opportunity. He will watch closely the progress of events with a view to seize the favorable opportunity to convert his demonstration into a real attack. In the event of success in the attack, the two divisions will endeavor to connect with each other as soon as possible by gaining ground to the right and left as rapidly as the movement of General Thomas' troops will enable General Hascall to move to the right and as General Cox, by his own success may be enabled to drive back the enemy's flank.

The first success being gained, it is desirable to mass the corps as much as practicable so as to strike heavy blows where they will be most effectual. During the morning General Cox will leave one brigade near General Hascall's right, with a view of its joining him at the proper time by moving directly across the valley, and, in the mean time, to meet any demonstration the enemy may make between the two divisions.

During the morning the commanding general will be at the telegraph office near corps headquarters. Division commanders will report frequently the progress of their movements and whatever else may be of interest. [*O.R.*, XXXVIII, pt. 4, p. 604.]

Schofield to Sherman, 27 June 1864, 7:30 a.m.

Cox crossed another brigade over Olley's Creek at 4 a.m., and is pushing to clear the Sandtown road in front of Reilly, after which he will push along the ridge toward Hascall's right. [*O.R.*, XXXVIII, pt. 4, p. 616.]

Sherman to Schofield, 27 June 1864, 11:45 a.m.

Neither McPherson nor Thomas has succeeded in breaking through, but each has made substantial progress at some cost. Push your operations on the flank and keep me advised. [*O.R.*, XXXVIII, pt. 4, p. 616.]

Schofield to Sherman, 27 June 1864, 12:20 p.m.

General Cox has just reported in person. He has advanced to the crest of the main ridge, a mile or so beyond Olley's Creek, and within a mile of the main road running to the mill on Nickajack Creek. The ridge is extremely rough and densely wooded. There is no hope of moving a force along it so as to reach the flank of the enemy's main line to-day. To go by the road would throw Cox three or four miles from Hascall's right, much too far for a single division. The enemy's works can be distinctly seen, running up the slope of the ridge at least a mile beyond Hascall's right. I cannot hope to reach the enemy's flank without separating my division much farther than I deem at all prudent. I believe that Cox's present position threatens the enemy's left more seriously than a single division could possibly by abandoning that position and endeavoring to strike the left of his present works.

I am satisfied that I cannot do more in this direction without risking. I will await your orders before pushing any farther. Whether Thomas and McPherson succeed in breaking through or we have yet to resort to a flank movement, I believe Cox's present position far more valuable than any he can gain by moving toward the railroad. [*O.R.*, XXXVIII, pt. 4, pp. 617–618.]

Sherman to Schofield, 27 June 1864, 4:10 p.m.

Let Cox secure well the crossing of Olley's Creek on the Sandtown road, and take all advantage of that flank should we move in that direction; otherwise hold fast all you have, and remain on the defensive. [*O.R.*, XXXVIII, pt. 4, p. 618.]

Schofield to Brig. Gen. Jacob D. Cox, 27 June 1864, 5 p.m.

General Sherman directs that we make what we have gained as secure as possible and remain on the defensive. No material advantage has been gained anywhere except that gained by you. Thomas' losses are very heavy. . . . Make your position very strong. I regard it as the key to the next movement.

P.S. I have your dispatch of 4:30 p.m. I do not think the importance of the position you have gained can be overestimated, especially in view of the failure elsewhere and probable future movements. [*O.R.*, XXXVIII, pt. 4, p. 621.]

Sherman to Maj. Gen. H. W. Halleck, Washington, D.C., 27 June 1864, 8 p.m.

Pursuant to my orders of the 24th, a diversion was made on each flank of the enemy, especially on the Sandtown road, and at 8 a.m. General McPherson attacked at the southwest end of Kennesaw, and General Thomas at a point about a mile father south. At the same time, the skirmishers and artillery along the whole line kept up a sharp fire. Neither attack succeeded, though both columns reached the enemy's works, which are very strong. General McPherson reports his loss about 500, and General Thomas about 2,000; the loss particularly heavy in general and field officers. . . . The facility with which defensive works of timber and earth are constructed gives the party on the defensive great advantage. I cannot well turn the position of the enemy without abandoning my railroad, and we are already so far from our supplies that it is as much as the road can do to feed and supply the army. There are no supplies of any kind here. I can press *Johnston* and keep him from re-enforcing *Lee*, but to assault him in position will cost us more lives than we can spare. McPherson took today 100 prisoners, and Thomas about as many, but I do not suppose we inflicted heavy loss on the enemy, as he kept close behind his parapets. [*O.R.*, XXXVIII, pt. 4, p. 607.]

Sherman to Maj. Gen. James B. McPherson, 27 June 1864

Schofield's right division (Cox's) has gained a good position on the other side of Olley's Creek, and at the head of the Nickajack. If we had our supplies well up I would move at once by the right flank, but suppose we must cover our railroad a few days. [*O.R.*, XXXVIII, pt. 4, p. 622.]

Halleck to Sherman, 28 June 1864, 3:30 p.m.

Lieutenant-General Grant directs me to say that the movements of your army may be made entirely independent of any desire to retain *Johnston's* forces where they are. He does not think that *Lee* will bring any additional troops to Richmond, on account of the difficulty of feeding them. [*O.R.*, XXXVIII, pt. 4, p. 629.]

Sherman to Halleck, 29 June 1864

Our loss on the 27th will not exceed 1,500. As usual, the first reports were overstated. General Harker is dead. The wounded are doing well and most are already sent to the rear in cars. Some few of the dead and wounded were left in the enemy's hands close to his parapet. I am accumulating stores that will enable me to cut loose from the railroad for a time and avoid the Kennesaw Hill, which gives the enemy too much advantage. I will aim to get to the railroad below Marietta by a circuit or actually reach the Chattahoochee. Our right flank is now on the Sandtown road below Olley's Creek. [*O.R.*, XXXVIII, pt. 4, p. 635.]

Special Field Orders No. 31, in the Field Near Kennesaw Mountain, 1 July 1864, Headquarters, Military Division of the Mississippi

The object of the contemplated movement is to deprive the enemy of the great advantage he has in Kennesaw as a valuable watchtower from which to observe our every movement; to force him to come out of his intrenchments or move farther south. To obtain which end:

I. All army commanders will fill up their wagons at Big Shanty depot to the utmost capacity with provisions, ammunition, and forage. The chief quartermaster and commissary will give all necessary orders to clean out the depots in front of Allatoona, and so instruct that the locomotives and cars will come forward of Allatoona with great caution, and only when ordered by the chief quartermaster.

II. Major General Thomas will hold the ground below Kennesaw as far as Olley's Creek near Mt. Zion, Major General Schofield that from Olley's Creek to the Nickajack, and General McPherson will move his train and troops rapidly in a single march and as little observed from Kennesaw as possible to the Sandtown road, and down it to the extreme right, with one corps near the Widow Mitchell's and another near Ruff's Mill, on the Nickajack, and the third in reserve near the forks of the road.

III. Gen. Garrard's cavalry will cover the roads out of Marietta which pass north of Kennesaw, and General Stoneman's cavalry will occupy Sweet Water Old Town, coincident with the movement of McPherson. In case the enemy presses Garrard back by superior and overwhelming forces he will send one of his brigades to the flank of General Thomas and with the others fall back gradually toward Allatoona, disputing every foot of ground.

IV. Major General McPherson will threaten the Chattahoochee River and also the railroad and General Thomas will press the enemy close and at the very earliest possible moment break his lines and reach the railroad below Marietta. All movements must be vigorous and rapid, as the time allowed is limited by the supplies in our wagons. [*O.R.*, XXXVIII, pt. 5, p.14.]

Sherman to Halleck, 1 July 1864, 9:30 p.m.

General Schofield is now south of Olley's Creek, and on the head of Nickajack. I have been hurrying down provisions and forage, and tomorrow night propose to move General McPherson from the left to the extreme right back of General Thomas. This will bring my right within three miles of the Chattahoochee and about five from the railroad. By this movement I think I can force *Johnston* to move his army down from Kennesaw, to defend his railroad crossing and the Chattahoochee, when I will, by the left flank, reach the railroad below Marietta; but I cut loose from the railroad with 10 days supplies in wagons. *Johnston* may come out of his trenches and attack General Thomas, which is what I want, for General Thomas is well intrenched, parallel with the enemy, south of Kennesaw. I think Allatoona and the line of the Etowah are strong enough for me to venture this move. The movement is substantially down the Sandtown road, straight for Atlanta. [*O.R.*, XXXVIII, pt. 5, p. 3.]

Sherman to Halleck, 3 July 1864, 10 a.m. (received 5 p.m.)

The movement on our right caused the enemy to evacuate. We occupied Kennesaw at daylight and Marietta at 8:30 a.m. Thomas is moving down the main road toward the Chattahoochee; McPherson toward the mouth of the Nickajack, on the Sandtown road. Our cavalry is on the extreme flank. Whether the enemy will halt this side of the Chattahoochee or not will soon be known. Marietta is almost entirely abandoned by its inhabitants, and more than a mile of railroad iron is removed between the town and the foot of Kennesaw. I propose to press the enemy close until he is across the Chattahoochee River, when I must accumulate stores and better guard my rear. [*O.R.*, XXXVIII, pt. 5, p. 29.]

The Confederate army fell back to fortified lines in front of Smyrna, which they occupied on July 3 and 4 while final preparations were made on the lines in front of the Chattahoochee. They occupied those lines on July 5, and Sherman pressed forward quickly. Rather than try another frontal assault, he moved forces upriver and forced a crossing against a very light defense on July 9. Instead of attacking the Union bridgehead, *Johnston* decided to fall back behind Peachtree Creek.

By this time, the Confederate political authorities had lost confidence in General *Johnston*. He relinquished command of the Army of Tennessee to Lieutenant General *John B. Hood* on July 17, setting the stage for the next phase of the campaign for Atlanta, which is best studied in textbooks rather than on sites covered with modern development.

This concludes your tour of significant sites in the campaign for Atlanta. Most users of this guide will reverse their route on Cheatham Hill Road, John Ward Road, Dallas Highway, Burnt Hickory Road, Old Mountain Road, and Stilesboro Road to reach the Visitor Center or the major highways beyond.

APPENDIX. "THE GREATEST POSSIBLE IMPORTANCE": SHERMAN'S LOGISTICS IN THE ATLANTA CAMPAIGN

Jay Luvaas

On March 2, 1864, Maj. Gen. Ulysses S. Grant was promoted to the rank of lieutenant general and placed in command of all Union armies. Maj. Gen. William T. Sherman succeeded him as commander of the Military Division of the Mississippi, embracing the departments of the Ohio, the Cumberland, the Tennessee, and Arkansas. The two had already corresponded about military matters, and when Grant departed for Washington several weeks later, Sherman accompanied him as far as Cincinnati, where they spent an evening in a hotel room discussing strategy and Sherman's role in the coming campaign. Grant then proceeded on to Washington and his duties there, while Sherman returned to establish his headquarters at Memphis. They were agreed as to Sherman's mission: Confederate Gen. *Joseph E. Johnston's* army was his primary objective; his second was the important railroad center at Atlanta.[1]

Sherman's command was subdivided into four departments, each of which reported to him and was subject to his orders.[2] In modern parlance, he was an Army Group Commander, responsible for the movements of the Army of the Cumberland (88,000 present for duty on April 10), the Army of the Ohio (26,000), and the Army of the Tennessee (64,000)—in round figures a total of almost 178,000 men.[3] In addition, he had to maintain strong garrisons throughout the military departments and protect his line of communication, and with each advancing step toward Atlanta—his geographical objective—his effective forces in the field would diminish.

Distance was therefore the overriding problem. Since the early days of the war, Louisville and Nashville had served as the principal supply centers for Union forces in the west. From Louisville it was 185 miles by rail to Nashville, Sherman's base depot throughout the Atlanta campaign. It was another 150 miles from Nashville to Chattanooga, the starting point for the 1864 campaign in the west, and from there an additional 120 miles to Atlanta—the ultimate objective. Moreover, in contrast to previous campaigns in the west, the rivers would be of little use in moving men or supplies. Indeed, from Dalton to Atlanta the rivers flowed at right angles across Sherman's line of advance, adding to his operational problems.

PREPARATIONS

Sherman's official correspondence during the months preceding active operations reveals his approach to the problems. "Knoxville will be naturally supplied from Chattanooga, as its railroad is better than the long road from Camp Nelson," he explained in late March to Brig. Gen. Robert Allen, his chief quartermaster. "Of course, I believe in as few depots as possible, and those on a large scale, well guarded. These depots, I think, should be at Nashville, Chattanooga, Huntsville, and Decatur, the two former of course the principal. . . . We are on the offensive, and should not think of any defensive measure."[4] In the coming weeks Sherman visited his three army commanders to obtain all information possible before making decisions. "The problem of the supplies is the most difficult," he confided to Grant. Explaining further, he wrote:

> [T]he [rail]roads can now supply the daily wants of the army, but do not accumulate a surplus, but I think by stopping the carriage of cattle and men, and by running the cars on the circuit from Nashville to Stevenson and Decatur, it can be done with the present cars and locomotives. The superintendent of railroads here . . . the quartermaster . . . and myself will determine tonight. I find too many citizens and private freights along the road, which are utterly inconsistent with our military necessities at this time. I aim to accumulate in all April, at Decatur and Chattanooga, a surplus of 70 days' provisions and forage for 100,000 men.[5]

By early April Sherman was convinced that he would need all railroads in front of Nashville for military freight alone. Private freight or citizens therefore would not be permitted on military railroads until the needs of the army were met. All troops would march from Nashville. "Don't publish this information," Sherman cautioned the brigadier general commanding in Louisville. "Let the interested parties find it out."[6] On April 4 Sherman informed Grant's chief of staff, Brig. Gen. J. A. Rawlins, that he was making troops and cattle march and was reducing sutlers' and private business to gain railroad cars for surplus stores and forage. "I am endeavoring to persuade the railroad superintendent to run the cars in a circuit so as to work as an endless chain," he explained, "but the habit of running by a time-table is so strong that I find him disinclined."[7]

A day or so later Sherman contacted the quartermaster general in Washington, M. C. Meigs, to request that he send him a qualified quartermaster with whom he could freely converse, explain his plans, and analyze figures and reports. He would be "especially satisfied," he added, if he could have Gen. Robert Allen—in his judgment the ideal man "to direct the harmonious working of this vast machinery." Meigs agreed and promptly assigned Allen to Sherman's command.[8]

Allen perceived at once that Sherman's greatest difficulty would be to get supplies forward to advanced depots. "Up to the present moment," he noted, "the rolling stock on the roads leading out of Nashville has only been sufficient to transport the daily want. All the engines and cars to carry forward the surplus have yet to arrive from the East; they are coming at the rate of about 15 per day; from 1,500 to 2,000 are required to do the work." Meanwhile, the depots at Nashville were overstocked both with provisions and forage.[9]

Throughout April Sherman labored to round up supplies and troops for the coming campaign. He continued to draw all detachments and furloughed men to Nashville and to accumulate surplus stores to the front. On April 6 he issued General Orders No. 6—the regulation that would enable the military railroads to more fully supply his armies in the field. According to this document, no citizens or private freight would be transported by the railroads, nor would bodies of troops be carried if they could march. Civilian employees of the staff departments or the railroads would be conveyed only upon order of the commanding officer of one of the military departments. The same would apply for all citizens.

Express companies would be allowed one car per day each way to carry small parcels for soldiers and officers. The same would be permitted for sutlers' goods and officers' stores. When a sufficient surplus of stores had been accumulated at the front, this allowance might be increased—but not before. Stores for officers' messes would be carried only with the consent of the inspecting officer at Nashville. No horses, cattle, or other livestock would be transported by railroad except upon the written order of the commanding general of one of the three armies. Only on return trips could cars carry private freight, and then only if shipments did not interfere with the full working of the railroad. Provost marshals would have nothing to do with transportation by railroad; their passes would allow the bearer to go from one point to another, "but not necessarily by rail." Railroads were strictly for military purposes. If and when the rolling stock could be increased or an adequate accumulation of stores existed at the front, then the expanded facilities could be extended to passengers and private freight. Otherwise, citizens and sutlers would have to use wagons.

Sherman insisted that until the railroad could be relieved, all military posts within 35 miles of Nashville and within 20 miles of Stevenson, Bridgeport, Chattanooga, Huntsville, and Loudon must haul stores only by wagons. The general manager of the railroads and his agents and conductors would control the trains. The military guard would enforce good order.[10] On April 9 Sherman wrote Quartermaster General Meigs to assure him that his two representatives, Col. J. L. Donaldson and Mr. Anderson, were acting "in perfect concert" to provide the transportation of army supplies.[11] Later he explained: "When we move we will take no tents or baggage, but one change of clothing on our horses, or to be carried by the men and on pack animals by company officers; five days' bacon, twenty days' bread, and thirty days' salt, sugar, and coffee; nothing else but arms and ammunition, in quantity, proportioned to our ability. . . . We must not be led aside by any raids."[12]

Sherman received staunch support from Meigs in resisting pressure from civilians and other interested parties. "March your troops and devote the cars solely to transportation of military necessities," Meigs counseled, "and you will accomplish much." Civilians could give all kinds of "charitable, patriotic, benevolent and religious reasons" why they should be at the front. No matter: nothing but an "absolute and unchangeable" prohibition of all travel would solve the problem.[13] And as many were soon to discover, "charitable," "benevolent," and "religious" were not words often associated with Sherman.

Several days later he received a confidential message from the Adjutant-General's Office in Washington.

> The following instructions, *which will not be printed*, are furnished by order of the Secretary of War for your information and guidance, and are to be sent by you to the officers under your command, to whom they will apply.
>
> 1. Generals commanding armies and army corps in the field will take the proper measures to supply, so far as may be possible, the wants of their troops in animals and provisions from the territory through which military operations are conducted.
>
> Private property so taken will be receipted and accounted

for in accordance with existing orders. Special care will be taken to remove horses, mules, livestock, and all means of transportation from the hostile districts infested or liable to be infested by guerilla bands of rebels.

2. Commanding officers will establish proper regulations in accordance with the usages and customs of war for the enforcement of this order.

Please acknowledge receipt,

I am, sir, very respectfully, your obedient servant,

E. D. Townsend, Assistant Adjutant-General[14]

Could it be that Sherman's reputation in the postwar South is due to his effective application of what in today's parlance would be considered national military policy? There is little doubt that the topic was discussed when Grant and Sherman shared views in the Cincinnati hotel. During the Vicksburg campaign, Confederate cavalry had captured Grant's base at Holly Springs, yet he managed to collect sufficient food and forage to sustain his army. Later, when Grant's forces crossed to the east bank of the Mississippi south of Vicksburg, temporarily giving up their line of communication, they had experienced little difficulty living off the land. Sherman had initially considered the plan too risky, but success obviously had made him a believer.

In Special Orders No. 35, issued on April 25, 1864, Sherman explained to his army commanders how they could maintain the Line of Communications.

A small force in a block-house, disencumbered of baggage and stores not needed, can hold their ground and protect their point against any cavalry force until relief comes. They should be instructed to fight with desperation to the last, as they thereby save the time necessary for concentration.

Small reserves capable of being shifted to a way-point by a train of cars should be placed judiciously and instructed. The main reserves will be at Nashville, Mufreesborough, Columbia, Decatur, and Stevenson, from which places they can be rapidly transported to the point of danger.

Danger to our line of communication is most to be apprehended from the West, and most care must be observed in that direction.

The Tennessee River will be patrolled by gun-boats, both above and below the Shoals. General Schofield will, as heretofore, look to his left and rear, General Thomas to his immediate rear, including Duck River and Columbia, and General McPherson to his right rear, especially Decatur and from the direction of Florence.

On notice of danger the commanding general of the reserve at Nashville will promptly provide for the emergency, and see that damages, if done, are quickly repaired, but all officers are cautioned against the mischievous and criminal practice of reporting mere vague rumors, often sent into our lines by the enemy for his own purposes. . . . An army of a million men could not guard against the fabulous stories that are sent to headquarters. Officers must scrutinize and see with their own eyes or those of some cool, experienced staff officer before making reports that may call off troops from another quarter, where there may be need of them.

When troops are entrenched or well covered by block-houses, a surrender will entail disgrace, for we have all seen examples when a few determined men have held thousands in check until relief came or the necessities of the enemy forced him to withdraw.[15]

Three days later, Sherman moved headquarters to Chattanooga, the starting point for the campaign, and notified authorities in Washington that his troops were ready to take the field. A week later—on the same day that Maj. Gen. George G. Meade's Army of the Potomac marched into the Wilderness of Virginia—the Atlanta campaign began.

By this time five months' worth of supplies had been accumulated at Nashville, but as the chief quartermaster pointed out, "Chattanooga is now the vital point; a failure there, and all that is accomplished is a failure."[16] To President Lincoln, who had written recently on behalf of the "suffering people" in the area, Sherman explained:

We have worked hard with the best talent of the country and it is demonstrated that the railroad cannot supply the army and the people too. One or the other must quit, and the army don't intend to, unless *Joe Johnston* makes us. The issues to citizens have been enormous, and the same weight of corn or oats would have saved thousands of the mules, whose carcasses now

corduroy the roads, and which we need so much. We have paid
back to Tennessee ten for one of the provisions taken in war.

I will not change my order, and I beg of you to be satisfied
that the clamor is partly humbug, and for effect.

Sherman assured Lincoln that every man willing to fight would get a
full ration: the others should go away, and he would offer them free passage
on the railroad.[17]

By the end of April, Sherman informed the quartermaster general
that, thanks to the cooperation of his office, Nashville was "abundantly
supplied." Now the problem was to feed the men and animals on the front
line and build up an adequate surplus for their departure. He noted, however, that in Thomas's department, some 230,000 rations had been issued
to citizens that month. These, he thought, were of doubtful use. He would
much prefer to have the rations in government warehouses at Chattanooga
and Ringgold. "If I could only count on a few more days," he asserted, "I
would have a thirty days' start, but I may have to move on the 2d of May
with barely enough to warrant the move, and beef-cattle and salt, on which
we may have to live, come forward too slowly."[18]

From the first, Sherman had recognized that logistics would be his
most difficult problem. But he had studied the census records, and he knew
that Georgia had a million inhabitants. "If they can live," he reasoned, "we
should not starve." If the enemy disrupted his line of communications he
would feel "perfectly justified in taking whatever and wherever we can
find."[19]

EXECUTION

Sherman's logistics for the campaign essentially depended upon one
railroad. As two officers at Fort Leavenworth pointed out in 1911, "Over
this single line of railroad the provisions, clothing, and camp equipage, forage for animals, arms, ammunition, and ordnance stores, re-enforcements,
and all the varied miscellaneous supplies required for a great army engaged
in an active campaign, were sent to the front; by it were returned the sick,
wounded, and disabled, and discharged soldiers, refugees, freedmen, captured prisoners, and materials deemed advisable to send to the rear."[20]

In a series of orders issued early in the campaign, Sherman revealed
how he proposed to create conditions that would enable the railroad adequately to support his three armies in the field. His experience and his
logistical experts pointed toward one tendency that would need to be con-

trolled: having limited railroad transportation with General Orders No. 6, he needed to limit the number of wagons accompanying the soldiers so that the forage requirements for draft animals did not overwhelm his limited resupply capacity. Each commander of an army, division, or brigade would indicate in orders beforehand the number of wagons needed for the various headquarters and subdivisions of command. "In no event were tents, chests, boxes or trunks to be carried," Sherman wrote in one of these orders. Wagons would be reserved for ammunition, cooking utensils, and provisions—Sherman specified bread or flour, salt, sugar, coffee, and bacon or salt pork. Meat was to be gathered in the country or driven on the hoof, and officers would "enjoy" the same food as enlisted men. One or two ambulances and one wagon would be allocated to each regiment, and all wheeled vehicles would be made up into trains of convenient size, commanded by a quartermaster and accompanied by a proper escort. Officers in charge of wagon trains operated under detailed instructions in order to keep them closed up, doubling on the roads whenever wide enough, and parking in fields along the roads, "so that the long periods of standing in a road, which fatigue the troops so much, may be avoided."[21]

Limiting the number of personnel who would draw on the railroad for support was also an important consideration. Any commander reporting an effective strength greater than he could immediately parade for battle would be considered guilty of having submitted a false report under the Articles of War. Save for "unarmed cooks, teamsters, pioneers, and laborers," all other noncombatants with the army who depended upon army supplies would be treated as "useless mouths" and sent north of Nashville.[22]

"On the whole I feel encouraged," the chief quartermaster at Chattanooga admitted on the eve of the campaign. "I think I shall be able to supply the army, and [I] see no grave mistake, or any want of foresight being shown." Sherman would have a movable column of 80,000, and he would now advance "if he has to eat his mules."[23] As usual, the logisticians' campaign had begun before active field operations, but they knew—as did Sherman—that the first ten days of forward movement were crucial.[24]

Sherman also knew the importance of setting a personal example. As he set off on the campaign, he wrote: "My entire headquarters transportation is one wagon for myself, aides, officers, clerks, and orderlies. I think that is as low down as we can get until we get flat broke, and thenceforward things will begin to mend. Soldiering as we have been doing it for the past two years, with such trains and impediments, has been a farce, and nothing but absolute poverty will cure it."[25]

The transition from logistical buildup to active operations is seen most clearly in the actual operation of the railroad. During the buildup, trains operated south of Nashville in convoys of four ten-car trains running at speeds of about 10 miles per hour. Four such convoys each day provided capacity of 1,600 tons per day, enough to allow for frequent accidents, meet daily requirements, and build up the stockpiles necessary for the campaign. To make the convoy system work in spite of equipment failure and unforeseen delays, sidings capable of holding five to eight trains were built about every 8 miles along the route—about 19 miles of sidings north of Ringgold before the campaign began. To keep trains fueled and moving, 45 water tanks were constructed, and materials and work crews were positioned to push forward similar improvements as Sherman's armies advanced.[26]

And the railroad did indeed keep pace as the three armies advanced. Colonel W. W. Wright, who directed the transportation, remained most of the time with Sherman. The retreating Confederates damaged or destroyed most of the bridges and miles of track, but under the supervision of Cols. Adna Anderson and E. C. Smeed, the Union Construction Corps soon repaired or rebuilt the bridges, and the advance continued. The reconstruction of the railroad bridge over the Chattahoochee provides a classic example—800 feet long and nearly 100 feet high, it took the Construction Corps but four and a half days to complete.[27] Frequent enemy raids might disrupt the flow of traffic, but the Construction Corps quickly repaired the damage and kept the lines open. In a matter of hours—or at most a few days—Sherman's trains were running again.

According to one authority on the military use of railroads, the Atlanta campaign provided "the greatest and most direct evidence" up to that time "of the possibilities of rail-power in warfare." When Sherman approached Atlanta, he was 360 miles from his main base of supplies, yet the trains kept running on what he himself described as "a poorly-constructed single-track railroad."[28] Sherman was inclined to be more forgiving than many commanders where tactical errors occurred, "knowing that the enemy's resistance and counter-action is the most incalculable factor in war." Rarely, however, would he tolerate delay in moving supplies: with "foresight, preparation and initiative," he insisted, material obstacles could always be overcome.[29] By his ruthless scrapping of transport and equipment, Sherman was able to restore mobility. As an historical footnote, when the British army in 1931 devoted its principal training exercises to experiments in the reduction of military transport, the exercise was officially known as "a Sherman march."[30]

Once into the campaign, Sherman seems to have paid little attention to logistics. He was fully occupied maneuvering his three armies against a skillful opponent. Rarely did he deal with supplies in daily correspondence, which now was dominated by operational or tactical considerations. Occasionally he might remind a subordinate that "a railroad in the end saves but little time in moving troops." Its main purpose, he insisted, "was to supply us."[31]

By May 9 the railroad had been repaired as far as Tunnel Hill, where a new depot was formed. Because Sherman needed all of his trains just to move supplies, the troops had to march. On May 15 Sherman announced that Dalton, Georgia, would be the new supply depot, but he permitted the railroad superintendent to bring forward trains hauling ammunition or special articles "up to the very rear of the army." He also alerted his army commanders to make sure that they kept on hand ten days' supply of meat and bread and that they foraged as much as possible, "keeping their mules in good shape because of the probability of a long march."[32] A week later, General George Thomas's Army of the Cumberland was given the responsibility of guarding all railroads in the rear.[33]

On May 16 Resaca was designated the new depot for supplies: all empty trains would be sent to that point, loaded as quickly as possible, and moved forward on the route taken by the Army of the Tennessee.[34] "We were abundantly supplied and our animals are improving on the grass and grain fields," Sherman assured his superiors in Washington. "Everything . . . is progressing as favorably as we could expect."[35] Two days later the army entered Kingston. "Tomorrow cars will move to this place," Sherman informed Halleck, "and I will replace our stores and get ready for the Chattahoochee. The railroad passes through a range of hills at Allatoona, which is doubtless being prepared for us, but I have no intention of going through it. I apprehend more trouble from our long trains of wagons than from the fighting."[36]

With the rebuilding of the Oostenaula bridge at Resaca the next day, Sherman's trains could get to Kingston. "Back us up with troops in the rear," he ordered General J. D. Webster in Nashville, "so I will not be forced to drop detachments as road guard, and I have an army that will make a deep hole in the Confederacy."[37] On May 21 President Lincoln telegraphed the governors of states in the upper Midwest, urging them to forward recently enlisted 100-day troops to "sustain General Sherman's lengthening lines."[38] On that same day, Sherman informed Halleck:

Weather very hot and dusty. We, nevertheless, by morning
will have all our wagons loaded and be ready for a twenty days'
expedition. I will leave a good brigade at Rome—a strong, good
point; about 1,000 men to cover this point, but will keep no
stores here to tempt an enemy until I have placed my army about
Marietta, when I will cause the railroad to be repaired up to that
point.

I regard Resaca as the stronghold of my line of operations
until I reach the Chattahoochee. . . . I will allow three days
to have the army grouped around Dallas, whence I can strike
Marietta, or the Chattahoochee, according to developments.[39]

On May 23 the chief quartermaster at Chattanooga informed the quartermaster general that Sherman would resume movements with his entire
command the next day: "He assured me emphatically that he was supplied
with everything that he wanted, and said no army . . . was ever better provided. . . . The general takes with him in his wagons twenty days' supplies,
which can be made to answer thirty in an emergency. Transportation in
good order. Mules in fine, serviceable condition. In the absence of the
army a full supply will be accumulated at this point."[40]

Even though General *Johnston* effectively blocked Sherman's flank
move through Dallas, the stalemate on the Dallas–New Hope Church line
was not prolonged. Sherman had forces back on the railroad near Acworth
by June 6, and he immediately gave the necessary orders to reconstitute
supplies at the front. To Halleck he reported that "the cars now come to
the Etowah River and we have sent back to replenish our supplies for a ten-
days' move to commence on . . . the 9th."[41] By June 11 the Etowah bridge
had been rebuilt and it was determined that supplies now would be accumulated at Allatoona Pass or even brought right up to the lines.[42]

All the while, Sherman had to cope with Confederate cavalry in his
rear, but although he suffered damage to the railroad—which was promptly repaired—the supply of food was still good, the forage for the horses
"moderate," with growing wheat, rye, and oats in the fields supplementing
the good grass in the valleys of the Etowah and the Oostenaula.[43] Sherman
no longer felt a need to use forage for horses at the front "unless they are
good artillery and cavalry horses."[44]

On June 26 he issued Special Field Orders No. 29, assessing the logistical situation after six weeks of strenuous campaigning.

The question of supplies to an army of this size is one of the greatest importance, and calls for a most rigid economy. By comparing issues by the commissary department and the reports of army commanders of effective strengths for duty . . . it is found that a quantity of provisions is issued daily equal to from 50% to 75% over the effective strength.

This proportion is entirely too large in our present situation, and either the quantity must be reduced or the number of non-effectives be brought within reasonable limits by sending servants and others to the rear. Twenty-five percent is deemed a large and reasonable limit, and the chief commissary of the army in the field, as well of all the garrisons and detachments dependent on the railroads south of Nashville, will see that issues are limited to that figure. The chief commissaries will be furnished with field reports from superior headquarters, and will call the attention of the proper commanding officers when requisitions exceed the number of men and officers for duty with twenty-five percent added.

When, from interruption to railroads or any other cause, supplies cannot be equal to this standard, the commissaries will make issues as near as possible for each ten days in advance, and must scale their issues so that all parts of the army receive a fair proportion of each article. When deficiencies occur in the bread or small rations, the commissary may increase the allowance of fresh beef, if on hand. Unarmed cooks, teamsters, pioneers and laborers are the only proper non-effectives with the army. All other persons dependent on our supplies are useless mouths which we cannot afford to feed, and should be sent north of Nashville. Twenty-five percent is the maximum allowance for this class of non-effective but useful laborers specified, and even these should be armed.[45]

The next day Sherman asked General Thomas if he was willing to move against Fulton, cutting himself loose from the railroad. "When do you wish to start?" was the curt response.[46]

Operations had now brought Sherman's armies to the vicinity of Kennesaw Mountain. Communications were relatively secure, and before long, Sherman would be knocking at the doors of Atlanta.

LESSONS LEARNED

In his "after-action" report, Sherman asserted that his chief quarter-master and chief commissary had "succeeded in a manner surprising to all of us in getting forward supplies. I doubt if ever an army was better supplied than this, and I commend them most highly for it."[47] And in his *Memoirs* Sherman summarized the "lessons learned" from this experience. "The 'feeding' of an army is a matter of the most vital importance," he de-clared, "and demands the earliest attention of the general intrusted with a campaign. . . . He must give the subject his personal attention, for the army reposes in him alone, and should never doubt the fact that their existence overrides in importance all other considerations. Once satisfied of this, and that all has been done that can be, the soldiers are always willing to bear the largest measure of privation."[48]

A modern officer who studied Sherman's logistics at the U.S. Army War College asserted that the Atlanta campaign was a "real model" for rear area operations.

> Sherman demonstrated a real talent for extremely thorough planning . . . focusing not exclusively on the front lines but on all aspects of the campaign. . . . The extremely long line of communication through unfriendly territory . . . and the fact that there was only a single railroad for the last 120 miles does not appear to have an equal. Certainly there were other campaigns that went deep into enemy territory, but these did not provide for any resupply from friendly bases. The task was made more difficult by the amount of supplies that had to be moved daily.
>
> Not only was this a daring gamble; it was also an amazingly successful gamble. At no time did Sherman's troops suffer from the lack of supplies.
>
> The type and degree of planning that went into this campaign are also exceptional. There were not a lot of other examples that provided a clue for the planning. This is particularly true when considering the planning for the operation and security of the rear area. There was little left to chance and the end result was an extremely successful rear area operation. There are a great many parallels between Sherman's campaign and modern rear area doctrine.[49]

Another War College student concluded from his research that this first modern general "showed great ability to make decisions and supervise his army in a manner easily recognizable to modern military analysis."

> His plans did not always work out in exact detail—few plans do—but his sound planning and the innate flexibility he built into them enabled his army to drive *Johnston* out of strong positions and eventually to accomplish his mission.
>
> From March to May there was the challenge of increasing the flow of supplies to the forward base of Chattanooga, building an adequate depot there that would be able to support an army of 100,000 men, securing his rear area (Kentucky and Tennessee initially) against guerrilla action, and developing a streamlined force capable of marching on Atlanta. . . .
>
> During the actual campaign . . . Sherman had to continue dealing with many of these problems. In addition he had to provide for the security of a new area, taking all actions necessary to keep his supply line—a single rail line—open. Even while he planned and fought the campaign to the front Sherman managed the battle to the rear area dealing with guerrilla actions, movements of units throughout a very extensive Rear Area, repair and maintenance of a much-threatened rail line, control of a sometimes hostile population and the maintenance of his force in spite of the enlistment expiration of many . . . regiments. That he was successful is the direct result of his planning and his direct supervision.[50]

Still another study at the Army War College, written by Lt. Col. Alfred C. Channels, Jr., concluded that Sherman "seemed to be a great captain ahead of his time." Channels wrote: "Today's military leader can gain tremendous insight into the operational level of war by studying Sherman and the Atlanta Campaign. His meticulous planning, thorough preparation and brilliant execution gives shape to today's doctrine and exemplifies the tenets of initiative, agility, depth and synchronization. The principles of campaign planning can be 'lifted' directly from the Atlanta Campaign."[51]

NOTES

1. William Tecumseh Sherman, *Memoirs of General W. T. Sherman*, 2 vols. (New York: Library of America, 1990), p. 467. Hereafter cited as Sherman, *Memoirs*.

2. Ibid., p. 463. Steele's Department of Arkansas was not a factor in the campaign.

3. Ibid., p. 472.

4. Sherman to Brig. Gen. Robert Allen, chief quartermaster, Louisville, March 24, 1864. *The War of the Rebellion: A Compilation of the Official Records of the Union and Confederate Armies* (Washington, D.C.: Government Printing Office), Series I, vol. XXXII, pt. 3, pp. 141–142. Hereafter cited as *O.R.*, with the appropriate volume number.

5. Sherman to Grant, April 2, 1864, ibid., p. 220.

6. Sherman to General S. G. Burbridge, April 2, 1864, ibid., p. 237.

7. Sherman to Brig. Gen. J. A. Rawlins, April 4, 1864, ibid., p. 247.

8. Sherman to Gen. M. C. Meigs, April 6, 1864, ibid., p. 270.

9. Allen to Meigs, April 12, 1864, ibid., p. 330.

10. General Orders No. 6, April 6, 1864, ibid., pp. 279–280.

11 Sherman to Meigs, April 9, 1864, ibid., p. 311.

12. Sherman to Gen. George H. Thomas, April 11, 1864, ibid., p. 323.

13. Meigs to Sherman, April 20, 1864, ibid., p. 434.

14. E. D. Townsend to Sherman, ibid., pt. 4, pp. 250–251. Emphasis added.

15. Special Orders No. 35, April 25, 1864, ibid., pt. 3, pp. 496–497.

16. Meigs, ibid., pt. 4, p. 4.

17. Sherman to Lincoln, ibid., pt. 4, pp. 33–34.

18. Sherman to Meigs, April 26, 1864, ibid., pt. 3, p. 503.

19. Sherman to Grant, April 10, 1864, Sherman, *Memoirs*, p. 492.

20. Captain Duncan K. Major, Jr., and Captain Roger S. Fitch, *Supply of Sherman's Army during the Atlanta Campaign* (Leavenworth, Kan.: Fort Leavenworth Press, 1911), p. 41.

21. Military Orders of General William T. Sherman, 1861–65 (Washington, D.C.: War Department, 1869), pp. 234–236. Cited hereafter as Sherman, *Military Orders*.

22. Ibid., p. 261.

23. Col. J. L. Donaldson to Meigs, May 1, 1864, *O.R.*, XXXVIII, pt. 4, p. 4.

24. Sherman to James Guthrie, President, Louisville and Nashville Railroad, May 1, 1864, *O.R.*, XXXVIII, pt. 4, p. 4.

25. Sherman to Meigs, May 3, 1864, *O.R.*, XXXVIII, pt. 4, p. 20.

26. Duncan and Fitch, *Supply of Sherman's Army*, p. 41. James A. Huston, *Sinews of War: Army Logistics, 1775–1953* (Washington, D.C.: Center of Military History), p. 207.

27. Francis Trevelyan Miller, ed., *The Photographic History of the Civil War*, 10 vols. (New York: The Review of Reviews Co., 1911), V, pp. 298–302.

28. Edwin A. Pratt, *The Rise of Rail-Power in War and Conquest: 1833–1914* (London: P. S. King and Son, 1916), pp. 34–35.

29. B. H. Liddell Hart, *Sherman: Soldier, Realist, American* (New York: Frederick A. Praeger, 1958), p. 235.

30. Jay Luvaas, *The Military Legacy of the Civil War: The European Inheritance* (Chicago: University of Chicago Press, 1959), p. 222.

31. Sherman to McPherson, May 10, 1864, *O.R.*, XXXVIII, pt. 4, p. 125.

32. Special Field Orders No. 7, May 15, 1864, ibid., pt. 4, p. 200.

33. Special Field Orders No. 8, May 16, 1864, ibid., pt. 4, p. 216.

34. Special Field Orders No. 11, May 16, 1864, ibid., pt. 4, p. 218.

35. Sherman to Maj. Gen. H. W. Halleck, May 17, 1864, ibid., pt. 4, p. 219.

36. Sherman to Halleck, May 19, 1864, ibid., pt. 4, p. 248.

37. Sherman to Gen. J. D. Webster, May 19, 1864, ibid., pt. 4, p. 249.

38. Lincoln to governors Morton, Yates, Stone, and Lewis, ibid., pt. 4, p. 274.

39. Sherman to Halleck, May 21, 1864, ibid., pt. 4, p. 274.

40. Allen to Meigs, May 23, 1864, ibid., pt. 4, p. 299.

41. Sherman to Halleck, June 7, 1864, ibid., pt. 4, p. 428.

42. Sherman to Halleck, June 11, 1864, ibid., pt. 4, pp. 454–455.

43. Sherman to Grant, June 18, 1864, ibid., pt. 4, p. 508.

44. Special Field Orders No. 27, June 20, 1864, ibid., pt. 4, p. 543.

45. Special Field Orders No. 26, June 29, 1864, ibid., pt. 4, pp. 601–602.

46. Thomas to Sherman, June 27, 1864, ibid., pt. 4, p. 611.

47. Report of Maj. Gen. W. T. Sherman, June 8, 1864, ibid., pt. 1, p. 84.

48. Sherman, *Memoirs,* p. 880.

49. Lt. Col. William Kyle III, "Rear Area Operations during Sherman's Atlanta Campaign" (Carlisle Barracks, Pa.: U.S. Army War College, 1991), pp. 36–37.

50. Lt. Col. John R. Scales, "Planning Sherman's Operations in North Georgia" (Carlisle Barracks, Pa.: U.S. Army War College, 1993), pp. 18–19.

51. Lt. Col. Alfred C. Channels, Jr., "Harmony of Action—Sherman as an Army Group Commander" (Carlisle Barracks, Pa.: U.S. Army War College, 1992), pp. 29–30.

ORDER OF BATTLE

UNITED STATES ARMY

MILITARY DIVISION OF THE MISSISSIPPI, MAJOR GENERAL WILLIAM T. SHERMAN, U.S. ARMY, COMMANDING

ARMY OF THE CUMBERLAND
Maj. Gen. George H. Thomas

IV ARMY CORPS
Maj. Gen. Oliver O. Howard

FIRST DIVISION
Maj. Gen. David S. Stanley

First Brigade (Maj. Gen. Charles Cruft)
(Col. Isaac M. Kirby)
21st Illinois
38th Illinois
31st Indiana
81st Indiana
1st Kentucky
2nd Kentucky
90th Ohio
101st Ohio

Second Brigade
(Brig. Gen. Walter C. Whitaker)
96th Illinois
115th Illinois
35th Indiana
84th Indiana
21st Kentucky
40th Ohio
51st Ohio

Third Brigade (Col. William Grose)
59th Illinois
75th Illinois
80th Illinois
84th Illinois
9th Indiana
30th Indiana
36th Indiana
84th Indiana
77th Pennsylvania

Artillery (Capt. Peter Simonson)
(Capt. Samuel McDowell)
(Capt. Theodore Thomasson)
5th Indiana Light Battery
Pennsylvania Light Battery B

SECOND DIVISION
Brig. Gen. John Newton

First Brigade (Col. Francis T. Sherman)
    (Brig. Gen. Nathan Kimball)
    36th Illinois
    44th Indiana
    73rd Illinois
    74th Illinois
    88th Illinois
    15th Missouri
    24th Wisconsin
    2nd Missouri
    28th Kentucky (until 28 May)

Second Brigade (Brig. Gen. George Wagner)
    100th Illinois
    40th Indiana
    57th Indiana
    97th Ohio
    28th Kentucky (from 28 May)

Third Brigade (Brig. Gen. Charles G. Harker)
    (Brig. Gen. Luther P. Bradley)
    22nd Illinois
    27th Illinois
    42nd Illinois
    51st Illinois
    79th Illinois
    3rd Kentucky
    64th Ohio
    125th Ohio

Artillery (Capt. Charles Aleshire)
    (Capt. Wilbur Goodspeed)
    1st Illinois Light Battery M
    1st Ohio Light Battery A

THIRD DIVISION
Brig. Gen. Thomas J. Wood

First Brigade (Brig. Gen. August Willich)
    (Col. William H. Gibson)
    25th Illinois
    35th Illinois
    89th Illinois
    32nd Indiana
    8th Kansas
    15th Ohio
    49th Ohio
    15th Wisconsin
    124th Ohio

Second Brigade (Brig. Gen. William B. Hazen)
    59th Illinois
    6th Indiana
    5th Kentucky
    6th Kentucky
    23rd Kentucky
    1st Ohio
    6th Ohio
    41st Ohio
    71st Ohio
    93rd Ohio

Third Brigade (Brig. Gen. Samuel Beatty)
    (Col. Frederick Knefler)
    79th Indiana
    86th Indiana
    9th Kentucky
    17th Kentucky
    13th Ohio
    19th Ohio
    59th Ohio

Artillery (Capt. Cullen Bradley)
    Bridges' Illinois Light Battery
    6th Ohio Light Battery

XIV ARMY CORPS
Maj. Gen. John M. Palmer

FIRST DIVISION
Brig. Gen. Richard W. Johnson
(Brig. Gen. John H. King)

First Brigade (Brig. Gen. William P. Carlin)
(Colonel Anson G. McCook)
104th Illinois
42nd Indiana
88th Indiana
15th Kentucky
2nd Ohio
33rd Ohio
94th Ohio
10th Wisconsin
21st Wisconsin

Second Brigade (Brig. Gen. John H. King)
(Col. William Stoughton)
11th Michigan
15th U.S. (6 companies)
15th U.S. (9 companies)
16th U.S. (4 companies)
18th U.S. (8 companies)
18th U.S. (4 companies)
19th U.S. (5 companies)

Third Brigade (Col. Benjamin Scribner)
(Col. Josiah Given)
37th Indiana
38th Indiana
21st Ohio
74th Ohio
78th Pennsylvania
79th Pennsylvania
1st Wisconsin

Artillery (Capt. Lucius Drury)
1st Illinois Light Battery
1st Ohio Battery I

SECOND DIVISION
Brig. Gen. Jefferson C. Davis

First Brigade (Brig. Gen. James D. Morgan)
10th Illinois
16th Illinois
60th Illinois
10th Michigan
14th Michigan
17th New York

Second Brigade (Col. John G. Mitchell)
34th Illinois
78th Illinois
98th Ohio
108th Ohio
113th Ohio
121st Ohio

Third Brigade (Col. Daniel McCook)
(Col. Oscar F. Harmon)
(Col. Caleb J. Dilworth)
85th Illinois
86th Illinois
110th Illinois
125th Illinois
22nd Indiana
52nd Ohio

Artillery (Capt. Charles Barnett)
2nd Illinois Light Battery
5th Wisconsin Light Battery
Detachment-2nd Minnesota Battery

THIRD DIVISION
Brig. Gen. Absalom Baird

First Brigade (Brig. Gen. John B. Turchin)
19th Illinois
24th Illinois
82nd Indiana
23rd Missouri
11th Ohio
17th Ohio
31st Ohio
89th Ohio
92nd Ohio

Second Brigade (Col. Ferdinand Van Derveer)
(Col. Newell Gleason)
75th Indiana
87th Indiana
101st Indiana
2nd Minnesota
9th Ohio
35th Ohio
105th Ohio

Third Brigade (Col. George P. Este)
10th Indiana
74th Indiana
10th Kentucky
18th Kentucky
14th Ohio
38th Ohio

Artillery (Capt. George Estep)
7th Indiana Light Battery
19th Indiana Light Battery

XX ARMY CORPS
Maj. Gen. Joseph Hooker

FIRST DIVISION
Brig. Gen. Alpheus S. Williams

First Brigade (Brig. Gen. Joseph F. Knipe)
5th Connecticut
3rd Maryland Detachment
123rd New York
141st New York
46th Pennsylvania
3rd Wisconsin

Second Brigade (Brig. Gen. Thomas H. Ruger)
27th Indiana
2nd Massachusetts
13th New Jersey
107th New York
150th New York

Third Brigade (Col. James S. Robinson)
82nd Illinois
101st Illinois
45th New York
143rd New York
61st Ohio
82nd Ohio
31st Wisconsin

Artillery (Capt. John D. Woodbury)
1st New York Light Battery I
1st New York Light Battery M

SECOND DIVISION
Brig. Gen. John W. Geary

First Brigade (Col. Charles Candy)
    5th Ohio
    7th Ohio
    29th Ohio
    66th Ohio
    28th Pennsylvania
    147th Pennsylvania
    73rd Pennsylvania
    109th Pennsylvania

Second Brigade (Col. Adolphus Buschbeck)
    (Col. John T. Lockman)
    33rd New Jersey
    119th New York
    134th New York
    154th New York
    27th Pennsylvania

Third Brigade (Col. David Ireland)
    (Col. George A. Cobham)
    60th New York
    78th New York
    102nd New York
    137th New York
    149th New York
    29th Pennsylvania
    111th Pennsylvania

Artillery (Capt. William Wheeler)
    (Capt. Charles C. Aleshire)
    13th New York Light Battery
    Pennsylvania Light Battery E

THIRD DIVISION
Maj. Gen. Daniel Butterfield

First Brigade (Brig. Gen. William T. Ward)
    102nd Illinois
    105th Illinois
    129th Illinois
    70th Indiana
    79th Ohio

Second Brigade (Col. John Coburn)
    20th Connecticut (until May 29)
    33rd Indiana
    85th Indiana
    19th Michigan
    22nd Wisconsin

Third Brigade (Col. James Wood)
    20th Connecticut (from May 29)
    33rd Massachusetts
    136th New York
    55th Ohio
    73rd Ohio
    26th Wisconsin

Artillery (Capt. Marco B. Gary)
    1st Michigan Light Battery I
    1st Ohio Light Battery C

Unattached Army Units

Reserve Brigade (Col. Joseph W. Burke)
    (Col. Heber Le Favour)
    10th Ohio (until May 27)
    9th Michigan
    22nd Michigan

Pontoniers (Col. George P. Buell)
    58th Indiana
    Pontoon Battalion (until June 17)

Siege Artillery (Capt. Arnold Sutermeister)
    11th Indiana Battery

ARMY OF THE TENNESSEE
Maj. Gen. James B. McPherson

XV ARMY CORPS
Maj. Gen. John H. Logan

FIRST DIVISION
Brig. Gen. Peter J. Osterhaus

First Brigade (Brig. Gen. Charles R. Woods)
26th Iowa
30th Iowa
27th Missouri
76th Ohio

Second Brigade (Col. James A. Williamson)
4th Iowa
9th Iowa
25th Iowa
31st Iowa

Third Brigade (Col. Hugo Wangelin)
3rd Missouri
12th Missouri
17th Missouri
29th Missouri
31st Missouri
32nd Missouri

Artillery (Maj. Clemens Landgraeber)
2nd Missouri Light Battery F
4th Ohio Light Battery

SECOND DIVISION
Brig. Gen. Morgan L. Smith

First Brigade (Brig. Gen. Giles A. Smith)
55th Illinois
111th Illinois
116th Illinois
127th Illinois
6th Missouri
8th Missouri
57th Ohio

Second Brigade (Brig. Gen. Joseph Lightburn)
83rd Indiana
30th Ohio
37th Ohio
47th Ohio
53rd Ohio
54th Ohio

Third Brigade (Col. John M. Oliver)
48th Illinois
99th Indiana
15th Michigan
70th Ohio

Artillery (Capt. Francis DeGress)
1st Illinois Light Battery A
1st Illinois Light Battery B
1st Illinois Light Battery H

XVI ARMY CORPS
Maj. Gen. Grenville M. Dodge

SECOND DIVISION
Brig. Gen. Thomas W. Sweeney

First Brigade (Brig. Gen. Elliott W. Rice)
  52nd Illinois
  66th Indiana
  2nd Iowa
  7th Iowa
  66th Illinois
  81st Ohio

Second Brigade (Col. Patrick E. Burke)
  (Col. Robert N. Adams)
  (Col. August Mersy)
  9th Illinois Mounted Infantry
  12th Illinois

Third Brigade (Col. Moses E. Bane)
  7th Illinois
  50th Illinois
  57th Illinois
  39th Iowa

Artillery (Capt. Frederick Welker)
  1st Michigan Light Battery B
  1st Missouri Light Battery H
  1st Missouri Light Battery I (until 39th Iowa
  May 22)

FOURTH DIVISION
Brig. Gen. James C. Veatch

First Brigade (Brig. Gen. John W. Fuller)
  64th Illinois
  18th Missouri
  27th Ohio
  39th Ohio

Second Brigade (Brig. Gen. John W. Sprague)
  35th New Jersey
  43rd Ohio
  63rd Ohio
  25th Wisconsin

Third Brigade (Col. William T. C. Grower)
  25th Indiana
  17th New York
  32nd Wisconsin

Artillery (Capt. Jerome B. Burrows)
  1st Michigan Light Battery C
  14th Ohio Light Battery
  2nd United States Battery F

XVII ARMY CORPS
Maj. Gen. Francis P. Blair

THIRD DIVISION
Brig. Gen. Mortimer D. Leggett

First Brigade (Brig. Gen. Manning F. Force)
  20th Illinois
  30th Illinois
  31st Illinois
  45th Illinois
  12th Wisconsin
  16th Wisconsin

Second Brigade (Col. Robert K. Scott)
  20th Ohio
  32nd Ohio
  68th Ohio
  78th Ohio

Third Brigade (Col. Adam G. Malloy)
  17th Wisconsin
  Worden's Battalion

Artillery (Capt. William S. Williams)
  1st Illinois Light Battery D
  1st Michigan Light Battery H
  3rd Ohio Light Battery

FOURTH DIVISION
Brig. Gen. Walter Q. Gresham

First Brigade (Col. William L. Sanderson)
  32nd Illinois
  23rd Indiana
  53rd Indiana
  3rd Iowa (3 companies)
  12th Wisconsin

Second Brigade (Col. George C. Rogers)
  14th Illinois
  15th Illinois
  32th Illinois
  41st Illinois
  53rd Illinois

Third Brigade (Col. William Hall)
  11th Iowa
  13th Iowa
  15th Iowa
  16th Iowa
  15th Ohio Light Battery

Artillery (Capt. Edward Spear)
  2nd Illinois Light Battery F
  1st Minnesota Battery
  1st Missouri Light Battery C
  10th Ohio Light Battery

ARMY OF THE OHIO
Maj. Gen. John M. Schofield

XXIII ARMY CORPS
Maj. Gen. John M. Schofield

FIRST DIVISION
Brig. Gen. Alvin P. Hovey
(Division disbanded on June 9; units assigned to 2nd and 3rd Divisions)

First Brigade (Col. Richard Barter)
  120th Indiana
  124th Indiana
  128th Indiana
  130th Indiana
  99th Ohio

Second Brigade (Col. John McQuiston)
  (Col. Peter T. Swaine)
  123rd Indiana
  129th Indiana

Artillery
23rd Indiana Light Battery
24th Indiana Light Battery

SECOND DIVISION
Brig. Gen. Henry M. Judah
(Brig. Gen. Milo S. Hascall)

First Brigade (Brig. Gen. Nathaniel C. McLean)
   (Brig. Gen. Joseph A. Cooper)
   80th Indiana (until 8 June)
   91st Indiana
   13th Kentucky (until 8 June)
   25th Michigan
   45th Ohio (June 8–22)
   3rd Tennessee
   6th Tennessee

Second Brigade (Brig. Gen. Milo S. Hascall)
   (Col. John R. Bond)
   (Col. William E. Hobson)
   107th Illinois
   80th Indiana (from June 8)
   13th Kentucky (from June 8)
   45th Ohio (May 11–June 8)
   11th Ohio
   118th Ohio

Third Brigade (Col. Silas A. Strickland)
   14th Kentucky
   20th Kentucky
   27th Kentucky
   50th Ohio

Artillery (Capt. Joseph C. Shields)
   22nd Indiana Light Battery
   1st Michigan Light Battery
   19th Ohio Light Battery

THIRD DIVISION
Brig. Gen. Jacob D. Cox
(Col. James W. Reilly)

First Brigade (Col. James W. Reilly)
(Maj. James W. Gault)
   112th Illinois
   16th Kentucky
   100th Ohio
   104th Ohio
   8th Tennessee
   63rd Indiana
   65th Indiana
   24th Kentucky
   103rd Ohio
   5th Tennessee (until June 5)

Second Brigade (Brig. Gen. Mahlon S. Manson)
   (Col. John S. Hurt)
   (Col. Milo S. Hascall)
   (Col. John Casement)
   (Col. Daniel Cameron)
   65th Illinois

Third Brigade (Brig. Gen. Nathaniel McLean)
   (Col. Robert K. Byrd)
   (Col. Israel Stiles)
   11th Kentucky
   12th Kentucky
   1st Tennessee
   5th Tennessee

Dismounted Cavalry Brigade
   (Col. Eugene Crittenden)
   16th Illinois
   12th Kentucky

Artillery (Maj. Henry W. Wells)
   15th Indiana Light Battery
   1st Ohio Light Battery D

CAVALRY CORPS
Brig. Gen. Washington Elliot—
Chief of Cavalry, Army of the Cumberland

FIRST DIVISION
Brig. Gen. Edward M. McCook

First Brigade (Col. Joseph B. Dorr)
 8th Iowa
 4th Kentucky Mounted Infantry
 2nd Michigan
 1st Tennessee
 1st Wisconsin

Second Brigade (Col. Oscar LaGrange)
 (Lt. Col. James Stewart)
 (Lt. Col. Horace Lamson)
 2nd Indiana
 4th Indiana

Third Brigade (Col. Louis Watkins)
 4th Kentucky
 6th Kentucky
 7th Kentucky

Artillery
 18th Indiana Horse Artillery Battery

SECOND DIVISION
Brig. Gen. Kenner Garrard

First Brigade (Col. Robert Minty)
 4th Michigan
 7th Pennsylvania
 4th United States

Second Brigade (Col. Eli Long)
 1st Ohio
 3rd Ohio
 4th Ohio

Third Mounted Infantry Brigade
 (Col. John Wilder)
 98th Illinois
 123rd Illinois
 17th Indiana
 72nd Indiana

Artillery
 Chicago Board of Trade Battery

THIRD DIVISION
Brig. Gen. Judson Kilpatrick
(Col. Eli Murray)

First Brigade (Lt. Col. Robert Klein)
 3rd Indiana
 5th Iowa

Second Brigade (Col. Charles Smith)
 8th Indiana
 2nd Kentucky
 10th Ohio

Third Brigade (Col. Eli Murray)
 (Col. Smith Adkins)
 92nd Illinois Mounted Infantry
 3rd Kentucky
 5th Kentucky

Artillery
 10th Wisconsin Battery

STONEMAN'S CAVALRY DIVISION
Maj. Gen. George Stoneman –
Commanding Cavalry, Army of the Ohio

First Brigade (Col. Israel Garrard)
9th Michigan
7th Ohio
6th Indiana
12th Kentucky

Second Brigade (Col. James Biddle)
16th Illinois
5th Indiana

Third Brigade (Col. Horace Capron)
14th Illinois
8th Michigan
McLaughlin's Ohio Squadron

Independent Brigade (Col. Alexander Holeman)
1st Kentucky
11th Kentucky

Artillery
24th Indiana Battery

CONFEDERATE STATES ARMY

ARMY OF TENNESSEE
General Joseph E. Johnston

HARDEE'S ARMY CORPS
Lt. Gen. William J. Hardee

CHEATHAM'S DIVISION
Maj. Gen. Benjamin F. Cheatham

Maney's Tennessee Brigade
    (Brig. Gen. George E. Maney)
1st and 27th Tennessee
4th Confederate
6th and 9th Tennessee
41st Tennessee
50th Tennessee

Strahl's Tennessee Brigade
    (Brig. Gen. Otho F. Strahl)
4th and 5th Tennessee
19th Tennessee
24th Tennessee
31st Tennessee
33rd Tennessee

Wright's Tennessee Brigade
    (Col. John Carter)
8th Tennessee
16th Tennessee
28th Tennessee
38th Tennessee
51st and 52nd Tennessee

Vaughn's Tennessee Brigade
    (Brig. Gen. Alfred J. Vaughn)
11th Tennessee
12th and 47th Tennessee
29th Tennessee
13th and 154th Tennessee

CLEBURNE'S DIVISION
Maj. Gen. Patrick R. Cleburne

Polk's Brigade
  (Brig. Gen. Lucius Polk)
  1st and 15th Arkansas
  5th Confederate
  2nd Tennessee
  35th and 48th Tennessee
  3rd Confederate

Govan's Arkansas Brigade
  (Brig. Gen. Daniel C. Govan)
  2nd and 24th Arkansas
  5th and 13th Arkansas
  6th and 7th Arkansas
  8th and 19th Arkansas

Lowrey's Brigade
  (Brig. Gen. Mark P. Lowrey)
  16th Alabama
  33rd Alabama
  45th Alabama
  32nd Mississippi
  45th Mississippi

Granbury's Texas Brigade
  (Brig. Gen. Hiram M. Granbury)
  6th and 15th Texas Cavalry
  7th Texas
  10th Texas
  17th and 18th Texas Cavalry
  24th and 25th Texas Cavalry

BATE'S DIVISION
Maj. Gen. William B. Bate

Smith's Brigade
  (Brig. Gen. Thomas B. Smith)
  37th Georgia
  4th Georgia Sharpshooters
  20th Tennessee
  30th Tennessee
  15th and 37th Tennessee

Lewis' Kentucky ("Orphan") Brigade
  (Brig. Gen. Joseph H. Lewis)
  2nd Kentucky
  4th Kentucky
  5th Kentucky
  6th Kentucky
  9th Kentucky

Finley's Florida Brigade
  (Brig. Gen. Jesse J. Finley)
  1st and 3rd Florida Cavalry
  1st and 4th Florida
  6th Florida
  7th Florida

WALKER'S DIVISION
Maj. Gen. William H. T. Walker

Mercer's Georgia Brigade
  (Brig. Gen. Hugh Mercer)
  1st Georgia
  54th Georgia
  57th Georgia
  63rd Georgia

Gist's Brigade
  (Brig. Gen. States R. Gist)
  8th Georgia Battalion
  46th Georgia
  16th South Carolina
  24th South Carolina

Jackson's Brigade
    (Brig. Gen. John R. Jackson)
    47th Georgia
    65th Georgia
    5th Mississippi
    8th Mississippi
    2nd Georgia Sharpshooters
    1st Georgia Sharpshooters

Stevens' Georgia Brigade
    (Brig. Gen. Clement H. Stevens)
    1st Georgia Confederate
    25th Georgia
    29th Georgia
    30th Georgia
    66th Georgia

HOOD'S ARMY CORPS
Lt. Gen. John B. Hood

HINDMAN'S DIVISION
Maj. Gen. Thomas C. Hindman

Deas' Alabama Brigade
    (Brig. Gen. Zachariah C. Deas)
    (Col. John C. Coltart)
    19th Alabama
    22nd Alabama
    25th Alabama
    39th Alabama
    50th Alabama
    17th Alabama Sharpshooters

Manigault's Brigade
    (Brig. Gen. Arthur M. Maginault)
    24th Alabama
    28th Alabama
    34th Alabama
    10th South Carolina
    19th South Carolina

Walthall's Mississippi Brigade
    (Brig. Gen. Edward C. Walthall)
    (Col. Samuel Benton)
    24th and 27th Mississippi
    29th and 30th Mississippi
    34th Mississippi
    41st Mississippi
    44th Mississippi
    9th Mississippi Sharpshooters

Tucker's Mississippi Brigade
    (Brig. Gen. William F. Tucker)
    (Col. Jacob H. Sharp)
    7th Mississippi
    9th Mississippi
    10th Mississippi

STEVENSON'S DIVISION
Maj. Gen. Carter L. Stevenson

Brown's Tennessee Brigade
    (Brig. Gen. John C. Brown)
    3rd Tennessee
    18th Tennessee
    26th Tennessee
    32nd Tennessee
    45th and 23rd Tennessee

Cumming's Georgia Brigade
    (Brig. Gen. Alfred Cumming)
    2nd Georgia State Line (from June 15)
    34th Georgia
    36th Georgia
    39th Georgia
    56th Georgia

Reynolds' Brigade
    (Brig. Gen. Alexander W. Reynolds)
    58th North Carolina
    60th North Carolina
    54th Virginia
    63rd Virginia
    46th Alabama

Pettus' Alabama Brigade
    (Brig. Gen. Edmund W. Pettus)
    20th Alabama
    23rd Alabama
    30th Alabama
    31st Alabama

STEWART'S DIVISION
Maj. Gen. Alexander P. Stewart

Stovall's Georgia Brigade
    (Brig. Gen. Marcellus A. Stovall)
    (Col. Abda Johnson)
    1st Georgia State Line
    40th Georgia
    41st Georgia
    42nd Georgia
    43rd Georgia
    52nd Georgia

Clayton's Alabama Brigade
    (Brig. Gen. Henry D. Clayton)
    18th Alabama
    32nd and 58th Alabama
    36th Alabama
    38th Alabama

Gibson's Louisiana Brigade
    (Brig. Gen. Randall L. Gibson)
    1st Louisiana
    13th Louisiana
    16th and 25th Louisiana
    14th Battalion Louisiana Sharpshooters
    19th Louisiana
    20th Louisiana

Baker's Alabama Brigade
    (Brig. Gen. Alpheus Baker)
    37th Alabama
    40th Alabama
    42nd Alabama
    54th Alabama

POLK'S ARMY CORPS
Major General Leonidas Polk
(Major General William W. Loring)

LORING'S DIVISION
Maj. Gen. William W. Loring
(Brig. Gen. Winfield S. Featherston)

Featherston's Mississippi Brigade
(Brig. Gen. Winfield S. Featherston)
    3rd Mississippi
    22nd Mississippi
    31st Mississippi
    33rd Mississippi
    40th Mississippi
    1st Mississippi Sharpshooters

Adams' Mississippi Brigade
    (Brig. Gen. John Adams)
    6th Mississippi
    14th Mississippi
    15th Mississippi
    20th Mississippi
    23rd Mississippi
    43rd Mississippi

Scott's Brigade
(Brig. Gen. Thomas M. Scott)
   27th Alabama
   35th Alabama
   49th Alabama
   55th Alabama
   57th Alabama
   12th Louisiana

FRENCH'S DIVISION
Maj. Gen. Samuel G. French

Ector's Brigade
   (Brig. Gen. Matthew D. Ector)
   29th North Carolina
   39th North Carolina
   9th Texas
   10th Texas Cavalry
   14th Texas Cavalry
   32nd Texas Cavalry

Cockrell's Missouri Brigade
   (Brig. Gen. Francis M. Cockrell)
   (Col. Elijah Gates)
   1st and 4th Missouri
   2nd and 6th Missouri
   3rd and 5th Missouri
   1st and 3rd Missouri Cavalry

Sears' Mississippi Brigade
   (Brig. Gen. Claudius W. Sears)
   (Col. William S. Barry)
   4th Mississippi
   35th Mississippi
   36th Mississippi
   46th Mississippi
   7th Mississippi Battalion

WALTHALL'S DIVISION
Maj. Gen. Edward C. Walthall

Reynolds' Arkansas Brigade
   (Brig. Gen. Daniel H. Reynolds)
   1st Arkansas Mounted Rifles
   2nd Arkansas Mounted Rifles
   4th Arkansas Mounted Rifles
   9th Arkansas Mounted Rifles
   25th Arkansas Mounted Rifles

Cantey's Brigade
   (Brig. Gen. James Cantey)
   17th Alabama
   26th Alabama
   37th Mississippi

Quarles' Brigade
   (Brig. Gen. William A. Quarles)
   1st Alabama
   4th Alabama
   30th Louisiana
   42nd Tennessee
   46th and 55th Tennessee
   48th Tennessee
   49th Tennessee
   53rd Tennessee

ARTILLERY
Brig. Gen. Francis A. Shoup

HARDEE'S CORPS ARTILLERY
Col. Melancthon Smith

Hoxton's Battalion
  (Maj. Llewelyn Hoxton)
  Phelan's Alabama Battery
  Perry's Florida Battery
  Turner's Mississippi Battery

Hotchkiss' Battalion
  (Maj. Thomas R. Hotchkiss)
  Key's Arkansas Battery
  Goldwaite's Alabama Battery
  Shannon's Mississippi Battery

Martin's Battalion
  (Maj. Robert Martin)
  Bledsoe's Missouri Battery
  Beauregard's South Carolina Battery
  Howell's Georgia Battery

Cobb's Battalion
  (Maj. Robert Cobb)
  Gracey's Kentucky Battery
  Mebane's Tennessee Battery
  Slocomb's Washington Louisiana Battery

Palmer's Battalion
  (Maj. Joseph Palmer)
  Lumsden's Alabama Battery
  Anderson's Georgia Battery
  Havis' Georgia Battery

HOOD'S CORPS ARTILLERY
Col. Robert F. Becham

Courtney's Battalion
  (Maj. Alfred R. Courtney)
  Garrity's Alabama Battery
  Dent's Alabama Battery
  Douglas' Texas Battery

Elridge's Battalion
  (Maj. John W. Eldridge)
  Oliver's Eufala Alabama Battery
  Fenner's Louisiana Battery
  Stanford's Mississippi Battery

Johnston's Battalion
  (Maj. John W. Johnston)
  Corput's Cherokee Georgia Battery
  Rowan's Georgia Light Battery
  Marshall's Tennessee Battery

Williams' Battalion
  (Lt. Col. Samuel C. Williams)
  Kolb's Barbour Alabama Battery
  Darden's Jefferson Mississippi Battery
  Jefress' Virginia Battery

POLK'S CORPS ARTILLERY
Lt. Col Samuel C. Williams

Myrick's Battalion
  (Maj. John D. Myrick)
  Cowan's Mississippi Battery
  Barry's Lookout Tennessee Battery
  Bouanchard's Louisiana Battery

Storrs' Battalion
  (Maj. George S. Storrs)
  Ward's Alabama Battery
  Guibor's Missouri Battery
  Hoskins' Mississippi Battery

Preston's Battalion
(Maj. William C. Preston)
Tarrant's Alabama Battery
Lovelace's Selma Alabama Battery
Barrett's Missouri Battery

Waddell's Battalion
(Maj. James F. Waddell)
Emery's Alabama Battery
Bellamy's Alabama Battery

CAVALRY CORPS
Maj. Gen. Joseph Wheeler

MARTIN'S DIVISION
Maj. Gen. William T. Martin

Allen's Alabama Brigade
(Brig. Gen. William Wirt Allen)
1st Alabama
3rd Alabama
4th Alabama
7th Alabama
51st Alabama
12th Alabama Battalion

Iverson's Brigade
(Brig. Gen. Alfred Iverson)
1st Georgia
2nd Georgia
3rd Georgia
4th Georgia
6th Georgia

KELLY'S DIVISION
Brig. Gen. John H. Kelly

Anderson's Brigade
(Brig. Gen. Robert H. Anderson)
3rd Confederate
8th Confederate
10th Confederate
12th Confederate
5th Confederate

Dibrell's Tennessee Brigade
(Col. George G. Dibrell)
4th Tennessee
8th Tennessee
9th Tennessee
10th Tennessee
11th Tennessee

Williams' Brigade
(Brig. Gen. John S. Williams)
2nd Kentucky
3rd Kentucky
9th Kentucky
2nd Kentucky Battalion
Allison's Tennessee Squadron
Hamilton's Tennessee Battalion

Hannon's Alabama Brigade
(Col. Moses W. Hannon)
53rd Alabama
24th Alabama Battalion

HUMES' DIVISION
Brig. Gen. William Y. C. Humes

Ashby's Tennessee Brigade
(Col. Henry M. Ashby)
1st Tennessee (formerly 6th Tennessee)
2nd Tennessee
5th Tennessee
9th Tennessee

Harrison's Brigade
(Col. Thomas H. Harrison)
3rd Arkansas
4th Tennessee
8th Texas
11th Texas

JACKSON'S DIVISION
Brig. Gen. William H. Jackson

Armstrong's Mississippi Brigade
  (Brig. Gen. Frank C. Armstrong)
  1st Mississippi
  2nd Mississippi
  28th Mississippi
  Ballentine's Mississippi Regiment

Ferguson's Brigade
  (Brig. Gen. Samuel W. Ferguson)
  2nd Alabama
  56th Alabama
  9th Mississippi
  11th Mississippi
  12th Mississippi Battalion

Ross' Texas Brigade
  (Brig. Gen. Lawrence Ross)
  1st Texas Legion
  3rd Texas Legion
  6th Texas Legion
  9th Texas Legion

Jackson's Division Artillery (Capt. John Waites)
  Croft's Columbus Georgia Battery
  King's Missouri Battery
  Waddell's South Carolina Battery

Wheeler's Horse Artillery (Lt. Col. Felix H. Robertson)
  Davis' Georgia Battery (1 section)
  Huwald's Tennessee Battery
  Huggins' Tennessee Battery
  White's Tennessee Battery
  Callaway's Arkansas Battery

INDEX